THE CONSTITUTIONAL HISTORY
OF ENGLAND TO 1216

THE MACMILLAN COMPANY
NEW YORK · BOSTON · CHICAGO · DALLAS
ATLANTA · SAN FRANCISCO

MACMILLAN & CO., LIMITED
LONDON · BOMBAY · CALCUTTA
MELBOURNE

**THE MACMILLAN COMPANY
OF CANADA, LIMITED**
TORONTO

THE
CONSTITUTIONAL HISTORY
OF ENGLAND TO 1216

BY

WILLIAM ALFRED MORRIS, Ph.D.

**PROFESSOR OF ENGLISH HISTORY IN THE
UNIVERSITY OF CALIFORNIA**

New York
THE MACMILLAN COMPANY
1930

SET UP AND ELECTROTYPED BY J. J. LITTLE & IVES COMPANY
· PRINTED IN THE UNITED STATES OF AMERICA ·

To my classes in constitutional history,
1908-1929

PREFACE

The writer's experience has convinced him that students of English constitutional history may be materially assisted by an account more wieldy than that of Stubbs, which nevertheless presents some detail and also embodies the results of the scholarship of recent years. To the topics covered by the first volume of Stubbs' *Constitutional History*, to which the scope of the present volume corresponds, eminent scholars have contributed so much in the past forty years, sometimes with such divergent conclusions, that the student needs new guidance through a development which is none too easy to trace. This statement implies no depreciation of the merits of the scholar who created the teaching subject. Stubbs is the great master whose diligent application, solid scholarship, and sound judgment have laid all workers in the medieval portion of the field under a weighty and permanent obligation. No one who attempts to survey the literature of the field can fail to appreciate the fact.

The more considerable recent accretions to knowledge of the subject up to Magna Carta have pertained to the Anglo-Saxon period and the Norman period rather than to that of the Angevin kings, although in the last-named field, which Stubbs so signally made his own, notable advance has been made through the study of judicial and financial history as well as that of administrative organization and of Magna Carta and the various questions which it presents. It is, however, in the first eleven chapters of this work rather than in the remaining five that the greatest deviation from the older standard account will be found. The unfortunate fact is that the work of Stubbs most needs revision just in those parts which are read first.

No doubt the most useful function of a work like the present one is the weighing and the integration of results already attained. This is hardly the place to propound new and striking theories even were the writer capable of doing so. The presentation of historical facts none the less must keep in mind the sources upon which they rest. The writer has re-examined the main body of these to test the views which he has accepted, and he has endeavored to fill in gaps and to add some new material. In the treatment of most topics he has of necessity followed the conclusions of well-known authorities. At first, the student's acquaintance with these is more likely to be of value to him than an extended study of source materials. A reference to the sources, however, is ultimately necessary if he is to attain independence of judgment, and the attempt has been made to encourage both lines of approach.

A complete review of secondary materials the writer does not claim to have accomplished. Arguments and points of view long superseded and inadequate surveys of an earlier time in the main have been passed over. Little good could come from reviving Thierry or much of Freeman, and Gneist is no longer very helpful. The debt to Stubbs, Liebermann, and Round as well as to Maitland, Chadwick, Boehmer, Vinogradoff, Haskins, G. B. Adams and others will be obvious to the reader. The treatment of Angevin finance is founded on the work of J. F. Baldwin and S. K. Mitchell, and that of local government largely recapitulates the writer's own conclusions published elsewhere. A countless number of possible, or even useful, footnote references to authorities have necessarily been omitted, and the fact implies no judgment that all or even most of these are without merit. Completeness of reference was impossible, and the highest utility was the only possible criterion of selection.

This holds also for the bibliographical notes appended to the respective chapters. Beginners need to be directed to the better books rather than to be given wide bibliographical information. The ready accessibility of the notable work of

Charles Gross, *The Sources and Literature of English History to about 1485,* renders it unnecessary to make the bibliographical sections more complete.

Certain special obligations of the writer are so great that they must be noticed here. First among these is his debt to the teaching and the influence of his master, Professor Charles Gross, whose former students two decades after his work has ceased will doubtless recognize in these pages ideas and interpretations gained in his classroom. The author's thanks are due to Dr. Ernest Barker, the then Principal, and to other authorities of King's College, London, whose kind invitation some years ago to deliver a series of lectures on the Norman and the Angevin constitution, marks the genesis of this volume. Through the genial friendship and sunny good nature of the lamented Professor Tout one chapter profited by receiving his attention. Mr. Charles G. Crump contributed valuable suggestions. Professor James F. Willard was kind enough to go over the entire manuscript in its earlier stage of preparation, and C. H. Williams read all the page proof. A number of other friends have read several chapters. They have saved the writer from some error; that he has not allowed too much of it to escape him is his earnest hope.

W. A. M.

London,
June, 1930.

CONTENTS

PART I. INTRODUCTION

PART IV. ADMINISTRATIVE AND CONSTITUTIONAL DEVELOPMENT UNDER THE ANGEVIN KINGS, 1154-1216

PART I
INTRODUCTION

CHAPTER I

THE SOURCES OF THE ENGLISH CONSTITUTION AND THE PROCESS OF ITS GROWTH

The English constitution of today has been described frequently and correctly as based partly upon statute law, partly upon common law, and partly upon custom or convention which has not yet become law. Until the modern period the enactment of statute was not an ordinary method or working change in the organs or usages of government. English institutions, indeed, are much older than recorded enactment of any kind. For an understanding of the earlier history, for instance, of kingship, the assemblies and the army, the scholar is thrown purely upon usage, however determinable. The history of English government in its earlier stretches depends much upon custom, very little upon legislation. Although from the seventh century onward the dooms or laws of various Anglo-Saxon kings began to modify in some measure the operation of government, so far as these are extant they touch but slightly the more important developments. The administrative usage which in this earlier period bent the line of institutional growth to conform to practical necessity has never ceased to be a potent force in constitutional history. Convention which is entirely extra-legal in its effect, but which responds to popular feelings and desires, still holds steady the English governmental system and still prescribes some of its basic features.

The common law system as established in the twelfth and thirteenth centuries accepted not only earlier legislation and basic agreements such as Magna Charta and other charters of liberty, but along with these existing institutions wherever the

3

law touched them. Embedded deeply, then, in the common law
are many of the customs of the past, some of which may be
set forth even at the present day in judicial decisions. The
rights of Englishmen and the powers of government in particular have been defined in this way. The usage of the past
has been constantly applied and continued with legal sanction.
Only about two hundred years ago, the judges even rendered
decisions to justify grave restrictions upon the freedom of the
press and to uphold the right of the crown to dispense with
enacted statute. But judicial decisions have also assured the
tenant in villainage a common law right to his holding, guaranteed to a jury the right to bring in a verdict according to
their view of the facts, and declared that no slavery can exist
in England. In the seventeenth century especially it was regarded as the duty of a judge to support the claims of the
monarch in matters of state. Since 1714 the judiciary has been
independent and often a prominent agency for vindicating the
principles of English liberty.

Enacted statute but recently has become one of the principal
agencies of constitutional change. In this it represents the attempt to meet actual problems and to conform with popular
desires. The seventeenth century produced some important
legislative declarations of constitutional principle, but it was
hardly until the period of the Reform Act of 1832 that the
enactment of statute was largely employed as a means of
modifying existing institutions. From the reign of Henry III
(1216-1272) this process was of course used occasionally to
place restraints in the interest of popular liberty upon the king
or his officials in their conduct of affairs. But until 1640 the
English monarch was for so much of the time absolute that
constructive and continuous policies of administration were
necessarily emanations from his authority. Until the nine-
teenth century, if exception is made of the period of the
Puritan Revolution and the Revolution of 1688, statute remained only an occasional means of settling a disputed constitutional issue or problem.

It is essential that the historian regard the English constitution as a constantly developing organism, shaped by the tradition of the past and modified by the practical or popular demands of any given period. The experiments of kings or their administrators until the seventeenth century provided nearly all the solutions of difficult problems. But administrative needs often led to the infringement of popular liberties and thus demanded readjustment. Bishop Stubbs has well said that from the Norman period on the constitution represents a balance between administrative pressure and popular liberty.

"The English constitution," says Stubbs, again speaking of administrative experiment, "is the result of a series of happy accidents." Its stability has been maintained by the tendency of the English people to follow in the ways of their fathers and by a high regard for law. It may be altered at any point by the usual legislative process and is, therefore, classified among the flexible modern constitutions as opposed to the rigid ones, which are based upon a single document establishing a frame of government and which rest upon a sanction theoretically superior to that of ordinary statute law.

For a thousand years the English constitution has changed every century in important particulars which have affected materially the balance of forces determining its general character. At any period it is a compromise between former practice and present needs. In the constitutional system of no other European country are past and present more intimately associated than in England. Though much of the constitution of today is comparatively recent, the beginnings of practice and experience with limited monarchy date from the fourteenth and fifteenth centuries. The present land law of England, it has often been shown, goes back more than six centuries. When Englishmen in the seventeenth century wished to combat the claims of a would-be absolutist king, they appealed to great constitutional guarantees of the thirteenth century as they had been interpreted in the fourteenth. With only minor exceptions every age has built upon the foundation left by the preceding age.

The history of the English constitution is that of a continuous growth which is almost unparalleled. Beginning with the institutions of the barbarous Angles and Saxons, when they settled in the Britain of the fifth century, it traces a development which in the course of fourteen centuries produced the most democratic type of monarchy which the world has yet known. Such continuity is impossible except in a state comparatively free from foreign invasion, from civil war and from political revolution. This growth is of much interest to the peoples of western Europe because it has produced two institutions basic to their liberty, namely constitutional monarchy and the cabinet system. It is important to English-speaking peoples across the sea because they have inherited from the mother country many of their offices, their governmental usages and their doctrines of liberty.

Within the past fifty or sixty years this concept of the continuity of English constitutional history has been gaining ground; but only a very few scholars have as yet essayed to trace the entire development. Such a continuous sweep necessitates the treatment of the field from an institutional point of view. Hallam, who published his constitutional history in 1828, was concerned chiefly with the constitutional conflicts of the period which he treated. It was reserved for Bishop Stubbs in his great work on the medieval constitutional history of England, the first volume of which was published in 1874, to deal with his subject as the continuous development and interaction of the more important institutions of government. The student of English constitutional history must know the functions and powers of the various organs of government, such as the crown, the parliament, the courts, the church, the various local governing bodies. But he must also know how the various branches of government originated, how they changed from time to time, how they operated together as parts of one system, and how one dominated or influenced others.

This idea of a constitution as an institutional framework of government is of course quite different from another which is met in current usage. In recent times it has been customary to regard the English constitution merely as a series of conventions or regulations according to which the sovereign carries out the popular will as expressed through parliament. As a clue to development this would of course be entirely inadequate, for the theory is of very late origin and the conception upon which it is based excludes from consideration many institutions which have lain at the foundation of English government. From the historian's point of view the constitutional history of England must consist in the main of the history of its more prominent institutions of government.

A continuous survey is necessary to correct errors in viewpoint. The obvious fact that the greatest of all of England's contributions to government has been constitutional monarchy must not be permitted to obscure the periods of strong monarchy which have transmitted and moulded English institutions; nor should the long-continued sway of a ruling class be ignored by a democractic age. No portion of the chronological development may be omitted without decided loss. The frequent neglect of the Tudor and Stuart period because of its strong monarchy, so out of harmony with the present, makes it impossible to understand the foundations of modern English liberty. One of the greatest needs of the present time is a better knowledge of English kingship and the organization of the executive from remote times to the present. This will correct common errors of viewpoint such as those likely to be encouraged, for instance, by Stubbs' account of the earlier constitution, which by dwelling upon parliament and briefly passing over the executive tends to give a wrong impression concerning the relative importance of the two. A continuous institutional treatment period by period in the light of materials made available especially by the research of the last four decades is essential to a balanced and adequate view of the growth of the English constitution.

CHAPTER II

GERMANIC ORIGINS

The initial problem of institutional origins in England is one of survivals. The Romans began the actual conquest of Britain in 43 A. D., and occupied it until the withdrawal of the imperial officials about the year 410. It is doubtful how far the Celtic inhabitants were romanized and how far the conditions of the early period of Anglo-Saxon conquest, extending approximately from 450 to 600, made possible a commingling of romanized Britons with Germanic invaders. It may still be held with confidence that the foundation of early English life and civilization was Germanic.

Arguments in favor of Roman influence upon Anglo-Saxon institutions have often been made, but these have usually rested upon conjecture.[1] The greatest authority on Roman civilization in Britain has been able through archaeological research to reconstruct many of its material and artistic features; but concerning the institutional system of the Roman era and the organization of administrative centres about the towns he finds little information.[2] Britain was a frontier region, the administration of which appears in some ways to have deviated from what was normal in other provinces of the Roman Empire. It was romanized in the urban centres and in part outside, but just how far is unknown;[3] moreover, there are evidences that Celtic elements were still quite alive.[4] One is hardly convinced by the argument that a specific phase of Anglo-Saxon institutional life is Romanic in origin

[1] Coote, *The Romans of Britain*, affords a striking example.
[2] Haverfield, *Romanization of Roman Britain*, chap. 6.
[3] Haverfield, *Cambridge Medieval History*, I. 370, 375-376.
[4] Vinogradoff, *Growth of the Manor*, 38-42.

8

because it bears external similarity to something known to have existed in another part of a wide empire.

Some presumption against Roman survivals is created by the disorder known to have existed in Britain between the withdrawal of Roman authority in 410 and the beginning of the Anglo-Saxon settlement, which according to tradition dates from the year 449. Roman rule for at least two centuries before its termination had to bear the onslaughts of the still barbarous Celts of the North. The attack seems to have lost nothing of its force in the fifth century. The few surviving accounts of the times show that the romanized population was assailed by the untamed Picts and Scots. After the Roman withdrawal the cities for a time retained political authority, but found decentralization a great disadvantage. The dwellers in these are represented as timid and without initiative, resources, and military skill to defend themselves. Just prior to the beginning of Anglo-Saxon occupation the present England was subjected to invasions from the north [5] in face of which Roman institutions, customs, and culture must have received a shock. The romanized area was probably reduced in extent. According to tradition it was the inability of a British leader of southern Britain to defend his people against the Picts which induced him to receive on friendly terms the Germanic leaders Hengist and Horsa.

The few known facts concerning the invasion and settlement of the Jutes, Angles and Saxons from across the North Sea in the century between 450 and 550 strengthen the belief that the somewhat scanty survivals of the Roman political system were inconsiderable in their influence upon the invaders. It is probable that the destruction of cities on the southern coast was not so great as was once supposed; [6] moreover, it is difficult to believe with Freeman [7] that among the new settlers there came no appreciable admixture of Celtic blood. A

[5] See Gildas, sects. 19, 20; Bede, *Historia Ecclesiastica*, book I, sects. 12-14.

[6] *Victoria County History*, Hampshire, I. 376-377.

[7] Freeman, *Four Oxford Lectures*, 74-85.

British writer assumed in the sixth century that some of the
subjugated population were enslaved by the conquerors at an
early time.[8] Yet Freeman and the Germanist school of historians present a very strong case when they point out that
in England survivals of Celtic language, custom and institutional life are extremely few. The refugee Gildas, writing in Brittany about 540, is moralizing when he tells of
the bloodshed and destruction which have overtaken the
British Celts on account of their sins.[9] Still he represents
the country, apparently the west and southwest, as devastated
by the inroads of the conquerors, and he with many other
civilized Britons was fleeing before the Germanic attack.
The struggle had moved from east to west, but, excluding
one long interval of peace, it had continued a century. One
may be sure of a peaceful contact between the two peoples
only in the seventh century, and then along the frontier of
Anglo-Saxon settlement toward the western edge of the island
and along borders of Wales and Devonshire. It is fairly certain that the English, like the Danes of a later time, ravaged
beyond the bounds of their own territory. Furthermore aloof-
ness on the part of the unconquered Britons appears in the
fact [10] that they did not preach Christianity to the pagan
intruders.

The Anglo-Saxon conquest of Britain presents a striking
instance of the lapse of a once civilized land into barbarism.
The material civilization and useful arts known to the Romans
disappeared.[11] The Latin language and the Christian religion
retired with the retreating Celts to the extreme west. Gildas
says that the cities of Britain lie dismantled and uninhabited,[12]
and later history bears out the statement. Roman political
organization vanished with its centres. Before the year 600

---

[8] Gildas, ed. Hugh Williams, sec. 25; cf. Bede, *Historia Ecclesiastica*,
I. 15.
[9] Gildas, ed. Williams, sects. 24, 25.
[10] Bede, *Hist. Eccles.*, I. 22.
[11] *Cambridge Medieval History*, I, 381.
[12] Gildas, ed. Williams, sec. 26.

Roman urban and commercial life had given place to the rural economy of Germanic tribesmen, and the mechanism and methods of Roman political organization had been replaced by those of a tribal nature. It is probable that the invaders borrowed an improved plan of tillage which was of Celtic or Roman-Celtic origin,[13] but for the life or government of cities they were not yet ready. With the written law codes of Rome, as well as its contralized governmental organization and its paid standing army, they did not come in contact, and of these they could hardly have learned much from the Britons. Some Roman influence returned with the monks who came to convert the English to Christianity at the end of the seventh century and the earlier part of the eighth. Through the church this was long continued, but it was no longer the influence of imperial Rome. Anglo-Saxon speech, customs and law are clearly Germanic. It is in Germany and not at Rome that the beginnings of English institutions of government must be sought.

Early Germanic life and institutions were first described in detail by the Roman historian Tacitus in his work entitled *Germania,* written about the year 98 A. D. It is hardly probable that he knew the tribes on the North Sea from which the invaders of Britain descended, but so much of what he says applies to the Teutonic peoples of a later time, including the Angles and Saxons, that the type of political organization which he describes may be accepted in general as accurate. A much briefer account is found in Cæsar's *De Bello Gallico,* written almost exactly a century and a half earlier. This is valuable chiefly because, when compared with the account of Tacitus, it gives some idea of the drift of civilization and society in the regions beyond the Rhine which the Romans had never occupied. It seems clear that in the period between the two accounts Germanic life ceased to be nomadic and the

[13] Vinogradoff, *Origin of the Manor,* 35-36, 83-87; Pettit Dutaillis, *Studies Supplementary to Stubbs, Constnl. Hist.,* I. 10-14; cf. *Cambridge Medieval History,* I. 387.

various tribes became settled on the land, practicing some agriculture. In the same period political organization was improved. Cæsar knew a state of affairs in which chiefs, who acted as judges locally in the various cantons or subdivisions, constituted the only permanent magistracy within the tribal area. Over the tribe as a whole he says that there was none except in war time, when a leader was chosen who had the power of life and death. By the time of Tacitus this situation had changed, for the various tribes were headed either by chieftains or in some cases by kings.

The whole organization of the tribal unit was primitive and imperfect. Tacitus could not fail to be impressed with the differences between this and the Roman state with its written laws, its standing army, its system of taxation, its numerous officials, and its highly organized administration. In the Germanic tribe there was nothing like taxation. The principal services of the state, judicial and military, were self-supporting. In whatever capacity the tribesmen assembled, they came armed, for war was a regular part of their activity. Law was the immemorial custom of the tribe, handed on as oral tradition, declared and enforced in popular assemblies or folkmotes, both of the whole tribe and its various cantons. There was a self-developing or common law system in contradistinction to the Roman system of code law. The state was not yet strong enough to deal with private injuries. These the clan of the injured person avenged, accepting a monetary compensation. Even manslaying was compounded by the payment of *wergeld* or man-money. The allotment of land was also made to family or clan groups, and these were employed to a considerable extent in the organization of the army, which consisted of the whole body of freemen of the tribe. Sentences imposed upon offenders against the tribe, such as traitors and deserters, were carried out by the priesthood upon the assumption that the gods rather than the secular power had been injured.

Tribal society in Germany presents class distinctions, and

degrees of right already depended upon these. The ordinary freemen, who must have constituted the great majority in such communities, largely formed both the army and the assemblies. They were entitled to the full rights of tribesmen in law and in the allotment of lands. There was, however, a noble class with larger landed rights and, at least at a later time, a greater *wergeld*. It was customary for each of the various chieftains to gather about him a following of young warriors whom Tacitus calls the *comitatus*. These were bound by a sacred oath to defend and protect their chief and regarded it as a disgrace to come unharmed out of battle. They received arms and horses from their leader, as well as the bounty which he provided from the plunder acquired in war. The class of freedmen had less right than the freemen, and Tacitus, with conditions at home in mind, goes out of his way to say that they are of little importance. At the bottom of the social scale were the slaves, a class recruited not merely by the usual sources, such as birth and captivity in war, but also by debt, for the Germans according to Tacitus were given to gambling and frequently lost their liberty in this way. Servitude was predial, and each slave had his separate household. Tacitus shows that from the economic point of view he resembled the Roman *colonus* or serf rather than the Roman slave. If the master killed a slave, as he sometimes did in sudden wrath, the deed went unpunished, for the slave had no *wergeld* and no clan to avenge him. The trend of early Germanic society, so it has been shown by Stubbs,[14] is determined by the class which is to be regarded as dominant, the nobles imparting an aristocratic, the freemen a democratic and the slaves a servile character. The inference from the account of Tacitus, as well as from the analogy of early tribal usage in general, is that the influence of the great body of freemen was still very strong.

Of the Germanic village community (*vicus*) Tacitus says little. The allotment of land by kindred groups, described by

[14] Stubbs, *Constitutional History*, I. 36-37.

Cæsar, implies that the village was constituted by such an unit. It seems fairly clear that it consisted usually, like later Germanic communities, of the village proper in which stood the detached dwellings of the inhabitants with garden plots, while the agricultural lands which they tilled and the meadow and woodland lay roundabout. Tacitus mentions a scheme of shifting tillage which is possibly the original of the two-field and three-field systems known in later days. A hot dispute has raged between the advocates respectively of tribal and of individual ownership of these village lands. But lands were plentiful, and all that the individual required was their use. The question was probably of little importance at the time. It seems clear, however, that each tribesman regarded his dwelling as his own,[15] and presumably also the plot of land on which it stood. Nothing is known concerning village organization. The village had no court of its own, and whatever organization existed seems to have been concerned with agricultural rather than political interests.

The local unit for purposes of government was the canton, called in Latin the *pagus* and in modern German the *gau*. For these districts were held assemblies in which as early as the time of Cæsar the chiefs rendered justice and settled controversies arising in the various villages. Tacitus says that these magistrates were chosen in the general assembly of the tribe. They were aided in their work, according to the same authority, by a hundred associates, an expression which may possibly refer to the men of a division known as a hundred, although the existence and character of the early Germanic hundred are in dispute. The *pagus*, however, also sent a hundred[16] picked men to the army, and the word hundred in this relation was no longer a mere number but now an expression of honor.

The central organization of the tribal divisions was loose.

[15] Tacitus, *Germania*, cap. 16: *suam domum.*

[16] Cæsar (*Gallic War*, IV. 1) says that each canton among the Suebi sent a thousand.

Some were ruled by chieftains, some by kings. Kings were distinguished by descent from the gods, but had very little power when judged by the Roman standard. The early Germanic ruler was strong primarily in proportion as he showed courage, valor, and leadership in warlike enterprise. A general power of constraining subjects seems to have been lacking. According to Cæsar, however, the leader in war time had power of life and death.

The political centre of this tribal organization was the great assembly. This Tacitus calls a *concilium*. The German word was no doubt some form of the word *thing* or *ding*. This body consisted of all the tribe who were entitled to bear arms. Here the youth assumed arms when his right to do so was formally recognized. The assembly was but the army meeting in council. Its decisions were those of a primitive tribal democracy. Tacitus does not tell how often this body met, but the usage of Germanic peoples at a later time suggests once a year except in cases of emergency. Meetings were held either at the new or the full moon. Silence was proclaimed and order maintained by the priests. Business was prepared in advance by the chieftains. Those who addressed the body spoke in order of rank, the king first or, if there was none, the chieftains. Decision was given by acclamation, by shouting to express disapproval of a proposal, by clashing of spears to show approval.

Along with questions of peace and war and general policy the great assembly dealt also with high questions of justice. Here accusations might be brought and capital offenses prosecuted. Here also crimes against the state, such as treason and desertion were tried. Offenses of cowardice and bodily lust were punished by the same process. Homicide and lesser personal injuries were punished by fine and *wergeld* payment, and, though ordinarily left to the clan, these were matters which came up in the assembly, the state apparently acting as arbiter to end clan feuds. No one except the priests was allowed to put a culprit to death, to imprison him or to beat him with stripes. For the lighter offenses the penalty was a certain number of horses or cattle. A part of these went to the king or tribe for its trouble in settling the case, a part to the injured person as compensation for the wrong he had suffered, or in case of homicide to the relatives of the slain.

In conclusion it may be emphasized that the institutions of the early Germans stood out in contrast to those of the Romans because of their primitive character. The tribal type of democracy prevailed except so far as its decisions were swayed by warlike chieftains. Law was the self-developing custom of the tribe, enforced and applied by the men of the whole assembled community. Taxation did not exist, and the army was the body of freemen. Kingship was weak and not everywhere existent, local political areas were controlled from the centre. As contrasted with Celtic institutions, the Teutonic showed a far stronger police and judicial power. The type was persistent and reproduced itself with variations in many a Germanic state, including those of the Angles and Saxons in Britain.

AUTHORITIES

The outstanding earlier work on Roman Britain was H. C. Coote, *The Romans in Britain* (1878). This attempted to show a considerable survival of Roman institutions in the Anglo-Saxon period, but the conclusions were conjectural and based largely upon analogy. The greatest authority on Roman civilization in Britain is F. J. Haverfield, whose views are presented in his *Romanization of Roman Britain* (1905), and more fully as to political organization and the Anglo-Saxon conquest in his *Roman Occupation of Britain* (revised by George Macdonald, 1924). He also contributed a useful chapter on Roman Britain to the *Cambridge Medieval History* (vol. I, chap. 13A, 1911).

The Roman accounts of early Germanic institutions appear in Cæsar, *De Bello Gallico* (book IV. chaps. 20-26; book V. chaps. 1-23) and in Tacitus, *Germania*. The most detailed exposition of the subject, that of Georg Waitz, in his *Deutsche Verfassungsgeschichte* (vol. I. 1844), pictures a democratic society. The theory of the free village community owning land in common was applied to Germany by G. L. Von Maurer in his *Geschichte der Markenverfassung in Deutschland* (1856). This view was stoutly assailed by Fustel de Coulanges, in

Questions Historiques (1893) and *Recherches sur quelques Problèmes Historiques* (1885, 2nd ed. 1894), although J. Flach in *Les Origines de l'Ancienne France* II. 47-62 (1893), has strongly criticized Fustel's arguments. A useful popular study of early Germanic society is F. B. Gummere, *Germanic Origins* (1892).

A contemporary idea of the Germanic conquest of Britain is afforded by Gildas, *De excidio et conquestu Britanniae*, written by a Celtic refugee in Brittany about 540, but the actual information given is slight. The best edition is that by Joseph Stevenson (English Historical Soc., 1838). There is a Celtic version (with translation) edited by Hugh Williams (Cymmrodorion Soc., 1899). Nennius in his *Historia Brittonum*, written about 796, gives bits of information derived from Celtic sources. The earlier dates in Bede and the Anglo-Saxon Chronicle depend upon tradition rather than accurate information. The earlier view of the Anglo-Saxon conquest of Britain is set forth by Edward A. Freeman in his *Norman Conquest* (I. 8-22), and restated in his *Four Oxford Lectures* (1888). With this J. R. Green agrees in *The Making of England* (1882). The brief account by Stubbs in his *Constitutional History* (I. chap. 4) is still highly useful. A more recent point of view is presented by Sir Paul Vinogradoff, who in book I. chap. 2, of his *Origin of the Manor* (1905) shows the probability that some purely Celtic elements survived Roman rule to influence the Germanic invaders. There are some critical observations in H. M. Chadwick, *The Origin of the English Nation* (1907). A good account for the use of the student is the chapter in the *Cambridge Medieval History* (I. chap. 13B, 1911) by F. G. M. Beck. There are useful suggestions regarding the period of the Anglo-Saxon invasions in Charles Oman, *England Before the Norman Conquest* (chaps. 11, 12).

PART II
THE ANGLO-SAXON FOUNDATIONS

CHAPTER III

THE INSTITUTIONS OF THE EARLY ENGLISH KINGDOMS TO 871

The Angles, Saxons, and Jutes who migrated from the continent to Britain were closely allied peoples. Their languages, it is now held, were practically the same. The West Saxons in the ninth century were said to speak not Saxon, but English, the tongue of the Angles. Indeed, the social systems and institutions of the Angles and the Saxons as well as their language were so much the same that they have been regarded by one scholar as of a single Anglo-Saxon nationality from the time of settlement.[1] It was only among the Jutes who settled in Kent that the social classes mentioned in the laws differed sharply from those of the other kingdoms.

A familiar passage in Bede explains that the people of Kent were of Jutish origin, that from the Saxons came the people of Essex, Sussex, and Wessex and from the Angles the East Anglians, Middle Anglians, and Northumbrians. This useful statement does not attempt to account for all the English kingdoms. There were at least ten of these in the seventh century,[2] although the number declined to six or seven in the eighth century and to four in the ninth. Few of these vanished at once upon being subdued by others. From the fifth century the more powerful English monarchs established their lordship over neighboring states. The smallest kingdoms tended to disappear, but a number of those still more important were ruled by under-kings subject to their more powerful neighbors. Finally, in the ninth century, the dependent states were fully absorbed and ceased to have separate existence.

The settlement of the Jutes in Kent, beginning about 450, was followed by their occupation of the Isle of Wight and the coast of

---

[1] Chadwick, *Origin of English Nation*, chap. 4.
[2] Beck in *Cambridge Medieval History*, I. 389. In some districts two kings reigned at the same time (Chadwick, *Origin of English Nation*, 155-156).

Hampshire. The first Saxon kingdom mentioned is Sussex, which tradition holds was founded in 477 by a leader named Aelle, said to have been the earliest king who exercised lordship over other English peoples.[3] The kingdom of Wessex was probably established about 515 as the result of a migration up the valley of the Thames. Its first ruler to attain hegemony over other peoples was Ceawlin, who is mentioned in the period between 560 and 570.[4] An East Saxon kingdom was established about London, but nothing is known of it until near 600, in which period tradition tells that the grandson of the first king was already ruling.

The outstanding facts in the political history of the English toward the close of the sixth century are the supremacy of Kent and the rise of the power of the Angles. The greatest Kentish king was Ethelbert (560-616), who is said to have become lord of the regions as far north as the Humber, including the kingdoms of the East Saxons and the East Angles.[5] Bede terms such a ruler, who exercised authority in wide territories beyond his own kingdom, a *bretwalda*, a word which means wielder of Britain. Ethelbert in 596 received Augustine and other Roman monks who came to convert the English to Christianity. Not only did the Kentish people soon accept the new faith, but the influence of Ethelbert brought its adoption also by the East Saxons.

The kingdom of the East Angles was apparently an important one from the days of Offa, who was its reputed founder. One of his descendants, Redwald, is represented as a strong ruler, who apparently about the time of the death of Ethelbert, established his authority over neighboring peoples.[6] On the east coast north of the Humber the Angles established two kingdoms, Deira in the present Yorkshire and Bernicia in Durham and Northumberland. The reign of Ida, the first king of Bernicia, began according to tradition in 547, and a Celtic writer says that it marked the end of the migration of the English from their earlier homes across the North Sea.[7] One of Ida's successors some years before 600 united the northern Angle kingdoms, and thus became king of Northumbria. Ethelfrith, who

[3] Bede, *Historia Ecclesiastica*, II. 5.
[4] Leeds, *Archæology of A.-S. Settlements*, 49-63; *Cambridge Medieval History*, I. 389-390. But cf. *Eng. Histor. Rev.*, XXX. 105-107.
[5] Bede, II. 3, 5.
[6] Bede, II. 5. For traditional genealogies of early kings, Nennius, sect. 57, ff.; Florence of Worcester, *Chronicon*, I. 247-276.
[7] *A.-S. Chronicle*, 547; Nennius, sect. 56.

came to the Northumbrian throne about 593, harried the British Celts far and wide and by 613 established his power as far to the south and west as Chester.

The seventh century is characterized by the conversion of the pagan English kingdoms and the struggle for supremacy between two Angle states, Northumbria and Mercia. The latter was an inland kingdom, that of the Middle Angles, which first appeared in the valley of the Trent. Until after the year 650 its struggle with Northumbria was influenced by the religious situation. Under Edwin, king of Northumbria (617-633), the northern English were won to Christianity (627) by Roman missionaries from Kent. Edwin's lordship was extensive, and he is said to have asserted it everywhere except in Kent. He was killed in battle by Penda, a pagan king of Mercia who had greatly enlarged that kingdom and who joined forces with a non-Christian Welsh ruler.[8] Northumbrian power was re-established by Oswald (634-642), renowned for bringing Celtic monks from the Isle of Iona to restore the Christian faith. Oswald's power was widely recognized, but he was unsuccessful in the struggle with his Mercian rival, though aided by the East Angles and the West Saxons, both now Christian. His successor, Oswy (642-670), finally overcame and killed Penda (655) and for a short time controlled the Mercian kingdom, where Celtic monks had already been received (653). The supremacy of Northumbria, however, soon declined before Mercian power. Penda's grandson, Wulfhere (658-670), extended his authority southward to the Thames, exercised dominion over the East Saxons, and even defeated the West Saxons.

The conversion of the southern English was completed by the Roman monks in the seventh century, that of Wessex dating from 635. The last kingdoms to be won to Christianity were Sussex (681), the kingdom of the Hwicce in southwestern Mercia, and the Jutish kingdom in the Isle of Wight (686).

Christianity strengthened the power of rulers, a fact which is especially clear in the case of Northumbria. The Christianized kings often insisted upon the appointment of friendly bishops and occasionally prevented or effected the division of dioceses to further their own plans. Moreover, the influence of the clergy was thrown in favor of the stronger kings. At the famous council of Whitby in 664 the mastery of King Oswy ended the rivalry between the Celtic and

[8] Bede, II. 20; cf. Corbett in *Cambridge Med. Hist.*, II. 543-544.

the Roman branches of the church in England and brought the Angle as well as the other kingdoms under the ecclesiastical headship of the Roman see. Theodore of Tarsus, archbishop of Canterbury (669-690), was thus able to become the first great organizer of the English church. He brought about an increase in the number of its bishoprics from seven to fourteen, as a result of which the stronger kingdoms except Wessex no longer constituted single dioceses. In Wessex the division came in 705. Theodore also greatly advanced the organization of parishes and in 673 called the first council of the entire English church, thus establishing a national organ to regulate its affairs.

The eighth century was that of Mercian supremacy. The kings of Mercia made no attempts to extend their dominion to the north, devoting their attention to the midlands and the south. Ethelred (675-704) annexed Lindsey at the expense of Northumbria and established his overlordship in Kent. The famous King Offa (757-796) brought the Mercian state to the height of its power. The kings of Kent, and apparently at times even those of Wessex, were his vassals. His authority extended also to Sussex; he annexed the kingdom of the East Angles; and he also devastated South Wales, and threw up a famous earthwork against the Welsh to delimit his western boundary.

The ninth century is marked by the supremacy of Wessex and the invasions of England by the Danes. Wessex appears as a weak kingdom in the seventh century until the last pagan king, Ceadwalla (684-688), reduced Sussex and brought to an end the Jutish kingdom in Hampshire. His successor, Ine (688-726), the greatest of the early West Saxon rulers, set up a kinsman as under-king in Sussex and conquered West Somerset from the Welsh. The power of the West Saxon state, nevertheless, was soon eclipsed by that of Mercia, and Wessex came more or less under the influence of Offa. Its permanent greatness was established only about a century after Ine's time by Egbert (802-839). He laid waste Cornwall, where he reduced the Welsh to dependence. Kent broke away from Mercia and received his son as under-king, and Sussex and Essex, also throwing off their Mercian allegiance, accepted his authority. In 825 the East Anglians slew the Mercian king in battle and re-established their independence. With their aid Egbert next overran Mercia and became overlord of all England south of the Humber. In 829 the king of Northumbria offered homage to ward off attack, and Egbert thus became the first overlord of all England, although he never established his authority in Northumbria and his control in Mercia seems to have been temporary. It is, therefore, wrong to call him the first king of England.

The real unity of English peoples came later through the Danish invasions. Beginning in 793 with an attack on Northumbria, the viking raids began to reach West Saxon territory in Egbert's time. Under Ethelwulf (839-858), his son and successor, they became more frequent in all parts of England and began to aim at the conquest of the country. The struggle grew in intensity in the reigns of three of Ethelwulf's sons, and only the fourth, Alfred (871-899), was able to check the course of invasion in Wessex. Just prior to his accession, in 870, the Northmen conquered East Anglia and in 874 drove the Mercian king from his throne. Two years later, after devastating Bernicia, they allotted Deira to Danish colonists. Outside the West Saxon lands there remained English only an isolated part of Bernicia besides western Mercia, which remained temporarily under an English vassal of the Danes.

The accession of Alfred in 871 is a favorable point at which to terminate a survey of early English institutions. Sussex and Kent had already been incorporated in Wessex, to which kingdom western Mercia was soon attached. Political unity under a single king henceforth prevailed among the English, and the old local separatism, at least for a time, was at an end. From the dawn of the authentic history of the Anglo-Saxon kingdoms to Alfred's reign is a period of slightly over three centuries; but for the first half century of this, preceding the arrival of the missionaries from Rome, there is no body of written record. Indeed the institutions of the English may scarcely be traced at all through documentary evidence except for about two centuries before Alfred. Moreover the extant sources practically confine the investigation to the four kingdoms which successively occupied the dominant position, namely Kent, Northumbria, Mercia, and Wessex. Their governmental systems show marked features of similarity which justify the treatment of them in one composite account. This similarity appears in its most striking form when a comparison is made between the institutions of Mercia and those of Wessex in the eighth century.

Evidence upon which satisfactory conclusions regarding English institutions may be founded is scanty before the tenth century. As a factor in constitutional history the destruction of the kingdoms of Mercia, Northumbria and East Anglia at the hands of the Danes has been too little appreciated. This not only eliminated the rivals of Wessex, but it destroyed the Angle institutions which prevailed throughout the greater part of England. In tracing these the historian has practically no aid from survivals as he has in the case of Wessex. For Northumbria there is hardly any material except an occasional reference in a chronicle. The code of King Offa of Mercia, the only known legislator from whose work assistance for this task might be sought, has been lost. A certain number of land charters and a few references in Bede and the Anglo-Saxon Chronicle are about all the Mercian materials that remain. For the Kentish kingdom before it was overrun by the Mercians, and then in the time of King Egbert by the West Saxons, there are only a few land charters and the laws of some of the Kentish kings of the seventh century. Even for early Wessex, although the laws of Ine are extant and Bede and the Anglo-Saxon Chronicle as well as numerous charters may be consulted, the account which may be pieced together is at best only imperfect and indistinct.

The social systems found in the Kentish laws of the seventh century and in those of Ine of Wessex show a general correspondence to what is mentioned in Tacitus, but there is greater detail and some local variation. There were slaves, freemen and nobles. Above the nobles were *aethelings* or princes of the royal family. From among such princes the rulers of provincial subdivisions of the larger kingdoms were chosen, and it is probable that in the smaller kingdoms they constituted the real nobility.[9]

Ranks in society were hereditary, although the freeman

[9] Corbett in *Cambridge Med. Hist.*, II. 566.

might rise to higher status by acquiring a sufficient amount of land. Each rank had its own *wergeld,* which was very much greater for the higher classes than for the ordinary freeman. Next beneath the *aethelings* stood a class of lesser nobles, called *eorlish* or gentle-born. Among these were the *gesiths,* whose *wergeld* in Wessex was twelve hundred or, for one class, six hundred shillings. Although extremely little information about them exists, the word *gesith* means companion, and the Latin equivalent is *comes.* The *gesiths,*[10] therefore, correspond to the *comitatus* of the early Germanic chieftain, and may be assumed to have been attendants of princelings and kings, from whom some of them received lands. In the Wessex of Ine's time, however, *gesiths* owed military service whether they held lands or not.[11]

Gesiths are mentioned only in the early period, and in their place came to stand the class known as thegns, who also formed a second rank of aristocracy about kings and other men of high rank. The word thegn is derived from *degen,* which means a warrior. There were several grades of thegns, but the two most prominent in Wessex bore *wergelds* respectively of twelve hundred and six hundred shillings. The higher class of these were king's thegns, apparently never very numerous, but so important that they attended meetings of his council. The thegns who attended king Cynewulf of Wessex are mentioned in a well known passage of the Anglo-Saxon Chronicle which relates events of the year 755. A body of thegns fought to defend the king of Wessex against assailants who slew him. Others attacked the murderers, amongst whom were some of their own kindred, refusing to serve the victorious leader, declaring that no kinsman was as dear to them as their lord, and waging the struggle to the death. There is not so much known concerning thegns who served persons other than the king, but as early as Alfred's time there are men-

[10] As to gesiths, Chadwick, *Studies on A.-S. Institutions,* 378-383; also *Origin of English Nation,* 166-170; Corbett, *Cambridge Med. Hist.,* II. 566.

[11] Laws of Ine, sec. 51.

tioned mounted thegns (*radcnihts*) whose *wergeld* was six hundred shillings and who rode on their lords' errands.[12]

Welshmen in Wessex were rated according to the amount of land they held, the highest class ranking with the lower grade of thegns, the lowest class, without land, decidedly below the ordinary freemen. The clergy ranked with the nobility, the priest with the thegn, the bishop with the alderman, and the archbishop in some regions with the king.[13]

The ordinary freeman was known as the *ceorl*. In West Saxon and Mercian law his *wergeld* was two hundred shillings. He was referred to as the *twihynde* man, the man whose life was worth two hundred shillings, as opposed to the *twelfhynde* or the *sixhynde* man, whose life was worth respectively twelve hundred or six hundred shillings. From an early time men of this class owed service in the *fyrd* or general military levy and in the building of bridges and fortifications. In the time of King Egbert these obligations were said to rest upon all ordinary freemen.[14] It is clear that some men of this legal rating were fairly important persons. Even about the year 600 there were *ceorlish* men who had loafeaters or dependents.[15]

Anglo-Saxon records throughout show the presence of men in bondage. In the laws of Kent, but there only, is mentioned also a class known as *laets*, which appears among other Teutonic peoples and which probably corresponded originally to the freedmen of Tacitus. In Kent there were three grades among these, the highest standing fairly well up in the social scale. That slavery existed among the Anglo-Saxons from the time of their settlement in England is assumed by Gildas who speaks of the reception of some of the defeated Britons into

---

[12] Chadwick, *Studies on A.-S. Institutions*, 88-89. As to the king's thegns, *ibid.*, 308-318; as to the early relation of *gesith* to thegn, *ibid.*, 333-354.

[13] This is according to the *Northleoda Lagu*, the law of the Danish kingdom of the North. Cf. Kemble, *Saxons in England*, I. 286.

[14] Birch, *Cartularium*, no. 389; Kemble, *Codex Diplomaticus*, nos. 1033, 1035.

[15] Laws of Ethelbert, sec. 25.

servitude.[16] The *Wealh* or Welsh slave is a familiar figure
in the early Anglo-Saxon laws. The *esne* or paid slave also
appears. The slave in the ordinary sense was called a *theow*.
The laws of Ine require that the *theow* be freed if compelled
to work on Sunday by his master's command. The freeman who
labored on Sunday without his lord's command and the family
who had knowledge of and consented to theft on the part of
its head, according to the same code, were reduced to servitude.
Some men were also enslaved because of conviction for crime,
and at a later time there is mention of those who bent their
heads for food in evil days.[17]

This elaborate social scheme shows an aristocratic form
of society which bears strong evidence of the influence of a
nobility consisting of princes, chieftains and their military
attendants during and following the settlement in England of
the Germanic invaders. Similar social systems existed in this
age among the Teutonic peoples on the continent. They indicate that the body of ordinary freemen had declined in influence since the time of Tacitus,[18] and that political control
had largely passed to princes and nobles.

As a result of the scarcity of sources constitutional historians formerly attempted to bridge the gap between the
early Germans and the tenth century by assuming a more
or less conjectural development, based largely upon analogies
drawn from Tacitus, but particularly upon the importance
of the family group or *maegth,* and of the free Germanic village community, which they called the mark.[19] It was formerly
assumed that the free village community or mark of the early
English tribesmen was the active factor in political development. Kemble in particular held that the local units of government were formed in England by the growth and federation

[16] Gildas, sec. 25; Bede, *Hist. Eccles.,* I. 15.
[17] Ine, sec. 24; Kemble, *Saxons in England,* I. 496-497.
[18] See Chadwick, *Origin of English Nation,* chap. 7.
[19] The word mark means boundary rather than the district within its
confines. Cf. the Anglo-Saxon *mearc,* in the laws of Hlothaere and
Eadric, sec. 15; Maitland, *Domesday Book and Beyond,* 354-355.

of marks. Upon the theory that the latter were constituted by bodies of kinsmen it has been customary to regard kinship and tribal law as the most important bonds of social and political coherence. This view too largely ignores the influence of personal lordship and that of the king.[20]

The English village community, the smallest territorial unit, is often called the township and, since the Norman period, has been known also as the vill. The most common Anglo-Saxon name was *tun*. This was given especially to the nucleated village. The village of scattered homesteads which prevailed in some districts was known as a *ham* or hamlet. According to Bede the amount of arable land which was allotted to each household was known as a *hwisc* or hide. Kemble believed that these early communities were self-governing and originally all-important in local affairs, and that each was settled by a number of households descended from a common ancestor. He held that the name of the village consists of a patronymic, followed by a suffix, such as *ham, ton*, or *wick*. Harlington, according to this theory is the village of the Harlings, Walsingham that of the Walsings.[21] Recent study of English place names tends to show, however, that what Kemble took for a patronymic is in many cases either a folk name or the name of a proprietor to whom the land was allotted.[22]

It must be recognized that the kindred group, or *maegth*, as it was called, was highly important in early English law. It avenged injuries upon one of its members by taking up the feud and exacting reparation. It seems to have been a landholding group and to have exercised guardianship over some of its members. But there appears little reason to assume that villages and *maegths* as a rule were coincident. So far as known, those who paid the *wergeld* when a person was slain were not the whole paternal kindred of the slayer, but

[20] See Chadwick, *Origin of English Nation*, 154-158.

[21] Kemble, *Saxons in England*, I. 58-59 and appendix A.

[22] Mawer and Stenton, *Introd. to Survey of English Place Names*, part I, 50-54. See also Round, *Commune of London*, chap. 1.

the immediate relatives both paternal and maternal.[23] The *maegth* of the father for this purpose was not identical with that of the son, for each generation introduced a new maternal group. The *maegth* for landholding purposes must have been different in membership and composed only of descendants in the male line. Lordship was probably quite as potent a factor in affairs as was the *maegth*. At any rate it is clear that before 700 the influence of the lord, the growing power of the monarch, the influence of monasticism and the opposition of the church to tribal and family feuds, were all working to lessen the influence of the kindred group.

The settlement of the invaders in free villages seems to have been the rule. Early English place names are group names, and the emphasis is thus upon the people settled in a given place.[24] Nevertheless, beside the free villages without lords there appeared dependent villages. The conception of dependence upon a lord on the part of his follower stands out strongly in the English folklore of the period,[25] just as it does in the case of the Germanic *comitatus*. The landlord is also mentioned in the laws of the seventh century. The laws of Ethelbert of Kent, dating from about 600, speak of the king's *tun* as well as that of the *gesith*.[26] The laws of Ine specify quantities of produce which are to be rendered from ten hides of land, apparently the usual holding the more well-to-do had received of the king. Other provisions declare that certain amounts of land shall be brought under cultivation by persons who have received estates also of smaller sizes. These same laws, moreover, show that tillers of the soil received of lords land on which they lived and for which they gave rent and services;[27] they show that the more important grade of *gesiths* were landholders and that Welshmen in

[23] Phillpotts, *Kindred and Clan*, 224.
[24] *Introd. to Survey of English Place Names*, ed. Mawer and Stenton, 54.
[25] Chadwick, *Origin of Eng. Nation*, 166-171.
[26] Laws of Ethelbert, sects. 5, 15.
[27] Laws of Ine, sects. 51, 64-66, 67, 70: 1.

Wessex ranked according to the amount of land they held;[28] they show that lords held much land, and give intimation that the social standing as well as the wealth of these lords had a relation to the amount of land they held.

Before the year 700 the lord, or *hlaford,* as he was called in old English, was the protector of many West Saxon freemen. Their dependence upon him and his responsibility for their good conduct were already recognized in law. If the dependent moved away without the lord's permission and was discovered, he had to return and make amends to the lord by paying what was then the heavy sum of sixty shillings.[29] The *gesith* had a responsibility to the king or to his lord when his dependents were guilty of wrongdoing.[30] When a lord's man was killed, he shared in the *wergeld* that was paid.[31] From the evidence in the laws it appears that many men were already dependent upon lords. This dependence was not necessarily abject, nor need one suppose that it was the rule. In the Wessex of Ine's time much of it seems to be due to the settlement of lands taken from the Celts, made over by royal grants to individual thegns,[32] and allotted by the latter to peasant cultivators. For the other kingdoms of the same period there is no sufficient evidence upon which conclusions may be based.

The view has been presented by Seebohm that the typical Anglo-Saxon *tun* was not a free village, but one held by a lord and tilled by serfs upon a plan borrowed from that of the Roman *villa.*[33] This theory requires little attention, for it rests upon conjecture. It not only implies a survival of Celtic population upon the land after the Anglo-Saxon conquest, but it also involves the improbable assumption that a great part of the English invaders were not free men. The defect in See-

---

[28] Laws of Ine, sects. 32, 45.
[29] *Ibid.,* 39.   [30] *Ibid.,* 22, 50.   [31] *Ibid.,* 21, 70.
[32] With Corbett, in *Cambridge Modern History,* II. 567-569, and Chadwick, *Origin of English Nation,* 158-161, cf. Vinogradoff, *Growth of the Manor,* 126-130; Oman, *England before the Norman Conquest,* 361-365, Guilhiermoz, *L'Origine de la Noblesse,* 90.
[33] Seebohm, *English Village Community,* chaps. 6, 8.

bohm's line of proof is that he reads back thirteenth century conditions into the early English period and assumes that these are derived from Rome.[34] The drift in England for centuries was not from serfdom to freedom, but exactly the reverse. The real significance of Seebohm's work today is in its emphasis upon the aristocratic as opposed to the democratic forces in early English society.

There is little indication that the free village community was the germ from which Anglo-Saxon political institutions developed; on the contrary there is much proof of the power of kings and other war leaders. In historic times the *tun* rendered its quota of troops and of taxes to a central power. Like the *vicus* of Tacitus, it had no court of its own, but belonged to a judicial division which included a group of villages. The only autonomy which appears at all likely is that which touched the economic life of the village and had to do with its agrarian and agricultural arrangements. It is possible, but not certain, that a village meeting was necessary for these purposes.[35] Later manorial history seems to show a certain sense of equality among peasant landholders preserved by the agrarian scheme, even in villages which were not free but which were dependent upon lords.[36]

The earliest English kings were probably more powerful than has been supposed. Stubbs regarded them as originally war leaders of small bands,[37] but according to tradition kingship appeared in the various regions only some time subsequent to the settlement of the invaders. It has been shown [38] that

[34] For refutation of Seebohm, Maitland, *Domesday Book and Beyond*, 221-222; Vinogradoff, *Growth of Manor*, book I, chap. 2; book II, chap. 1.

[35] For the communal system of tillage, see Nasse, *Agricultural Community of the Middle Ages*, 15-30. Vinogradoff, (*Growth of Manor*, 185-196) assumes a village meeting on a basis of much later evidence. Cf. Maitland, *Domesday Book and Beyond*, 147-150. A village meeting in the Danelaw prior to 1066 seems very probable (Stenton, *Documents, Social and Economic History of the Danelaw*, pp. lxi-lxii).

[36] Maitland, *Domesday Book and Beyond*, 150; Vinogradoff, *English Society in Eleventh Century*, 475-477.

[37] Stubbs, *Constitutional History*, I. 71-72.

[38] Chadwick, *Origin of English Nation*, chap. 6.

long before the migration a strong kingship existed among the Angles on the continent. The Anglo-Saxon conquest, at least after the earlier years, seems to have been effected by large bodies of men, and Bede's statement [39] that in his time the land of the Angles on the continent was still said to be deserted, indicates his belief that this people migrated as a body. The early kings were often ambitious rulers, the narrow extent of whose domain made them intent not only on conquering Celtic territory, but also on acquiring lordship over other English peoples beyond their own borders. This latter process, as shown above, is believed to have begun before the year 500. War leadership is the main aspect of early monarchy as it appears in Bede and the Anglo-Saxon Chronicle. Success in war and the subjugation of new territories increased the power of kings. After the conversion of the English the influence of the church was also important. The position of the ruler was strengthened by the Christian doctrine of obedience to the powers that be. The clergy were opposed to the strife between *maegths* and favored monarchs strong enough to secure order and afford them protection. The stronger kings, the overlords, the *bretwaldas*, as Bede well shows, had their sympathy and support, for they could better meet these conditions. Moreover, they could afford to endow the church with lands as the lesser kings could not. "Inevitably, then, if unconsciously," says Corbett, "the clergy stood for fewer and larger kingdoms, and instilled into the minds of the victorious kings ideas which may be called imperial." [40] Members of the clergy aided the kings, moreover, in administering the larger states and were undoubtedly of great assistance in working out systems of taxation and tribute.

Just what powers these rulers exercised beyond those of military leadership is not clear, but it is certainly Bede's idea that in their hands was lodged the government of the people. He represents Edwin as effecting a most unusual observance

[39] Bede, *Hist. Eccles.*, I. 15.
[40] W. J. Corbett, *Cambridge Med. Hist.*, II. 549-550.

of the public peace in Northumbria; he tells of kings who admitted or expelled Christian missionaries; and he says that
one of the kings of Kent destroyed idols and caused Lent to
be observed.[41] The guidance of affairs rested with the head of
the state.

The type of monarchy was in various ways backward and
primitive. Kings were sometimes displaced by conspiracies
of the nobles. This was true especially in Northumbria, but
in Wessex there is said to have been no instance of a son's
succeeding his father for a century and a half.[42] The Mercian
kings of the eighth century are the first who seem to stand
out as really powerful rulers. The king's wealth was chiefly
in land and its produce, but his resources were greater than
those of his subjects both in variety and in amount. Like the
Frankish ruler, he regarded these and his powers as well in
a personal rather than a public light. His lands, his public
authority and his special personal protection were conferred
upon individuals when he saw fit. In England, however, there
is no trace of the marked absolutist trend which Frankish
monarchy in Gaul acquired from a romanized environment.
The Anglo-Saxon king does not appear as a sovereign judge,
and he is never found supporting his position by claims nor
theories based upon Roman law. There was as yet no law of
treason. Offenses against the king's dignity and person were
still atoned for by money payments, as in the case of other
men of rank, except that the payment was heavier. Even for
the slaying of the king compensation could legally be made.
A *wergeld* was assigned to the Mercian king and probably to
the heads of other states also, for this usage is found among
other Germanic peoples.[43] The amount was fixed, however, at
a very high figure and no one could pay it, so in practice the
penalty imposed upon the regicide would be death.

The monarch admitted some places, persons or classes of

[41] Bede, *Hist. Eccles.*, III. 8.
[42] Stubbs, *Constitutional History*, I. 152.
[43] Liebermann, *Gesetze*, I. 462-463; cf. pp. 458-459 and II. 732-733.

persons to his special protection (*mundborg*). This was an outgrowth of the authority of the head of the Germanic household, and apparently was not very different from that offered by the nobility and the prelates, except that it was more widely extended and the sums exacted for its breach were greater.[44] As early as the time of King Ethelbert there was an especially heavy fine in the *tun* of the Kentish king for striking a person. A law of King Ine [45] established a special kind of security within the king's house. The man who fought there forfeited his property and his life as well if the king so required. From these beginnings was developed the idea of the king's special peace which had great possibilities for the future.

In important matters the monarch is found consulting councillors called *witan*. These constituted an aristocratic body, not a popular assembly of freemen like that described in Tacitus. They correspond rather to the gathering of chieftains. The earliest laws, those of King Ethelbert of Kent, speak of the king's calling his people to him, but this may refer only to military summons.[46] The only available evidence shows that the earlier *witan* comprised the *aethelings*, or princes of the royal family, including those who ruled provinces, and the king's nominees, including his thegns.[47] From the seventh century a few prelates were in attendance and occupied a prominent position. King Ine legislated, as the introduction to his code states, with the aid of his bishops, his officials in charge of provinces [48] (*ealdormen*) and the more distinguished counsellors of the kingdom. King Offa is mentioned as assenting to an act along with his bishops, abbots and magnates.[49] A careful study of the *witan* of this king has

[44] See Chadwick, *Studies on A.-S. Instns.*, 115-123; Lavisse, *Histoire de France*, II. 109.   [45] Sec. 6.

[46] See Chadwick, *Origin of English Nation*, 156-157; Liebermann, *National Assembly*, 12.

[47] Chadwick, *Studies on A.-S. Instns.*, chap. 9.

[48] A grant of Cynewulf of Wessex *cum caterva satraparum* (Birch, *Cartularium*, no. 299) describes the whole body of *witan*.

[49] *Ibid.*, no. 231; in no. 272 with the council of bishops and *senatores*. Cf. a grant of Brihtric of Wessex with the testimony of bishops and *optimates* (*ibid.*, no. 282; Kemble, *Codex Diplomaticus*, no. 180).

shown that they included the bishops, a few abbots, and about a dozen others, and that they rarely numbered thirty, even when joined with those of Kent.[50]

It has been doubted whether the witan constituted a political control or check upon the king as Stubbs and earlier writers assumed. A body of high clergy, provincial governors, normally the king's relatives, and *thegns* who were royal followers or officials, was not likely under ordinary circumstances to hold such power. That they did so under kings like Ine and Offa is quite improbable. When there was need, the *witan* might choose the king, but this does not imply the right to dispose and replace him, although there are instances of this.[51] The known functions of this body in relation to the king were almost exclusively those of counsel. Its members aided him in legislation, assented to his grants of lands, advised him in regard to relations with other states or the pope or the archbishop of Canterbury,[52] and sometimes exercised a judicial function.[53] That they formed a deliberative body is shown through Bede's account of an assembly held by King Edwin in 626 to discuss the adoption of Christianity, and through Eddi's mention of a session held by a king of Northumbria in 705, which debated the question of the banishment of Bishop Wilfrid.

Anything resembling a grant of taxes to the king is notably lacking. His support was largely provided by income from his lands and by a tribute,[54] both apparently rendered in food or other produce and known by the name of *feorm*. Sums imposed for theft and offenses against the king's peace also formed part of his income.[55] By the time of Egbert the king of

[50] Corbett, *Cambridge Med. Hist.*, II. 569.
[51] Stubbs, *Constitnl. Hist.*, I. 153-154.
[52] Liebermann, *National Assembly*, 60-62.
[53] Birch, *Cartularium*, nos. 387, 390; Kemble, *Codex Diplomaticus*, no. 1034.
[54] *Vectigal.* See Maitland, *Domesday Book and Beyond*, 234-241; Miss Demarest, in *Eng. Histor. Rev.*, XXXV. 78-89; Vinogradoff, *English Society in Eleventh Century*, 143, and *Growth of Manor*, 240, no. 35, suggests that the tribute came to take the form of a *landgafol* or land tax.
[55] Ine, sec. 73; Chadwick, *Studies on A.-S. Instns.*, 115-117.

Wessex was also receiving a portion of the *wergeld* of the slain stranger.[56] The food rent or *feorm* due the king is illustrated in the laws of Ine,[57] which specify a fixed amount of various kinds of provision to be rendered by estates of ten hides of land. West Saxon and Mercian charters of the earlier part of the ninth century frequently mention the king's *feorm* as being employed for his own support or entertainment, for the maintenance of his visitors, officials, and messengers, or for that of his horses, dogs, hawks, falcons and their keepers.[58]

Certain public services were maintained by an obligation resting upon all freemen. The three ordinary ones were later known as the *trinoda necessitas* or threefold necessity. They included the building of bridges, the repair of fortifications and service in the military levy (*fyrd*). These are mentioned in Mercia as early as the seventh century,[59] but they also appear in Kent [60] and long persisted in Wessex. Under King Offa there seems to have existed in Mercia another general obligation, that of doing fosse work against the king's Welsh enemies.[61] These public services in time came to be regarded as due in the first instance from land and only in a secondary sense from individuals.

The military system is an obscure matter throughout the whole Anglo-Saxon period, especially so before the time of Alfred. It is difficult to believe that in the days of the conquest of a new land military service was not rendered generally by the body of the freemen. The retention of the principle of this obligation for ages shows the importance attached to it. Yet a general levy of freemen was almost impossible except in a limited area, and the army which it produced was relatively inefficient. The fighting men employed as a rule, so

[56] Birch, *Cartularium*, no. 413; Kemble, *Codex Diplomaticus*, no. 236.
[57] Sec. 70: 1.
[58] Chadwick (*Studies on A.-S. Instns.*, 101 and note 1) collects evidence from the charters.
[59] Maitland, *Domesday Book and Beyond*, 235; cf. William of Malmesbury, *Gesta Regum*, I. 83-84.
[60] See Birch, *Cart.*, nos. 161, 243; Kemble, *Cod. Dipl.*, nos. 1003, 1013.
[61] *Ibid.*, no. 161; Birch, no. 264.

one must believe, were of a more expert type. Early English
society afforded in the *gesiths* and thegns a class whose business was largely that of war, and who provided at least the
nucleus [62] of a specialized force. Frequent references in the
Anglo-Saxon Chronicle to expeditions of mounted men indicate that in the eighth and ninth centuries select troops
were employed. Furthermore, military service from the seventh
century was conceived of as resting upon land,[63] an idea which
furthered the selection of men to perform military service by
making it possible to call out one man for a certain arable
unit. One document, indeed, reveals a usage which required
one man for six hides of land.[64] The fact that lords had lands
let out to dependents facilitated these arrangements. Some recent writers believe that even in this period military service
had become due primarily to lords and was exacted by them.[65]

From the seventh century onward it was customary in
giving an idea of the size or importance of a district, large or
small, to say that it had so many hundred hides of land.
These reckonings were well known, and Bede gives them
for the lands of various peoples quite remote from his northern
home. Thus the original Mercian land in the valley of the
Trent counted as 12000 hides, the Isle of Wight as 1200. There
is scarcely room to doubt that these figures represent some
official assessment. The hidages of whole kingdoms such as
Sussex and Essex are recorded.[66] A document known as the
Tribal Hidage gives the reckoning in hides of the various regions under Mercian supremacy as they stood in the seventh
century.[67] Such a hidage scheme appears later in Wessex from

[62] Chadwick (*Origin of English Nation*, 158-162) believes they constituted the entire force; but see Vinogradoff, *English Society in Eleventh
Century*, 23-31. The *ceorl* of Ine's time owed service (Ine, sect. 51).
[63] Maitland, *Domesday Book and Beyond*, 235-236.
[64] Birch, *Cartularium*, no. 201.
[65] Chadwick, *Studies on A.-S. Instns.*, 102; *Origin of English Nation*,
160; cf. Vinogradoff, *Growth of Manor*, 129.
[66] See Corbett, *Cambridge Med. Hist.*, II. 550-551.
[67] Corbett, *Transactns., Royal Histor. Soc.'* n. s. vol. 14; *Cambridge
Med. Hist.*, I. 544-545; Brownbill in *English Histor. Rev.*, XXVII. 625-
648; Kemble, *Saxons in England*, I. 81-82.

the time of Alfred and was used there in allotting fiscal and military obligations. Some of the later hidage figures show a correspondence with the earlier ones. Corbett has presented a strong case to show that even in the seventh century hidages were the basis upon which Mercian military levies and tributes were exacted.

English local government prior to the tenth century is an exceedingly difficult topic, and there is only slight allusion to its administrative geography. A local ruler, called *praefectus* and mentioned toward the close of the seventh century in Northumbrian towns,[68] seems to be the official mentioned later in the same region under the title of high reeve. The divisions of Mercia were tribal areas which were gradually joined to the original kingdom. Over these ruled *ealdormen*, who were no doubt originally under-kings and later *aethelings*.[69] They enjoyed a *feorm*, as did the king, and had a right to demand that their huntsmen and servants should receive food.[70] These *ealdormen* are mentioned in the Anglo-Saxon Chronicle as the military leaders of their respective districts, and five of them were killed in 825 in the noted battle fought with the East Anglians.

Wessex was a more solidly compacted state than its rival, although the Jutish portion of Hampshire seems to have been incorporated only late in the seventh century and Celtic areas to the west even later. The creation of West Saxon administrative subdivisions apparently followed more artificial lines than that in Mercia. There were already under-kings in the seventh century, and in a kingless period from 673 to 684 these ruled the various parts of Wessex.[71] There can be little doubt that the territorial subdivisions which they held corresponded to the shires which are mentioned a few years later in the laws of King Ine. The word shire, in Anglo-Saxon *scir*, meant share or part, and may be regarded as a

[68] Eddi, *Life of Wilfred*, secs. 36-38.
[69] W. J. Corbett, *Cambridge Med. Hist.*, II. 569.
[70] Heming, *Chartulary* (ed. Hearne), I. 31, 47.
[71] Bede, IV. 12; Chadwick, *Studies*, 284-290.

province or division of the kingdom allotted to a member of the royal family.[72] By the time of Ine the head of a West Saxon shire was called an *ealdorman*. He was its chief judicial official and by the laws of this king was threatened with dismissal if he failed to punish crime.[73] According to the Anglo-Saxon Chronicle he was also the military commander who led the men of his shire against the Mercians and the Danes. Royal dues both in produce and in labor [74] were rendered to him. In Wessex as in Mercia he and his subordinates were entitled to a *feorm* derived from certain lands. His relation to these and other matters of administration shows a reason for his place among the *witan* of the king's council.

The small kingdoms subjected by Wessex were gradually reduced to the status of shires. Under-kings were replaced by members of the West Saxon royal family. Ethelwulf, the son of Egbert, is mentioned as king of Kent, and one of Ethelwulf's sons in turn is said by Florence of Worcester to have held this region with Surrey and Sussex until he became king in 860. Thenceforth *ealdormen,* and not under-kings, are mentioned in the regions which had constituted separate states. The mediatized kingdom like Sussex or Kent thus became a shire of Wessex.

To trace any systematic administrative subdivision of the shire in this period is impossible. It has been customary to assume that a Germanic unit of local government known as the hundred was introduced by the Anglo-Saxon settlers,[75] but there is no mention of hundreds in the earlier English records, nor indeed is there any allusion to a comprehensive arrangement of small judicial areas of any kind until after the death of Alfred. A hundred hides of land, or, more probably at first, a Germanic hundred of a hundred and twenty hides,

---

[72] Corbett, *Cambridge Med. Hist.*, II. 566. For other explanations see Oman, *England before the Norman Conquest*, 371-372.

[73] Ine, sec. 36:1.

[74] Kemble, *Cod. Dipl.*, nos. 196, 210, 277; Birch, *Cart.*, nos. 357, 487.

[75] Stubbs, *Constitnl. Hist.*, I. 104-105; Vinogradoff, *Growth of Manor*, 144-145; Corbett, *Cambridge Med. Hist.*, II. 570.

seems to have constituted an early administrative reckoning employed by kings for military and fiscal purposes. There are bits of evidence which show the village or single estate reckoned at ten hides,[76] yet an administrative plan of this sort does not necessarily involve division of the shire into the judicial and police districts later known as hundreds.[77] The laws of Ine mention persons other than the *ealdorman* who are judges, but there is no other clue to popular assemblies held generally for groups of villages. This may possibly be explained by the fact that the laws and the royal land charters are concerned with the king's affairs rather than with those of local communities. The evidence of Tacitus and later Anglo-Saxon usage both point to the existence of such local assemblies. Officials of the *ealdorman* known as reeves probably held them for primitive territorial divisions, which it is impossible to identify with the administrative areas mentioned at a later day.

Early subdivisions of shires are mentioned only in one connection. Certain territories were administered from royal *tuns,* where local agents of the king resided and, at least in Alfred's time, held courts. It is quite probable that this mode of government was originally employed only on the king's estates and in the collection of his dues, the rest of the shire being left to the *ealdorman* to administer with the aid of his own officials. The writer who about the time of Alfred translated Bede into Anglo-Saxon thought of the king's *tun* as the residence of a royal official.[78] It has been shown [79] quite convincingly that in Kent and elsewhere an administrative district was centred in the king's *tun.* In Kent these districts were larger than *tuns* and seem to have corresponded to the divisions later known as lathes. In Mercia the king's vill is mentioned especially as a place where tribute was due and

[76] Laws of Ine, sec. 70:1; W. J. Corbett, *Cambridge Med. Hist.,* II. 550.

[77] Chadwick, *Studies,* 244-248.

[78] *Ealdor:* Seebohm, *Tribal Custom in A.-S. Law,* 420.

[79] *Studies on A.-S. Instns.,* 249-262.

where criminals were held to responsibility.[80] In Wessex a little before Egbert's time an official known as the king's reeve was performing his duties in the neighborhood of a royal *tun*,[81] and, according to the laws of Alfred a century later, a reeve had charge of the king's prisoners there.[82] An old tradition that the West Saxon ruler rendered justice in person may be accounted for by the fact that his reeve who held a court was stationed at the royal vill, where the king was often in residence.[83] Alfred was thus able to correct his reeves by word of mouth when they erred in matters of judgment,[84] as he could not have done under later conditions.

The king's reeve or *gerefa*, who was in charge of administrative work at the royal *tun*, was probably in the beginning an officer of the royal household.[85] In the laws of King Ine he appears as the king's personal fiscal agent, and there can be little doubt that he was much the same as the fiscal official (*procurator* or *exactor*) who according to both Mercian and West Saxon charters exacted public services and, according to the latter, also collected sums due because of criminal offenses.[86]

His functions were of much the same nature as those of a

[80] Cf. the charter of King Cenwulf in Kemble, no. 210, and Birch, no. 357; also Heming, *Chartulary*, 101-102. Labor dues at royal *villulae* are mentioned in a grant of Offa in 892 (Birch, no. 848). A charter of King Wiglaf (Birch, no. 416) indicates that the royal *tun* was a *burh* where wall work was performed (*liberabo a pastu regis et principum et ab omni constructione regalis ville*).

[81] *A.-S. Chron.*, 787.

[82] Laws of Alfred, 1: 2, 1: 3.

[83] Under the early kings of Kent justice appears to have been done in ordinary matters at the king's hall (Withred, 22; cf. Hlothaire and Eadric, 7, 16). Under Ine the king and his reeve are said to settle upon the composition to be paid for theft (Ine, 73).

[84] Asser, ed. Stevenson, sects. 91, 106.

[85] Cf. the *praefectus* of the king of Kent, Bede, *Eccles. Hist.*, IV. 1; Larson, *King's Household in A.-S. Period*, chap. 4.

[86] Kemble, *Cod. Dipl.*, no. 196; Birch, *Cartularium*, no. 351. In a charter of the Mercian King Bertwulf of the year 828 (Kemble, *Cod. Dipl.*, no. 242) occur *praefecti* who can hardly be anything but reeves. So the West Saxon *exactor* in Birch, no. 449. In a grant of King Ethelwulf made in 847 (Kemble, *C. D.*, no. 260; Birch, *Cart.*, no. 451) : *vi exactorum operum sive poenalium causarum furisque comprehensione*.

contemporary class of reeves, called the *ealdorman's gingran* or juniors, who in Mercia had a share in the *feorm* exacted, and who, at least in the time of Alfred, presided over assembly-courts or *gemots*.[87] In Alfred's reign the king's reeves, like the *ealdormen*, are known to have held such assemblies in which they pronounced judgment.[88] Accusation of guilt was made before them, and certain persons were led to them to be placed in suretyship.[89] Such royal agents, exercising local, fiscal, judicial, and presumably also police, functions were clearly persons of importance and of great usefulness.

The assemblies or *gemots* in which justice was done, like those of the early Germans, were popular assemblies or folk-motes.[90] Asser mentions in Alfred's time difficulties which arose because of discontent with the conduct of the *ealdormen* and the reeves presiding in these assemblies.[91] The one held by the *ealdorman* in Wessex was almost certainly a shire *gemot* or county court, although there is no specific information cencerning it until a later time.

In the law enforced by popular judgment in these bodies may be traced survivals of early Teutonic usage. Payment for homicide was exacted by the *maegth* or kindred group of the slain, which thus supplemented the functions of the government. For personal injuries fines, or *bots* as they were called, were also required. The code of King Ethelbert of Kent, the first of the Anglo-Saxon codes, consists largely of a list of payments for manslaying or bodily injuries. The same scheme is prominent in the laws of Alfred nearly three centuries later. The law of Ine required that a thief be punished by death unless he redeemed himself with the amount of his *wergeld*. In addition to the sum exacted by the kindred, the

---

[87] As in Birch, *Cart.*, nos. 357, 487; Kemble, *Cod. Dipl.*, nos. 210, 277. Cf. the *subditi* of kings and *principes* (Heming, *Chartulary*, 47, 69, 70, 101-102). See also Alfred, secs. 38, 38: 1, 38: 2.

[88] Asser, ed. Stevenson, sec. 106.

[89] Alfred, secs. 22, 34.

[90] See Birch, *Chartularium*, no. 201.

[91] Asser, ed. Stevenson, sec. 106: *in contionibus comitum et praepositorum.*

state demanded also a fine or *wite* for its services in hearing the case which came before the *gemot*. Men's oaths as well as their *wergeld* varied in value according to their rank in society.

The early Anglo-Saxon political scheme, though backward and unformed in many ways, shows much advance upon that described by Tacitus. It retains, especially in its legal and judicial usages, some primitive features. The state has nevertheless gained much by the growth of kingship and by a stronger assertion of monarchical authority. The king, though far from claiming absolute authority, has extended his power from the centre outward. He has improved upon a tribal military system; he has devised a scheme of tribute or rent akin to taxation; he has introduced his own reeve in local administration and his control has reached further into the province of the *ealdorman's* authority. On the other hand, the aristocratic elements represented by a nobility and by dependence upon lords are prominent and influential. The former of these forms the greatest practical check upon the monarch's power. Some phases of tribal democracy none the less seem to be retained in the constitution of the *tun* and stand out clearly in the local assemblies which do justice according to traditional custom. The Anglo-Saxon, like the early Germanic, system presents features of control by king, nobility and freeman. The successive vicissitudes of the three factors largely mark the course of English constitutional history.

AUTHORITIES

The sources for the constitutional history of the period consist of laws, land charters, and chronicles. The extant laws are those of several kings of Kent and of Ine of Wessex. The laws of the Anglo-Saxon kings are in the nature of enacted supplements to the existing body of customary law. They were edited by Benjamin Thorpe (*Ancient Laws and Institutes*, 1840), whose work often presents a philological rather than an institutional interpretation. A better edition of the laws is that by Reinhold Schmid (*Gesetze der Angelsachsen*, 1858). This contains a glossary which presents useful discussion of old English institutions. The best and most scholarly edition is the notable work of

Dr. Felix Liebermann (*Gesetze der Angelsachsen,* 1898-1916). This is in three volumes, the first of which presents in parallel columns the various texts of the laws. The second volume consists in large part of an encyclopedic glossary which systematically treats many Anglo-Saxon institutions. An eclectic text of the laws, more readily available and with English translation, is presented in two recent works, F. L. Attenborough, *The Laws of the Earliest English Kings* (1922) and Agnes J. Robertson, *The Laws of the Kings of England from Edmund to Henry I* (1925).

The land charters of the Anglo-Saxon period are chiefly royal documents. Many were issued by the king with the advice of his *witan,* whose names often appear as witnesses. The only collection covering the whole period to 1066 is that edited by J. M. Kemble and published under the title *Codex Diplomaticus aevi Saxonici* (6 vols., 1839-1848). The *Cartularium Saxonicum,* edited by W. de Gray Birch (3 vols, 1883-1893), covers the period only to 975, but includes some documents not published by Kemble. Several useful volumes, notably, Thorpe, *Diplomatarium Anglicum Aevi Saxonici* (1865), Earle, *English Land Charters* (1888), and Harmer, *Select English Historical Documents* (1914) present collections of selected charters.

The *Anglo-Saxon Chronicle* took its present form about the year 900. The earlier portion is crabbedly annalistic. Some parts from about 750 give detail and show more first-hand information on the part of the writer; but the earlier years of the *Chronicle* present a traditional account, and its chronology of the Anglo-Saxon conquest is not trustworthy. The most important, and almost the only, authority for the history of the early English kingdoms is Bede, *Historia Ecclesiastica Gentis Anglorum.* This is extremely useful for the period extending from slightly before the arrival of the Roman missionaries in 597 to the year 731. There are many editions. A good one is that edited by Joseph Stephenson (*English Historical Society,* 1838); the edition by Charles Plummer (1896) is of unusual importance.

The first systematic work on early English institutions was that of J. M. Kemble, *The Saxons in England* (2 vols., 1849, 2nd ed. 1876). This stressed the importance of the *maegth* and assumed that the free Germanic mark was the starting point of political development in England. The second notable account was that of William Stubbs in his *Constitutional History of England* (3 vols., 1874; various subsequent editions) which cautiously followed Kemble's theory concerning the earlier period. J. R. Green in his account of the Anglo-Saxon conquest, *The Making of England* (1882), and Edward A. Freeman in his various works were more largely influenced by the same views. J. H. Round in chap. I of his *Commune of London* (1899) assails much of

Kemble's contention in regard to the settlement of the English village communities.

The first notable English writer to question the general viewpoint of Kemble was Frederick Seebohm, who in his *English Village Community* (1883) contended that the early English village was predominantly serf and not free. This view was attacked by F. W. Maitland in his *Domesday Book and Beyond* (1897) and by Paul Vinogradoff in *The Growth of the Manor* (1905). Both of these works contain useful material on early English society. The latter especially holds, like Stubbs, that the type of institutional system mentioned in Tacitus, including a Germanic hundred, existed in England from the days of Germanic settlement.

The first important work to deal with Anglo-Saxon institutions generally from a new point of view was H. M. Chadwick, *Studies on Anglo-Saxon Institutions* (1905). It presents a detailed examination of the sources which shows that early English government, as revealed in documents, was marked by monarchical and aristocratic rather than popular influence. Chadwick finds no evidence of the existence of the hundred before the tenth century, and holds that it is not safe to build up a supposititious political system for the early Anglo-Saxons upon a basis of analogies drawn from Tacitus. He has still more sharply challenged the views of the Germanist school of writers in his work, *The Origin of the English Nation* (1907). Liebermann also rejects the traditional account of the hundred.

The most useful brief account of Anglo-Saxon history to the time of Alfred is presented in chapters of the *Cambridge Medieval History*, vols. I-III (1911-1922). The "Teutonic Conquest of Britain" (I. chap. 13) is by F. G. M. Beck, the remainder of the account, by W. J. Corbett (II. chap. 17; III. chap. 14). This includes material on institutions and the composition of society, and presents in brief compass the best balanced treatment of these topics. It should be compared with F. M. Stenton's article "The Supremacy of the Mercian Kings" in *English Historical Review*, XXXIII. Mr. Corbett's particular specialized contribution was his study of the Tribal Hidage (*Transactions of Royal Historical Society*, n.s. XIV, 1900). Another important study of this document has been made by J. Brownbill (*English Historical Review*, XXVII. 1912; XL. 1925).

Local government has been treated in detail by Kemble, Stubbs, Chadwick, and Liebermann. A careful study of this side of the Anglo-Saxon system is presented by Miss Helen M. Cam in her *Local Government in Francia and England* (1912). There are useful suggestions in chap. 4 of L. M. Larson, *The King's Household in England before the Norman Conquest* (Bulletin, University of Wisconsin, no.

100, 1904). The introductory chapter of W. A. Morris, *Medieval English Sheriff* (1927) deals with the king's reeve.

The student will find it interesting to read an account of early Frankish institutions for the sake both of comparisons and contrasts with Anglo-Saxon institutions. Lavisse, *Histoire de France,* vol II (1903) affords a good brief account of the Gallic law and Frankish society (pp. 107-115), and chapter 4 is devoted to the institutions of the Merovingian period.

CHAPTER IV

THE CENTRAL GOVERNMENT, 871-1066:
KING, WITAN, AND ROYAL HOUSEHOLD OFFICIALS

Wessex was saved from Danish conquest by Alfred (871-899).
Viking successes elsewhere left him the sole national leader of the
English. In 872 he made a peace with the Danes by which they
agreed to withdraw from his territories, but in 877 the invasion was
renewed by the Danish king, Guthrum, and other leaders. The defeat
of Guthrum the next year was followed by a peace made at Chip-
penham, according to which he agreed to accept baptism and to
withdraw from Wessex. About 879 Ethelred, who ruled the unconquered region of western Mercia, gave allegiance to Alfred to
gain his aid. Henceforth Ethelred was no longer known as king but
as *ealdorman,* and the English were united under one ruler. Guthrum
established a kingdom in Essex and East Anglia, but the eastern
midlands as well as the land between the Welland and the Humber
were ruled by more or less independent viking leaders, known as
jarls, who maintained themselves in fortified towns or boroughs. The
region in which the conquerors established their customs and institutions came to be known as the Danelaw. Alfred reorganized the
military system of Wessex, built up a system of fortresses or
boroughs, and in 885 gained London at Guthrum's expense. In 892
he was assailed by a multitude of vikings who had been forced out
of Frankish territories, but he resisted so successfully that in 896
they gave up the struggle. Henceforth Wessex was prepared to
assume the offensive.

Alfred's son, Edward the Elder (899-925), began the subjugation
of the Danelaw. The process required in all about fifty years, but
when completed made the ruler of Wessex the king of England.
Edward was aided by his sister Ethelfled, the widow of the
ealdorman Ethelred. As the English advanced into Danish territory,
they erected boroughs to hold the frontier. In 918 they gained Northampton and Leicester, and the Danish leaders in Cambridge, Hunt-

ingdon and East Anglia made their submission to Edward, accepting
him as their lord. In the course of another year, the English king
became the overlord of all the Danes as far north as the Humber.
In 920 he received the homage also of the English ruler who remained
in Bernicia and the Danish king in Yorkshire.

Edward's son, Athelstan (925-939), annexed the latter kingdom
and in the battle of Brunanburh in 937 broke up a league against
him, formed by the Scottish king, consisting also of Britons, Irish
vikings, and the Danes in northern Britain. Athelstan took the title
king of all Britain, and set up a new administrative organization in
the southern Danelaw. His brother, Edmund (939-946), for a short
time lost York and the region of the five Danish boroughs of the
northern midlands, but regained this ground and strengthened his
position by making over the troublesome Norwegian community of
Cumberland to the Scottish king. Edmund's successor suppressed a
final attempt of the Danes of Yorkshire to regain their independence,
and in 954 placed this region under the English high reeve at Bamborough. The northern Danelaw retained its own laws, but England
now constituted a single kingdom. This reached the height of its
power under Edgar (959-975), the son of Edmund, whose reign is
known chiefly for its ecclesiastical reforms under the leadership of
Dunstan, archbishop of Canterbury.

In the reign of Ethelred (978-1016), son of Edgar, came a period
of decline. A new series of viking invasions began in 991. Time and
time again the invaders were induced to depart by the payment of
a large sum of money. The northern regions remained Danish, and
the king's power there was not great. Scandinavian kingdoms had
now taken shape in Sweden, in Norway and in Denmark, and after
1002, Sweyn, the king of Denmark, formed a definite plan for the
conquest of England. Within a few years the realm was unable to
withstand his onslaught, especially when in 1013 he was received
by the Danes in Yorkshire and overran Wessex. Ethelred fled to
Normandy, his wife's country, and only the early death of his rival
prevented the latter from reigning as king of England. The attempt
at conquest was continued by Sweyn's son, Canute. In the midst
of the struggle Ethelred died and his son Edmund, known as Ironside,
who had proved a competent leader, was chosen king. He arranged to
divide the kingdom with Canute, but his death soon left the Dane
in control.

Canute (1017-1035) ruled England as an English rather than as a Danish king. He also acquired Denmark and a considerable Scandinavian empire, but resided chiefly in England. He married the Norman Emma, the widow of Ethelred, and governed according to the laws of Edgar, which were formally adopted in 1018.[1] The various regions of the kingdom were placed under strong *jarls* or earls, about six in number. At first these were all foreigners. After a time Wessex and Mercia were given respectively to the English earls, Godwin and Leofric. The English rulers of Bernicia were also retained, but East Anglia, Yorkshire, and western Mercia were ruled by Scandinavian earls. Canute, who had become a Christian, from 1020 governed England largely according to the wishes of the bishops. At his death his Scandinavian empire broke up, and England's direct connection with Denmark ceased.

The reigns of Canute's two sons, Harold (1035-1040) and Hardacanute (1040-42), were unimportant. At the death of the latter the *witan* of his kingdom, setting aside the Danish claimant to the throne, chose as their ruler the son of Ethelred and Emma, Edward (1042-1066), who at a later time came to be known as Edward the Confessor. Under his rule the great earls were powerful figures in the realm, whose ambition reinforced the separatist tradition of their respective regions. The greatest of these, Godwin, increased his influence by gaining three additional earldoms for his sons, one in East Anglia, and one at the expense of Mercia. The king preferred the culture of Normandy, where he had been brought up. Moreover, he appointed a number of Norman prelates, gave an earldom to his Norman nephew, and in other ways employed his mother's countrymen to reduce the power of Godwin's family. A breach developed, and in 1051 the powerful earl took up arms. The earls of Mercia and Northumbria, his rivals, aided the king, and Godwin and his sons were outlawed and became exiles. The next year, however, they returned and regained their position, a turning of the tables which resulted in the flight of most of the king's foreign followers, and the domination of the house of Godwin over Edward for the rest of his life. After the death of the great earl, the king attempted without much success to play off other earls against his successor, Harold. In 1065, Tostig, the brother of the latter, was given an earldom in Northumbria, only to be expelled by

[1] *Anglo-Saxon Chronicle*, 1018.

a popular uprising. At the Confessor's death in 1066, Harold was chosen king to the exclusion of the claims of the late king's relative, William, duke of Normandy. The new king had to face first a Norwegian invasion of the north aided by Tostig. Hardly was this defeated, when he had to deal with a Norman invasion of the south. Unsupported by the rival earls of the house of Mercia, Harold was defeated and slain by Duke William near Hastings in October 1066, and the Norman Conquest followed.

Increasing respect for kingship and increasing claims in its behalf are apparent in the tenth century. The leadership of King Alfred and his descendants in the national cause was of great advantage. A treason law of Alfred for the first time afforded the protection to the king which the usages of *wergeld* could not give. By the new law,[2] he who plotted against the king's life, or harbored his enemies, was liable in his life and all he possessed. This was exactly the same penalty as that imposed in Alfred's law for plotting against one's lord. The doctrines of personal lordship were being appropriated by the crown to extend its claims over all men. Edward the Elder, acknowledged as lord by the men of various Danish districts, by Mercian subjects of his sister and by northern kings as well, asked that his *witan* enter into his vassalage.[3] Moreover, a law of Edmund required that all swear fealty to the king "as a man ought to be faithful to his lord." [4] The monarch thus came to make a strong personal claim to fidelity upon every man in the realm.

Kingship in some cases remained elective, although the crown was in general hereditary. The king was inducted into office with the religious ceremonies of crowning and anointing at the hands of a bishop or archbishop. According to the coronation oath used in the tenth century [5] he promised to preserve the church and all Christian men in true peace; to forbid

[2] Laws of Alfred, sec. 4.
[3] Liebermann, *National Assembly in A.-S. Period*, 27.
[4] III Edmund, 1.
[5] See Liebermann, *Gesetze*, I. 214-217; A. J. Robertson, *Laws of Kings of England*, 42.

robbery and unrighteous deeds; and to enjoin equity and mercy in all judgments.

The king was the commander-in-chief who called out and sometimes personally led [6] the armed forces of the kingdom. He presided over the *witan*, sought their advice in various matters and legislated by their counsel. The officers of church and state he regarded as his officers, and he claimed wide powers in appointing and dismissing them. In the laws of Ine the king threatened the *ealdormen* with loss of their shires for failure to punish crime, but three and a half centuries later, when Edward the Confessor gave the Northumbrian earldom to Tostig, local tradition was too strong and the intruder was expelled. Reeves and sheriffs were among the king's own officials, and there are also numerous known instances in the eleventh century of his appointing bishops and abbots. He was the guardian of the peace of the realm. It was his to execute the law and protect the realm from invasion. If, like Ethelred, he failed to do this he was not accounted a good king.

The royal power was employed in the tenth and eleventh centuries to supplement the general peace (*frith*) by extending the king's peace (*grith*) to cover particular cases or classes of cases. This was done in part through legislation but also through the monarch's special grant and through proclamation made by his officials such as earls, sheriffs, and reeves.[7] Payments required for breach of the king's peace were unusually heavy, so his protection was the more effective. This as yet extended merely to certain persons, places and seasons, but it was capable of ready expansion and was in the course of time destined to become coincident with the national peace.

The ancient principle of the king's *mundborg* was exemplified as late as the Confessor's reign in a royal grant which placed the men of a monastery under the ruler's special pro-

[6] Ethelred, 35; *Domesday Book*, I. 172: *edictu regis.*

[7] *Domesday Book*, I. 252; *ibid.*, 280b, 298b: *pax data regis vel sigillo ejus; ibid.*, 262b: *pax data manu regis vel suo brevi vel per suum legatum.*

tection.[8] A law of Ethelred placed widows under the king's peace,[9] and another made him protector and avenger of strangers.[10]

Of the places covered by the king's peace the king's residence is the first to be mentioned. The man who fought there was at the king's mercy, and liable in his property and life.[11] According to Canute's law the penalty for this offense held also for breach of *grith* in the army.[12] Men were under the special peace in attending the meetings of the local courts, and also in going and returning.[13] The king's peace was extended to churches, partly by legislation[14] and partly by the king's special act.[15] As early as Alfred's day violation of the right of sanctuary in a church was equivalent to infraction of the king's peace.[16] This also protected dwellings[17] and certain highways and navigable streams.[18] Maitland contended that the same held for boroughs, but the evidence is insufficient to establish this as a rule.[19] The king's peace also protected certain seasons of the year. It ran for several days at Christmas, Easter and Pentecost.[20] For certain offenses in Lent, as well as on Sunday, Christmas or Easter, a double compensation was required. In the Confessor's time, the king's peace not only prevailed at these important periods in the church calendar, but in some localities at other seasons.[21]

[8] Kemble, *Codex Diplomaticus*, no. 904.

[9] V Ethelred, 21; VI Ethelred, 26.

[10] VIII Ethelred, 33; II Canute, 40. Above, p. 38.

[11] Ine, 6; II Canute, 59. For the distance the peace extended about the king's residence, Liebermann, *Gesetze*, I. 390-391.

[12] II Canute, 61.

[13] II Canute, 82.

[14] V Ethelred, 10:1; VIII Ethelred I. 5:1; Kemble, *Codex Diplomaticus*, no. 904: God's *grith* and mine.

[15] I Canute, 2:2.

[16] Alfred, 5.

[17] The *burh* here may be only the king's house.

[18] *Domesday Book*, I. 1, 2, 280; cf. *Leges Edwardi Confessoris*, 12.

[19] Maitland, *Domesday Book and Beyond*, 185; II Edmund, 2; III Ethelred, 1:2; Domesday Book, I. 154b; Liebermann, *Gesetze*, I. 471.

[20] *Leges Edwardi Confessoris*, 12; cf. *Ramsey Chronicle* (Rolls Ser.), 163. It also prevailed during Rogation days.

[21] Alfred, 5:5; II Canute, 47; cf. *Domesday Book*, I. 262b; *ibid.*, I. 1 (Michaelmas to St. Andrew's Day).

From an early time infraction of the king's peace gave rise to several unusually important crimes, among which were breach of the king's protection especially extended, invasion of, or assault upon, a dwelling, and waylaying and assaulting a man upon a highway.[22] In the eleventh century Englishmen in Wessex and Mercia made amends to the king for these by the high monetary penalty of five pounds.[23] There were other offenses which yielded to the king the same amount, but the list seems to have varied locally. All these were the precursors of the later pleas of the crown, standing out in marked contrast to the more ordinary cases.

The king's relation to the administration of justice amounted to a superiority without much direct control. There is no satisfactory evidence that the monarch was the fountain of justice in the same sense as the king of the Norman period, who either sat personally to pronounce judgment or else authorized members of his court to go out and hold trials. The old English king was in a way regarded as head of the judicial system. The local courts were considered his courts, yet it is doubtful whether he thought of himself as the highest judge. Alfred has sometimes been represented as meting out justice personally in a sort of patriarchal fashion, but a well-known document which relates that he caused a judgment to be revised,[24] does not show that he exercised strictly judicial functions nor held a special court.

The monarch was under a moral obligation to enjoin equity and mercy. He was sought by the person who failed to obtain justice in the local assemblies, or who believed that the penalty imposed upon him was unduly severe. Individuals were for-

[22] The respective Anglo-Saxon names are, *mundbryce* or *borhbryce*, *hamsocne*, and *forestal*. Chadwick, *Studies on A.-S. Institutions*, 115-117: *Codex Diplomaticus*, no. 310. Cf. II Canute, 12; *Leges Henrici*, 80 : 1, 2, 4, 11. *Hamsocne* is the *hamfare* or *hainfare* (Haskins, *Norman Instns.*, 28) of the Norman period.
[23] II Canute, 12, 58, 62; *Domesday Book*, I. 172, 252; cf. IV Ethelred, 4 : 1; II Edmund, 6.
[24] Kemble, *Codex Diplomaticus*, no. 328; Birch, *Cartularium*, no. 591; Harmer, *English Historical Documents*, 30-32, 60-63. For comment, Lees, *Alfred the Great*, 254-256; Adams, *Essays in A.-S. Law*, 23-24.

bidden by the law of Edgar and of Canute to approach the
king unless the local courts had failed to settle their cases.[25]
The monarch intervened in various ways to secure justice.
He exercised the prerogative of mercy.[26] He might dismiss or
otherwise punish corrupt or ignorant officials responsible for
unsatisfactory decisions.[27] Against outlaws or powerful offenders he wielded the peace (*frith*) by armed force.[28] Moreover, he took cognizance of some judicial matters, apparently
both when judgment had actually been given in the local
courts, and when it was pending. In such cases the king's
messenger was sometimes sent to the shiremote with the
royal writ.[29]

As against the assumption of the existence of a royal court
to which appeals might be taken,[30] the older and opposing
view must still be upheld. The chronicles of certain great
churches, such as Ramsey, Ely, and Worcester, tell of suits
in the local courts touching church lands. It is almost certain
that, if the king had heard appeals and rendered decisions in
a court of his own, these accounts or some of the royal charters
would make allusion to the fact. Yet the only procedure mentioned is a reference of some phase of the matter to the *witan*
or the shiremote.[31] The *witan* seem to be the only central
court available in such cases.[32] Although the king alone might
claim jurisdiction over his thegn[33] and probably also over
holders of bookland,[34] this seems to have been exercised
through the national assembly.[35] From the time of Canute

[25] III Edgar, 2; II Canute 17, 19, 19: 1.   [26] III Edgar, 2: 1.
[27] III Edgar, 3; cf. Asser, *Life of Alfred* (ed. Stevenson), sec. 106.
[28] II Ethelred, 6; II Canute, 13.
[29] Kemble, *Codex Diplomaticus*, no. 693; cf. nos. 755, 898, 929.
[30] Liebermann, *National Assembly*, 68-69.
[31] Alfred once permitted an oath to certain facts, but this could well
have been taken in a folkmote. See references in note 24.
[32] See *Liber Eliensis*, 122; cf. Kemble, *Codex Dipl.*, no. 693.
[33] III Ethelred, 11.
[34] He alone had the fines for their offenses (I Ethelred, I. 14).
[35] Stubbs, *Constitutional Hist.*, I. 146. As to the *theningman's* court
of Edgar's time see Kemble, *Cod. Dipl.*, no. 1258; Birch, *Cart.*, no. 1296;
translation. Adams, *Essays in A.-S. Law*, 348-349. Liebermann (*National Assembly*, 69) regards this as an officials' court, but the members
mentioned are *witan*.

is mentioned a military assembly which seems to have consisted of the king's Danish troops or later of his household guard.[36] So far as evidence goes, this body affords the only examples prior to the Norman Conquest of the rendition of justice by a curial as opposed to a national assembly.

The old English king was the national executive who had much power in every department of government, not excluding the church. The manner in which he availed himself of his positon of course depended upon his vigor and ability. The tenth century was a period largely of youthful kings and the eleventh century a period mainly of weak ones. Liebermann has remarked that under a weak prince the word king meant nothing but state or commonwealth. In such cases power obviously rested with the *witan,* in whom lay the principal limitation upon royal authority.

The national assembly of the English kingdom consisted of the *witan.* The word is the plural form of *wita,* one who knows. The name *witenagemot* or assembly of the counsellors, used by modern historians, does not appear in the laws or the charters. The word *micel gemot* or great assembly was sometimes employed as a designation, though it might also denote an ecclesiastical assembly. The Latin name is *sapientes* or wise men, although this is not an accurate translation [37] of the Anglo-Saxon word *witan.* Besides the national assembly, provincial assemblies of *witan,* which are survivals of various early kingdoms such as Northumbria and East Anglia,[38] continue to be mentioned occasionally until the Norman conquest. Among the Danes in England the army or the fleet sometimes exercised similar powers.[39]

The *witan* formed a regular assembly summoned by the king, and was not merely a chance assemblage as was once

[36] Larson, *King's Household,* 165-167. See below, note 39.
[37] Liebermann, *National Assembly in Anglo-Saxon Period,* pp. 7-8.
[38] As in *A.-S. Chron.,* 1004.
[39] In 1014 the fleet chose Canute king; in 1036 thegns and the *lithsmen* of London chose Harold. In 1049 (*A.-S. Chron., Cotton Tib.,* 13 Bl) the king and all the army declared Sweyn an outlaw. Cf. below, p. 87.

believed. Mention in the laws of the king's gathering his *witan* about him [40] implies initiative on his part. As Liebermann shows, the assembly was likely to meet each year at a different place, if not at a different season, so summons of some sort was necessary to give notice concerning the meeting place. In 1048 Edward the Confessor is said to have sent for his *witan* to assemble at Gloucester. There seems usually to to have been at least one meeting a year, and in a few known instances two, three or even four within the space of twelve months. Meetings occurred more frequently at Christmas, Easter or Whitsuntide than at other seasons.

The exact number of *witan* who were present on any occasion is not known. In the tenth century about fifty on the average witness the king's grants. In one instance a hundred subscribe. The principle upon which the body was constituted was always aristocratic. It consisted partly of a high official nobility, partly of the king's personal dependents. His near relatives, including his wife, his mother, his sister or his daughter, are often mentioned as present. Next in rank came the archbishops and bishops. The abbots of some of the monasteries were also included, and occasionally a few ecclesiastics, royal chaplains for instance, who ranked below the prelates. Liebermann [41] concludes that the clerical element in the *witan* when weighed against the lay element was decidedly preponderant in influence. The secular nobility included the *ealdormen,* who ruled over the shires and ranked next to the royal family. Like the bishops, they introduced a fixed provincial principle into the composition of the assembly. A majority of the *witan* in attendance in the tenth century were the king's thegns, and among these were included various royal household officials. Edward the Elder undertook to bring all the *witan* under the crown's vassalage. For a long time before the Norman conquest many of those who sat in the national assembly were vassals of the king and important

[40] II Athelstan, Epilogue; I Edmund, prologue.
[41] *National Assembly in A.-S. Period,* 30.

landowners holding of him. Even a bishop was sometimes classified as a king's thegn.[42]

The witan presents phases both of dependence upon the king and also of independence. He determined the time and place of meeting. He presided, put his questions, proposed his measures and finally dismissed the assembly.[43] The thegns at least were his personal dependents. In the tenth and eleventh centuries the bishops and abbots in a good number of cases were the king's appointees. Yet prelates and ealdormen were committed to particular institutional or local points of view which prevented them from becoming subservient. The former, moreover, held office for life and the latter, except in unusual cases, by hereditary tenure. It was necessary that a king should get on with the higher *witan* of his predecessor.

The functions of the assembly in the tenth and the eleventh centuries were varied. Kemble in holding that it had "a right to consider every public act which could be authorized by the king," [44] seems to give too favorable an impression of its importance. Not all the numerous functions attributed to the *witan* for a period of four centuries could well have been performed at one period. Due allowance must be made, moreover, for the fact that the initiative rested primarily, and the executive power entirely, with the king. One may agree with the conclusion of Chadwick, that the functions of the body were never properly defined.[45]

In the exercise of one or two powers the *witan* rose superior to the king. When an emergency left the kingdom without an executive, they assumed control.[46] When there was a questionable succession to the throne, they decided the choice to be made. Hereditary succession of males was the rule, but in the tenth century the brother of a deceased king was regu-

---

[42] *National Assembly in A.-S. Period*, 35.
[43] *Ibid.*, 20.
[44] Kemble, *Saxons in England*, II. 204. Kemble admits (*ibid.*, 204) that a king might not make public questions of some matters.
[45] Chadwick, *Studies on A.-S. Instns.*, 355.
[46] Liebermann, *National Assembly*, 58-59.

larly crowned to the exclusion of a young child. The question arose at the death of Alfred concerning the succession of his son as against that of the son of one of his brothers who had previously reigned. In the eleventh century unusual situations appeared in the recall of Ethelred II in 1016, after he had taken flight from England, in the succession of the Danish Canute, in that of Edward the Confessor, who excluded the Danish line, and, more irregular still, that of Harold the son of Earl Godwin, who was designated by the *witan* as king, upon the death of the Confessor. Chadwick has held that such designation did not consist of formal election but only of recognition by individuals.[47] But, whatever the form, election was in some cases a necessity. Some sort of deliberation often preceded designation.[48] It seems necessary to hold with Liebermann [49] that election could sink into ceremonial form only when the succession was settled before a king's death or when his eldest son, his brother or his brother's son survived without a rival.

Another power exercised by the national assembly was legislative. Among the Anglo-Saxons, as among the early Germans, law consisted in the first instance of legal custom. There was little need for legislation to supplement this, and the amount enacted when judged by present day standards was extremely small. From the days of Ethelbert of Kent the *witan* participated in this process of enacting new laws. In the tenth century they deliberated concerning such legislation, and this after its adoption was promulgated by the executive branch of the government.[50] The prologue to Alfred's laws represents that king as causing to be written down the laws of an earlier period and as rejecting those which the *witan* did not approve. The laws of Athelstan show the *witan* advising the king that

[47] Chadwick, *Studies*, 357-360.

[48] As to the Confessor's election, Liebermann, *Gesetze*, I. 533. Conditions were imposed upon the return of Ethelred. See also *A.-S. Chron.*, 1035.

[49] *National Assembly in A.-S. Period*, 54-56.

[50] Davis, *Eng. Histor. Rev.*, XXVIII. 425.

the public peace was not well enough observed and repeatedly considering with him measures to improve the situation. On some occasions the king is said to ordain new laws by the counsel of the *witan*, in other cases these are mentioned as enacted both by the king and *witan*.

In a third category may be placed powers relating to foreign policy and to peace and war. Treaties with continental powers are more than once said to have been considered by the *witan*. Alfred's treaty of peace with the Danish king Guthrum is recorded as ordained by king and *witan*. The same is true of the treaty between Edward the Elder and Guthrum's realm, and that between Ethelred and the leaders of the Northmen in 991.[51] In 994 Ethelred and his *witan* entered into the famous arrangement with the Danes by which they were tendered provisions and a payment of £15,000 on condition that they desisted from plunder. Similar agreements were made with the sanction of the national council in 1002, 1006 and 1111. The payment of danegeld in 1112 to carry out the last of these agreements seems to have been supervised by the *witan* themselves. The assembly in this period is mentioned as taking counsel with the king regarding the military levy, the movements of the army and the fleet, and the defense of the realm in general. The authority of the *witan* was thus joined to that of the king because of the peril of the times,[52] but also because of lack of confidence in King Ethelred.

The *witan* exercised certain appointive powers, although these seem often to have fallen to the king alone. The national council was sometimes consulted concerning ecclesiastical appointments. In the tenth century these are often said to be made by the king and the *witan*. The Anglo-Saxon chronicle records that in 1044 an abbot was elected by the *witan*, but it states, on the other hand, that in 959 the king gave Dunstan the bishopric of Worcester. In the eleventh century the king is often said to appoint bishops, some of whom were priests from his chapel. In 1043 Edward the Confessor de-

[51] II Ethelred, prologue.   [52] Kemble, *Saxons in England*, II. 225.

cided privately upon the appointment of an abbot. In two instances the same king appointed an earl of Northumbria. Liebermann shows that there is a good amount of evidence in favor of the appointive power of the *witan*,[53] but the king could hardly have shared this with them except when he wished to call for their aid.

Much clearer, and probably much more independent of the crown, stands the high judicial power of the *witan*. This included jurisdiction both in civil and in criminal causes. It seems to have been marked off from the jurisdiction of the ordinary courts by being limited to causes of national import and to those which touched the king, members of the *witan* and the king's thegns.[54] In numerous instances in the eleventh century the assembly pronounced outlawry.[55] Earl Godwin and his sons were thus outlawed in 1051, and before this body the earl, after overcoming his enemies in 1052, cleared himself of the charges against him and procured the outlawry of archbishop Robert and various other Frenchmen. Kemble finds an instance in which the lands of a certain man condemned for treason by judgment of the *witan* were bestowed upon the king.[56] Civil causes were also decided by them..[57] King Alfred asked the *witan* to declare the law in a matter affecting his succession to certain lands which his brother had held.[58]

Finally, the *witan* wielded important fiscal powers. The usage by which they ratified the king's grants of land has often been explained upon the basis of assent to the substitution of a privileged form of land tenure for ordinary tenure. There was, however, a national significance in such acts, for the king in granting away public property was lessening the resources and powers of the state. Such grants were usually

[53] Liebermann, *Natnl. Assembly*, 63-64.
[54] *Ibid.*, 70.
[55] A later account represents the king as pronouncing outlawry *ore suo* (*Leges Edwardi Conf.*, 6.1).
[56] *Saxons in England*, II. 228-29.
[57] As in Kemble, *C. D.*, nos. 327, 1078.
[58] Kemble, *C. D.*, no. 314.

attended by exemption from public services and often conferred upon the grantee quittance of certain fiscal obligations. Their actual effect, therefore, was to transfer fiscal
rights from the king to a subject or a church. Moreover,
they sometimes conferred exemption from the obligation to
attend the local courts and thus lessened the judicial income
of the monarch and indirectly authorized the setting up of
private jurisdictions. In the tenth century the approval of
such grants was no mere formality, and it was regarded as
advisable to influence individual members to gain their assent.[59] In this one finds the *witan* showing the clearest traces
of independence as against the king. By the eleventh century, however, evidence of such an attitude is lacking.

The national council, beginning in 991, authorized the only
direct tax mentioned in the Anglo-Saxon period, the danegeld. Tribute to the Danes had sometimes been rendered
locally in the age of Alfred, but this was not a national tax.
Danegeld was levied for two distinct purposes. A tributary
danegeld was paid to the Danes in Ethelred's time to pur-
chase a cessation of plundering, and a stipendiary danegeld
was levied from the time of Canute to pay the Danish army
and fleet retained in England. This geld was a land tax, levied
upon the official hidage of the hundred, the vill often being
roughly estimated for the purpose at five or ten hides.[60] Since
the purpose of the tax in its later form was to meet a yearly
payment, the trend must have been toward a regular levy,
but this did not become annual.[61] The story that Edward the
Confessor abolished it in 1052 seems to be true, for about
this time he dismissed the last of the Danish fleet.[62] Certain
lands were devoted to the support of the force still retained
as housecarls[63] or household guards.

[59] Liebermann, *Natnl. Assembly*, 26-7, 74.
[60] See Round, *Feudal England*, 103.
[61] Liebermann, *Gesetze*, II. 345 (6).
[62] Cf. *A.-S. Chron.*, 1047 (1049), 1050, 1052; also Vinogradoff, *Eng.
Society in Eleventh Century*, 18-20.
[63] *Domesday Book*, I. 75 (Devon).

National finance was ordinarily the king's affair. Alfred's will shows that the king had a considerable amount of treasure in coin. With the exception of danegeld his revenues were, in the eleventh century, fixed unless he granted away their sources. The most important of these was his income from lands, his *feorm* or *ferm* as it comes to be termed. In Ethelred's time this was still a provender rent.[64] By the reign of Edward the Confessor it is described in terms of monetary value and seems to be paid chiefly in cash. For the purposes of administration, the *feorm* was allotted to groups of manors, from the head one of which it was collected. The unit of the joint contribution was the amount of produce sufficient to provide entertainment for the king and his retinue upon their progress one day out of each year.[65] Sheriffs in the time of the Confessor were sometimes paying specified sums each year for the royal manors of the county and also for boroughs.[66] Included annually with this *ferm* or rent from demesne manors and royal boroughs, was the ordinary income from the courts of the shire and its hundreds. By the Confessor's day this was beginning to be estimated also at a fixed sum.[67] The sheriff did not as yet farm of the king for one sum the demesne, the borough and these judicial perquisites, but he is sometimes recorded as paying one sum each year which covers revenues arising from two of these sources.[68] Financial administration was being simplified by a trend toward the lumping of these together in one *ferm* for the whole county. This plan never embraced the special forfeitures due the king, notably the lands of persons outlawed or convicted of serious offenses [69] and the five-pound payments for grave

[64] *A.-S. Chron.*, 1006; cf. Athelstan, Alms (Charities), 1-2.
[65] Round, *Feudal England*, 109-115; Birch, *Cartularium*, no. 271. It is probable that this was an ancient rent or *gafol* in food at one time based on hides (Demarest, in *E. H. R.*, XXXV, 78).
[66] Round, *Commune of London*, 69-74.
[67] *Domesday Book*, I. 262. Here the amount of the earl's third is given.
[68] Round, *Commune of London*, 72-73; Morris, *Med. Eng. Sheriff*, 32.
[69] II Canute, 13, 57, 77 : 1; Kemble, *Codex Diplomaticus*, no. 591. Wreckage of ships also belonged to the king (*ibid.*, no. 853).

breaches of his peace. The latter could not well be estimated in advance by the year and were collected and turned over to the treasury as separate items.[70]

In addition to the income from the royal demesne and that from judicial fines, another important source from 991 to 1052 was the danegeld. A fourth source was afforded by the profits of the coinage,[71] a fifth by tolls. The latter might include import dues,[72] road tolls, or a tax upon sales in boroughs or market towns.[73] Another source of profit to the king was a *heriot*, a render in horses, arms and money [74] required at the decease of an earl or royal thegn, and probably originating in an old usage by which the professional warrior received his military accoutrement from his lord, to whom it reverted at his death. Finally, a certain part of the king's income was derived from miscellaneous sources, some in commutation of services or public work, some in minor customary payments of various sorts.[75]

To the king still belonged the old public services which are known as the *trinoda necessitas*, namely borough and bridge work, and military duty in the *fyrd* or national military force. In the time of Ethelred there is mention also of an obligation to maintain ships and provide men for the king's naval service (*shipfyrd*).[76] This was a burden upon land. Three hundred hides provided a ship, and by an order of the year 1008, eight hides supplied a helmet and a coat of mail. Maritime communities sent a man for every five hides.[77] The general military levy of the men of a county was called

[70] Morris, *Med. Eng. Sheriff*, 30.
[71] *Domesday Book*, I. 75, 172.
[72] IV Ethelred, 2. Mentioned under Ethelbald of Mercia (Birch, *Chart.*, nos. 149, 152; Kemble, *C. D.*, no. 84).
[73] Kemble, *Saxons in England*, I. App., pp. 501, 509; Ballard, *Domesday Boroughs*, 73, 74, 111.
[74] II Canute, 71a.
[75] Morris, *Med. Eng. Sheriff.*, 33-34; Maitland, *D. B. and Beyond*, 78-79, 156.
[76] V Ethelred, 27; VI Ethelred, 32:3; II Canute, 10.
[77] *A.-S. Chron.* 1008; Vinogradoff, *Eng. Society in Eleventh Cent.*, 31-32; *Domesday Book*, I. 100.

out in emergencies,[78] but ordinarily in the eleventh century
the army was constituted on a more restricted plan. In the
time of the Confessor and probably much earlier this was
based upon land assessment. According to Domesday Book,
a fighting man was sent for every five hides of land, and each
hide that he represented contributed two shillings toward his
maintenance.[79] This is mentioned, however, only in Wessex.
In the Danelaw, where the land was generally in the hands
of small freeholders, the allotment of service necessarily
followed a different plan, and the levy was made up less of
professional warriors.[80] The boroughs, as a rule, were responsible for a fixed number of fighting men (*burhware*),
who were often highly efficient fighters.[81] Canute's Danish
army and fleet were maintained at the national expense. Most
of them were dismissed in 1018, although a smaller Danish
force, apparently numbering some three or four thousand,
continued to be supported in the same way. This was increased in size by Hardacanute, then reduced, and finally dissolved, at least as a naval force, in 1050.[82]

The permanent nucleus of the king's fighting force from
the time of Canute was formed by this force of paid troops,
fighting at first either on land or sea.[83] These were in time reduced to the proportions of a household guard, known as *housecarls*, and as such were retained until 1066.[83] The earls and the
better class of king's thegns were expected to have horses and
a rather elaborate equipment in swords, spears, shields, helmets and coats of mail, which indicates their leadership in

---

[78] As Ethelred's levy in Wessex and Mercia (*A.-S. Chron.* 1006) cf.
expeditio popularis (*Chron. Monast de Abingdon* I. 51, 53).

[79] For two months. Vinogradoff, *Eng. Soc. Eleventh Century*, 30-31;
Domesday Book, I. 56b.

[80] Vinogradoff, *Eng. Soc. Eleventh Century*, 29-30, 35-38.

[81] Maitland, *Domesday Book and Beyond*, 190-191.

[82] *A.-S. Chron.* 1018, 1039, 1040, 1047 (1049), 1050, 1052; Vinogradoff,
Eng. Soc. Eleventh Century, 17-19; Ramsay, *Foundations of England*,
I. 413-416.

[83] Larson, *King's Household*, 153, 169-171; Vinogradoff, *Eng. Soc.
Eleventh Century*, 19-20. The Danish warriors have been characterized
as horse marines.

the military profession. At times there appears evidence that their followers also were mounted men, although in actual battle the English troops dismounted and fought on foot.[84] The earl was still the commander of the forces of the county, but the sheriff might take his place.[85] The king's thegns stood in a prominent place next to the earl.[86] It was assumed that the greater thegns had followers with five hides of land for which they rendered the king service.[87] The grouping of the forces followed a plan which was in part quasi-feudal. In the time of Canute men are mentioned as attending their lords upon an expedition by land or sea and as fighting in their presence.[88] The men of various lords, churches, or boroughs formed distinct military units.[89] On the eve of the Norman Conquest the forces of Wessex, except when a general levy was called, must have consisted of well equipped, well trained men, selected largely from among the thegns or other tenants of important landholders. Those of the Danelaw, on the other hand, seem to have come from among the small landholders who upheld the more popular tradition of the *fyrd*.

If the attempt be made to analyze the Anglo-Saxon constitution, it is apparent, first of all, that the monarch was the directing power. "Anglo-Saxon monarchy is monarchy limited by the *witan's* counsel," [90] but only the minority or striking personal weakness of the king could leave control to the *witan*. In the reign of the boy kings of the tenth century they doubtless held the reins. Ethelred was compelled to depend upon them first by his youth and then by his incompetence. A charter issued by him in 994 refers to the *witan* as directing affairs.[91] That they did so at later periods of his war with

[84] II Canute, 71a ; Beck, *Eng. Histor. Rev.*, XXI. 776.
[85] Morris, *Med. Eng. Sheriff*, 27.
[86] *A.-S. Chron.*, 894.
[87] Liebermann, *Gesetze*, I. 456-57 ; Stubbs, *Select Charters*, 65.
[88] II Canute, 77, 78.
[89] Thus, the men of the bishop of Winchester at Taunton (*Domesday Book*, I. 87b). So the Welsh of Archenfield (*ibid.*, I. 179). See also Maitland, *Domesday Book and Beyond*, 159, 308.
[90] Liebermann, *National Assembly*, 23.
[91] Kemble, *Cod. Dipl.*, no. 687 ; Liebermann, *National Assembly*, 23.

the Danes and after his flight from England in 1014, is clear, but these times of crisis were exceptional.

There is no evidence that a competent ruler fell under their domination. The king was the first of the *witan.* He held the vantage ground of initiative in calling them and laying his proposals before them and that of executive power in enforcing their decisions. Consultation with them accorded with precedent and was essential to the proper conduct of the government. It had on its side the commendable usage of the best and strongest rulers. Edgar enacted a whole series of laws by advice of his *witan,* nor does this imply lack of real deliberation and of some initiative even under a strong ruler. Athelstan consulted his *witan* frequently about means to improve the public peace, sometimes upon their insistence.[92] Although there is evidence of hot discussion in the national assembly,[93] there is no hint of conflict with the king. In general it did not impose its policy upon the monarch. There is evidence that just the opposite situation sometimes existed. Laws which were passed for the protection of the poor against powerful lords, were clearly distasteful to the *witan.* Athelstan required them to give pledges to preserve the peace in their own shires.[94] Alfred felt it advisable to say he would hold no grudge against any of them on account of a conscientious expression of opinion in a judicial matter in which he was personally interested.[95] Hardacanute seems to have procured a heavy danegeld from a subservient assembly.[96] In the reign of Edward the Confessor the *witan* reversed its sentences against Godwin and his sons when the king became reconciled with them.

The checks upon the sovereign's will in the Germanic constitution were incidental and not consciously devised.[97] There

---

[92] Liebermann, *National Assembly,* 67-68.
[93] *Ibid.,* 52.
[94] Liebermann, *National Assembly,* 68; VI Athelstan, 8, 9.
[95] Kemble, *Cod. Dipl.,* no. 314.
[96] *A.-S. Chron.,* 1039.
[97] G. B. Adams, *Origins of English Constitution,* 3, note 2.

lay upon Anglo-Saxon monarchy the restrictions of law and usage. Stubbs describes these as constitutional forms which hedged in the king, but adds the important conclusion that "they were very easy to break through and were broken through with impunity." [98] Kings might in some matters be capricious and despotic. The worst and weakest kings were guilty of irresponsible acts of tyranny. Ethelred in 986 laid waste the diocese of Rochester and in 1102 commanded that the Danes be slain. Hardacanute, when the people of Worcester rose and slew the king's agents sent to collect an unpopular geld, caused the shire to be ravaged. [99] Edward the Confessor took up a private quarrel of his sister's husband and made the inexcusable demand that Earl Godwin attack the men of Dover. [100] The power of the great earls from the time of Canute placed a very practical restraint upon the conduct of the ruler, but neither this nor the influence of the national assembly reduced the king to the position of the limited monarch of modern times. The principal factor in the establishment of English constitutional monarchy was destined to be national control of the king's income, and this was impossible because his income was regarded as purely personal.

The king carried on his every day business through his household organization. [101] The *praefectus* or high reeve of early times has been regarded as an incipient *major-domo*. As late as Ethelred's reign an official bearing the title high reeve was a person of the very highest rank, [102] and some high reeves performed important military duties. In the tenth century, so it has been shown, England differed from the Germanic states of the continent in having not four but only three important household dignitaries, namely the butler, the steward and the chamberlain. The office of butler is

[98] Stubbs, *Constl. Hist.*, I. 157.

[99] *A.-S. Chron.*, 1041.

[100] *Ibid.*, 1048 (1050).

[101] See L. M. Larson, *The King's Household in England before the Norman Conquest* (Bulletin Univ. of Wisconsin, no. 100) ; J. H. Round in *Eng. Hist. Rev.*, XIX.

[102] *A.-S. Chron.*, 1001; Larson, *King's Household*, 114-115.

older than Alfred's reign. The king's steward or *dapifer* of
the Confessor's time had duties similar to those of the dish
thegn (*disc thegn*) of the tenth century. More prominent in
administration was the chamberlain, originally the bower-
thegn (*burthegn*), who was the keeper of the royal chamber,
including the wardrobe and the treasure. Audience with the
king was sought through this official.[103] One of the chamberlains of Edward the Confessor is mentioned as depositing a
charter in the royal treasury, but this hint that the treasury[104]
was more than a strong box is probably misleading, for it
comes from a later period. The treasurer remained a subordinate of the chamberlain for more than half a century after
the Norman Conquest.[105] A fourth great office, that of the
staller (*stallr*) or master of horse, Larson, an unusually competent judge, holds to be Norse in origin,[106] hence probably
new in the period of the Danish kings. His position seems to
be much like that of the Norman constable. Under Edward
the Confessor an official known as the *strator* performed
functions of the later marshal.[107]

A secretarial department was included in the organization
of the king's chapel.[108] Palace priests were apparently doing
the king's clerical work in the tenth century, and by 950 these
already took rank next after the three great palace officials.
The technical form of old English documents makes it clear
that, at least from the early years of the Confessor, there
was a trained body of clerks constituting a secretariat or
chancery in the continental sense, although it was not so

---

[103] Larson, *King's Household*, 124-131.

[104] *Gazaphulacium* (*Ramsey Chronicle*, 170-171); Tout, *Chapters in Administrative History*, I. 73; see also Larson, *King's Household*, 132-133.

[105] Below, p. 203. At the Norse court of St. Olaf, who may have followed the usage of Ethelred, the king's chaplain acted as treasurer (Larson, *King's Household*, 197-198), but the early treasurers in England were laymen.

[106] Larson, *The King's Household*, 146-152. In Domesday Book (I. 151) Bondi the staller is called *constabularius*.

[107] Round, *Eng. Hist. Rev.* XIX. 90-91.

[108] For this and the chancery, Larson, *King's Household*, chap. 6.

designated.[109] A royal document, issued in 1050, is witnessed by eight priests.[110] The importance of the king's chapel in administration is shown by the fact that four of Canute's chaplains were made bishops and that this reward was conferred upon no less than eight of the king's priests of the reign of Edward the Confessor.[111] Some organization of this clerical force is indicated by a reference to royal secretaries who in Canute's time were under the direction of Bishop Ethelric. It is an obvious but somewhat neglected fact that the official documents of the Norman kings of England continue old English forms. In this the English usage generally speaking excelled the Norman. The king's seal (*insegel*) mentioned in the time of Ethelred was, as has been suggested, probably a signet. It is only in the time of Edward the Confessor that there appears a great seal [112] which is impressed in wax to authenticate the king's documents inscribed upon parchment. The first known chancellor is mentioned in this reign, and the fact suggests that both this title of the head of the king's chapel and the use of the great seal were importations from the continent.[113]

The existence of a separate court council before the Norman Conquest is not established by existing evidence.[114] The counsellors mentioned in the reign of Edward the Elder were his *witan*,[115] and the counsel or *raed* mentioned in Canute's reign was that of the same body.[116] In the reign of Edward the Confessor a small group of prominent officials and household

[109] Stevenson, *Eng. Histor. Rev.*, XI. 731; Davis, *Regesta, introd.*, pp. xi, xii, xv.

[110] *Ibid., introd.*, p. xiv.

[111] *Ibid.*, p. xiii.

[112] The monks of Ramsey (*Ramsey Chron.*, 161, 167), who knew that King Edgar used no seal, rejoiced in a sealed charter of King Edward. Charters issued at the *scriptura* attached to the king's chapel were sometimes deposited there along with the relics (*ibid.*, 172).

[113] Cf. Davis, *Regesta*, p. xiii. Canute and the Confessor employed in the chapel some Lotharingian priests. The great seal appears in France under Henry I and in the Empire a little earlier (Tout, *Chaps.*, I. 124).

[114] See G. B. Adams, *Council and Courts*, xxi-xxii.

[115] Kemble, *Cod. Dipl.*, no. 336; Birch, *Cartularium*, no. 602.

[116] Liebermann, *National Assembly*, 8-9, 12.

dignitaries appeared to witness the king's writs,[117] but there is no proof that they gave collective counsel.[118] On the other hand the personal opinion of powerful ecclesiastics often prevailed with the king,[119] and three earls are said to have advised him in 1043 to seize his mother's treasures.[120] In too many cases the Anglo-Saxon king remained to the end like Ethelred, a *raedeless* king, a king without counsel.

Institutional improvement in the eleventh century did not suffice to make central government very effective. The king's hold on local administration and justice in Anglo-Saxon England was not firm, despite his control over the sheriff. The growth of vassalage and the rise of hereditary earldoms, rooted in local provincial tradition and strengthened by quasi-feudal conditions, made the situation worse. The personal weakness of the kings subsequent to Canute, made a *witan* in which the earls dominated policy a real check upon monarchy and a baneful influence in government. Even the king's hold upon the national army was affected by the principle of personal lordship, which again favored the power of the earls, the most powerful lords of the realm. Much of the ruler's income had been granted away, and the plan upon which both the king's *feorm* and the danegeld were levied was an antiquated one. When to these factors were added the blundering and pettiness of the rulers of the period, the effect was a weak monarchy.

AUTHORITIES

The sources for kingship and the *witan* are in the main the laws, the charters and the Anglo-Saxon Chronicle, as noted at the end of the last chapter. The Anglo-Saxon Chronicle is of more value from the

[117] Kemble, *Cod. Dipl.*, nos. 904, 908. No. 956 seems to be witnessed by the *witan* but also by the housecarls, the king's priests, and the *burhware* of Lincoln.

[118] Liebermann (*Natnl. Assembly*, 17-18) assumes that they are a council.

[119] Luard, *Lives of Edward the Confessor*, Rolls Series, 399; *Gesta Abbatum Monasterii S. Albani*, Rolls Series, 38.

[120] Florence of Worcester, *Chronicon, anno* 1042. See William of Malmesbury, *Gesta Regum*, I. 229, as to those who advised the execution of Edward's brother, Alfred.

time of Alfred. By the eleventh century continuations were being made in different churches. These were of course not uniform, and thus they supplement one another. Twelfth century chroniclers sometimes included accounts of the Anglo-Saxon period, and the most useful of these later accounts are in the *De Gestis Regum* of William of Malmesbury (ed. William Stubbs, Rolls Series, 1887-89), dating from 1125, and the *Chronicon* of Florence of Worcester (ed. B. Thorpe, English Historical Soc., 1848-49) who wrote a little before 1120. Domesday Book, the great survey of England prepared in 1086, makes occasional allusion to various usages and institutions and to the king's rights as they existed before 1066.

The oldest detailed study of the Anglo-Saxon king and the *witan* was published by Kemble, in volume II of his *Saxons in England*. Kemble strongly emphasized the importance of the *witan*. His estimate of its influence and power as against that of the king has been accepted only in part by more recent writers. Stubbs in his *Constitutional History* (I. chap. 6) gives a good general account. The work by Dr. Felix Liebermann, *The National Assembly in the Anglo-Saxon Period* (1912), goes much more fully into this subject, and presents additional material as well as some new conclusions. Chadwick in his *Studies on Anglo-Saxon Institution* (1905) devotes some attention (chap. 8) to the constitution of the national assembly, but chiefly for the period before Alfred's time.

The most complete account of the king's household is L. M. Larson, *The King's Household in England before the Norman Conquest* (Bulletin of the University of Wisconsin, no. 100, 1902). J. R. Round also dealt with this subject in *The English Historical Review*, vol. XIX. A treatment by W. H. Stevenson of the old English chancery also appears in the same journal, XI. 731-44 (1896). T. F. Tout in his *Chapters in Medieval Administrative History* (vol. I, 1920) presents useful conclusions concerning the Anglo-Saxon treasury and chancery (chap. 2, sec. 2; chap. 4, secs. 1, 2). These matters are also carefully treated in the introduction (pp. x-xv) to *Regesta Regum Anglo-Normannorum* (ed. H. W. C. Davis, 1913). The most useful brief account of the political history of the period is that by W. J. Corbett in the *Cambridge Medieval History* (III. chap. 14, pp. 352-370; chap. 15).

CHAPTER V

LOCAL GOVERNMENT, 871-1066:
THE HUNDRED, THE SHIRE, AND THE BOROUGH

The organization of local government through shires, hundreds and boroughs is one of the chief constitutional contributions of the Anglo-Saxon period. The contact between central and local government was not very close under the old English monarchs, and herein lay one weakness of their rule. The defect was not repaired before the Norman Conquest, so it was left to foreign rulers to inaugurate a process of centralization. In the local centres some of the ideas and methods of primitive democracy were retained, although control became limited to the thegns and other landholders.

The *tun*, so it has been shown earlier, was an agricultural rather than a political unit. It had no *gemot* which rendered folkright. Traditionally its men performed police duty, but its head man or reeve is not mentioned until the time of Ethelred. There are indications that none existed in rural free villages as late as the reign of Edgar.[1] A unit known as the tithing, which consisted in theory of ten men and from the latter half of the tenth century performed police duties under a tithingman subject to the head of the hundred,[2] seems to have become coextensive with the *tun* of Wessex. Villages under the control of lords, known later as manors, were sometimes exempted by the king's grant from the jurisdiction of the courts of shire and hundred, and from certain payments usually levied there. This enabled the lord in some instances

[1] VII Ethelred, 2:5; I Edgar, 4; Maitland, *Domesday Book and Beyond*, 147-149. For the manorial reeve or *villicus*, Bede, IV. 24; the lord's reeve, Ine, 63.
[2] VI Athelstan 3-4; I Edgar, 2, 4; VII Ethelred, 2:5; II Canute, 20.

to establish a manorial court for his tenants, and his reeve to levy upon them fines which had hitherto pertained to the public *gemots*. The jurisdictional privileges thus assumed were described in general by the words *sake* and *soke*. The Anglo-Saxon ecclesiastic or other lord who obtained such a grant probably did not always establish a court to enforce his claims, for it is quite possible that his judicial perquisites were often turned over to him by the public officials who ordinarily imposed and collected them. It is clear none the less that in numerous instances manorial courts were established by the eleventh century.[3] These were thus outside the regular scheme of justice, which, from the time of Edgar at the latest, was carried on through the organization of the hundred, the shire and the borough.

The question of the administrative subdivision of the shire prior to the reign of Edgar is extremely difficult. Until recently it has been assumed that the smaller unit for which a *gemot* was held, justice rendered, and local administration organized from first to last was the hundred. Various writers including Stubbs have held that the hundred in England was a primitive unit perpetuating a Germanic division known as the hundred (*hundertschaft*).[4] Vinogradoff assumes that the English hundred was Germanic, that it consisted of a hundred households, and that it was so called because it provided a hundred men for the *fyrd*.[5] Corbett, on the other hand, has emphasized a reckoning by hundreds of hides of land for fiscal purposes and seeks in these the origin of later hundreds.[6] Nothing is known of a corresponding judicial or police unit before the tenth century. If one assumes the existence of

[3] Maitland, *Domesday Book and Beyond*, 135, 276-278; W. J. Corbett in *Cambridge Med. Hist.* III. 405-408.

[4] For the arguments concerning the origin of the hundred, Liebermann, *Gesetze der Angelsachsen*, II. art. "Hundred." For an argument in favor of the primitive hundred in England, Henry Adams, *Essays on Anglo-Saxon Law*, 5-18.

[5] Vinogradoff, *Growth of Manor*, 144; *English Society in Eleventh Century*, 29.

[6] Corbett, "The Tribal Hidage" in *Trans. Royal Histor. Soc.*, n. s., XIV. 187-230.

primitive groups of villages for which public courts were held, these must have been older than the hidage assessment. It is thus unlikely that they were identical with later hundreds or were so named.[7]

Liebermann points out that prior to the tenth century there is no evidence of the existence in England of a local unit of government known as the hundred.[8] He observes that Bede used other words in speaking of minor territorial subdivisions and that the writer who about 870 translated his work into Anglo-Saxon did not use the word hundred. The first mention of a judicial and police area so named occurs slightly before 950.[9] It is difficult to account for the rise of the hundred in Wessex, but it seems that until about 930 or 940 another, though possibly a somewhat similar, type of minor political subdivision prevailed. Prior to the reign of Alfred, as shown in an earlier chapter, the known area of local administration smaller than the shire was one centered in the king's *tun*. Over this district was set the king's reeve, who exercised fiscal, police and judicial functions.[10] He had charge of prisoners,[11] and from the time of Alfred, if not earlier, he held an assembly court or *gemot* which was a part of the national scheme of justice.[12] In the laws of Edward the Elder is mentioned for the first time a general scheme of local courts held by reeves. Each of these was required to hold a *gemot* every four weeks; they enforced folkright, and they dealt not only with criminal but also with civil cases; they saw

[7] Round, *Feudal England*, 97-98. The title of King Ethelwulf, *rex occidentalium Saxonum centuriorum* (Kemble, *Cod. Dipl.*, no. 241; Birch, *cart.* no. 426) may imply that a military arrangement was based on hundreds of hides.

[8] Liebermann, *Gesetze der Angelsachsen*, II. 516-517. Round, (*Feudal England*, 97, note 177) shows that an assessment which reckoned vills at five or ten hides was probably necessary to meet the obligations which formed the *trinoda necessitas*.

[9] III Edmund, 2.

[10] Above, pp. 42-44.

[11] Alfred, 1 : 2-3.

[12] Asser (ed. Stevenson, sec. 106) : *contiones comitum et praepositorum.* See Chadwick, *Studies on A.-S. Instns.*, 235 ; Morris, *Med. Eng. Sheriff*, 5-6.

that each plea was assigned a term; and they declared judgment. Not all of these could have been located in royal *tuns*, and many must have been subordinates of the *ealdormen* set over districts of much earlier origin and of an extent and designation now unknown. Apparently the king and the *witan* were now for the first time making definite regulations for old-time popular assemblies held for such areas.

From the time of Alfred the organization by royal *tuns* takes on a new form. Well within a half century after his death it is the borough which appears as the active centre of the king's local administration. This change was brought about by the Danish wars. Alfred in his effort to hold Wessex against the Danes devised a new military administration. The fortifications at royal *tuns* were reconstructed or newly built.[13] Boroughs or fortress towns were garrisoned as a permanent feature of the military scheme, apparently in imitation of Danish usage. In 895 the Danes were defeated by the borough forces (*burhware*) of Chichester.[14] It is clear from the Anglo-Saxon Chronicle that in the reigns of Alfred's successors new boroughs served as military bases for the conquest and occupation of the Danelaw, and that the Danes held out in similar centres. Danish boroughs were seats of civil government in the midlands. A document known as the Burghal Hidage, which dates from the early tenth century, lists without regard to shires the boroughs of Wessex, along with Oxford, Worcester and Warwick, and assigns to each a certain number of hundreds of hides of land, evidently charged with their upkeep.[15] The laws of Athelstan show that these districts were employed for civil purposes.[16] The borough rather than the king's *tun* is now the centre which is mentioned. Those who render tithes of the king's income are the reeves in each

[13] Asser, *Life of Alfred* (ed. Stevenson) sec. 91.

[14] *A.-S. Chron.* 895; *Eng. Histor. Rev.*, IV. 729.

[15] Birch, *Cartularium*, nos. 297, 297A, 297B, 1335; see Maitland, *Domesday Book and Beyond*, 502-506; Chadwick, *Studies*, 204-209; Oman, *England before the Norman Conquest*, 469-470; Corbett, *Cambridge Med. History*, III. 357. See below, p. 90.

[16] Chadwick, *Studies*, 219-227; cf. 236.

borough.[17] Those who are enjoined to ride, to enforce court process and to execute judgment on the thief, are the men who belong to the borough.[18] It is not necessary to believe that this burghal type of organization any more than the older one of the king's *tuns* superseded the shires in the south of England,[19] for the shires appear later by the old names, but a plan of burghal organization originally Danish, did give rise to new English shires formed in the midlands.[20]

The police and judicial territory known as the hundred is first mentioned in a law of Edmund's reign (940-946). A law attributed to Edgar,[21] but possibly enacted a little earlier, makes detailed regulations concerning the sessions, the usages, the police work and the criminal jurisdiction of the hundred, and includes the provision that it is to render justice as does any other court. This creates the presumption that the legislator is introducing a new kind of organization and making its judicial usages uniform with those of older units. Liebermann assigns the formation of the hundreds to about the time of Athelstan,[22] and believes that it has some relation to groups of a hundred men each for police and other purposes, mentioned in the burghal district about London by an ordinance of this reign.[23] Liebermann's view that the hundred of Wessex as it appears in history was thus organized in the period of the reconquest of the Danelaw is incapable of direct proof, but it is in several ways the most satisfactory explanation that has been offered. The hundred fulfilled a demand for better enforcement of the peace, which appears constantly in Athelstan's laws. It embodied ideas suggested in an ordinance of

[17] I Athelstan, prolog.

[18] II Athelstan, 20 : 1-4.

[19] See Chadwick, *Studies*, 224-226. The reeve's district is called a *scir* in VI Athelstan 10, 8 :4. Chadwick is inclined to believe that a change came through emphasis upon earldoms which included more than one county.

[20] *A.-S. Chron.*, 918: Thurferth the jarl and the nobles and all the army which belonged to Northampton north as far as the Welland.

[21] I Edgar, 1-9; Stubbs, *Select Charters*, 70-71.

[22] Liebermann, *Gesetze*, II. 518-519; cf. III. 118.

[23] VI Athelstan, 3-4; Stubbs, *Select Charters*, 67.

that reign. It was apparently organized because the king's burghal districts did not cover the whole realm and declined in importance with the conquest of the Danelaw as they were found too large for effective government. The head of the hundred performed various public functions which appear earlier under the direction of the king's reeve located at the royal *tun* or the burghal centre.[24] So far as one can see new judicial regulations and a new type of police organization were also being imposed upon ancient groups of villages, outside the king's special sphere, for which local reeves had been holding courts.

The hundred of Wessex appears in the eleventh century as a district for the collection of danegeld. Hundreds in the south of England, however, are often small [25] and rated at far less than a hundred hides. Here a territorial hundred and a hundred hides of land were not co-extensive.[26] The name hundred, therefore, seems to be that of an area [27] which included a hundred men, like the police group of Athelstan's London ordinance. The hundreds in the Mercian and Danish regions annexed by Alfred and his successors were, on the other hand, clearly laid out to correspond to assessment areas. In the western or English part of Mercia and in parts of the Danelaw may be found many territorial hundreds assessed at a hundred hides. The hundreds of the former region were taking final shape in the later part of the tenth century. Three hundred hides of land held by the bishop of Worcester accounted for three of the hundreds of this shire.[28] The hundreds of the Danelaw were formed about the time of Canute and super-

[24] Morris, *Med. Eng. Sheriff*, 20-21.

[25] Kent has 71, Sussex, 68. On the other hand Lancashire has but 7 and Staffordshire 5. The area of the hundred ranges from ⅛ to 18 square miles (Liebermann, *Gesetze*, II. 517).

[26] Stubbs, *Select Charters*, 68-69; Von Schwerin in *Zeitschrift der Savigny Stiftung für Rechtsgeschichte*, vol. 29 (1908), 280, ff.

[27] Chadwick (*Studies*, 224-228) suggests, however, that the idea of the hundred was borrowed from the Danes in England.

[28] Round in *Victoria County Hist.*, Worcester, I. 237-238; Maitland, *Domesday and Beyond*, 451-55, 459. Maitland thinks that the hundreds here may be traced to the earlier part of the tenth century.

seded older organizations in that region. They were grouped
to fit into a fiscal or military scheme of assessment,[29] probably to support the Danish troops in England. Everywhere
the hundred came ultimately to serve both a judicial and a
fiscal purpose.[30]

Not all the shires were subdivided into hundreds. In certain
northerly shires of the Danelaw, the corresponding subdivision
is known as the wapentake.[31] The judicial functions of the
wapentake, so far as evidence shows, were exactly the same
as those of the hundred. In the four northernmost shires,
Northumberland, Durham, Cumberland, and Westmoreland,
which were organized only in the twelfth century, there are
no hundreds nor wapentakes. These counties were divided
into wards instead, although by the thirteenth century the
king's officials were treating these like hundreds for administrative purposes. Cornwall was originally divided into Celtic
districts known as *cantrefs*. After the English conquest of
this region in the ninth century these were called shires, but
later came to be known as hundreds.[32]

The head of the hundred was the hundred reeve, who exercised judicial, fiscal and police powers. He is called the hun-
dredman in the law of Edgar, where he is directed to take
the lead in pursuing the thief, and in Domesday Book, where
he appears as a collector of the danegeld.[33] Later history
fails to confirm the view of Stubbs[34] that this was a different
officer from the hundred reeve who presided in the *gemot*.

[29] Stenton, *Manorial Structure in Northern Danelaw*, 87-90; Douglas,
Social Structure of East Anglia, 57, 191. See Corbett, *Trans. Royal
Histor. Soc.*, XIV. 210-220.
[30] Stenton, *Docs. of Hist. of Northern Danelaw*, introd., pp. lxiii-lxv;
Vinogradoff, *Eng. Society Eleventh Century*, 102-103; Corbett, *Cambridge Med. History*, III. 368.
[31] Here the name hundred appears as a unit of land reckoning consisting of twelve carucates (Vinogradoff, *Eng. Society in Eleventh Century*,
103-104; Round, *Feudal England*, 53).
[32] Corbett, *Cambridge Med. Hist.*, III. 345. In Yorkshire and Lincolnshire at a later time appeared larger judicial areas, known as *trethings*
or thirds, today called ridings. Kent had subdivisions, which included
hundreds, known as lathes, and Sussex similar divisions called rapes.
[33] Round, *Feudal England*, 53-54.   [34] *Constnl. Hist.*, I. 113.

Such a combination of powers in the hands of Anglo-Saxon reeves was usual. The official who stood at the head of the wapentake was also a reeve.[35] There are various indications that in the eleventh century at least the hundred reeve was the subordinate and agent of the earl or the sheriff.[36] In the hundred of Edgar's time were appointed twelve transaction witnesses, two or three of whom were expected to be present when all buying and selling was done.

The hundred court or *gemot* met once in four weeks. In the time of Edward the Confessor the sheriff as well as the reeve might preside,[37] a circumstance which reveals the former as the superior, the latter as the subordinate. According to the law of Canute every free man was expected to belong to a hundred, but by the time of Edward the Confessor only freemen with a certain amount of land were expected regularly to attend its sessions.[38] A fine was imposed upon members of the assembly who failed to attend in response to summons.[39] The term for hearing causes was set by the reeve. In conformity to the general usage of assembly courts of folkmoots of the Germanic type, judgments were found according to customary law by the men of the hundred.[40] The causes and procedure in the hundred mentioned by the laws almost invariably have to do with criminal justice, but other matters came up. The *wite* or fine for failure to pay danegeld was apparently imposed here,[41] and judgment given in some land cases and other civil matters.[42]

[35] III Ethelred, 3 : 1-2.

[36] See Chadwick, *Studies*, 234. In fiscal matters he was apparently accountable to the sheriff (Morris, *Med. Eng. Sheriff*, 30) ; so in judicial matters (see below, p. 156). An earl might convene several hundreds jointly (*Liber Eliensis*, 123, 130) and thus supersede their reeves.

[37] Kemble, *Cod. Dipl.*, no. 840.

[38] Below, note 66; cf. Vinogradoff, *Eng. Soc. in Eleventh Century*, 98.

[39] Ballard, *Domesday Boroughs*, 53 ; *Domesday Book*, I. 179.

[40] *Domesday Book*, I. 269b. *Diiudicaverunt homines hundreti: ibid.*, II. 424.

[41] Round, *Feudal England*, 53.

[42] *terra . . . quae remanet regi per iudicium hundret: Domesday Book*, II. 99. See the tradition of Queen Edith's appeal to a hundred to protect her rights (Kemble, *Cod. Dipl.*, no. 918) ; also Vinogradoff, *Eng. Soc. in Eleventh Century*, 97, n. 3.

The shire (*scir*), the largest and most important subdivision of the kingdom was of West Saxon origin.[43] The word county, at present a synonym for shire, is derived from the Latin *comitatus*, through the French *comté*, and did not appear in England in this sense until after the Norman conquest.

The shires of England with respect to origin fall into three main groups, those of the south and southeast, those of the midlands, and those of the extreme north. Those of the south are much the oldest. The older shires of Wessex date back to the seventh century. In the early ninth century the smaller kingdoms, Kent, Sussex and Essex, became assimilated to the West Saxon shire organization. All of the shires south of the line of the Thames except Cornwall are mentioned by their present names before the time of Alfred. Cornwall was then a recently conquered Celtic region.

The midlands were organized into shires after their reconquest from the Danes in the tenth century, and the process was not complete until about the end of the reign of Ethelred.[44] After the beginning of his reign the region of the former Danish confederation of the five boroughs of Derby, Leicester, Lincoln, Nottingham and Stamford, still had one court and apparently one *ealdorman*.[45] In the midland region the shire originated in a Danish, in western Mercia an English, burghal area. This organization about boroughs is shown in the fact that the midland shires are named for their boroughs and their names are formed by adding the suffix 'shire' to the name of the principal town.

The northernmost shires were not organized until the eleventh or twelfth century. These are Lancashire, Westmoreland, Cumberland, Northumberland, and Durham. At the date of the Norman Conquest much of this region was still in the

---

[43] Above, p. 40.

[44] C. S. Taylor in *Trans. Bristol and Gloucestershire Archaeol. Soc.*, 1898, pp. 32, ff; Oman (*Essays in History* presented to R. L. Poole, 90) shows that Winchecombeshire was added to Gloucestershire in the time of Ethelred.

[45] III Ethelred, I. 1.

hands of the Scots. It was only after the occupation of Carlisle in 1092 that the whole of the present counties of Lan-
caster and Cumberland became English.

The official head of the shire prior to the tenth century was
called the *ealdorman*, a word which means chief man.[46] In
the Latin charters his title is *princeps* or *dux*. Originally he
appears as an under-king[47] and his office in some cases was
hereditary. From at least the time of Ine he was the head
of the judicial system of the shire. He was also the war leader
of the men of the shire.[48] Both judicial[49] and military functions inhere in the office throughout its history.

In the tenth century the *ealdorman* gave way to the earl,
who exercised the same powers, but who was usually set over
several shires instead of one. Until the time of Alfred there
was apparently an *ealdorman* over every shire, but under
Alfred's successors for some reason, possibly either the activity
of borough areas, reducing the importance of shire administration, or the necessity of organizing the Danelaw, the number
declined.[50] By the time of Edgar in Danish regions the word
earl was already a synonym for *ealdorman*.[51] The title is derived from the Scandinavian *jarl*. By Edgar's time *ealdormen*
had come to constitute a small aristocratic circle, in most
cases closely allied by birth or marriage with the royal family.
In the eleventh century the title *ealdorman* was no longer
used, and that of earl took its place. By the later years of
Ethelred there were but four of these officials. With the rule
of Canute the position of the heads of the four great administrative divisions was amalgamated to that of the Danish

---

[46] In Kemble, *Cod. Dipl.*, no. 95 (Birch, *Cart.*, no. 171) Peter is the
ealdorman of the apostles.

[47] *Victoria Co. History Somerset*, II. 179; Chadwick, *Studies*, 286-290.

[48] As in *A.-S. Chron.*, 837, 845, 851, 860, 871.

[49] Thorpe, *Diplomatarium*, 376; *Liber Eliensis*, 139; Wulfstan, *Homilies*
(ed. Napier), 148, 263; H. W. C. Davis, *Eng. Histor. Rev.*, XXVIII.
421. If an offender abjured the realm before the earl or the sheriff this
official had power to recall him and restore him to the peace (*Domesday
Book*, I. 298b).

[50] Chadwick, *Studies on A.-S. Instns.*, 171-197.

[51] *Ibid.*, 161-63.

jarl.[52] Henceforth they often ruled more or less in the spirit
of viceroys. There were six or seven [53] in the time of Edward
the Confessor, in whose reign their power was sometimes a
menace to the state. Their relation to local administration is
shown by the fact that they were entitled to the third penny
of the ordinary judicial income of the shire and hundred
courts,[54] and usually also to a third of the king's income from
boroughs.[55] Certain manors were attached to the office and
served to increase the power of its holders.

From about the reign of Edgar the sheriff appears as an
associate of the *ealdorman* in shire government. The word
sheriff is derived from the old English *scirgerefa* or shire-reeve.
Stubbs supposed that his office was originally elective, its
origins presumably running back to the primitive mark. Chadwick and Liebermann [56] have shown, however, that the office
is not to be regarded as a primitive one. It can be traced only
in the later tenth century, and the *scirgerefa* is mentioned by
this title in no extant document earlier than the reign of
Canute.

The office continues the tradition and functions of the king's
reeves who in the earlier years of the tenth century were set
over certain subdivisions of the county. These officials not
only exercised judicial functions, but they were responsible
for the maintenance of order. They proclaimed the peace.
They headed the men of the community in the pursuit of
thieves and executed justice upon them. They also brought
under suretyship persons of bad reputation and served as witnesses to transactions. Moreover, the king's reeves were fiscal
officials. The publicans of the New Testament are called *gere-
fan* in Anglo-Saxon religious literature. The reeves were toll-
collectors, and they received court fines and took possession of
the confiscated chattels of felons. According to the laws of

[52] Larson, *Canute the Great*, 114-115.
[53] Freeman, *Norman Conquest*, II. 555-568.
[54] Ballard, *Domesday Boroughs*, 41-43.
[55] Stubbs, *Constnl. Hist.*, I. 126.
[56] Liebermann, *National Assembly*, 36; Chadwick, *Studies*, 229-231.

Athelstan they distributed the king's alms. There are frequent complaints about their unjust exactions.[57]

There is no evidence that one of these reeves was set over a whole shire until in the tenth century, when the *ealdormen* declined in number as they came to rule several shires.[58] Under such conditions the *ealdorman* or earl could not personally attend to all the duties of administration in so large an area. The sheriff was the deputy who appeared to assist him. The office is mentioned just as the burghal areas are declining in importance and borough government shrinks to its later limits. The rise of the sheriff, like that of the hundred, thus fits into a general reorganization of local government consequent to the reconquest of the Danelaw.

Like the earlier reeves, sheriffs were appointed and removable by the king. A few of them in the reign of Edward the Confessor held important positions in the royal household. In so far as he was a fiscal and police official, the sheriff was distinctly the representative of the king as opposed to the earl, who was a provincial ruler.[59] But in the exercise of some of his functions, notably those of a judicial and military nature, he was clearly the representative of the earl. As a judicial official he is found holding sessions of the shire court, presumably in the earl's absence,[60] and upon occasion he might hold sessions of the hundred court. As a police official he made arrests, assisted in proclaiming the king's peace, and aided in the maintenance of order. As a military official he had the right to enforce the performance of local guard duty (*inward*). At least in western counties he led the levy of his shire against Welsh incursions. One Anglo-Saxon sheriff is known to have fallen with King Harold in his struggle against the Normans. As a fiscal official the sheriff collected the rents and dues from

[57] Morris, *Med. Eng. Sheriff*, 11-14.
[58] Chadwick, *Studies*, 192, 231.
[59] For the work of the sheriff, Morris, *Med. Eng. Sheriff*, 21-39.
[60] In Canute's proclamation of 1020 (Liebermann, I. 274; Stubbs, *Charters*, 75) the reeves are to judge right judgments by the witness of the bishop and are to do such mercy as the bishop thinks right.

the royal estates and was responsible for court fines levied
in the courts of the shire and hundred. He was apparently
supervisor of the collection of danegeld, was custodian of the
royal estates and enforced services and payments due the
king. He had a right, in some districts at least, to demand
animals for the king's transport service.[61] Upon the occasion
of the king's visit to the shire the sheriff was the official who
saw that he had a bodyguard and who provided for the
royal convenience and safety.

The sheriff was a useful official whose work was exceedingly
varied. In the eleventh century he acted as the earl's representative, and thus held powers beyond those which he wielded
in his old capacity as king's reeve. On the eve of the Norman
Conquest he was rapidly gaining control of the administration
of the shire. The office was important as a centralizing institution, and of such there were few in the Anglo-Saxon
period. Through the sheriff the king exercised some direct
control over local affairs. This co-ordination of central and
local government was very imperfect, but its possibilities were
great.

The county court or shiremote was the judicial centre of
the county. According to a well-known passage in the law of
Edgar it met twice a year, and the bishop and *ealdorman* were
present to administer ecclesiastical as well as secular law. In
the law of Canute there is intimation that more frequent
sessions might be called if necessary.[62] By the time of Ethelred
the sheriff might take the ealdorman's place as presiding official, and by the time of Edward the Confessor he seems to
have been the usual president.[63] Until a much later period
judgments were given by the assembled men of the county,
but by the eleventh century the actual attendance was limited.
This body is sometimes referred to as the shire *witan*.[64] The
king's writs which went to the county court were addressed

[61] As in *Domesday Book*, I. 189-190.
[62] III Edgar, 5 : 1; II Canute, 18.
[63] Morris, *Med. Eng. Sheriff*, 24-25.
[64] Wulfstan (ed. Napier), 173.

to the bishop, earl, sheriff, and the thegns of the shire. The thegns clearly did not constitute the entire membership,[65] but by the time of Edward the Confessor regular attendance was confined to landholders who possessed some degree of economic independence.[66] In the later tenth century the county court in Danish regions might be regarded as an assembly of the military force (*here*) of the shire.[67] It is probable that in this period a *tun* was already represented occasionally in the courts of shire and hundred by its reeve and four men, for men of four neighboring vills were being employed in Ethelred's time in the investigation of certain matters arising in one of these village communities.[68]

Excepting great men, whose causes might come before the *witan*, Englishmen prior to the Norman Conquest found the shiremote the highest court open to them. The available information presents it as active chiefly in civil cases, especially land cases.[69] Matters touching ecclesiastical law were also heard here in the bishop's presence. Some causes came up through failure of the complainant to gain a hearing in the hundred court.[70] The king sometimes sent his writ suggesting action in certain causes. The shire assembly was not without jurisdiction in criminal matters. Judgment in one important type of case through failure of justice in the hundred was

[65] Kemble, *Cod. Dipl.*, no. 731 : all my thegns *twelfhynde* and *twihynde;* *Ramsey Chartulary*, Rolls Ser., II. 79 : all the *witan* and *holden* (faithful) of Hants ; Kemble, no. 732 : these things are known to the doughty men of Kent, nobles and *ceorls*.

[66] Moteworthy men are classed with the fyrdworthy and foldworthy (Kemble, *Cod. Dipl.*, no. 853). A grant of William Rufus to the church of Bury St. Edmunds states that only those men are to be constrained to attend the courts of shire and hundred who had land enough to be worthy to go to the courts of shire and hundred in the Confessor's time (*Eng. Histor. Rev.*, XXIV. 421 ; Davis, *Regesta Regum Anglo-Normanorum*, no. 393).

[67] Vinogradoff, *Eng. Soc. Eleventh Century*, 97, note 3 ; Birch, *Cart.*, III. 369 : *on ealles heres gemot on Hamtone*.

[68] IV Ethelred, 15 ; Gross, *Select Coroners' Rolls*, Selden Soc., p. xxxviii.

[69] Kemble, *Cod. Dipl.*, nos. 898, 929 ; Thorpe, *Diplomatarium*, 346, 376 ; Vinogradoff, *Eng. Soc. Eleventh Century*, 97, n. 3 ; 98, n. 1.

[70] II Canute, 19.

given here. The county assembly like the *witan* declared an outlaw (*nithing*) the person [71] guilty of a grave offense or the offender who did not appear to answer an accusation after his presence was formally demanded according to custom.

Official publicity and probably some administrative action also were gained through the medium of this same assembly. The community might be made witnesses of wills and the formal transfer of land through the execution of such acts in the shiremote.[72] The king, moreover, availed himself of this means to publish his acts. In the tenth century new legislation was proclaimed here.[73] Notice of the king's grants in writ form, directed to the officials and thegns of a given shire, indicate that these were designated for publication in the same way. It is probable that the county also had functions pertaining to taxation, particularly the danegeld, and that it apportioned to each hundred its proper quota.

The third unit in the regular scheme of local government was the borough. This was a town or municipality to be distinguished from the village of the *tun* or manor, of which it was likely to be an outgrowth. Little dependence may be placed in various *a priori* theories which have been advanced concerning the history of the early English towns. The view, for instance, that municipal organization in this period was associated with gilds [74] may be abandoned because of lack of evidence and because of improbability that commercial activity in Anglo-Saxon days was sufficiently advanced to maintain a gild system. It has been held that Roman town life survived the conquest to influence the English,[75] but it is im-

---

[71] I Ethelred, 1, 9a; Liebermann, *Gesetze*, I. 392-393; *Domesday Book*, I. 252, 262b, 298b; *siquis pro aliquo reatu exulatus fuerit a rege et a comite et ab hominibus vicecomitatus: ibid.*, I. 336b.

[72] Thorpe, *Diplomatarium*, 346; cf. Vinogradoff, *Eng. Soc. in Eleventh Century*, 251.

[73] Davis, *Regesta*, p. xi.

[74] Brentano, introd. to *English Gilds*, ed. Toulmin Smith, p. xciii. The few gilds known before the Norman Conquest were not merchant gilds (Gross, *Gild Merchant*, I. 181-191), the only type which could have constituted a possible foundation of municipal organization.

[75] The assumption of Coote, *Romans of Britain*, 358, ff.

possible to believe that they had as yet reached a stage of civilization which could sustain urban activities and organization. Even London under the Kentish kings seems to have been under the control of a wick or village reeve who was an official of the court.[76] Finally, the borough has been regarded as springing entirely from military conditions.

The Anglo-Saxon word for borough (*burh*) originally meant a fortification. Military necessity is not the sole explanation of the rise of English towns, but it is the one best recorded. In the early laws the house of the king or noble, located no doubt in his *tun*, is called his *burh*.[77] Another type of stronghold employed the walls of Roman towns, which were repaired.[78] Thus Canterbury appears in the eighth century as a place of refuge,[79] and the name means the borough of Kentishmen. A public obligation to do wall work (*burhbot*) has been traced back to the end of the seventh century. One of Offa's charters shows that it was performed at the king's *tun*, and in Egbert's day it was one of the three public services required of all West Saxon freemen.[80] There are known instances even in the last days of Anglo-Saxon rule of borough maintenance through the labor of the men of the county.

There is no indication that English town life or organization was of much importance before the time of Alfred. The Danish wars of his day led to a reorganization of the military system which led to the rise of some towns. The palisaded residence at the king's *tun* grew into a fortification of national importance. Permanent garrisons were maintained in the boroughs. Under Alfred's successors both English and Danish boroughs became the strategic centres in the struggle for the Danelaw. In some counties there was but one borough of central importance,[81] and this in the midlands became the seat

[76] Cam, *Francia and England*, 38.
[77] Ine, 45; Alfred, 40.
[78] Ballard, *Domesday Boroughs*, 104-105.
[79] *Ibid.*, 106-107.
[80] Above, p. 28. For detail, II. Athelstan, 13.
[81] Maitland, *Domesday Book and Beyond*, 186-187; Ballard, *Domesday Boroughs*, 4-10.

of county government. Under Alfred's succcessors appears a
new plan of meeting burghal obligations, which probably dated
from his time. Some lords acquitted their obligation to do
wall work by maintaining in the borough houses which were
regarded as annexed to some manor and in which were kept
men to do the repair work. Burghal military service was in
some cases provided by a special class of tenants who held
houses in the town.[82] These arrangements, however, could not
have prevailed everywhere, for in the time of Edward the Confessor every hide of land in Cheshire still sent a man to do the
wall work at Chester.[83] Some of the king's thegns who rendered service for five hides of land were established in
boroughs.[84] They must not be regarded as the whole population, for even in the tenth century commerce had become
an important factor in the life of towns. The lands within the
town might be owned by numerous proprietors, but the
boroughs were directly under the monarch, and a source of
profit to him. In four or five cases prior to the Norman Conquest they had passed under the control of churches,[85] but
this was only a slight deviation from the rule of subjection
to the royal authority.

The government of boroughs and counties is differentiated
in a law of Edgar, in which the borough is seen to possess
a court meeting not twice, but three times a year.[86] At a
later time intermediate sessions were held, as in the shire.
In some of the towns of the former Danish region there were
twelve men, known as lawmen, whose duty was to serve as
judgment finders.[87] Conveyance of land was sometimes witnessed here as in other *gemots*.[88] The chief official of the
borough was the reeve or portreeve,[89] as he was often called.

[82] Ballard, *Domesday Boroughs*, 31-36, 107-108; cf. *Domesday Book*,
I. 179.
[83] *Domesday Book*, I. 262b; Ballard, *Domesday Boroughs*, 35.
[84] Stubbs, *Charters*, 65. As to the burh-gate seat, see Maitland, *Domesday Book and Beyond*, 190.
[85] Tait, *Eng. Histor. Rev.*, XLII. 322-323.
[86] III Edgar, 5:1.   [87] Ballard, *Domesday Boroughs*, 51-53.
[88] Bateson, *Borough Customs* (Selden Soc.), I. introd., xiii.
[89] Kemble, *Anglo-Saxons*, II. 174-175; IV. Ethelred, 7.

As a fiscal official he represented the king, and he might also exercise military functions.[90] According to the laws of Edward the Elder and of Athelstan, he was a witness to sales, and thus able not only to vouch for lawful possession of goods but to collect the toll at the same time. The law of Edgar required that twelve transaction witnesses be appointed to witness sales in the smaller boroughs and thirty-six in the larger.[91]

The Anglo-Saxon borough belonged, then, to the national scheme of government and made not the slightest pretension to an independent status as did the free cities of the continent. The king's peace covered the offense of fighting or stealing in his boroughs. It is said to have prevailed in the streets of some of them. Maitland believed that this was the rule, and that the peace and security thus assured had much to do with the rise of town life and trade.[92] In the eleventh century the boroughs lost much of their military importance, and their development depended upon trade and peaceful pursuits.

The chief Anglo-Saxon courts in ordinary cases were those of the shire and the hundred. In the tenth century the meeting of the *gemot* was announced seven days before it was held.[93] Canute forbade the transaction of its business on Sunday as well as the taking of oaths and ordeals on that day.[94] *Gemots* were under the king's peace.[95] Their function was the enforcement of public law. The rendering of decisions rested with the whole assembly, although in the Danish regions judgment, following Scandinavian usage, seems often to have been given by twelve lawmen[96] (*thegns*). In some instances also an equal number of judges of fact was chosen

[90] Ballard, *Domesday Boroughs*, 91.

[91] IV Edgar, 4, 5.

[92] Maitland, *Domesday Book and Beyond*, 185, 190; Liebermann, *Gesetze*, I. 471 (15).

[93] II Athelstan, 20.

[94] Liebermann, *Gesetze*, I. 275; also on feast days and fast days (I Canute, 17).

[95] Even men going to and coming from the *gemot* (II Canute, 82).

[96] III Ethelred, 13:2; Vinogradoff, *Eng. Soc. in Eleventh Century*, 5-6.

by each side of the controversy and judgment rendered by these.[97]

The local courts dealt with offenses against the king or the state, but this was a minor part of their activity. Anglo-Saxon law had to do largely with private injuries incurred through manslaying, mayhem, wounding or cattle theft. In most of these cases initiative rested with the injured, in homicide cases with the family of the slain, who were required to abandon the feudright when the first installment, a tenth, of the *wergeld* was paid.[98] After 1066 the usage still prevailed by which the complainant summoned his adversary before witnesses, giving him, it seems, at least seven days to answer in the assembly.[99] If he failed to appear, he was summoned again. For non-appearance after the third summons he was subject to a contempt fine, known as the king's *oferhyrness*, which was quite heavy in amount.[100] The accused, when once he responded, might be placed in suretyship to guarantee his appearance for trial at the proper time.

So difficult was it to bring into court irresponsible persons without property that Anglo-Saxon lawgivers devised a special system of suretyship or *borh*, as it was called, to meet this situation. From an early time is traceable the principle that the offender's lord is responsible for him.[101] A law of Athelstan required that the kindred of the lordless man of whom no satisfaction could be obtained, should find for him a lord to produce him if required. The law of Edmund prescribed that men of bad reputation and those accused of offenses be compelled to be under pledge. The laws of Athelstan and Edgar held lords responsible for the men on their lands. By the time of the last-named king the plan was so far developed that every man not of the propertied class was required to have a standing surety (also called *borh*) to produce him in case

---

[97] *Chron. Ramsey Abbey,* 79.
[98] Liebermann, *Gesetze,* I. 392-393. This was the *healsfang.*
[99] *Leges Henrici Primi,* 7 : 4 ; 59 : 2b.
[100] II Athelstan, 20.
[101] Ine, 22.

he committed an offense.[102] By a regulation made later [103] lords were responsible especially for producing members of their own household. A passage in the law of Canute, so it is shown by Liebermann,[104] implies that responsibility for general peace suretyship or *borh*, had fallen upon the tithing which earlier appears in the laws as a group of ten men with police duties. It was natural that a lord should strive to place this burden upon his dependents' fellow villagers, yet there is no definite knowledge of the means by which such *borh* was constituted in the last decades of Anglo-Saxon rule. There is reason to believe that various plans were followed,[105] and it is unsafe to assume that English *borh* had generally developed into the frankpledge system found in Norman England.

The defendant once in court, the trial began with the fore-oath [106] of the injured person, which made formal complaint. This was unnecessary when the injury was palpable, as when he exhibited a wound in court. If the accused formally denied the charge, as usually occurred, judgment proceeded upon this conflict of oath [107] and was determined by the assembled free-men, or, in some of the *gemots* of the Danelaw, by the twelve lawmen.[108] Judgment consisted in a decision as to the kind of proof the defendant must produce. Ordinarily this was by compurgation or the ordeal and was determined by the previous reputation of the accused. If the offender was caught in open theft, trial was unnecessary and he might be summarily executed.[109] This along with housebreaking, arson, secret killing and treason to one's lord [110] was classed as a

---

[102] III Athelstan 7; IV Edgar, 3; I Ethelred, 1; II Canute, 20, 25. Cf. II Edward, 3; also Morris, *Frankpledge System*, 19.
[103] II Canute, 31.
[104] II Canute, 20; Liebermann, *Gesetze*, II. 744.
[105] Morris, *Frankpledge System*, 20-29, 39. Below, p. 175.
[106] II Athelstan, 23 : 2.
[107] Pollock and Maitland, *History English Law*, II, 600, 608-609. The father of the deaf and dumb man had to pay compensation for his misdeeds, since he could neither confess nor deny them (Alfred, 14).
[108] III Ethelred, 3 : 1; 13 : 2. Ballard, *Domesday Boroughs*, 53.
[109] Ine, 12; II Canute, 4a : 2.
[110] III Edgar, 7 : 3; II Canute, 64.

botless crime, that is to say, one for which no financial restitution was permissible.

Exceptional modes of proof are occasionally mentioned. In land cases it might be made by a charter or other record. For the clergy there were peculiar forms, but ordinarily, if the reputation of the accused was satisfactory,[111] the test allotted was that of producing a certain number of compurgators or oath-helpers to swear that their principal's oath was clean and guileless.[112] The requisite number varied, but seems usually to have been six or a multiple of six.[113] The oath of a *twelfhynde* man was worth that of six *ceorls*,[114] and some oaths also weighed according to the amount of land or property possessed by the swearer. If the accused failed to produce the required number of compurgators or if he bore a bad reputation, proof was demanded by ordeal. This was a mechanical test, imposed upon the theory that God would not let the innocent suffer, and it was often called the judgment of God. Trial by battle does not appear among the Anglo-Saxons. The forms of ordeal employed for laymen were those of cold water, hot water, and hot iron. The accuser designated which of the three should be used.[115] All were in charge of the clergy and were preceded by three days of fasting on the part of the accused. On the day of the ordeal was held a special religious service which included prayers, adjuration of the water or fire to reveal the guilty, and exhortation of the accused to tell the truth.[116] When the defendant was a man of bad reputation or his offense a heinous one, he went to the threefold ordeal,[117] in which the hot iron carried was three times the

[111] II Canute, 22. According to the laws of Ethelred (I, 2) and Canute (II Canute, 30 : 1), either the lord with two thegns or the reeve might give testimony on this point.
[112] Liebermann, *Gesetze*, I. 398-399.
[113] IV Ethelred, 3 ; III Ethelred, 13 ; Alfred and Guthrum, 3.
[114] Liebermann, *Gesetze*, I. 462-463.
[115] III Ethelred, 6 ; see Attenborough, *Laws of Earliest English Kings*, 170-73.
[116] II Athelstan, 23 ; Liebermann, *Gesetze*, I. 401-416.
[117] II Canute, 30 ; II Athelstan, 4, 5, 6 : 1 ; I Edgar, 9 ; III Ethelred, 3 : 4.

usual weight or the stone to be reached in the boiling water was suspended at more than the usual depth.

Throughout the period the family of the injured, especially in cases of homicide, claimed and collected a money compensation. To them was rendered the *wergeld* of the slain, the feud ceasing when the first installment was paid.[118] To payment for personal injury was added also the *wite* or court fine which went to the state. For wounds personal compensation, known as *bot*, was paid according to a fixed scale, depending upon the kind of injury, and the *wite* was also exacted. The price of the property involved, and the *wite* atoned for theft. As already observed, the *wergeld* of the thegn was six times that of the *ceorl*, and the scale of payments generally varied according to the rank in society of the injured. As an Anglo-Saxon writer puts it, law went by ranks.[119] The amount of the *wergeld* was different in the northern Danelaw from that in Mercia and Wessex.[120] In the Danish period the criminal who committed a grave offense or who became a fugitive was proclaimed an outlaw, if he did not appear in accordance with the law of summons. He then was said to bear a wolf's head and might be slain with impunity. Originally a sort of declaration of hostility against the offender[121] who committed an unusually grave offense, outlawry came to be employed as a means of enforcing the authority of courts. When the freeman's offense was botless, or, when he was unable to pay the amount imposed for his offense, the penalty was mutilation or death. Loss of the tongue was by one law fixed as a possible penalty for stirring up sedition and by another for false accusation leading to loss of property or reputation.[122] Loss of the hand was the penalty for some crimes.[123] From the time of Ine the man accused of theft and at last caught in the act

[118] Liebermann, *Gesetze*, I. 392-393.

[119] *Ibid.*, I. 457; Stubbs, *Select Charters*, 65.

[120] Cf. Liebermann, *Gesetze*, I. 392-393, 458-463.

[121] Edward and Guthrum, 6 : 6; II Athelstan, 2 : 1; Birch, *Cartularium*, no. 1131. See Pollock and Maitland, *Hist. Eng. Law*, I. 43; II. 449.

[122] Alfred, 32; III Edgar, 4; II Canute, 16.

[123] II Athelstan, 14 : 1.

or else proved guilty at the ordeal lost a hand or a foot.[124] In Canute's time the offender who failed at the ordeal forfeited his hands or feet and for more serious offenses his eyes, his nose, his ears, his upper lip or his scalp.[125]

The characteristics of Anglo-Saxon legal procedure are thus the initiative of the parties, the passivity of the state, judgment by popular assemblies, judgment before proof, the burden of proof on the accused, and proof by mechanical test. As a scheme for enforcing justice this seems peculiarly irrational. The compurgators swore merely to a set formula [126] and not to tell the whole truth. Doubtless there was much perjury, but the plan was not without its advantages. The matters sworn to were usually of common knowledge in a small community in which neighbors knew what went on. Moreover the impressive ritual used at the ordeal was designed to produce confession through fear of eternal punishment.

AUTHORITIES

The laws furnish the principal source material on local government from Alfred to 1066, but they are occasionally supplemented by the charters, and by passages in the Anglo-Saxon Chronicle, and in *Domesday Book*. Concerning this see the notes at the end of chapters III, IV, above. There are a few useful references in Asser, *Life of Alfred*. The best edition is that by W. H. Stevenson (1904).

The traditional theory of the development of English local institutions from early Germanic origins is presented by Kemble, *Saxons in England* (I. chaps. 2, 3). Stubbs in his *Constitutional History* (I. chap. 5) gives a more careful treatment, which is tinged here and there by the views of Kemble. A much more critical treatment of the subject begins with H. M. Chadwick, *Studies on Anglo-Saxon Institutions* (1905), which is largely devoted to the social system and to local institutions. The chapters dealing with the earl and the local administrative system (chaps. 5-7) are epoch-making. They present an entirely new view of minor local subdivisions which rejects the existence in England of a primitive Germanic hundred, and lays stress on neglected facts and institutions. Liebermann, in vol. II of his *Gesetze* largely

[124] Ine, 18, 37.
[125] II Canute, 30 : 4-5.
[126] See Liebermann, *Gesetze*, I. 398-399.

agrees with these views. Probably the most notable of Liebermann's
discussions is on the origin of the hundred (art. "Hundred") and the
tithing (art. "Zehnerschaft"). W. J. Corbett in his paper on "The
Tribal Hidage" (*Trans. Royal Historical Society,* new series, XIV)
deals with the relation between the hundred of record and the scheme
of hidage assessment. Sir Paul Vinogradoff, *English Society in the
Eleventh Century* (1908), in section II. chap. 1, gives a useful treatment
of the county and the hundred. For the local institutions of the Danelaw, material is presented by F. M. Stenton, *Types of Manorial Structure in the Northern Danelaw* (Oxford Studies in Social and Legal
History, II. 1910), and in his introduction to *Documents illustrative of
the Social and Economic History of the Danelaw* (*British Academy
Records of the Social and Economic History of England and Wales,* V.
1920), as well as by D. C. Douglas, *The Social Structure of Medieval
East Anglia* (*Oxford Studies in Social and Legal History,* IX. 1927).

A brief and more compact treatment of local institutions will be
found in Miss H. M. Cam, *Local Government in Francia and England*
(1912), and of some specific subjects in W. A. Morris, *The Frankpledge
System,* chap. 1 (1910) and *The Medieval English Sheriff to 1300,* chap.
2 (1927). The classical account of the old English borough is F. W.
Maitland, *Domesday Book and Beyond,* essay I. sect. 9 (1897), although
its conclusions are not generally regarded as adequate. Maitland presents material of a more general nature in his *Township and Borough*
(1898). Additional material is presented by Adolphus Ballard, *The
Domesday Boroughs,* especially pp. 104-124 (1904), and more recently
by James Tait in the *English Historical Review,* vol. 42 (1927).

CHAPTER VI

THE CHURCH AND THE FEUDAL TREND IN RELATION TO THE STATE

A survey of the old English political system calls for a consideration of the relations between church and state and also of the series of changes by which, so far as public obligations were concerned, the nobility came to stand between their free dependents and the state. In both instances usages and conditions came in part as the result of a gradual extra-legal development; but many of these by the end of the tenth century had crystallized into law and appeared in the codes of the various kings.

Relations between the English kings and the papacy were not unfriendly, neither were they close. From the earlier days petitions and letters were sent to the papacy as a matter of course, but from 787 to the time of Edward the Confessor only two papal legates visited England. With the reign of the Confessor, who introduced continental ideas and appointed Normans and other continentals to bishoprics, relations began to grow closer. This was not true, however, with respect to Peter's pence,[1] a payment which had been rendered to the papacy at intervals, apparently since the reign of King Offa and for Wessex since the year 855. The annual amount came to be fixed at a penny a hearth.[2] In Alfred's day Peter's pence was borne to Rome by a special envoy,[3] and a stringent law of Edgar provided for its collection. In the eleventh century, however, the payment was discontinued. One papal right exer-

---

[1] See II Edgar, 4 : 1-3.
[2] Rev. O. Jensen, in *Trans. Royal Histor. Society*, new ser., XIV. 178-183, 187-188; see I Canute, 9.
[3] *A.-S. Chron.*, 888-890 (889-891).

cised was that of conferring upon the two archbishops the *pallium* or badge of office, a vestment necessary upon important occasions. This enabled the pope to accept or reject the person chosen to this office and to exercise some influence upon elections. In the time of Edward the Confessor the *pallium* was for a time denied to Aldred of York because he had been transferred from the see of Worcester to the archbishopric without papal leave.[4] The deposition in 1052 of Robert, the Norman archbishop of Canterbury, created an irregularity in the succession and left the English Stigand for a time unable to procure his insignia of office. His ultimate reception of the *pallium* at the hands of an antipope was accounted a schismatic act.[5] The exercise of the metropolitan power by an archbishop who was regarded as wrongfully in possession thus arrayed the papacy against King Harold and gave moral support to the Norman Conquest.

The constitutional history of the Anglo-Saxon Church from the eighth century shows a trend toward secularization which increased rapidly in the tenth and eleventh centuries. From the time of Edgar, ecclesiastical organization was in various ways subjected to state control. This made for efficiency when the devastating effects of the Danish wars required reparation, but in the eleventh century the higher church officials were too obviously associated with political affairs. The church was losing in freedom of action, and the effect is seen in relaxed spiritual energy and lowered standards.

In the seventh century, following the conversion of the English of the various kingdoms, church and state have usually been regarded as independent. Although it is clear that kings interfered in various ways in the government of the church in England the latter attained unity of action long before the various kingdoms were combined. Under Archbishop Theodore (669-690) all the dioceses came to recognize the headship of Canterbury, and provision was

---

[4] *Historians of York*, ed. Raine, III. 6.
[5] *A.-S. Chron.*, 1052, 1058.

made in 673 for the holding of national councils to regulate ecclesiastical affairs. Moreover, the dioceses, which hitherto had been identical with the various kingdoms, were broken up and gained in central direction as they ceased to comprise the chief political divisions of the land. The synod of Theodore's time was the first national assembly in England and was the forerunner of the national *witenagemots* and parliaments.[6] Ecclesiastical organization was in advance of political organization and might well afford a lesson to ambitious rulers.

This administrative unity was not retained. The Northumbrian archbishopric of York, permanently established in 735, interfered with the headship of a single metropolitan and the scheme for general councils of the English church. King Offa, moreover, to increase the prestige of the Mercian kingdom in 787 effected the creation of a third archbishopric, that of Lichfield. This, however, did not outlive the first archbishop, and came to an end in 803, the rights of Canterbury being restored. The rise of the West Saxon hegemony about this time seems to mark a further movement in the direction of secular control.

This is clear in one respect from the time of Alfred, when the Danish invasions isolated the church in most of the former Angle kingdoms and in portions of the midlands all but wiped it out. Henceforth general synods of the older sort were not held. Legislation for the church came more and more to be enacted by the king upon consultation with assemblies of prelates. This type of council shaded off by degrees [7] into the *witan,* of which the same prelates formed a part. In the tenth and the eleventh century it was usual to legislate for the church through the national assembly. Edgar and Canute enacted codes dealing with ecclesiastical affairs which both in detail and in bulk are quite comparable to their secular codes. Even when assemblies of ecclesiastics drew up regulations,

[6] Hunt, *Hist. English Church,* 139.
[7] Liebermann, *National Assembly in A.-S. Period,* 15-17.

they were enacted by royal authority.[8] In England no collection of ecclesiastical canons seems to have embodied the general usage of the church. The national assembly sometimes interfered in the internal affairs of the church, as when in 975 it aided the monks in their struggle against the secular clergy, enabling them to replace the latter in some of the cathedral chapters.[9]

In another direction the control of the crown increased. There is evidence from the earliest period that at times the influence of the monarch in the appointment of bishops and abbots was powerful. Under Alfred and his strong successors the appointment of these became an important secular concern. The election of bishops nominally by the clergy or the whole people of the diocese, and of abbots by the whole conventual body, is mentioned,[10] yet the king often named bishops and abbots, sometimes, Liebermann believes regularly, upon consultation with the *witan*.[11] From the time of Canute clerks who had been found useful in the king's service were rewarded with bishoprics. Under Canute's sons and Edward the Confessor the crown or a great noble dictated appointments. In 1048 the king appointed a bishop by writ and seal.

Under the Confessor appointments were made for personal reasons, and the signs of secularization were numerous. There was complaint of simony.[12] Some ecclesiastics spent much time in secular employment, and dioceses were occasionally held in plurality.[13] The union of existing dioceses and the re-

---

[8] Hunt, *Hist. of English Church*, 316; Liebermann, *National Assembly*, 17.   [9] *Ibid.*, 62.

[10] Dunstan was chosen archbishop, according to the *Ramsey Chronicle* (I. 25), *voto totius cleri et populi cum favore regis*. A charter of Ethelred (Kemble, *Codex Diplomaticus*, no. 714) provides for the election of an abbot *cum regis consilio*.

[11] Liebermann, *National Assembly*, 63-64; Hunt, *Hist. of Eng. Church*, 313-315. Edward the Confessor made a formal grant to the monks of Bury St. Edmunds of the right to elect their abbot (*Eng. Histor. Rev.*, XXIV. 425).

[12] Malmesbury, *Gesta Pontificum*, 35, 150, 170, 205, 251; *A.-S. Chron.*, 1044 (1043); Symeon of Durham (Rolls Ser.), I. 91, 92.

[13] Malmesbury, *Gesta Pontificum*, 150, 249, 251.

moval of their seats were matters for which, as in the past, the permission of the king or of both the king and the *witan* was sought.[14] It is related that Dunstan once received his episcopal lands from the king. In some instances the bishops of King Edward's time received their charges through the royal writ.[15] In a few cases the government expelled bishops from their sees and replaced them with others. Moreover, church lands sometimes passed into the hands of laymen in the royal favor.[16]

The direction of the clergy in secular affairs was nevertheless greater than that of the government in ecclesiastical affairs. Distinct as was the work of the state from that of the church, it was permeated in many ways by clerical influence. Even in the days of the pagan kingdoms the priesthood had been influential. In Christian England prelates served as the king's ministers, and the archbishop of Canterbury usually enjoyed a priority of position among the advisers of the West Saxon monarch. Bishops and abbots formed a considerable and an influential part of the national assembly, and had a hand in framing legislation not only for the church but for the realm in general. Just as the bishop's association with a kingdom from early times gave him a national significance, so in the south of England his later association with one of its subdivisions gave him importance in local government. From the time of Edward the Elder the dioceses of Wessex corresponded in general to its shires, hence the bishop of the tenth century was a shire bishop who ranked as a shire official of the highest importance. Furthermore, the clergy were essential to the administration of justice, since the ritual and conduct of the ordeal were in their hands. After the rise of the parish system in the seventh and eighth centuries.[17]

[14] Böhmer, *Kirche und Staat*, 50, and n. 5; Liebermann, *National Assembly*, 62-63.

[15] *Ibid.*, 63; Böhmer, *Kirche und Staat*, 49-50.

[16] *Ibid.*, 77; Morris, *Med. Eng. Sheriff*, 36, and n. 153.

[17] Bede's account (IV. 27) shows that it did not yet exist in Northumbria about 685.

the parish tended to coincide with the village or *tun*. It is not surprising, then, that in Norman inquests soon after 1066 the parish priest appears as a person of importance in judicial affairs.

The bishop, in addition to his purely spiritual functions and his powers in disciplining the clergy,[18] was accorded in Anglo-Saxon law a remarkably influential position. This is illustrated by the law of Edgar which prescribed that he was to sit with the *ealdorman* in the county court where ecclesiastical as well as secular justice was to be enforced.[19] Justice to his flock as well as their social welfare was his concern. The evidence of episcopal control in secular affairs is strongest in the time of Canute. According to an old document, it pertained to the king and the bishop to see that a wrong done a stranger or a man in orders was righted.[20] A writer of the eleventh century [21] holds that it is the bishop's duty to appease strife and effect peace; that in cases of accusation he is to direct the test in oath or ordeal so no man wrong another; that every legal right is to be settled by the bishop's counsel and witness; and that just balances for weighing and exact measures for use in boroughs are to be assured by his supervision. A law applicable to the Danish districts provided that a criminal maimed by way of punishment, if alive in three days, might be given aid by the bishop's permission.[22] Specific enactments required him to exercise supervision over the judicial work of reeves. In some instances of the failure of these officials to enforce enacted law it was even made his duty to exact the monetary penalty imposed upon them.[23]

The close relations between church and state are also shown by the invocation of the civil power to aid in matters of ecclesiastical concern. Within a century of the conversion of

[18] As in the laws of Wihtred of Kent, cap. 6; Alfred, 21.

[19] III Edgar, 5: 1-2.

[20] Stubbs, *Select Charters*, 65.

[21] Institutes of Polity, 7, Thorpe, *Ancient Laws*, 426; Liebermann, *Gesetze*, I. 477.

[22] Edward and Guthrum, 10.

[23] III Edgar, 3. Cf. Athelstan, Alms (Charities), 2.

Kent, laws of this kingdom were enacted to put down certain heathen practices and to enforce the observance of Sunday and of fast days.[24] In the laws of King Ine, which belong to almost exactly the same period, a penalty is laid upon the guardian of a child that dies without baptism. The man who works on Sunday without his lord's command is to be reduced to slavery. The right of the criminal to seek sanctuary appears in these same laws,[25] although it was given broader application by the law of Alfred.[26] The laws enacted by Edward the Elder along with the Danish king Guthrum provided that heavy pecuniary penalties should be inflicted upon those who honored heathen practices by word or deed, and other sections were directed against pagan marriage customs and the non-observance of fasts and of Sunday.[27] The law of Canute once more forbade pagan worship [28] in its various forms. Other laws of the Anglo-Saxon kings also imposed penalties upon priests remiss in the exercise of purely spiritual functions,[29] and provided for the regulation of conventual life,[30] and for the enforcement of clerical celibacy.[31] A law of Ethelred [32] prescribes that the church tithe be divided into three parts and specifies the uses to which these shall be applied.

The material interests of the church were also safeguarded by the state. In the northern regions Peter's pence was collected in each wapentake by a priest and two thegns.[33] The requirement of the contribution of a tithe for the support of the church, first called for by the legatine councils held in England in 787, was made by Ethelwulf of Wessex in 855 and enforced by the laws of nearly all the kings of the tenth cen-

[24] Wihtred, sects. 9-14; so II Edgar, 5.
[25] Ine, sects. 2, 3, 5.
[26] Alfred, 2, 5; cf. I Canute, 2:3.
[27] Edward and Guthrum, 2, 4.
[28] II Canute, 5.
[29] Wihtred, 6; Edward and Guthrum, 3: 1-2.
[30] V Ethelred, 4-6.
[31] I Edmund, 1; V Ethelred, 9:1.
[32] VIII Ethelred, 6.
[33] Northumbrian Priests' Law, 57:2, Liebermann, *Gesetze*, I. 384.

tury. This from the time of Edgar was compulsory upon
tenants as well as lords.[34] Several enactments provided that
severe monetary penalties should be laid upon those who withheld the tithe.[35] In each parish was paid a commutation of
the first fruits of crops under the name of church-scot [36] and
mortuary dues under the name of soul-scot.[37] It was made the
duty of the reeves to see that these were rendered and to aid
the stewards of churches in enforcing such rights.[38] In the
early eleventh century the county court dealt with the man
who broke fasts and who did not rightly render alms.[39] The
same body seems to have given decisions concerning the
church-scot and the terms when it was due.[40] A half of the
composition for some offenses, such as adultery, non-payment
of tithes and false swearing on the relics, was by law conferred upon the bishop.[41]

The claims of the church to secular immunity as compared
with those of later times were light. The bishop exercised a
jurisdiction although this was of very limited scope. He gave
decisions in some matters involving offenses against morality.[42]
He adjudged the case of the priest who neglected or improperly
performed his ecclesiastical functions.[43] Disputes between
priests were by a canon reserved to ecclesiastical decision.[44]
The priest who was a party to false witness or perjury, or was
the associate of thieves, was subject to the bishop's judgment

[34] II Edgar, I :1.
[35] II Edgar, 3 :1; VIII Ethelred, 8; I Canute, 8 :2.
[36] Ine, 61; Canute's Proc. of 1027, sec. 16; I Canute, 10.
[37] VI Athelstan, 8 :6; I Athelstan, 4.
[38] I Athelstan, 4; VIII Ethelred, 32. Plough-alms (II Edgar, 1 :1; I
Canute, 8 :1), consisting of a penny a ploughland (VII Ethelred, 1 :2),
and dues to provide wax for maintaining lights in the churches (Edward and Guthrum, 6 :2-3; V Ethelred, 11; I Canute, 12) were also
rendered.
[39] Wulfstan, *Homilies*, ed. Napier, 173.
[40] Thorpe, *Diplomatarium*, 440.
[41] Alfred, 8; II Edgar, 3 :1; I Canute, 8 :2; II Canute, 36; *Domesday
Book*, I.1.
[42] II Canute, 53 :1. It is difficult to draw the line between the judicial
power and the power to enforce. penance. Cf. *ibid.*, 54 : 1.
[43] Wihtred, 6.
[44] Thorpe, *Ancient Laws*, 395.

concerning amends to be made both to God and to man.[45] According to a provision of the treaty between Edward the Elder and the Danes, the man in holy orders who committed a capital crime was to be arrested and his case reserved to the bishop's decision.[46] Eleventh century law assumed that the bishop would act if homicide or any other great crime was committed by a priest, for it prescribed that such an offender should be deprived of his office and banished, and also go on pilgrimage as far as the pope prescribed.[47]

The exemption of men in holy orders from secular jurisdiction was very far from complete. There are mentioned no separate ecclesiastical courts until after the Norman Conquest, and the bishop probably gave most of his judgments in the county court. No doubt his influence there settled many cases of clerics which were not reserved to his special decision. Priests were at an early time accorded the privilege of clearing themselves of accusations at the altar [48] by their own asseveration, and might use light forms of the ordeal.[49] They were not involved in the feud, nor did they pay *wergeld* for their kindred. Monks also left the law of their kindred behind them when they entered the service of the church.[50] The priest was subject to the ordinary law at many points. If he misconducted an ordeal, he was punished much as any other official.[51] In case of failure to make the prescribed amends for homicide, he might be declared an outlaw.[52] For negligence in purely spiritual functions, such as failure to bring the chrism or the withholding of baptism, he was liable to a fine.[53] Here his legal responsibility appears to have been similar to that of the civil official.

[45] VIII Ethelred, 27 ; I Canute, 5a :3.
[46] Edward and Guthrum, 4 :2.
[47] VIII Ethelred, 26 ; II Canute, 41. Cf. Alfred, 21.
[48] Wihtred, 18, ff ; VIII Ethelred, 19-24 ; I Canute, 5, 5a.
[49] I Canute, 5a :1-2c.
[50] Alfred, 21 ; I Canute, 5a ; 2b, 2d.
[51] Liebermann, *Gesetze*, I. 382.
[52] II Canute, 41 :2.
[53] Edward and Guthrum, 3 :2.

Anglo-Saxon law guaranteed the privileges and social status of the clergy as well as the peace of the church. The secular power forbade the extension of aid or protection to excommunicated persons so they might be constrained to submit to ecclesiastical requirements.[54] The penalty for the violation of the archbishop's or bishop's special protection (*mundborg*) was heavy, but not heavier than in the case of other personages of high rank.[55] For fighting or bearing false witness in the presence of the bishop the compensation exacted was likewise heavy.[56] The priest in good standing was entitled to the status and privilege of a thegn.[57] The clergy in general were protected by a law [58] which declared that he who killed a servant of the altar should be outlawed unless he made amends by pilgrimage and compensation to the kindred of the slain. The church edifice was protected by a special peace (*grith*), the violation of which, through the commission of homicide within church walls, was a botless offense.[59] One of the few distinct instances of immunity from the civil power occurs in the right of asylum for three days afforded by certain monasteries [60] and for seven days by consecrated churches. Violation of this right of sanctuary in the case of churches was by a law of Alfred made a breach of the king's peace.[61]

The secular burdens laid upon church property seem in general much the same as those of other property. In early Kentish law is broadly proclaimed the principle of the immunity of the church from rents.[62] Church lands in Wessex conferred by royal grant were regularly held to the obligations of the *trinoda necessitas*, nor is the opinion that they were exempt from danegeld [63] well founded. Release from the pub-

[54] VIII Ethelred, 42; II Canute, 66:1.
[55] Chadwick, *Studies on A.-S. Instns.*, 115-121; cf. Alfred, 3.
[56] Ine, 13; Alfred, 15.
[57] V. Ethelred, 9:1; VIII Ethelred, 28; I Canute, 6a:2a.
[58] II Canute, 39.   [59] I Canute, 2:3.   [60] Alfred, 2, 2:1.
[61] Alfred, 5, 5:1-4. Cf. VIII Ethelred, 1:1.
[62] Wihtred, 1.
[63] Makower, *Constnl. Hist. Church of England*, 10; *Leges Edwardi Conf.*, 11:1. Churches were assessed for the danegeld (Ballard, *Domesday Inquest*, 89-94).

lic burdens which fell upon their lands came only by grant of the king.

In the tenth century and also in the eleventh church and state in England were more closely bound together than in any other land of western Christendom. The church looked to the *witan* to regulate many of its affairs, including some of purely clerical import. The king, when he so desired, controlled the appointment of bishops and abbots, sometimes conferring office upon the former. The ordinary courts of shire and hundred disposed of many matters of ecclesiastical concern. The bishop possessed a certain independent jurisdiction in relation to his clergy, but it was of extremely limited extent. The king was the protector of the church and the clergy. The authority of the state was invoked to enforce the payment of church dues and the excommunication pronounced by the bishop. On the other hand, the influence and power of the clerical estate in temporal affairs were surprisingly great Apparently until a late period theirs was a powerful influence in the national council, and until the end of Anglo-Saxon rule matters of secular justice were settled under the eye of the bishop. The church constantly lost rather than gained independence of status, and its immunities were few; yet it was probably the strongest single force in the disposition of the ordinary affairs of the realm. As Böhmer has shown, the entire body politic assumed a theocratic character which materially distinguished it from those of the continent.[64]

The supremacy of the state which is manifest in its relations to the church appears also, although in lesser degree, throughout the feudalizing movement of the Anglo-Saxon period. So largely was this true, that it is not permissible in any strict sense to use the word feudalism, much less the expression feudal system, to describe any set of conditions which existed. From the political point of view the term feudalism denotes a peculiar set of usages prevalent in continental Europe, particularly the former Frankish lands, from the

[64] Böhmer, *Kirche und Staat*, 56.

tenth to the thirteenth century. Here a feudal scheme was based on the tenure of land whereby the personal obligation of man to lord tended to supersede the public bond between the subject and the state. The lord largely exercised functions of government with respect to his tenants who owed him various forms of service, including military service, in return for the land they held of him.

Feudalism in this sense was never prevalent in Anglo-Saxon England. Certain feudal elements, however, were well developed on English soil, although they were never combined into such a consistent scheme as that on the continent. These were sufficient to modify profoundly the relations of the state to the great body of freemen. They may be classified under three heads: (1) vassalage, or the personal dependence of man upon lord; (2) dependent land tenure, fixing an economic bond between man and lord, and enhancing the political obligations and status of the latter; and (3) the political immunity or private jurisdiction, establishing another form of control of lord over dependent.

The statements of Tacitus regarding the *comitatus* of the early Germanic chieftain and the conditions shown in early poems warrant the conclusion that the Anglo-Saxons brought some form of vassalage with them when they entered England. The relations of lords and their dependents stand out prominently in the laws of Ine.[65] Certainly in the later seventh century *gesiths* had lords.[66] Apparently they formed the *comitatus* of kings and other great persons. The king's thegns of a later day were also his personal dependents, many of whom rendered him special service for their land. Some who stood in close personal relationship served him at his hall and did his errands.[67] The earls were also regarded as the vassals of the king.[68] Lords other than the king were served by

---

[65] Above, p. 32. [66] Wihtred, 5; Ine, 50.

[67] Above, p. 27; cf. Liebermann, *Gesetze*, I. 456-457; Stubbs, *Select. Charters*, 65; Maitland, *Domesday Book and Beyond*, 163-164.

[68] This is the significance of the *heriot* rendered at their decease (II Canute, 71a; cf. Liebermann, *National Assembly*, 28-29; *Gesetze*, II. 501).

thegns, and thegns were regarded as vassals. Such dependence was not confined to the nobility. Not only the great men and the thegns, but apparently any man of standing, might receive an ordinary freeman and become his lord. Vassalage in the later laws, as in the earlier, is assumed to be the normal order.[69]

Men voluntarily placed themselves under a lord or a church to gain protection,[70] land or some other advantage. The process of entering this relationship is known as commendation.[71] In commending himself in the tenth century a man took a solemn oath to be faithful and true to his lord, on condition, so the formula runs, "that he keep me as I am willing to deserve and fulfill all that was agreed to when I became his man and chose his will as mine." [72] A law of King Ine directed that the man who moved away without his lord's permission was to be returned and to make to the latter a heavy payment.[73] In the earlier decades of the tenth century it was forbidden that anyone receive a man subject to another without the permission of him whom the dependent had been serving.[74] A man was required to be loyal to his lord. A law of King Alfred branded plotting against one's lord as a great crime for which the lord might take a man's life and all that he had. In the days of Edgar and Canute treason to one's lord was punishable only by death.[75] In Alfred's day a man might fight for his lord if attacked, and similarly a lord for his man, without incurring liability to the feud. A man might also fight for his relative if unjustly attacked, but not against his lord.[76] Men who were law-abiding might arrange to leave their lords and to seek others. A law of Athelstan's

[69] Above, p. 32; below, p. 112.
[70] The Latin term used is *tuitio* (*Domesday Book*, I. 50b).
[71] Maitland, *Domesday Book and Beyond*, 67-72.
[72] Liebermann, *Gesetze*, I. 396-397.
[73] Ine, 39.
[74] II Edward, 7; II Athelstan, 22; III Athelstan, 4.
[75] Alfred, 4:2 (cf. 1:1); III Edgar, 7:3; II Canute, 26. According to IV Edgar, 1:1-2 refusal to pay rent might become such an offense.
[76] Alfred, 42:5-6.

time declares that a freeman who has acted rightly in all respects toward his lord shall not be prevented from seeking a new one.[77] At least in the eleventh century a man might have more than one lord at the same time, for example, one as landlord, one as lord for judicial purposes or for acquitting service or taxes due the government.

Lordship over the lower classes tended to become permanent and hereditary because of its economic bearing. Many men held land of their lords from which they derived their subsistence, and thus they were in no position to leave nor to seek better conditions of life. At the dawn of authentic Anglo-Saxon history, in the reign of Ethelbert of Kent, both the king and the nobles were the possessors of *tuns*.[78] To the end of the period there possibly remained some free villages in Wessex, but the dependent or manorial type was never growing less in numbers and in the long run greatly increased. The available records presuppose a scheme under which agriculture was carried on by dependents. A lord might acquire control of part of the lands of a free village. Even in the time of Edward the Confessor men were seeking lords and, as the phrase ran, "taking their lands with them," [79] but this applies to the former Danelaw more largely than to the south of England. There was more or less servitude from the Anglo-Saxon conquest onward, and certainly some slaves were employed in tilling the lands.[80] But, despite Mr. Seebohm's argument to the contrary, it is well established that the majority of the tillers of the soil were *ceorls* who were legally free.[81] Such was the legal status of the typical dweller in the *tun*, the *tunesman*

[77] IV Athelstan, 5; cf. III Athelstan, 4:1.
[78] Ethelbert, 5, 13.
[79] Maitland, *Domesday Book and Beyond*, 71-74.
[80] See Seebohm, *Eng. Village Community*, 165-66. Corbett reckons that in 1065 fourteen or fifteen per cent. of the population were *theows* in Mercia, on the Welsh border seventeen per cent., in Cornwall twenty-one, and in the East Anglia only four (*Cambridge Med. Hist.*, III. 401).
[81] Even the lower class of peasants, the geburs, and the cottagers, paid hearthpenny on Holy Thursday, "as every freeman should do" (Ballard, *Domesday Inquest*, 109).

or *villanus,* to the latest days of the Anglo-Saxon rule.[82] There
had all along been a dependent class of peasants,[83] and the rest
drifted toward dependence. This decline was evidently advanced in West Saxon lands by the Danish wars. Ethelred's
laws assume that the ordinary man has a landlord and that
the man without means has a lord.[84] On the eve of the
Norman conquest free villages in England seem to have been
rare outside the Danish regions,[85] where much of the older
independence survived.

In the upper ranks of society there were employed forms of
dependent land tenure which assumed a more strictly feudal
character. At an early time some of the *gesiths* were rewarded
for their service with lands. Royal thegns often owed service
for lands which they held.[86] It was customary for men of
rank to confer land to be held upon certain specified terms.
The Anglo-Saxon called this *laen* or loan land. Some of these
loans were heritable and were held upon quasi-feudal conditions. Prelates sometimes made land-loans for the term of a
life, or even for three lives, to secure the protection of influential persons or the performance of services such as those of
the *trinoda necessitas.*[87] There is no evidence to show how far
down in the social scale the principle of land loans might be
extended.

The dues and services which the poorer English peasants
rendered their lords were often of a character which greatly
restricted their freedom of movement. The ordinary manorial
arrangement was for the lord to exact from the peasants who

[82] Maitland, *Domesday Book and Beyond,* 50-60.

[83] Chadwick (*Studies,* 404) holds that the West Saxon *ceorl* of the
seventh century was as much depressed as at any subsequent period.
But see above, p. 32.

[84] I Ethelred, 3:1; III. 7; VIIa. 5; cf. Vinogradoff, *Growth of the
Manor,* 214-216.

[85] For conditions in the Danelaw, Maitland, *Domesday Book and
Beyond,* 339-340; Stenton, *Documents of Social and Economic History
of Danelaw,* pp. lxi-lxiii; Douglas, *Social Structure of Medieval East
Anglia,* 209-210.

[86] Liebermann, *Gesetze,* I. 456-457.

[87] Maitland, *Domesday Book and Beyond,* 302-310.

held land of him certain dues and also labor upon the demesne
which he retained in his own hands. This plan seems to be as
old as the laws of Ine.[88] The terms upon which the lands were
tilled were customary and became hereditary. The *geburs* or
boors, the lower class of free peasants, about the time of
Canute are recorded in some districts as receiving their equipment and plough oxen from their lord and as laboring for him
in many cases two or three days a week and three days a
week in seed-time and harvest. The cottiers, who held less
land, were also at the lord's call one day a week and three
days in harvest.[89] This evidence comes only from larger estates
and not from those of the ordinary thegns,[90] but men who
were subject to such demands were almost in the position of
the serf, bound to the soil. The laws of Canute, show that the
line between freemen and *theowmen* was not very clear,
and that strong men for legal purposes were treating their men
as free, or as bond,[91] whichever was most advantageous. It is
easy to believe with Maitland [92] that in the eleventh century
large numbers had reached an abject stage of dependence
not far removed from actual serfdom.

The lords holding many villages were the king, the earls,
the great churches and the thegns. For the great numbers the
lay lord was a thegn. The laws of Ethelred so class manorial
lords other than the king.[93] A well-known document gives the
information that a man ranked as a thegn when he had five
hides of land which rendered service to the king and had an
establishment in keeping.[94] The dignity was not necessarily
exclusive, and to it a prosperous *ceorl* might aspire. Economic

[88] Seebohm, *Eng. Village Community*, 143.
[89] *Rectitudines Singularium Personarium*, Liebermann, *Gesetze*, I. 444-
47; Seebohm, *Eng. Village Community*, 129-133. For other evidence,
ibid., 154-55, 162-63.
[90] W. J. Corbett, *Cambridge Med. Hist.*, III. 405.
[91] II Canute 20 :,1.
[92] Maitland, *Domesday Book and Beyond*, 172, 323-332.
[93] VIII Ethelred, 8.
[94] Liebermann, *Gesetze*, I. 457 (cf. 460-61, 8:9); Stubbs, *Charters*,
65. W. H. Stevenson (*Eng. Histor. Rev.*, XII. 489-492) holds that a
thegn as here described was the holder of a manorial house.

status and social position, however, made the thegns the ruling class of the shire. It was assumed that a judge in districts under English law would be of thegnly rank;[95] moreover, the body of the county court was described in the king's writs as the thegns of the shire.

At an early time, so it has been shown above, Anglo-Saxon law seized upon personal lordship as a means of keeping the dependent classes in order. The lord's privileges and duties in this respect have been regarded as springing originally from the principle of his *mundborg* or protection. Thus in King Ine's time a lord was financially responsible if his man committed an offense and was entitled to compensation from him in such cases. One of the laws of this king declares that a noble-man shall have no portion of the fines of his men when he has not previously taken care to restrain them from evil-doing.[96]

Similar ideas and practices run through the Anglo-Saxon law codes to the time of Canute. Public justice and a lord's rights over his dependents were inextricably blended. The law of Ethelred shows the lord as legal protector of his men. He assumed initiative to establish for his man a reputation sufficient to save him from the threefold ordeal; he might even be called upon to clear himself of the accusation that he had advised his delinquent dependent to escape.[97] So largely was the lord responsible for his man that tenth century law forbade the person under accusation to leave his lord for another.[98] The lord's summons was a sufficient excuse for a man who did not appear in the hundred court [99] at the ap-pointed time. Lordship in considerable measure, as shown earlier, superseded kinship as the power to secure justice to offenders. An oft-cited law of Athelstan's reign required that the kindred of lordless men from whom no legal satisfaction

[95] III Edgar, 3 ; II Canute, 15 : 1.
[96] Ine, 50.
[97] Ethelred, 1 : 2, 8.
[98] II Edward, 7 ; II Athelstan, 22 : 2.
[99] I Edgar, 7 : 1.

could be obtained were to settle them in a fixed abode and find them a lord.[100] The scheme was extended by subsequent legislation until a lord was regarded as holding his men in suretyship (*borh*) and was liable for the property stolen by one of them, or else his *wergeld*, if he escaped while under accusation.[101] Upon the old-time corrective power of the lord a state, never too effective in such matters, encouraged the erection of a structure which intervened between it and most men of humble rank.

The position of the thegn as landlord caused the king to look to him to fulfill certain public duties which at an earlier time seem to have pertained to the free *ceorls*. The old-time obligations of the *trinoda necessitas*, which every man owed, had rested upon land. By the time of Canute the man who performed the service due the state from land was recognized as its full legal owner.[102] An eleventh century document described *fyrd* service, fortress work and bridge-repairing as duties which the thegn owed for his land,[103] but made no mention of such obligations when specifying those of the peasants. The king evidently looked to the thegn as the landholder to acquit these obligations. Thus military service was largely associated with thegnage. In the time of Canute it was enacted that if a man through cowardice deserted his lord on a military expedition the latter took back the land he had given him.[104] The rule by which five hides of land sent one man to the king's array [105] explains why the holder of this amount of land ranked as a thegn of Wessex. Here was a state of affairs which on the Continent lay at the very roots of feudalism, although there is every reason to believe that these conditions

[100] II Athelstan, 2. Cf. III Edmund, 7.

[101] Evidence on these points is assembled by Miss Cam, *Francia and England*, 96-98.

[102] II Canute, 79.

[103] Liebermann, *Gesetze*, I. 444; Seebohm, *Eng. Village Community*, 129.

[104] II Canute, 77.

[105] For a summary of the evidence, Cam, *Francia and England*, 145, n. 8.

did not prevail in the Danelaw.[106] Prelates sometimes made
land loans to liegemen for the term of three lives upon condition of the fulfilment of obligations which included military
service. Some grants of this kind made in Edgar's day were
quite clearly still operative in the time of Edward the Confessor, but the services rendered to his lord by the mounted
thegn or *cniht* of the western shires were in many ways different from those of the knight of the continent.[107] Moreover,
the linking of five hides of land with military service in England prior to 1066 was but partial.

Another form of public obligation involved in landlordship
was that of liability for ecclesiastical dues and danegeld. The
penalty for failure to pay church-scot was the severe one of
a twelve-fold payment, altogether too heavy for the ordinary
peasant to meet.[108] In the time of Ethelred it was required
that a lord should render the alms penny if his men would
not.[109] If a Northumbrian villager failed to pay his Peter's
penny, his lord was expected to do so and to take an ox from
him by way of repayment.[110] Maitland has held that payment
of the danegeld by the lord operated similarly to lower the
standing of the tillers of the soil.[111] Men sometimes commended themselves to lords that the latter might acquit such
obligations for them.[112] There is some evidence that the person
who paid the danegeld which was overdue thereby gained
title to the land.[113] The authorities did not, as Maitland believed, ignore the *villani* and look entirely to the landlord
for the danegeld,[114] yet ultimately he must have been respon-

[106] Vinogradoff, *Eng. Society in Eleventh Century*, 28-38.
[107] Maitland, *Domesday Book and Beyond*, 304-313; cf. *Rectitudines
Singularium Personarum*, in Seebohm, *Eng. Village Community*, 129;
Ballard, *Domesday Inquest*, 131.
[108] Maitland, *Domesday Book and Beyond*, 321-322.
[109] VIIa Ethelred, 5. Cf. VII Ethelred, 1:1-3.
[110] Northumberland Priest's Law, 59, Liebermann, *Gesetze*, I. 384.
[111] Maitland, *Domesday Book and Beyond*, 24-25, 54-56.
[112] For acquitting or "defending" the land (*Domesday Book*, I. 32b,
58; Maitland, *Domesday Book and Beyond*, 69, notes, 4, 5).
[113] *Ibid.*, 55-56 and n. 1.
[114] Ballard, *Domesday Inquest*, 134; Ballard, "An Eleventh Century
Inquisition," *Brit. Acad. Records of Social and Economic Hist.*, IV, p. xx.

sible. Moreover, he so stood between them and the state that
large numbers of the peasantry lost direct responsibility for
military service, borough repairs, bridge work, ordinary attendance at the courts of shire and hundred, and the payment
of ecclesiastical dues.

The third great factor in the feudalizing process was the
grant of an immunity by virtue of which the lord came to
supersede certain ordinary powers of the state and in some
cases to establish a jurisdiction over his tenants. The legal
authorization for such unusual powers was the king's charter
or book (boc). This was originally an instrument for dedicat-
ing land to the service of a church. Yet as early as the time
of Offa prominent laymen sometimes obtained land, "by
church right," [115] and these grants continued to be made to
laymen as well as churchmen.

Land held by this privileged tenure was known as bookland. One of its characteristics was that when it was held by
a layman he might dispose of it by will to others than his
kindred.[116] Land held by ordinary tenure, on the other hand,
known as folkland, was regarded as family land, and there
were restraints upon its alienation. It was not the land of the
folk, as once supposed, but rather land held by customary
folkright.[117] Bookland was also distinguished from folkland
by the fact that disputes concerning the latter came regularly
before the shiremote, while bookland belonged especially to
the king's province.[118]

Besides authorizing a special form of land tenure, land-
books also gave to their holders certain exemptions from
secular authority. These were sometimes extensive, although
they did not dispense with the three obligations of the trinoda
necessitas. The Mercian kings of the eighth century made

[115] Maitland, Domesday Book and Beyond, 242-244.
[116] Alfred, 41. According to II Canute, 79, land gained by rendering
military service for it was held as bookland. See Maitland, Domesday
Book and Beyond, 244-247.
[117] Vinogradoff, Eng. Histor. Rev., VIII. 1-17.
[118] II Canute, 13 : 1.

grants of land which almost freed the inhabitants [119] from attendance and payment at the ordinary courts, and seem to have placed immunists in a position to do justice to their men and accept the profits. King Egbert's charters seem to show that the profits of justice were granted to monasteries and churches and also to private persons. Summary powers over the thief taken upon the land were conferred in some grants. All this hints at the exercise of judicial powers by the immunist, but a charter of Edward the Elder in 904 leaves no room for doubt. It confers upon a bishop the right to hold over certain of his men all judgments in secular affairs as the power is exercised in matters pertaining to the king.[120]

Such jurisdictional power was known in the Anglo-Saxon period as *sake* and *soke,* or merely *soke.* The words *sac* and *soc* are used also in the same sense. The documents of the eleventh century show this power in private hands in many places. King Canute conferred upon his wife Emma *sake* and *soke* over eight and a half hundreds [121] and upon the archbishop of Canterbury *sake* and *soke* throughout his lands along with judicial superiority in certain important causes.[122] The laws of this king lay down the principle that to him belong the most important pleas [123] over all men in Wessex unless he grants these away also. He thus gives notice that these may not be assumed by individuals unless they have a specific grant from the king to that effect. The vague wording of old charter forms will no longer be accepted as authority.

It was formerly held that these jurisdictional grants until the time of Edward the Confessor conferred not the power to hold a court but merely the income from justice in certain

---

[119] Maitland, *Domesday Book and Beyond,* 269-277.

[120] Cam, *Francia and England,* 112-116.

[121] H. W. C. Davis, *Eng. Histor. Rev.,* XXIV. 418.

[122] Earle, *Land Charters,* 232.

[123] *Mundbryce, hamsocn, foresteal,, flymena-frymth* and *fyrd-wite* (II Canute, 12).

matters.[124] It is clear that in the Confessor's reign some churches held whole hundreds from some of which the sheriff was entirely excluded, and that numerous lords had powers of justice.[125] The opinion is now held that grants of full jurisdiction are as old as the eighth century. There can be no doubt that certain lords exercised their rights of *sake* and *soke* in courts which they held for their tenants, although such jurisdiction over a few men in a village probably did not involve this.[126] In some cases the lord's men were not called from their own village when they committed crime. In other instances his reeve judged them in petty, though not in the greater cases. To their powers, already great, the landholders upon occasion added that to hold seigniorial courts. They were in a semi-official position,[127] often intervening between their men and the state in judicial as well as in fiscal and military affairs.

There had thus developed in England prior to 1066 institutions and usages which, broadly speaking, were feudal, although many of these existed in Frankish lands prior to what is usually regarded as the feudal age. The old English state has been described as "a society of lords and men." [128] Between the peasants at the bottom of the scale and the king at the top there sometimes intervened two or three lords. Various kinds of service were being purchased by grants of lands. The manorial system, the economic basis of feudalism, was well established in the lands of old Wessex. There was a dependent peasantry, the lower ranks of which were without political importance and sometimes without direct political relations with the state.

The development of the scheme was none the less incomplete. Landlordship was not universal, and there were some

---

[124] Henry Adams, *Essays in A.-S. Law*, 33-54.
[125] Maitland, *Domesday Book and Beyond*, 87-89, 267-269; W. J. Corbett, *Cambridge Med. Hist.*, III. 405-408.
[126] Maitland, *Domesday Book and Beyond*, 96-97, 135.
[127] Cam, *Francia and England*, 116. Cf. I Edgar, 3.
[128] Maitland, *Domesday Book and Beyond*, 170.

free or lordless villages. In the Danelaw small landlords and free proprietors were so intermingled that villages disposed of their own affairs. In East Anglia this was not the exception but the rule.[129] Conditions were not yet stabilized, for at least the better class of freemen might go from one lord to another and sometimes transferred superiority over their lands at the same time. Men did not always hold land of their lords. As Maitland has shown, lordship and landlordship were not yet united.[130] Moreover, men were not necessarily subject to the jurisdiction of their landlord according to true feudal requirements. It was possible, as Domesday Book shows, to hold land of a lord and belong to the *soke* of the hundred or of some other lord.[131]

Of the relations between the better class of men and their lords, which were highly important from the political point of view, information is surprisingly scant. Although military service entered into the arrangement under which some held their lands, this was not so generally true as it became later in the case of the Norman nobility, nor did the Norman military requirements directly succeed the English nor rest upon the same basis. The thegn's correspondence to the knight of the continent was but superficial at best. The arrangement by which five hides of land furnished a fighting man was not essentially feudal and is mentioned only in part of England. Some of the elements which entered into continental feudalism were present, but, taken singly, they were not fully developed; moreover in many instances they were not yet combined. It is hardly possible that, if left to themselves, these Anglo-Saxon usages would have developed into the type of feudalism which existed on the continent.[132]

Upon the political power of the lord Anglo-Saxon monarchy

[129] Stenton, *Documents of Social and Economic History of Danelaw*, introd., pp. lix-lxi; Douglas, *Social Structure of Med. East Anglia*, 217-18.

[130] Pollock and Maitland, *Hist. Eng. Law*, I. 104, 172.

[131] For forms of possible relationship of one man to several lords, cf. Liebermann, *Gesetze*, III. 424 (6).

[132] G. B. Adams, *American Histor. Rev.*, VII. 11-35.

always imposed some effective restraints. He might render payments or perform military service for his dependent, or even exercise jurisdiction over him in a manorial court. The personal, political and military power of the earls was a menace by the time of Edward the Confessor. When King Edward proceeded against the earls of the house of Godwin, he prudently required that their thegns be given into his hand.[133] There was, however, no disintegration of the state, as in the Carolingian kingdom of the ninth and tenth centuries. Neither the towns nor the prelates gained in England the independence sometimes attained on the continent. The strongest bishop or earl was unable to found a government for a state. The principle of the independent power to raise troops was not recognized, despite the strong position of the great landholder in constituting his force for the national service. The right to wage warfare upon one's neighbors or against the king never existed. The king claimed the allegiance of all men regardless of their obligations to lords. The judicial powers of the immunists rested not upon usurpation of the functions of the state, but upon royal grants, however loosely these might be expressed or interpreted. Justice was not feudal, for it was not incident merely to the relation of lord to man. The failure of Anglo-Saxon feudalism to develop on the political side marks the wide gap which separates it from the continental type.

In various directions, none the less, the way was prepared in England for Norman rule. Quasi-feudal conditions were to render easy the introduction of continental feudalism. The *witan* already consisted largely, in theory at least, of the king's dependents who were in his fealty. The army of Wessex, if not feudalized, at any rate was founded upon landholding and constituted in part at the instance of the lord. The thegn who was a vassal of the king and who rendered him service, bore more than a remote likeness to the Norman baron, and the strong earl, in theory the king's dependent, was in some

[133] *A.-S. Chron.*, 1048 (1050).

ways comparable to the Norman count. Most men held land of lords, and some private jurisdiction had long existed. Some Norman methods of government seem to have been employed by King Edward. A few Norman, Fleming, and Lotharingian bishops worked for closer relations with Rome. Even the sheriff, the backbone of local government, the agent of the king, the least feudalized element in the whole system, had his Norman counterpart. The institutional breach of 1066 and the years following was not so great as has sometimes been supposed. Much that was English was preserved. The boldness, the initiative, the confident strength of Norman monarchy in England, as well as the novelty of the machinery and usages employed by it, mark the distinction between the old and the new.

AUTHORITIES

1. THE CHURCH. For the period prior to the year 731 Bede, *Historia Ecclesiastica Gentis Anglorum* is the chief authority. The *Anglo-Saxon Chronicle* gives information especially concerning the bishops of the tenth and eleventh centuries. The legislation affecting ecclesiastical matters is embodied in the various collections of Anglo-Saxon laws, the best of which is F. Liebermann, *Gesetze der Angelsachsen.* The narrative history of the old English church is covered in William Hunt, *The English Church from its Foundation to the Norman Conquest.* Chapter 16 of this work deals in particular with the relations between church and state. The best study of this topic before the Norman Conquest appears in Heinrich Böhmer, *Kirche und Staat in England und in der Normandie im XI und XII Jahrhundert* (1899), chapter 2. Stubbs, *Constitutional History of England,* I, chapter 8, is a brief treatment of the Anglo-Saxon church from the institutional viewpoint. Felix Makower, *The Constitutional History and Constitution of the Church of England* (translation, 1895) in sections 1-5 also deals with the same subject.

2. FEUDAL TENDENCIES. The source materials consist largely of the land charters of the Anglo-Saxon kings, published originally by Kemble in his *Codex Diplomaticus Aevi Saxonici* and issued in a new edition as far as the year 975 by Birch in his *Cartularium Saxonicum.* The laws (see above, p. 45) add some information. Domesday Book throws much light upon landholding and the social system of the days of Edward the Confessor.

The fullest account of Anglo-Saxon feudalism is presented by F. W. Maitland in his *Domesday Book and Beyond* (1897). A useful brief account is given by Miss Helen M. Cam in her *Local Government in Francia and England* (1912). A succinct and scholarly treatment also appears in sec. 2 of Julius Hatschek, *Englische Verfassungsgeschichte* (1913). George B. Adams in the *American Historical Review*, VII. 11-35, shows basic differences between Anglo-Saxon and continental feudalism. J. H. Round in *English Historical Review*, XII. 492-494, shows differences in the two military systems. Frederic Seebohm, *The English Village Community* (1896, 4th ed.), is still useful for its presentation and analysis of materials illustrating the obligations and position of the Anglo-Saxon peasants. His main thesis, that the Anglo-Saxon agrarian scheme was originally operated by serfs, but that the drift was toward freedom, has been refuted by Maitland and by Sir Paul Vinogradoff, *The Growth of the Manor* (1905). Vinogradoff in an article in the *English Historical Review* (VIII. 1-17) overturned the older conception of folkland and gave to it the accepted definition. In his *English Society in the Eleventh Century* (1908) he introduces much material which explains social and political conditions on the eve of the Norman Conquest. The older idea of private jurisdiction in the Anglo-Saxon period is presented by Henry Adams in his treatise on Anglo-Saxon Land Law in *Essays in Anglo-Saxon Law* (1876).

It is highly instructive to compare feudal developments in England prior to 1066 with those in France. The latter may be traced out in some detail in Jacques Flach, *Les Origines de l'Ancienne France*, vols. I., II. (1886, 1893). There is an excellent brief account of the origins of the feudal regime on the continent in Lavisse, *Histoire de France*, II. (1903), pp. 414-439.

PART III

NORMAN MONARCHY AND INSTITU-
TIONAL INNOVATION, 1066–1154

CHAPTER VII

NORMAN INSTITUTIONS AND THE INTRODUCTION OF CONTINENTAL FEUDALISM IN ENGLAND

The defeat and death of King Harold in the battle of Hastings, October 1066, was followed at the succeeding Christmas by the coronation of William of Normandy as king of England. The duchy of Normandy, according to tradition, dates from 911 when the Frankish king, to check the inroads of the vikings, received the homage of their leader Rollo. The duchy, which then included only the region of the lower Seine, within some twenty years approximated its later extent. For a long time bands from the Scandinavian north continued to establish themselves in the country, but in the course of a century the colonists adopted the speech, the customs, and the legal ideas of their Frankish neighbors. Christianity was formally accepted by Rollo the year after his investiture. The viking leaders at first regarded themselves as the equals of the duke, but through the influence of the feudalized society about them their successors became his feudatories and rendered him military service, no longer fighting on foot, but on horseback as knights renowned for their skill.

The fourth duke, Richard II (996-1026), furthered a reform of the monasteries along the well-known lines proposed at Cluny. His son, Robert I (1027-1035), also encouraged a movement among the Norman baronage to found new monasteries. In his time bands of Normans acting independently established the beginnings of a state in southern Italy. Duke Robert died while on a pilgrimage to Jerusalem, leaving the duchy to his illegitimate son William, then a child about eight years of age.

Duke William (1035-1087) with the aid of the king of France in 1047 defeated a league of barons formed in the interest of a rival prince, destroyed the unlicensed castles built during his minority, and henceforth appears as a powerful figure. He waged war against the count of Anjou, who had acquired Maine, and in 1064 established his overlordship over this county. He asserted his suzerainty over Brittany. He visited England in 1051 and claimed to have been named by his kinsman Edward the Confessor as his successor. Out of this claim came his invasion of England, his defeat of King Harold and his assumption of the kingship.

William had merely begun the conquest of the land in 1066. A series of rebellions in the southwest, the west, the north, and finally in the east, delayed the complete subjugation of England for almost five years. In 1069 the situation was complicated by the fact that the king of Denmark sent forces to Yorkshire to assert his claims. The revolt was punished by the king's thoroughly laying waste the region from York to Durham. He soon placed his Norman followers in possession of English lands upon feudal terms. Henceforth Normans and not English were the rebels against the king's authority. A revolt in 1075 was headed by Roger earl of Hereford and Ralph earl of Norfolk, who were soon defeated and dispossessed of their estates. In England as in Normandy William proved a strong ruler, maintaining order and rigorously putting down opposition. Normans were placed in office both in church and in state. A considerable measure of ecclesiastical reform was introduced. The English were largely dispossessed of their lands, but the principal grievances against King William's administration were his heavy financial exactions and the severity of the forest laws he introduced.

At the death of William the Conqueror in 1087 England and Normandy were separated, the latter going to his eldest son, Duke Robert, the former to his second son, William II (1087-1100), known as Rufus. The reign of William Rufus began with a revolt of the Norman baronage of England in 1088 in the interest of his brother Robert. This the king put down as he did also a subsequent uprising in 1095 under the leadership of Robert Mowbray, earl of Northumberland. In 1091 William compelled his brother, Duke Robert, to make over the control of much of Normandy. Five years later Robert mortgaged to William the whole duchy to gain funds needed to take part in the first crusade. In 1092 William overran the districts of Cumberland and Westmorland, heretofore a part of the Scottish kingdom. He aided the Norman barons against the Welsh, but was unsuccessful in North Wales, which he invaded in 1094. In South Wales the power of the barons was established as far as Pembroke. In 1098 the king began a war on the continent to conquer Maine. The rule of Rufus was not so just as that of his father. He was irreligious and venal. The exactions for his wars were heavy, and he placed novel impositions upon the church. His unscrupulous minister, Ranulf, known as Flambard, is famous for his management of these matters. The appointment of bishops and abbots to churches was postponed that the crown might appropriate their income during vacancies. The exactions of the king, along with his desire to control ecclesiastical policy, in 1097 virtually forced Anselm, the archbishop of Canterbury, to leave England.

Henry I (1100-1135), the youngest son of the Conqueror, upon the sudden death of Rufus seized the royal treasure at Winchester and three days later was crowned king at London. He at once issued a charter promising freedom from the exactions which Rufus had imposed upon the church and from the abuses of royal feudal rights which had characterized his rule. There was included also promise of a firm peace, of the observance of the laws of Edward the Confessor, and of various other popular concessions. The document, which was not observed in all respects, was designed to gain for the new king support against the opposition of his brother Robert. Moreover, Henry increased his popularity by his marriage with Matilda, a daughter of the king of Scotland, who was a descendant of King Alfred and thus popular with the English. In 1101 Robert returned, and a part of the feudal nobility in England rebelled in his interest. The king's differences with his brother were settled for the time by negotiation, and the rebels were suppressed and dispossessed of their estates. To mend relations with the church the king recalled Anselm, but they soon disagreed over the question of the lay investiture of prelates and the archbishop again went abroad. A settlement of the investiture question, hastened by the imminence of a struggle between Henry and Robert, was agreed upon in 1106 and officially proclaimed the next year. The crisis of the reign passed when at Tinchebrai in Normandy in 1106, Robert was defeated, to remain a prisoner until his death.

Normandy was now conquered and the king of England was again its duke. Henceforth Henry's rule in England was peaceful, although in 1116 his position on the continent involved him in a war with the king of France and the allies of the latter. To these in 1118 were joined various Norman barons who revolted to set aside the king of England in favor of Robert's son. Henry gained the victory, but had to suppress a second revolt in Normandy in 1123 and 1124. A final struggle with the French began in 1128, but after a brief period also ended fortunately for Henry. One of the greatest achievements of his successful rule was in the constitutional field. In England as well as in Normandy the reign was marked by notable advance in administration and improvement in its central organs.

Stephen of Blois (1135-1154), Henry's nephew, seized the throne in defiance of the claims of Matilda, daughter of the late king, who had been acknowledged by the barons as his successor and who was the wife of Geoffrey, count of Anjou. Stephen proved to be a weak ruler. He made concessions to the church to gain its support. In 1138 some of the barons in Normandy denounced him as a usurper and influenced others in England. The king of Scotland, the uncle of Matilda, seized the opportunity to invade Northumberland but was defeated in 1138 in the Battle of the Standard. In 1139 Stephen aroused the opposition of the prelates by arresting Roger, bishop of Salisbury, and his nephew, the bishop of Lincoln. The same year Matilda came to England, and a long period of conflict began. The reign became one of baronial license and anarchy. The barons changed from side to side to gain advantage, they built castles, some of them treated the people barbarously, and at times they laid waste much of the land. Matilda was proclaimed queen in 1141, but gave up the struggle and retired from England in 1148. Her son, Henry of Anjou, returned in 1153 to renew the contest. In the spring of 1154 it was agreed by the treaty of Wallingford that Stephen's mercenaries should be disbanded, and that administration reforms should be effected. Henry was also recognized as heir to the throne, to which he succeeded on Stephen's death six months later.

Norman institutional development in 1066 was in many ways of the same type as that of the Anglo-Saxons. An important point of difference was the influence in Normandy of Frankish usage which had incorporated some practices and legal conceptions of the Roman period. In many cases there were only minor differences between Norman and English machinery of government, and little conscious change was necessary. Institutional amalgamation came as a matter of course. The institutions of Normandy, so far as they may be traced, were on the whole less highly developed than those of England, but Norman legal ideas were more definite and central administration stronger. Those differences which were destined to have the greatest influence in English constitutional history may be included under two heads, namely the strong power of the Norman duke and the existence of an organized feudalism, which he not only kept in check on its political side but which he was able to turn to good account in administration.

Concerning the duke's household organization or *curia* little is known. Haskins in his notable work [1] shows that it was similar to that which appeared at the court of the French kings prior to 1060. The chief officials at the court of Duke William were the seneschal and the chamberlain. The butler was prominent as was also the constable, the marshal barely being mentioned in the duke's documents. It is safe to assume that the secretarial work was done by the clerks of the duke's chapel. There is little indication at this time of the existence of a chancellor or a seal, but both are mentioned earlier.[2] The treasury was known as the *camera*, and its head, as in England, was the chamberlain.

The greater *curia* or assembly of the duchy was attended by bishops, by counts and other men of high rank, by the household officers and by some others. This was a body of the great men, and they were the duke's vassals.[3] It was customary for the duke to hold an assembly at Easter and possibly at other seasons. Those in attendance attested the issue of the duke's charters, but it is not clear that they were asked to give their consent. The duke called upon them to give him counsel in various matters. They exercised a jurisdiction in civil matters affecting ecclesiastical and baronial affairs, also serving as a court to try barons for high crimes.

[1] *Norman Institutions*, chap. 1. The writer here follows closely this authority.
[2] *Ibid.*, 52-53; Tout, *Chapters in Administrative History*, 125-216.
[3] Pollock and Maitland, *Hist. English Law* (1899), I. 73.

The oath, the ordeal and the wager of battle were all employed and probably the sworn inquest as well.

The local government of the duchy, likely to be the weak point in a feudal state, was distinguished by the existence of an important administrative district known as the *vicomté*, or viscounty, which was public rather than feudal or domanial in character, although it was not so ancient nor so well established in tradition as was the English shire. The head of this territorial division, the *vicomte*, in various ways resembled the sheriff, but no superior, such as the English earl, intervened between him and the head of the state. The office in some instances had become hereditary, yet the duke's control in such cases was not relaxed. Unlike the English sheriff, the *vicomte* sometimes appears as a member of the great *curia* of the duchy. Like the sheriff he administered local justice, preserved order and collected for his district the revenues which pertained to the central government. Like the sheriff also he performed military duties as leader of the duke's forces. Moreover he served as guardian of the ducal castles.

The administrative control of the Norman ruler was in some ways more direct and his government more effective than that of his Anglo-Saxon contemporary. Usage both prior and subsequent to the Conquest shows him doing justice in person with the aid of certain of his attendants. Apparently even before 1066 he sent some of these to adjudicate causes in local courts.[4] His fiscal system had the advantage of no general tax like danegeld, but was unusually well developed for those days. It has often been pointed out that he had an income in ready money, from which he might make grants or allowances, at a time when the Capetian rulers made grants only in kind. The sources of his income seem to have been numerous. Among them were mills, salt-pans, fishing-rights, also wreckage, treasure-trove and the profits of the coinage. Prominent also were the income from justice and the feudal

[4] Adams, *Council and Courts*, 70-73, 92-94.

dues. The *vicomte* rendered a definite farm for the ordinary
revenues of his district. For other revenues separate accounting was made as in England.

Before 1066 there may be traced in Normandy some of the
characteristic features of French feudalism. The obligations
of homage, the ceremony by which a man became the vassal
of a lord, and of fealty, by which the man took oath to be
faithful to his lord, were well understood.[5] It is not clear that
all land was regarded as held directly or ultimately of the
duke, but vassalage and dependent land tenure abounded.
So far was it customary for the lords to confer lands upon
their men, that more than two decades before 1066 it was
necessary for a church council to prohibit bishops from granting estates of the church as benefices to laymen. Instances in
which a lord granted to his man a portion of the lands he
held of an overlord are known to have occurred well before
1066, and in some cases more than one lord stood between
the holder in possession and the ultimate holder. The Norman
counts, the greatest feudatories of the duke, in the early
eleventh century were only five or six in number and represented collateral lines of the ducal family. They seem usually
to have administered their own territories without much intervention from the ducal *vicomte*.[6]

Certain financial claims of the duke upon his vassals, known
as the feudal incidents, were recognized, notably in the feudal
relief, a payment made by the heir of a vassal to gain possession of the lands of his deceased relative. The payment to a
lord for his consent to the marriage of the heiress of his
vassal was another of the incidents in Normandy.[7] The duke
already made demand upon his vassal for special financial
aid in certain contingencies, although these aids differed
somewhat from the three so well known at a later day, namely
the aid required to pay the lord's ransom when he was taken

[5] Orderic Vital, ed. le Prevost, II. 294.
[6] Corbett, *Cambridge Med. Hist.*, V. 485-486.
[7] Baldwin, *Scutage and Knight Service*, p. ix.

captive, and those taken respectively when the lord's eldest son was knighted and when his daughter was married.[8]

The barons, that is to say the men or vassals, of the duke held their lands by military service, which was also due from the bishops and the heads of the older abbeys. To support this service, in some cases holdings or parcels of land, known as knights' fees, had been set aside. Fiefs rendering to the lord the service of groups of ten, or probably five, knights,[9] seem to have been usual, the lord in turn providing the duke with a part of these for his needs and a lesser proportion to acquit the military obligation which the latter owed his feudal superior, the French king. The period for which this military service was due each year at the vassal's cost was forty days. The duke also had the right to call out the general levy in case of invasion.

It is clear that the duke of Normandy found feudalism useful both in its fiscal and its military aspects. Moreover, he was able to maintain restraints upon the power of his barons. He retained control of the coinage. Castles might be built only with his permission, and they had to be turned over to him upon demand. Norman nobles showed turbulent traits, and the right to carry on private war existed, but it was held within limits. The ducal supremacy was also maintained in matters of justice. In Normandy barons as such possessed a jurisdiction which was feudal in character, but powers of justice in the more important pleas might rest in baronial hands only by virtue of the duke's grant. Certain offenses, such as assault in the duke's court or his host, crimes against pilgrims and those against the coinage were reserved exclusively to his jurisdiction. Offenses involving the penalty of death or mutilation and matters involving trial by duel per-

[8] In one instance a lord had an aid from his vassal to ransom himself from captivity, or to redeem his land forfeited by the duke or the abbot from whom he held it, or to ransom his son if captured in the service of the duke or abbot (Haskins, *Norman Institutions*, 22).

[9] Round, *Feudal England*, 259-60; Haskins, *Norman Institutions*, 17-21.

tained to the ducal jurisdiction, but were sometimes granted
to vassals.[10] From the duke's grants of jurisdictional powers
it is possible to learn how much he had to give.

The political genius of the Norman dukes, particularly of
the conqueror of England, is strikingly revealed in the fact
that although in their state feudalism was well developed,
probably more so than in any other European state of the
time, yet ducal power was strong and ducal administration
effective. The barons were not permitted to destroy public
order nor to wrest from the head of the state his powers of
justice nor the sources of his income. Over the Norman church
the duke also exercised control wherever his own rights and
authority were involved, not only appointing bishops and
abbots but even interfering with the action of church councils. The substitution of so masterful a regime for the weak
rule which had characterized the reign of the Confessor,
meant the regeneration of English monarchy and laid the
basis for constitutional progress.

Before examining the strong monarchy founded in England
by the Conqueror, it will be well to notice the other fundamental change which came with his rule, namely the introduction of Norman feudalism. Round[11] long ago destroyed
Freeman's contention that this was brought about not in the
reign of William I but in that of his successor, William
Rufus. Feudal usages which are known to have existed in
Normandy were introduced among King William's Norman
followers within a short period after the battle of Hastings.
It is admitted that these represented in many ways an early
type of feudalism in a formative stage.[12] Its establishment
in England was one thing, the working out of its details and
its legal theory quite another. The feudal world lived by usage.
The time of testing and of fixing precedents probably came
not so much in the Conqueror's day as in that of his suc-

---

[10] Haskins, *Norman Instns.*, 28-30.
[11] Round, *Feudal England*, 225-314.
[12] G. B. Adams, *Origin English Constn.*, **32.**

cessors, within about a generation after 1066. The rights which the lord believed to be involved in the homage and fealty of the vassal were most likely to find concrete assertion when the heir of the latter succeeded to the fief. Only after the lapse of time were King William's Norman followers and their sons to know their exact status as feudatories in England.

The Conqueror acted according to the feudal custom of Normandy with which he was familiar. One immediate motive in introducing this in England was obviously military. The maintenance of the king's rule in his new realm depended upon his ability to suppress the various rebellions of the English. Within a brief period the warriors who had followed him to England desired to return to their homes across the Channel.[13] The basic principle of feudalism was that of an exchange, the granting of land in return for service. The men who had won the victory at Hastings expected to be rewarded with lands, and King William naturally provided himself with the requisite military forces by a process of enfeoffment. The lands at his disposal were abundant. There is mention of a time in 1067 when the English redeemed their lands,[14] but this can refer only to an exceptional class of cases, for Domesday Book shows few English thegns still in possession. The issue of the battle with King Harold and the subsequent coronation of William placed at his disposal the whole of the royal demesne. The estates of the English nobility who had fought against him, many of whom had fallen in Harold's last fight, he claimed as a matter of course, apparently without formal judgment.[15] The uprisings which followed led to new confiscations. The Anglo-Saxon Chronicle under the year 1067 tells that the Conqueror gave away every man's lands.

[13] Orderic Vital, II. 167, 186. Not all were Normans. There were Bretons, Poitevins, and Burgundians (*ibid.*, II. 125).

[14] *A.-S. Chron.*, 1066; Maitland, *Domesday Book and Beyond*, 60, and note 4.

[15] *Gesta Abbatum Mon. S. Albani*, I. 48. But cf. Bigelow, *Placita*, 1-2. There is a tradition of a formal inquest to determine who the English rebels were (*Dialogus de Scaccario*, Oxford ed., 100).

The service of a specified number of knights from the estates granted to his greater vassals or barons was probably required from the beginning. Later evidence shows that in this reign the barons set aside knights' fees in Norman fashion.[16] What happened on the lands of the church is fairly clear. Upon bishops and abbots in England the king also imposed military service. The abbot of Ely, whose loyalty had not been above suspicion, was required by William to provide for the needs of forty knights.[17] The unfriendly abbot of St. Albans had to set aside some of the lands of his church to provide knight service.[18] The chronicler of Abingdon Abbey tells that William required this church to furnish knights, and represents them as holding lands which had been in possession of thegns who fell at Hastings.[19] William thus compelled the prelates to receive military tenants. A document which has lately come to light shows an abbot granting a fief to a baron who was to provide several fully equipped knights for service within the realm at the summons either of the abbot or the king.[20] A later chronicler tells that the king in 1070 imposed upon the great churches a definite allotment of military service, and the statement has been accepted by good authority.[21] Just prior to Pentecost 1072, William is known to have called out the new feudal array. The writ which he issued to the abbot of Evesham on this occasion bade the latter bring up the five knights he owed for his abbey, and also notify those under his jurisdiction to bring the knights whose service they owed. There is some evidence that a similar summons was issued to bishops and to other abbots.[22] A century and a half later the tenant-in-

---

[16] Round, *Feudal England*, 157, 295-296; Vinogradoff, *English Society in Eleventh Century*, 41 and n., 1. Cf. Round, *Archaeological Journal*, LIX. 150-155.

[17] *Liber Eliensis*, 275; Round, *Feudal England*, 300.

[18] *Gesta Abbatum Mon. S. Albani*, I. 50.

[19] *Chron. Monast. Abingdon*, II. 3-6.

[20] *English Historical Review*, XLII. 246-247.

[21] Matthew Paris, *Hist. Anglorum*, I. 13; Round, *Feudal England*, 298.

[22] *Ibid.*, 301; Davis, *Regesta*, no. 63; Adams, *Council and Courts*, 36; cf. *Liber Eliensis*, 224.

chief was still responsible to the king for the total number of knights due from his barony, whether he provided them directly or derived them from under-tenants. The service of his barons supplied the king's array.

The specific allotment of knight service made by the Conqueror to his various tenants-in-chief, including bishops and abbots as well as lay barons, seems to have remained unchanged after his time. Those who held lands directly of the king provided him with a force of five or six thousand knights[23] whom he might assemble at their expense for a definite term of service each year, probably forty days as in Normandy. Exact quotas of knights required from English baronies are ascertainable first in 1166, just a century after the Conquest. It is clear, however, that the amount of service due had become traditional by the time of Henry I, and this was the case in Normandy still earlier.[24] The record of 1166 shows, for instance, that the two archbishops, the bishops of that day and twenty-four abbots owed military service.[25] The obligation did not rest upon the other abbots, nor did it rest upon them at a later time.[26] There is every reason to believe that this basis of military service was that established by the Conqueror. The number of knights required had to fit into the scheme of organization by fives or tens which prevailed in the Norman army. Under the plan recorded in 1166 the number due from a barony or one of the greater churches was practically always five or a multiple of five. In numerous instances it ran as high as forty or sixty.[27] Earl Robert of Gloucester, the son of Henry I, owed the service of a hundred knights, but he had acquired several baronies. Most of the barons acquitted themselves by providing from ten to twenty-five knights. The figure had been arbitrarily fixed, for it did not depend very definitely upon the amount

---

[23] Round, *Feudal England*, 289-292; Mitchell, *Studies in Taxation*, 4.
[24] Round, *Feudal England*, 257-262; cf. 296-297.
[25] *Ibid.*, 249-251.
[26] H. M. Chew, *Eng. Histor. Rev.*, XLI. 163-164.
[27] Round, *Feudal England*, 253-256.

of lands held. This fact also seems to reveal the work of William the Conqueror.

A man might provide for the service he owed in one of two ways. He might quarter knights upon his demesne, the land he retained after making grants to his vassals, thus making them a charge upon it; or he might designate specific lands to support them and grant these upon feudal terms as knights' fees.[28] Furthermore, tenants-in-chief arranged with their barons for quotas of knights in return for lands. Knights' fees were being established in the Conqueror's time, both upon lay baronies and upon the lands of bishoprics and abbeys. Lanfranc, the archbishop of Canterbury, in 1072 established a considerable number. There is a well-known list, dating from about 1125, of the knights who had been enfeoffed on the lands of Peterborough Abbey.[29] The process of creating such fees continued long after the death of Henry I.[30] A knight's fee did not consist of a definite amount of land, but it was apparently supposed to yield an income of twenty pounds a year.[31]

Little is known concerning the process by which the Norman barons came into possession of the lands of the English. Domesday Book shows that the estate of a given thegn was usually conferred in its entirety upon a Norman. The baronies of the southern and midland regions might be largely reckoned in terms of vills or *tuns*, but many English lords had held parts of *tuns*, and these holdings also passed to their Norman successors. The more important vassals of the Conqueror received fiefs consisting of large numbers of villages, and usually including the lands of several Anglo-Saxon thegns. The exact form in which King William granted these lands is not known, but Domesday Book alludes to the issue of writs and the

[28] Round, *Feudal England*, 237.
[29] Davis, *Regesta*, no. 264; cf. *Domesday Book*, I. 4-5; *Chronicon Petroburgense*, Camden Soc. ed. T. Stapleton, 168 ff.
[30] Round, *Feudal England*, 237-242.
[31] Pollock and Maitland, *Hist. English Law*, I. 256-57; Round, *Feudal England*, 293-295; Vinogradoff, *Eng. Society in Eleventh Century*, 43-48.

sending of royal messengers to order sheriffs to place a lord in possession of lands and men. The writs might be proclaimed and formal delivery made in the county or the hundred court. In the absence of such public delivery the Domesday jurors were often unable to testify that the transfer had been made.[32] There is no hint of an attempt to enumerate the obligations assumed by the crown tenants other than those of a military nature. In all probability the usage prevalent in Normandy was taken for granted, and details were settled only with the lapse of time. Feudal practice was inclined to assume existing usage and to avoid needless discussion of detail.

The England of Domesday Book, twenty years after the Normans invaded the land, was a feudal England. The Domesday inquest shows that the king reserved to himself demesne lands in each county and remained the largest landholder. It was assumed, however, that he had conferred all other lands in the county [33] upon a certain number of barons and churches. The tenants-in-chief in turn gave lands to their barons, who often rendered military service to the immediate overlord. A Norman chronicler, writing in the time of Henry I, calls the barons who received fiefs from William I in England and Normandy the men, that is to say the vassals, of that king.[34] The marks of a feudal scheme are clear enough. The king was the ultimate landowner. Great lords who wished to give lands to the church had to have the king's consent, for full ownership was not theirs. What had taken place may be seen in the cases of the bishops and abbots. Their lands had not been confiscated, yet these were held, inferentially at least, from the king, and they provided him military service like lay fiefs. The newly elected bishop or abbot was placed in possession of his lands only after he had done homage to

[32] *Domesday Book*, I. 59, 60b, 62; II. 377; IV. 163, f. 175b; *Victoria County Hist.*, Suffolk, I. 379-380.

[33] *Hoc tripliciter; scilicet tempore Regis Aedwardi, et quando Rex Willelmus dedit; et quomodo sit modo: Domesday*, IV. 496-497; Stubbs, *Charters*, 86. Domesday arranges the lands under the names of tenants-in-chief.

[34] Orderic Vital, ed. le Prevost, III. 316.

the king and had received investiture [35] from him. The usages
of homage and fealty, by which a man became the vassal of
the king or some other lord [36] and swore loyalty to him, were
prevalent. To do homage to a lord and receive land from him
seems to have been the rule. In theory every man, except the
king, who held land held it of a lord. Allodial tenants are
mentioned, but these also had lords.[37]

All of this embodies ideas and customs that are unmistakably feudal. The existence of knight service, however, has
been correctly regarded as the one great technical proof of
the introduction of feudalism in England. This implies the
holding of land by military service and also homage and
vassalage to a lord; it exemplifies the render of feudal service
to this lord; moreover, it involves the typical feudal obligations which are represented by the feudal aids and incidents.

The feudal incidents are best known through their abuse
by William Rufus, but they existed in England, as in Normandy, before his reign. The right of the lord to bestow in
marriage the heiress of his vassal together with her lands, is
mentioned in Domesday Book.[38] In this is involved the lord's
power to exact a fine if she did not accept the husband of his
choice. The relief or payment made by the heir to be allowed
possession of his father's fief also appears. It is true that the
Anglo-Saxon *heriot* and various other payments not strictly
feudal in nature [39] were called reliefs by Norman writers.
According to Domesday Book the thegn who in northern shires
had more than six manors paid eight pounds directly to the
king and he who had six or less paid three marks to the
sheriff.[40] This seems still to be a *heriot*, but it certainly is

[35] Below, p. 250. For these usages see Luchaire, *Manuel*, 184-186, 273,
509-510; Seignobos, *Feudal Regime*, trans. Dow, 41-42.
[36] See Orderic Vital., ed. le Prevost, II. 294. In *Eng. Histor. Rev.*,
XLII. 247, a knight becomes a homo *feodalis* of an abbot with hands
joined. Cf. Malmesbury, *Gesta Regum*, II. 495; Round, *Calendar*, p. 530.
[37] Maitland, *Domesday Book and Beyond*, 151-154.
[38] Vinogradoff, *Eng. Society in Eleventh Century*, 244.
[39] *Leis Willelme*, 20-20:4. So also the reliefs of the allodiaries of
Kent, the burghers, and others (*Domesday Book*, I. 1, 269b, 280b, 298b).
[40] *Domesday Book*, I. 280b, 298b.

not far removed from a feudal relief. That the latter existed there can be no doubt, for William Rufus made it excessively heavy.[41] Henry I, when he professed to remedy this abuse in his coronation charter, laid down no rule except that the relief was to be just and lawful. A century later the amount of the relief paid to the king by a baron's heir for possession of his father's estates was still a matter of specific agreement.[42] William Rufus even demanded reliefs from the tenants of the bishopric of Worcester [43] when in 1095 he assumed its custody during a vacancy. The policy of exacting high reliefs from barons and of extending feudal claims to church lands is apparently responsible for the statement in the Anglo-Saxon Chronicle that this king wished to make himself the heir of every man, both clerk and lay.

Rufus stands accused not only of having abused his feudal rights by demanding an excessive payment from the feudal heiress for his consent to her marriage but of having required widows to marry that he might profit in the same way.[44] Henry I promised reforms in these respects, even undertaking to require nothing for the marriage of an heiress, though later he exacted both from heiresses and from widows the usual marriage fine.[45] In Henry's coronation charter is also mentioned another feudal incident which had been a source of oppression, the lord's right to the profits of wardship over a minor heir. Here the king promised that the actual guardian of the land and children of the deceased should be either the wife or some relative.[46]

[41] He exacted three thousand pounds from Robert of Bellême for the earldom of Shrewsbury (Orderic Vital, IV. 32). The king's right to the reliefs of his barons is mentioned in *Leges Henrici*, 10 :1.

[42] Glanville, IX. 4; *Dialogus de Scaccario*, Oxford ed., 155. For instances, *Pipe Roll* of 1130, 54, 55, 78, 87, 132, 158.

[43] Round, *Feudal England*, 309-310; Adams and Stephens, *Select Documents*, no. 5.

[44] Coronation Charter of Henry I, secs. 1, 3.

[45] *Pipe Roll* of 1130, 8, 26, 34, 37, 88, 92, 94; cf. the king's grant of an heiress with her possessions (Round, *Ancient Charters*, no. 6).

[46] This was not Norman usage (Pollock and Maitland, *Hist. Eng. Law*, I. 326). But cf. *Pipe Roll* of 1130, p. 119.

The typical feudal aids for the ransom of the lord, the knighting of his eldest son and the marriage of his eldest daughter, are scarcely mentioned in the Norman period. The Conqueror was not in a position to demand of his barons in England an aid for the knighting of his eldest son,[47] or the marriage of his eldest daughter.[48] Rufus was a king without son or daughter, and no Norman king required a ransom. The aid collected in 1110 for the marriage of King Henry's daughter to the emperor Henry V is the first and only one mentioned prior to 1154.

Existing information is too slight to warrant a conclusion as to how well established such usages were in the time of William the Conqueror. Much of the character of his policy must remain doubtful. The uncertainty of the situation may be attributed to the tyranny of William II, who made exorbitant claims upon tenants-in-chief. It is quite probable that the Conqueror's demands upon his barons were not very systematic and that his successor was able to take advantage of the situation before custom became settled.[49] In any event a definite working policy is traceable only in the third Norman reign. The law of England for crown tenants was probably the severest in Europe. Maitland presents the view that as a system it was worked out in the court of exchequer, in the time of Henry I, by the process of accumulating precedent upon precedent.[50] It still left to the king's determination questions of pressing importance to the tenant-in-chief.

The arrangements made by the king's barons and others with their vassals, although they provided part of the royal army, were largely beyond the range of crown interest. They developed according to the inclination and custom of men acquainted with continental feudalism, but scarcely ever are they mentioned. The general duty of observance of the obli-

[47] His youngest son alone is known to have been knighted when he was king (*A.-S. Chron.*, 1086; Orderic Vital, III. 267).

[48] She was a nun (Stenton, *William the Conqueror*, 180).

[49] Pollock and Maitland, *Hist. Eng. Law*, I. 325-26.

[50] *Ibid.*, I. 95-96.

gations between man and lord is strongly set forth in the time of Henry I.[51] Every man owes faith to his lord of life and limb and earthly honor and must preserve his lord's counsel in all that is honorable and proper, saving the faith due to God and the king. To kill one's lord is the greatest of all crimes. But if the lord takes a man's land from him or deserts him in mortal peril he loses his lordship. The principle that one may not withdraw his legal service from his lord appears in a work which is probably older.[52] The usage which brought the cause of the vassal into the court of his lord for adjudication was recognized.[53] Feudal law in general sanctioned the principle of appeal from lord to overlord in case justice was denied, and here the king sometimes became involved.[54] Outstanding examples of the king's intervention in the relations between his barons and their vassals appear in the Conqueror's exaction from under-vassals of an oath of fealty and in King Henry's charter of 1100, which extends to the rear vassals the benefit of its concessions. According to the charter of Henry I the vassals of the king's barons, like the king's barons themselves, are to pay only a just and lawful relief for their lands. They are also to observe the same regulations as the king regarding the wardships of heirs and the marriages of widows and heiresses. These acts mark an exception to the general policy of the Norman king regarding the lower reaches of feudalism. Feudalism was at its height, and the time for intervention had not yet come.

Anglo-Norman feudalism as it touched the crown differed in several respects from that of the continent. In the first place, the conquest of England followed by wholesale confiscations of lands made it possible to establish a more regular feudal scheme. Nowhere was this scheme more perfect than in England. In the second place, English feudalism, except

---

[51] *Leges Henrici*, 55:3; Pollock and Maitland, Hist. Eng. Law, I. 300.
[52] *Leis Willelme*, 32.
[53] See the writ of Henry I concerning county and hundred courts, sect. 3.
[54] *Pipe Roll* of 1130, p. 143.

during the weak reign of the Conqueror's third successor, Stephen (1135-1154), was never permitted to develop the decentralizing political phases which proved so dangerous in many a continental state. The Conqueror had the advantage of much experience in checking assertions of baronial independence when he assumed the English crown. Moreover, he and his two sons assumed and wielded vigorously the powers of an English king, which even under the weakest ruler had been sufficient to prevent the nobility from usurping the powers of the monarch or his officials. William I in the famous assembly as Salisbury in 1086 exacted an oath of allegiance to the king from the rear vassals,[55] by which they recognized him as liege lord and became bound to follow him against all others. Thus the principle was established in England that the obligation of the feudal vassal to the king was paramount, and he might not, as on the continent, follow his lord against the king.

English monarchy profited, moreover, from another peculiarity of the feudal scheme. The baronies which were established by the Conqueror in most instances did not lie in territorial blocks as was often the case on the continent. The lands of the greater Anglo-Saxon lords were to a large extent scattered, and the allotment to the greater Norman lord of one or more holdings of this kind produced a great barony or honor, as it is often called, which was not compact but formed of detached parts. The important Domesday tenants quite regularly held lands in several counties, and those with estates in five or six were by no means rare. A rather extreme case which appears in Domesday Book is that of Geoffrey de Mandeville, who held one hundred and sixty-six manors in eleven different counties. Such a state of affairs was clearly

[55] A.-S. Chron., 1086: the landowners of account; Henry of Huntingdon, 1086: the homage and fealty of all landholders whosesoever vassals (feudi) they were. The allegiance of all free men to the king (Ten Articles of William I, sec. 2) was different. See Pollock and Maitland, Hist. Eng. Law, I. 299-300. For homage to an abbot saving fealty to the king, Eng. Histor. Rev., XLII, 246, 247; for Norman usage, Valin, le Duc de Normandie, 61-63.

due more to accident than to design, and was furthered by
the piecemeal character of the conquest, but it retarded the
establishment of central baronial courts and the gathering of
baronial armies to operate against the sovereign.

A fourth difference between the situation in England and
that in Normandy is that in the years after 1066 there was
more community of interest between the king and the great
crown tenants. The Conqueror in rewarding those who had
been of greatest service to him was able to determine the personnel of the highest baronage. Upon their loyalty much depended, and William knew his men. His ability to place in
positions of power his friends and comrades in arms gave him
a strong hold upon affairs. It was chiefly when he and his
sons came to deal with the second generation of this new
nobility that there arose those serious differences which attended the operation of the system elsewhere. Because of
revolts of the English between 1066 and 1071 the Normans
could have had little feeling of security. To assure themselves
of their recently acquired wealth and position it was essential
that they stand solidly with the leader to whom they owed
these and who alone was strong enough to maintain himself
against a concerted rising of the subjugated people.

That King William did not fear this structure which he
had erected in England, but rather trusted in it, is evident.
This stands out nowhere clearer than in his willingness to
create some extensive territorial lordships. It is possible that
in Northumbria peculiar territorial arrangements facilitated
the formation of unusually large and compact fiefs.[56] At any
rate, in certain regions, notably on the Welsh and on the
Scottish border, the Conqueror recognized palatine earldoms,
the heads of which had control of justice and administration
much like a true continental *seigneur*. Such seems to have been
the situation in Cornwall [57] for a time under William's half-

[56] Joliffe, *Eng. Histor. Rev.*, XLI. 8-9.

[57] Davis, *Regesta*, p. xxxi. According to Orderic (III. 270) William's
other half-brother, Odo bishop of Bayeux, was palatine earl of Kent.
But there is no direct evidence of this.

brother, Count Robert of Mortain, upon whom the king conferred the greater part of the lands of the county, some seven hundred and fifty manors. Herefordshire was placed under the government of William fitz Osbern, a trusted official at the Norman court, and Shropshire similarly was entrusted to count Roger of Montgomery.[58] In Cheshire, the third county of the western border, another strong man, Hugh of Avranches, was created earl and set to hold back Welsh incursions. Upon earl Hugh was conferred not only the government of the county but practically all of its lands in addition.[59] Robert de Comines failed in an attempt to establish such a regime in Northumbria as did Walcher, bishop of Durham.[60] Robert Mowbray, nephew and heir of Geoffrey, bishop of Coutances, and earl of Northumberland, held great powers and possessions in the north until his rebellion under William Rufus.[61] By this time the palatine lordship of Durham under the bishop, who had his own sheriff, was also in process of formation.[62] In border districts hard to rule the combative feudal lord of the continental type exactly met the needs of the case so long as he was loyal. In the marches of Wales Norman power was established by the same means. It turned out that most of the palatine or semi-palatine lordships were short lived. Herefordshire was forfeited in 1075 because of the rebellion of the second fitz Osbern earl. Robert Mowbray's dominion was in 1095 ended by William Rufus under similar conditions. The feudal rebellion of 1102 enmeshed William, count of Mortain, son of Robert, the Conqueror's brother, and also Robert of Bellême, son of Roger of Montgomery, earl of Shrewsbury, and these great lords thus forfeited their lands and their status in England.

[58] Davis, *England under Normans and Angevins*, 31-32.
[59] *Domesday Survey of Cheshire* (Chetham Soc., ed. James Tait), 26-31.
[60] *A.-S. Chron.*, 1068; Florence of Worcester, anno 1080; Orderic Vital, II. 187. *Dux pariter provinciae et episcopus* (Malmesbury, *Gesta Pont.* 271).
[61] Orderic Vital, II. 223.
[62] Lapsley, *Palatinate of Durham*, 80-81.

To Norman feudalism England long owed most of her land law. The greater part of the lands were undoubtedly held by hereditary tenure as baronies or as knights' fees under the customary feudal conditions. But William the Conqueror and his successors made small grants of lands also to persons who rendered them personal household service. These persons were known as the king's serjeants, and later on they were said to hold not by barony nor by knight service but by serjeanty. Domesday Book shows that already the king's cook, his doorkeeper or his physician had received land in return for his services. By the time of Henry I serjeanties were becoming hereditary. Some of these now involved duties at the exchequer. The highest offices of the king's household, especially those of the chamberlain, the marshal and the constable, likewise became hereditary serjeanties. At a later time men are found holding serjeanties of mesne lords as well as of the king. Some of those existent at the end of the twelfth century represent the riding service which Anglo-Saxon thegns had rendered the king and other lords. Some rendered the most nominal kind of service, but others called for the performance of duties in war time and came to stand on much the same footing as knight's fees.[63]

Churches often held land by a tenure different from that of the ordinary baron which was imposed upon bishops and abbots after the Norman Conquest. When lands were given a church for a spiritual object, such as the repose of one's soul or for the service of saying masses to such an end, the tenure came to be reckoned purely ecclesiastical, and by the latter part of the twelfth century was called frankalmoign. Land thus held was said to be held in free alms.[64]

A more important form of tenure from the viewpoint of our

[63] Pollock and Maitland, *History of English Law*, I. 284-289. Later military usage made two serjeants equivalent to one knight (*ibid.*, 256).
[64] Pollock and Maitland, *Hist. Eng. Law*, I. 240-247; cf. Valin, *Le Duc de Normandie*, 59. The grantor might acquit the church of all service, but this could not affect the service due the overlord (Kimball in *Eng. Histor. Rev.*, XLIII. 341-353).

own day was that by which the small freeman held of his lord. This was the origin of our free and common socage which has become the finest of modern tenures. It seems to represent the tenure of the freemen or socmen of the Danish regions who recognized lords but were proprietors of lands.[65] Their status was perhaps not very different from that of the peasants in general, except that the unfree tenants, who constituted the great number and who came to be known as tenants in villainage, were bound by their services to the soil and in the twelfth century were regarded as holding their land merely at the lord's will. Another form of free tenure, known as tenure by burgage,[66] existed in boroughs, where lords gradually came to acquit their men of ordinary manorial obligations and to require them merely to pay quitrents for the lands they held.

From the standpoint of government feudal arrangements were of vast importance. They provided a professional force of mounted warriors equipped with lances, shields, helmets and coats of mail, which the overlord might call to serve at their own expense for a certain term each year. The feudal tenant, moreover, not only rendered service but also suit to his lord. The latter meant that he was expected to attend his lord's assembly, to give him counsel when called upon to do so, and to sit as a member of his lord's court along with his fellow vassals to render justice. Trial by one's peers was a fundamental principle of feudal justice which afforded the lord a means of trying the cases of his vassals and of fulfilling his obligation to do them justice.

Finally, the feudal aids and incidents increased the power of the lord and brought him an income. This, to be sure, could not be estimated by the year, for it was dependent upon certain contingencies which in the main arose only once in a life-time. The occasion of the knighting of the lord's eldest

[65] Stenton, *Types of Manorial Structure in Northern Danelaw*, 9-10, 13-14; Pollock and Maitland, *Hist. Eng. Law*, I. 291-295.
[66] Hemmeon, *Burgage Tenure*, 158-166; Pollock and Maitland, *Hist. Eng. Law*, I. 295.

son or the marriage of his eldest daughter entitled him to call upon his vassals to render him a feudal aid. For the third aid, that to ransom the lord when captured by his enemy, there was little occasion in Norman England. The feudal incidents also appeared only at long and uncertain intervals. Thus, it was the death of the tenant and the succession of his son which brought the feudal relief to the lord. The succession of an heir who was a minor prolonged the lord's control of his fief and produced the profits of wardship. The marriage of an heiress entitled the lord to the marriage fine unless she accepted the husband he selected for her. The failure of heirs at the death of a tenant enabled the lord to take over the property as an escheat and to grant it to another tenant who might pay a relief and render the necessary service. These profits brought the king a revenue which, when fully developed, was considerable. The system strengthened his political position by giving him control of the estates of heirs, of escheated fiefs and of the marriages of heiresses. It enforced loyalty and the performance of obligations on the part of crown tenants, for the lord might claim the forfeiture of the fief of a disloyal vassal or a vassal who defaulted in his obligations. An experienced ruler like the Conqueror, who knew how to counteract the adverse effects of feudalism, was able to make certain of its features the chief support of the royal power. Such they long remained in England.

The occupation of the English lands by a Norman nobility, moreover, served to keep in subjection the masses of the English people. The Anglo-Saxon lord, so it has been shown in the preceding chapter, was a figure highly important to the public peace. To him the state had long looked to aid in bringing to justice his dependents, and some lords through grants of *sake* and *soke* had gained jurisdictions of their own. The basis of public order afforded by lordship now ceased to be shifting and became fixed upon the soil by hereditary tenure. The feudalism of the continent recognized the right of the lord to do justice to the better tenants who were his vassals, but it also presupposed the right of the lord to exercise jurisdiction, in minor matters at least, over the peasants upon his lands. The Norman lord who succeeded a Saxon with powers of *sake* and *soke* was in a still stronger position and might wield justiciary rights which ordinarily belonged only to the crown and the courts of shire and hundred. The income from jurisdiction, whether in minor or greater causes, represented a mode of exploiting the peasantry. There can be no doubt that the Norman Conquest not only perpetuated the manorial courts already in existence but greatly increased their number. Norman lords of whole villages often maintained courts or hallmoots for their men and, in cases wherein Saxon lords held profits of *sake* and *soke* over men scattered in several places, sometimes held courts also for these.[67] This lessened the importance of the courts of the hundred, in which minor and criminal causes were tried, although usually the manorial court might assume only inferior jurisdiction and not necessarily supersede the more important powers of the hundred. Feudalism reduced the importance of the shire court by assigning to the courts of feudal lords cases between lord and vassal or the vassals of the same lord. But Norman sheriffs were no less intent upon the profits of jurisdiction than were Norman lords, and infringement upon the powers of the public courts was likely to be carefully watched. The continental usage which in some regions made all local justice feudal justice was averted. In Norman England the authority of the public courts was maintained. In but few instances do the records reveal in the hands of lords franchises from which the sheriff was entirely excluded.[68]

The economic subjugation of the English peasantry and their decline in the social and political scale were intensified by the Norman Conquest. Nominally no doubt the tillers of the soil remained upon the lands subject to the same obligations as formerly. Nevertheless the Norman lords who ac-

[67] Cf. *Leges Henrici*, 9:4.
[68] Cf. Vinogradoff, *Eng. Society, Eleventh Century*, 106-107.

quired the soil succeeded to the political control wielded by
the Anglo-Saxon thegns. The dwellers in the villages whose
services were agricultural, were even more sharply distinguished than before from their lords, who were now of another
race and whose services were noble or, as feudal law termed
them, honorable. The Conquest tended to depress the status
of the lower classes. Political policy favored the subjugation
of the English masses. To this influence was added the new
social pressure as well as increased economic subjection. It is
clear that even on royal manors, where the condition of the
peasantry was presumably most favorable, their burdens were
considerably increased by added exactions.[69] The revival of
the danegeld must also have served to reduce their status.
Many who had succeeded in maintaining a position of some
independence despite the trend of the Anglo-Saxon period,
sank to the level of the semi-servile class of the period before
the Conquest.[70] This was true even in the former Danish regions,[71] where the survival of freedom in 1066 was greatest.
Some freemen of the agricultural classes continued as landholders, enough to perpetuate socage tenure to a post-feudal
age, but unless one errs in interpreting Domesday statistics,
they were only about one-seventh of the number of English
peasants. The vast majority were so dependent that twelfth
century law came to regard them as tenants holding at the
will of the lord, with whose tenure the king's courts were
not concerned.

Legal writers of the time of Henry I still preserved the
tradition that the villager (*villanus*) was a freeman,[72] yet
the presence of actual serfs, the burdensome rustic duties including a fixed number of days' work each week, and the
hard discipline maintained by the lord's steward made the

[69] *A.-S. Chron.*, 1087; Round, *Victoria History*, Hampshire, I. 414.

[70] Maitland, *Domesday Book and Beyond*, 60-66; Ballard, *Domesday
Inquest*, 111, 133, 146-154, 264.

[71] See Stenton, *Types of Manorial Structure in Northern Danelaw*,
17-20, 90-91; Douglas, *Social Structure of Medieval East Anglia*, 218-19.

[72] Maitland, *Domesday Book and Beyond*, 43-44.

condition of villainage a very lowly one. In Domesday Book it was noted as a degradation when a freeman became a villain.[73] According to the French Leis Willelme, not later than the time of Henry I and possibly earlier, those who cultivated the soil were not to be harassed except for their legal rent and were not to be ejected from the land so long as they performed their legal service. They were not yet regarded as tenants at will, but naifs or villains had to carry out the form of service of the estate upon which they were born. If they departed, no one was to retain them nor their goods, and they were to be sent back to perform the service which was incumbent upon them.[74] Their general condition was that of the villain who in thirteenth century law was held to be a bondman. The change of attitude may have been due to a change of theories quite as much as a change of conditions.[75] A dangerous analogy might be drawn from the fact that most free peasants rendered the same kind of service as the serfs. Moreover, from the earlier part of the twelfth century the doctrine of the revived Roman law, that every man was either free or slave, must have had its influence. By the thirteenth century the great majority of Englishmen were no longer held at law to be free but unfree. Quite regardless of doctrines, it appears that a great number were actually in serfdom in the time of Henry I.

The situation presents one redeeming feature in that slavery tended to disappear after the Norman Conquest, and those in the lowest form of servitude were merged with the great mass of serfs on the lands of the lords.[76] The villain retained a position in the manorial court which still bore witness to his

[73] Vinogradoff, Eng. Society in Eleventh Century, 453. This seems to mean that he ceased to hold his land merely by paying rents and dues and became a tenant on a lord's demesne who must labor for him a certain number of days each week.

[74] Leis Willelme, 29-30; Maitland, Domesday Book and Beyond, 51; cf. Davis, England under Normans and Angevins, 39.

[75] See Stenton, Documents of Economic History of Danelaw, introd., pp. lxxviii-lxxx.

[76] Ballard, Domesday Inquest, 151-152, 160-161.

former standing as a free judgment-finder.[77] Representatives of his class were still important in matters of police, as petty local officials and even at inquests held by the king's order. English society, however, long ceased to be the great body of freemen who in early Germanic law wielded political control. This until the fifteenth century was exercised by the feudal lord. It was through those who held land by freehold, and especially by feudal, tenure that the spirit of self-rule was to be perpetuated for ages.

AUTHORITIES

The source material bearing upon the introduction and operation of Norman feudalism in England is widely scattered. It includes portions of *Domesday Book,* some of the royal writs and charters, various private documents and passages in the chronicles and in the legal writings of the period. These are described in the notes at the end of the succeeding chapters (chaps. VIII-X).

The standard account of the early Norman constitution is Charles H. Haskins, *Norman Institutions,* chap. I (1918). This is supplemented slightly by Lucien Valin, *Le Duc de Normandie et sa Cour* (1910). There is a summary in Haskins, *The Normans in History,* chap. 3 (1915), and a more extended one in F. M. Powicke, *The Loss of Normandy,* 48-67 (1913). Some material is provided in the account of Normandy by W. J. Corbett in the *Cambridge Medieval History,* V. chap. 15 (1926). Sir F. Pollock and F. W. Maitland, *History of English Law,* I. (1895; 2d ed., 1899) contains a useful chapter on "Norman Law" (chap. 3). The best account of continental feudalism as a system, though not confined to this period, is that by Achille Luchaire in his *Manuel des Institutions Françaises* (1892). Luchaire's *Institutions Monarchiques sous les Premiers Capetiens,* I. 1-53 (1883, 2d ed., 1891), deals with the obligations of the barons to the French King.

The establishment of continental feudalism in England by William the Conqueror was first demonstrated by J. H. Round in his classic essay entitled "The Introduction of Knight Service in England" published in his *Feudal England* (1895). This is an excellent study of feudal military service in the Norman period. The best account of feudal conditions in Norman England is that in the first eight sections of F. W. Maitland, *Domesday Book and Beyond* (1897), but much use-

[77] Maitland, *Domesday Book and Beyond,* 135; Vinogradoff, *Villainage,* 211-213, 297-300, and chap. 5. Cf. Ault, *Private Jurisdiction in England,* 138.

ful material was brought together by Sir Paul Vinogradoff in his *English Society in the Eleventh Century* (1908). A more popular treatment of many of these matters is that by Adolphus Ballard in his *Domesday Inquest* (1906). Special studies on land tenure and the status of the peasantry in the Danish parts of England are F. M. Stenton, *Types of Manorial Structure of the Northern Danelaw* (Oxford Studies in Social and Legal History, vol. II.), and D. C. Douglas, *The Social Structure of Medieval East Anglia* (the same series, vol. IX. 1927). Various phases of feudal law, including the law of the various land tenures, are covered in Pollock and Maitland, *History of English Law*. The chapter on feudalism by Sir Paul Vinogradoff, in the *Cambridge Medieval History,* III. 18, gives helpful background. A useful treatment of feudalism in its relation to government is given by George B. Adams in his *Origin of the English Constitution,* chap. 1 (1912) and in parts of his *Council and Courts in Anglo-Norman England* (1926). Adams was a strong champion of feudal interpretation in constitutional history. A brief summary of many of his views is presented in chapters 1, 3, and 8 of his *History of England, 1066–1216* (1905.)

CHAPTER VIII

LOCAL INSTITUTIONS IN THE NORMAN PERIOD

The Norman Conquest brought some centralization of control over the old English scheme of local government. The earl ceased to be the administrative head of the shire and left the sheriff, who was appointed by the king, with no local superior. The sheriff's control over the hundred, already apparent in the time of Edward the Confessor, was continued after the Conquest.[1] Moreover, the borough, a part of the national scheme of government and never in the position of a free city, was subordinated through its officials to the king.[2] The agencies of local government were subject henceforth to more or less central direction, and might be set doing the king's work when he saw fit. The needs of monarchy preserved the machinery of popular control when that control had all but disappeared. By the early years of the twelfth century, probably in the time of William Rufus, irregular sessions of the hundred and the shire were being held, apparently to further the sheriff's financial plans. Henry I in a noted writ issued a few years after the Battle of Tinchebrai directed the sheriffs that these courts were to be held at the same times and places as in the time of King Edward and not otherwise.[3] The king reserved the right to order the holding of special sessions for his own purposes, and from time to time directed the sheriff to lay various matters before the county court in regular session. Moreover, the king's justice might convene

---

[1] *Domesday Book*, II. 424: a sheriff at the hundred court. He may order a case to be heard there (*Chron. Monast. Abingdon*, II. 117). Cf. note 48.

[2] Ballard, *Domesday Boroughs*, 45-47; Tait, *Eng. Histor. Rev.*, XLII.

[3] Liebermann, *Gesetze*, I. 524; cf. *Leges Henrici*, 7:1.

several shires together [4] and the sheriff likewise several hundreds.[5] There was a correlation between central and local government which was to prove one of the most important features of the English constitution.

Within the manor the lord's reeve maintained order and enforced dues and services, and his steward held a court. It is impossible to form an estimate as to the prevalence of seigniorial courts after the Norman Conquest, but their work was varied, and they must have been very numerous. The lord's court was called a hallmote or *halimote*,[6] a fact which distinguishes it from the assemblies of the shire and the hundred convening in the open air. The jurisdiction which might be privately exercised was of three types,[7] a manorial jurisdiction over the lord's humbler tenants who tilled the soil; a franchisal jurisdiction, a portion of the authority of the public courts; and a purely feudal jurisdiction affecting interests of the lord and his barons or military tenants. In practice separate sessions of the lord's court were not essential to the maintenance of all these respective kinds of justice, and they might be more or less combined at the same session.

Anglo-Saxon lords with courts of their own had some jurisdiction over their agricultural tenants, but in Frankish lands the holding of a court even for free peasants was regarded as incidental to the lordship over a manor. This idea was perpetuated in Norman England. The lord valued the privilege because of the income it brought him, but it aided him in enforcing his claims upon the service and dues of the villagers, and it included minor causes and probably already a police authority to punish them for fighting and other lesser offenses.[8] This petty jurisdiction was by far the commonest form exercised by the lord's court. Even after the peasants

[4] *Liber Eliensis*, 256; *Domesday Book*, II. 238b.
[5] *Leges Henrici Primi*, 7 : 5; Ramsey *Chartulary*, Rolls Ser., I. 148.
[6] *Leges Henrici*, 9 : 4, 20 : 2; Vinogradoff, *Origin of the Manor*, 364-365.
[7] Ault, *Private Jurisdiction in England*, chap. 1.
[8] *Leges Henrici*, 33. Cf. Glanville, I. 2; Ault, *Private Jurisdiction*, 8.

came to be regarded as bondmen, they preserved something of the tradition of a folkmote, enforcing the custom of the manor and giving collective judgment in the old fashion.[9]

The greater lords, as in the Anglo-Saxon period, often possessed rights of franchisal justice. *Sake* and *soke* passed from English to Norman lords, and a writer of the time of Henry I shows that these powers are exercised by lords of importance.[10] An occasional prelate or other lord had gained control of a hundred, and some others had the right to do justice to their own men involving the ordeal by fire or by water.[11] In theory justice in criminal matters and other causes belonging to the public authority could be conferred only by grant of the English king, and Norman law held to the same principle.[12] The Norman king made occasional grants which gave to a lord the control of a hundred,[13] or conferred rights of *sake* and *soke* or released the men of a church from attending the courts of the shire and the hundred.[14] That there was some attempt to usurp public powers of justice is probable, but this was not altogether easy of accomplishment. The Norman sheriff was not disposed to forget the claims of the shire and hundred courts so long as the profits of their jurisdiction formed part of the revenues which he farmed. One of the causes of the rebellion of Earl Roger in 1075 was that sheriffs had tried causes on his lands.[15] The writer of the *Leges Henrici* was careful to specify that the king's jurisdiction in fiscal matters extended even to those who enjoyed powers of *sake* and *soke*.[16]

Feudal or baronial jurisdiction was more novel than the franchisal type and was also quite injurious to the public courts. Its establishment, moreover, required no grant of the

---

[9] See references, p. 154, note 77.
[10] *Leges Henrici*, 20 : 2. In *halimotes* according to *ibid.*, 9 : 4.
[11] *Leges Edwardi Confessoris*, 9-9 : 3.
[12] Above, pp. 134-135.
[13] *Chron. Monast. Abingdon*, II. 164; Davis, *Regesta*, nos. 106, 157.
[14] *Ibid.*, nos. 162, 244; Ramsey *Chart.*, Rolls Ser., I. 249.
[15] Davis, *Regesta*, no. 78.
[16] *Leges Henrici*, 24.

king. It rested upon the principle which required the lord to do justice to his feudal vassals by judgment of their peers, and therefore involved the more well-to-do elements in society. This jurisdiction might be exercised in a central court over vassals on the lord's various manors.[17] According to the *Leges Henrici* every lord had a right to summon his man to justice in his court even from a remote manor of his barony, but, if the lord held different fiefs, his man in one of these was not compelled to go into another to plead his case.[18] Cases involving feudal land tenure and military and other service to one's lord were thus automatically removed from the courts of the shire and the hundred. Henry I recognized the principle that land cases between vassals of the king or of one of the king's barons were to be tried in the court of the lord, but claimed for the county court such cases between vassals of different lords.[19] It is clear that the Norman kings were bent upon using the shire and hundred courts as a counterpoise to seigniorial jurisdiction.

The hundred court apparently suffered through these changes. A passage in the *Leges Henrici* hints that the number of judgment-finders was sometimes inadequate for the rendering of decisions, for it states that in such cases these were to be given by two or more hundreds.[20] Moreover, the assumption was made that qualified judgment-finders were to be landholders and lords,[21] all of which probably meant a diminution of the number who were eligible. The writ of Henry I dealing with local courts directed that all should come as in the time of King Edward,[22] but this also implied supremacy of the landed class.

[17] *Leges Henrici*, 9 : 4, show a distinction between *halimotes* and *curiae dominorum*.

[18] *Leges Henrici*, 55 :1-1b.

[19] Liebermann, *Gesetze*, I. 524 (sect. 3) ; Robertson, *Laws of Kings of England*, 286. According to *Leges Henrici*, 25 : 2, the latter class of cases would have gone to the defendant's court.

[20] *Leges Henrici*, 7 :5.   [21] *Ibid.*, 7 :2-3 ; cf. 29 :1, 1b.

[22] Liebermann, *Gesetze*, I. 524 (sect. 4). If a lord is absent his demesne is to be represented in the hundred by his steward or by the priest, the reeve and four better men of the vill (*Leges Henrici*, 7 :8).

The hundred did not cease to meet after the Norman Conquest. In the time of Henry I monthly sessions were still the rule, and they were still important in enforcing observance of the peace. According to a work written in French which professes to give the usage of the Conqueror, accusations of crime were made here as in the past.[23] When barons had not the power of holding judgment by ordeal, it was assumed to rest in the hundred.[24] In the time of Henry I two out of the twelve sessions each year assumed an unusual character. An especially full attendance was required, and on these occasions the peasants were placed in suretyship groups or tithings for the observance of the peace.[25] This particular activity of the hundred was probably directed by the sheriff, who is found regularly holding these special sessions some fifty years later.[26] That their business had not regularly fallen to the seigniorial courts is seen in the fact that the abbot of St. Edmunds obtained from Henry I a special charter specifying that his men were not to leave the lands of his own franchise to be placed in the tithings.[27]

Criminal justice and suretyship against crime did not comprise all the business of the hundred. There were men of humble rank whose civil causes came up here; and there were matters which had to come into the hundred court before they could be taken to any higher court.[28] Moreover, the fine when danegeld was not paid was imposed here.[29] That the hundred had not lost its importance in administration is also indicated by the fact that it appears as the unit of danegeld assessment, and Domesday documents show its reeves collecting danegeld.[30] Furthermore, the hundred reeve collected the king's *ferm* of the hundred, as the agent of the sheriff.[31]

[23] *Leis Willelme*, 51, 52; cf. 42 :1; so also *Leges Henrici*, 59, 6.
[24] *Leges Edwardi Confessoris*, 9 :3.   [25] *Leges Henrici*, 7 :4.
[26] Morris, *Frankpledge System*, 113-115.
[27] *English Historical Review*, XXIV. 427.
[28] Below, p. 171; also *Leis Willelme*, 42 : 1, 43.
[29] Round, *Domesday Studies* (ed. Dove), I. 117; *Feudal England*, 103.
[30] Round, *Feudal England*, 103. Round, in *Domesday Studies*, I. 117.
[31] *Victoria County History*, I, 389-390. So above, p. 64.

The third of the lesser units of local government, the borough, assumed new aspects in the Norman period. The introduction of the castle made the old plan of fortification of very minor importance for purposes of defense. It was apparently the new commercial movement of the time which raised new villages to burghal status.[32] Some of these grew up on the lands of lords other than the king.[33] The *Leges Henrici*, contrary to the provision of Edgar's law, state that borough courts are to meet twice a year.[34] It is obvious, however, that the privileges and organization of some boroughs now fell outside a uniform national scheme. The conditions and terms of the establishment of municipal organization were henceforth to be varied, and there could not be uniformity of type. As towns prospered, the king and other lords in England conceded special privileges in individual cases.

This is well illustrated in some well known instances. The well-known charter granted to London by Henry I, apparently about 1130,[35] well exemplifies the usage. It conferred fiscal autonomy and unique arrangements in government. It allowed the citizens to farm the county of Middlesex for three hundred pounds a year and to appoint their own sheriff and also a justice with the sole right of holding pleas of the crown. The husting or assembly was to sit once a week. Citizens were exempted from the payment of danegeld and murder fines. Moreover, they were not required to plead any case beyond the city walls nor to defend their causes by duel, and no one, even of the king's household, was to be billeted within the walls. In 1130 the burgesses of Lincoln paid two hundred marks of silver and four of gold to hold their city of the

[32] C. Stephenson in *American Histor. Review*, XXXII. 16, 20.

[33] *Ibid.*, 17. For examples, Stubbs, *Constnl. History*, I. 444, 447.

[34] *Leges Henrici*, 7 :4.

[35] The elective sheriff (sec. 1) seems to date from about 1130. The Londoners in 1130 owed one hundred pounds for this privilege. Page (*London*, 203-207) in tracing the succession of the justiciars of the city shows that those before 1130 were not of the burgess type and those at a later date were. See Liebermann, *Gesetze*, I. 524-26; Stubbs, *Sel. Charters*, 108-109.

king in chief [36] and thus to avoid dealings with the sheriff. It has been shown even from Domesday Book that the king entered into peculiar arrangements with some boroughs regarding taxation and military service.[37] Municipal liberties and organization were beginning to be introduced through special bargains, and much diversity was to be the result.

The borough officials mentioned in Domesday Book are called reeves or portreeves. The *Leis Willelme*, written in French, speak of the provost.[38] Most of the royal boroughs were under control of the sheriff, and the reeves were now in most cases their subordinates.[39] Until a much later time the sheriff was generally accountable for the dues and payments of boroughs. These were derived from land rents, market dues, the profits of the mint and the mill and some miscellaneous sums included in a *ferm*.[40] A third of these amounts in the Anglo-Saxon period had usually gone to the earl, the other two-thirds to the king. As the earl ceased to be head of the shire after the Norman Conquest, the king often acquired this third of borough profits.[41] Some boroughs were assessed to the danegeld, like rural properties, at a certain number of hides.[42] The village in becoming a borough did not always lose its connection with the hundred, although it sometimes did.[43] The grant of a special privilege often exempted the townsmen from the obligation to plead in a court ouside the borough.

The county of the Norman period still surpassed all other units of local government in importance as in extent. It of-

[36] Stubbs, *Constnl. Hist.*, I. 446.
[37] Ballard, *Domesday Boroughs*, 87-89; Stephenson, *American Histor. Rev.*, XXXII. 19.
[38] *Leis Willelme*, 2:1.
[39] Ballard, *Domesday Boroughs*, 44-47; Tait, *Eng. Histor. Rev.*, XLII. 330-332.
[40] As to the Domesday *firma burgi*, Round, *Domesday Studies*, ed. Dove, I. 135-136; as to the income from markets, *Victoria County Hist.*, Somerset, I. 422.
[41] Ballard, *Domesday Boroughs*, 41-43.
[42] *Ibid.*, 64-71.
[43] *Ibid.*, 102. Cf. Tait, *Domesday of Cheshire*, 32, n. 3.

fered great possibilities to a ruler bent upon central control, and in many ways it resembled the *vicomté* or viscounty, which had been of great service to the Norman duke. The control of its chief official over administration in the hundred and the borough afforded advantages which Norman rulers were not slow to utilize.

Within a few years after the Norman Conquest the sheriff became the nominal as well as the actual head of the shire. The battle of Hastings destroyed the earls of the house of Godwin. Edwin and Morkere, two of the earls of the Mercian line, retained a precarious hold in the midlands and in the north, but they had both vanished from the scene by 1071, as did Waltheof, earl of Northampton in 1076. Upon the Breton Ralph the Conqueror conferred an earldom in East Anglia, but his rebellion in 1075 along with Roger, son of William fitz-Osbern, palatine earl in Herefordshire, brought the end of both earldoms. No more of the old type were created. Henceforth no Norman earl was official head of a county except in the few palatinates of the north and west.[44] Even the king's brother, Bishop Odo of Bayeux, though for a time earl of Kent, did not exercise control over the sheriff of that county.[45]

This increase in the prestige and important of the sheriff's office [46] is shown in many ways, but in none more clearly than through the type of man now appointed to fill it. Although the sheriffs of Edward the Confessor's time who remained in office, and who had not fought with Harold against Duke William, were regarded in rightful possession of their offices, they practically all gave way to Normans within a period of five years. For the succeeding thirty-five years the sheriff was usually a baronial figure. Domesday Book does not make a business of naming sheriffs, but its scattered references to them show that in 1086 the heads of at least twenty counties

[44] Above, pp. 146-147.
[45] Morris, *Medieval English Sheriff*, 44.
[46] The account which follows is founded on the author's *Medieval English Sheriff*, chaps. 3, 4.

were of this type. Often the sheriff was one of the greatest barons, if not the greatest baron, in his county. He was strong enough to repress the subdued English, to bring recalcitrant feudal lords to order and often to crush rebellion. The period of the first two Norman reigns marks the highest point ever attained in the power of the sheriff. This was due largely to the confidence placed by the Conqueror in the men who held the office. Some had been his companions in arms. Many held extensive landed estates of him, either directly conferred or inherited from their fathers to whom the king had given them. The standing of some with the king is shown by the fact that they appear as his household officials or other administrative agents of the king at court.

The holding of the office by prominent feudatories might have become highly dangerous. The king was in no position freely to remove from office many sheriffs of this type. In more than a half dozen counties a son succeeded his father in the office. Moreover, some of the barons of Domesday Book long remained sheriffs. Most of the hereditary shrievalties persisted down to 1100 and in some cases to a later date. In Gloucestershire six members of one family successively filled the office, which they seem to have held continuously almost from the time of the Conquest, for a period of ninety years. A longer succession in Worcestershire may be traced in the family of Urse d'Abetot and that of his daughter's husband, Walter de Beauchamp. In Devonshire the Domesday sheriff was followed by his two sons, the younger holding the office until near 1130. In Kent Haimo the dapifer was also followed by two sons, although here the family tenure was not so long.

The attempt to counteract this trend seems to have grown out of the feudal rebellions of the time of William Rufus and Henry I. In the time of Rufus two sheriffs may be identified as new men, efficient administrators who rose to importance through the king's special favor. One of them, Hugh of Buckland, much employed about the business of the court, held at least three counties before 1100. The number of sheriffs belonging to the feudal baronage was further reduced by Henry I about the time of the battle of Tinchebrai. In 1109 or 1110 Hugh of Buckland governed eight shires, and five other trusted agents of the kings, all new men, controlled nine more. This unusual centralization was relaxed somewhat after a few years, but sheriffs of the newer type continued to increase in number and gradually displaced the incumbents who represented the older feudal families. By 1130 descendants of these lines held but very few counties. In 1129 and 1130 the king, apparently for fiscal reasons, gave over eleven counties to be administered jointly by Aubrey de Vere and Richard Basset, two important officials of the court. At this time the sheriffs of all but eight of the counties seem to have held some special post at court, and nearly all of them were officials of the newer type. These men who owed all to the king were bound to be loyal upholders of his policy. Moreover, there was now little difficulty in removing or exchanging sheriffs. In the system of governing the shires, as at court, the appearance of the new official nobility wrought marked changes.

The functions of the sheriff were even more numerous than in the Anglo-Saxon period. He was the judicial head of the courts of the shire, and was responsible for those of the hundred as well.[47] This position of the powerful Norman sheriff was alone sufficient to make him a great figure in local government. His duties in maintaining order were important, and here, as in judicial and military matters, he succeeded to the full power of the old English earl. He proclaimed the king's peace, he was responsible for maintaining order, he made arrests. In military affairs his position was even greater than in the past. In the local revolts of the time he is found heading the popular levy of his shire. He exacted the old obligation to render *inward* or local guard duty and *avera* or animals for transport service. In some of the counties the sheriff was the custodian of the principal castle and is sometimes mentioned

[47] Above, p. 156.

in Domesday Book as its builder. It often fell to him to exact the service known as castle-guard.

The head of the shire also executed royal writs and orders in a wide range of matters, including the enforcement of the decisions of the king's courts, the trial of specific causes assigned him, the procuring of a jury to ascertain facts in a given matter, the publication of writs generally, the protection of private rights, the disposition of lands in the king's hands, the recognition of rights, dues and privileges granted away by charter, and matters relating to the king's estates, his income and services due him. In many ways the king contrived to make the shrievalty an executive arm of the central government.

Its financial functions further illustrate the same fact. Here, as in the execution of the king's writs, the sheriff was purely a royal agent. His power was that of the old-time king's reeve who was the local custodian of the royal fiscal interests. Lands which fell to the king were taken into the sheriff's hands, and the usual process of alienating them was to give notice to him. He was charged with general supervision of the king's estates, and in the time of Henry I was held responsible at the exchequer if he did not keep them stocked or permitted them to depreciate in value. He collected the great bulk of the king's revenues. The chief of these were included in the farm of the county, a combination of income from royal estates and from the courts of shire and hundred.[48] Domesday Book shows that sheriffs were regularly acquitting this for a fixed annual sum, and it must have constituted their chief source of profit. The sheriff also collected sums derived from the special pleas of the crown, such as the five-pound forfeitures, which were not farmed.[49] Along with these went

---

[48] The reeve of the hundred here appears as his subordinate; *Burgus de Winchelcumbe reddit xx libras cum toto hundredo ejus villae. Durandus vicecomes apposuit lx solidos* (*Domesday Book*, I. 162).

[49] *Soca vero placitorum alia proprie pertinet ad fiscum regium . . . alia vicecomitibus et ministris regiis in firma sua, alia pertinet baronibus socam et sacam habentibus* (*Leges Henrici*, 9:11).

the murder fine laid upon the hundred. He was also in charge of the collection of the danegeld of his county and of many special dues. The money paid in commutation of local guard duty went into his hands; he sometimes handled payments made by lesser tenants of the crown; and, until the boroughs made separate arrangements, he collected the annual sums which they rendered the king and which often formed a part of the regular farm of the shire. The sheriff, moreover, served as a disbursing official of the king, providing hospitality and transportation for royal guests travelling through the country, and maintenance for the king's messengers. He was also charged with the payment of the annual sums which the king gave as charities, especially the fixed alms to churches.

Norman sheriffs in England were accused of much injustice. In the time of William the Conqueror they sometimes appropriated monastic lands, commandeered animals, and made wrongful claims to danegeld. As the officials who had most to do with farming out the dues from the king's lands, they were responsible for the heavy exactions upon peasants, of which the Anglo-Saxon Chronicle bitterly complains. They were so harsh and grasping in their dealings, that by the reign of Henry I the men of the towns were beginning to bargain with the king for the privilege of handling the annual sum due the crown and dealing directly with the exchequer. In the period immediately following the Conquest sheriffs often destroyed town houses to make room for the castle. However, outrageous their demands, there seems for a generation to have been no redress against them except on the part of persons influential enough to appeal directly to the king. They stood somewhat in the position of viceroys and expressed the crudeness of Norman rule. So long as they maintained order and paid his dues, the king was not greatly concerned with the exactions they laid upon peasants, burgesses, and monks.

When sheriffs joined in feudal rebellion, as happened in a few instances in the time of William Rufus, or when through bad management they depreciated the value of the king's estates, or when they did not promptly render to the king what was due him, the situation assumed a different aspect. Local autonomy which conflicted with the royal rights was well checked in the time of Henry I. The exchequer devised methods for holding sheriffs to strict fiscal accountability. It is evident that the king's justices in this reign were doing much to reduce the sheriffs to a subordinate judicial position. No doubt the motive was mainly fiscal, for through the justices the exchequer officials might know the exact sums due the king from the pleas of the crown. If these were levied by the sheriff in the county court, there was no adequate means of holding him to an accurate accounting. One great problem of the twelfth century monarchy was that of keeping the sheriff in check. It is clear that Henry I all but solved this. Under Stephen, however, confusion and disorder returned, and the sheriffs once more became troublesome.

The county court remained an important body. In the time of Henry I it was still convened twice a year, although there is mention of the rule, which was much older, permitting more frequent sessions if these were needed.[50] The sheriff soon became the sole presiding officer. Not only did the administrative earl vanish, but through the separation of the ecclesiastical from the secular jurisdiction the bishop lost his chief reason for attendance. In any event the sheriff was in control.[51] He summoned the court seven days in advance of the time of meeting,[52] he also summoned persons to answer there,[53] and he set special days for the hearing of causes.[54]

The identity of those who now attended and found the judgments in the county court is hard to determine. It is clear, however, that the landed class remained in control and that the duty of attending became more and more attached to certain lands. The theory of the writer of the *Leges Hen-*

[50] *Leges Henrici*, 7:4; 51:2. See above, p. 86.
[51] Morris, *Medieval English Sheriff*, 54-57, 89-90.
[52] *Leges Henrici*, 52:2a.   [53] *Ibid.*, 60:3.   [54] *Ibid.*, 41:2, 5.

rici[55] was that those in attendance were landlords or their representatives. In one passage he asserted that the king's judgment finders should be barons, by which he seems to have meant men of the county, who had freehold within it.[56] Others might be present, so he held, to represent lords or rather their lands, and among these he named the hundred reeve and the village reeve. This writer says that if a lord was not present, his steward might take his place, just as he is known to have done at a later time;[57] but if neither of these attended, the lord's demesne land was acquitted by the attendance of the priest, the reeve and four better men of the village as representatives of all who had not been summoned by name. It appears then, that some villains might attend the county court. The writer of the *Leges Henrici* says that they ought to have no part in the finding of judgment.[58] The reason for this seems to have been that they had no property of their own and, if they took part in a false judgment and thus incurred a fine, they were really forfeiting their lord's property.[59] It is nevertheless clear that these lesser men did sometimes participate in judgments,[60] although their right to do so was limited, in the causes of men of higher rank, by the principle that a man was to be judged by his peers.[61]

The appearance in the court of the shire, as well as that of the hundred, of the priest, the reeve and the four men of each vill, has been assumed to be the rule.[62] The statement of the *Leges Henrici* would establish the usage only under some circumstances, but there was another reason for the attendance of these persons in a representative capacity. About the time

---

[55] *Leges Henrici*, 7:2, 7. The king sometimes excused the men of certain lands from the duty of attending shire and hundred courts (British Museum, Faustina A iii, fol. 75d.).

[56] *Ibid.*, 29.

[57] Round, *Archaeological Review*, II. 67; Morris, *Early English County Court*, 104-105.

[58] *Leges Henrici*, 29; 29:1a.

[59] *Ibid.*, 29, 1b.

[60] Pollock and Maitland, *Hist of English Law*, I. 546.

[61] *Leges Henrici*, 31:7.

[62] Stubbs, *Constitutional History*, I. 425.

of Henry I, and apparently much earlier, it was the custom
to take the testimony of the men of four neighboring vills to
determine certain matters of fact. The priest, the reeve and
several of the better men of four vills adjoining a given
vicinity were employed in making special inquiry, especially
in clearing up matters bearing upon a man's possible connection with a crime.[63] A few representatives of the hundred were
also employed in the same capacity,[64] and in a charter somewhat later than 1120 there is reference to four men of the
wapentake who attend for purposes of the king's pleas.[65] It
is possible that all vills and hundreds were habitually represented in semi-annual sessions of the county which dealt with
criminal pleas,[66] but this is not clear, for part of these may
have been specially summoned from time to time as need arose.
The king's justices in the Domesday inquest employed as
jurors the priest, the reeve and six men of each vill and also
eight men of each hundred.[67]

The county court, far from being a decadent body as some
have supposed,[68] seems to assume new importance after the
Norman Conquest. It was still the highest tribunal open to
the great number. Only ecclesiastical cases, those of men great
enough to gain a hearing in the king's court, and those which
went to seigniorial courts, were altogether excluded. In some
respects its jurisdiction parallelled that of the hundred,[69] but
it heard causes also which could come up nowhere else. Pleas

[63] Gross, *Sel. Coroner's Rolls*, Selden Soc., p. xxxviii. According to
Leges Edwardi Confessoris (38:2) they give testimony as to a man's
reputation, and this assists him in clearing himself before the county
court (38:3); again (24, 24:1) they throw light on a man's rightful
or wrongful possession of property; or (20:3) on his accomplices. See
Gross, *ibid.*, xxxix, for a royal inquest by men of four vills.

[64] *Leges Edwardi Confessoris*, 38:2.

[65] *Monasticon* VI., pt. 3, p. 1272, no. 20.

[66] With the *placita generalia comitatuum* (*Leg. Hen.*, 7) cf. the *comitatus generalis* of a later time (Pollock and Maitland, *Hist. Eng. Law*,
I. 538-540).

[67] As to the latter, Round, *Feudal England*, 118.

[68] Davis, *Normans and Angevins*, 235; cf. Adams in *Amer. Histor.
Rev.*, VIII. 487-488.

[69] *Leis Willelme*, 43, 44.

of the crown were now regularly tried before the men of the county, who thus attracted some business from the hundred. Cases of failure to obtain justice had long gone to the county and continued to do so.[70] Judgments of hundreds and boroughs might be reconsidered in the county assembly and these bodies fined for false judgment.[71] Not all lords seem to have had courts,[72] and their failure to do justice meant action on the part of the public courts.[73] King Henry's order, that land cases between vassals of different lords be tried in the county court,[74] shows how this body filled another gap in the feudal scheme of justice. Furthermore, it was a court for enforcing many public obligations and claims of the sheriff to payments and service, and the king by his writ might bring some matters before it, as when he ordered the sheriff to make a jury inquest.[75]

The jurisdiction of the county court in criminal matters, if exception be made of offenses against one's lord and treason against the king, was now the most important in England. No doubt ordinary crimes in most cases continued to be punished in the hundred, but in the county court, as well as in the hundred, took place what was known as appeal,[76] that is to say, accusation of crime made by one person against another. A non-feudal offense on the part of a baron, even a baron with powers of *sake* and *soke,* did not of itself call for a state trial, and such cases are mentioned as coming before the county.[77] Franchisal justice was thought of as justice which excluded the sheriff,[78] and thus its equivalent belonged to his

---

[70] Above, pp. 55-56. *Leis Willelme,* 44:1; *Leges Henrici,* 7:6.

[71] *Leges Edwardi Confessoris,* 13:1; Morris, *Med. English Sheriff,* 97.

[72] Maitland, *Domesday and Beyond,* 102.

[73] Glanville, 1:2. The men of the abbot of Abingdon were by charter of Henry I (*Chron. Monast. de Abingdon,* II. 165) to plead outside the abbot's court only in case he failed to do them justice.

[74] Liebermann, *Gesetze,* I. 524 (sec. 3); Robertson, *Laws,* 286; but cf. *Leges Henrici,* 25:2.

[75] Morris, *Med. Eng. Sheriff,* 58, 90-91.

[76] Ten Articles of William I, sec. 6.

[77] *Leis Willelme,* 2:3.

[78] Morris, *Med. Eng. Sheriff,* 93.

province either directly or through his supervision of the
hundred.

The pleas of the crown formed one of the principal categories of business [79] at the semi-annual sessions of the county.
Even jurisdiction over main highways and navigable streams
was exercised by the county.[80] Theft, robbery, arson and other
crimes came before the sheriff for trial in the time of Henry
I, although these might also come before another agent of the
king.[81] Breach of the king's peace is mentioned in Domesday
Book as an offense punished by outlawry in the county assembly.[82] The practice of pronouncing outlawry here against
offenders [83] necessarily meant in many instances the disposition
of cases in which the hundred had failed to do justice. The
transfer of the pleas of the crown from the sheriff to the
justices of the king's court in the reigns of Henry I and Henry
II, obviously intended to reduce the power of the former, did
not discontinue trial of some of these before the county court.

The sheriff in disposing thus of the king's special business
acted as his justice. Certain passages in the legal works of the
reign of Henry I must be so construed,[84] and this idea still
appears at a much later time. Under the first two Norman
kings he was apparently the only justice who dealt systematically with pleas of the crown. Moreover, when the sheriff in
response to the king's writ empanelled a jury, or when he
took part in proceedings which involved trial by duel, he was
performing a function of the king's court. Some courts held
by the sheriff were regarded as the king's county courts,

[79] *Leges Henrici*, 7 : 3.

[80] *Leges Edwardi Confessoris*, 12 : 9-13 : 1.

[81] *Leges Henrici*, 66 : 9 : a justice. The term was one which might include the hundred reeve. See note 84.

[82] *Domesday Book*, I. 172. For the breach of the peace given by the
sheriff the penalty, however, was 100 shillings.

[83] Above, p. 88. Cf. *bebodenes utlage: Instituta Cnuti*, III : 46.

[84] *Amer. Hist. Rev.*, VIII. 490. *Leg. Edw. Conf.*, 3, 9, 20 : 1a, 36 : 3-5,
38 : 2, regard as a *justicia* or *justiciarius* the holder of the court of the
shire, the hundred, or that of the bishop. King Stephen addressed a writ
to the justiciars of two hundreds (Binham Chart., Brit. Mus., Claud,
D XIII, p. 41).

others, or even the same courts for other purposes, were regarded as popular county courts.[85] The king might even order the sheriff to convene the county court especially for his own business.[86]

The county court was also employed by Norman rulers as a forum for the proclamation of their writs, their legislation, and their grants.[87] Domesday Book in various passages assumes that the king's land grants are made known here.[88] The grants of privileges made by the Norman rulers are addressed to the county courts,[89] as also are their judicial decrees. The charter of liberties issued by Henry I was addressed in writ form to various county courts whither it was sent for publication.[90]

Popular control in the courts of shire and hundred had disappeared long before 1066, but they preserved something of self-direction in local matters. Their power to decide cases, though limited by seigniorial jurisdiction and that of the king's central court, remained for centuries. The shire court until the time of Henry II must be regarded as the greatest tribunal for the enforcement of folkright. Counties, however, varied in their legal rules sufficiently to embody some local custom. In the court of the palatinate of Herefordshire William fitz Osbern established a rule by which no knight was amerced more than seven shillings, whereas in other counties the amount was frequently twenty or twenty-five shillings.[91] Other differences in county legal usage are mentioned more

[85] G. B. Adams, in *Amer. Hist. Rev.*, VIII. 490. In *Monasticon*, VI. pt. 3, 1272, there is mention of a special procedure for the king's county courts.

[86] Above, p. 156.

[87] Morris, *Med. Eng. Sheriff*, 90.

[88] Above, p. 140.

[89] This is the meaning of the usual form of address to the sheriff and barons of a county (W. H. Stevenson, *Eng. Histor. Rev.*, XXI. 506-507; Morris, *Med. Eng. Sheriff*, 90).

[90] See Liebermann, *Gesetze*, 521; also Robertson, *Laws of Kings of England*, 276, note 2.

[91] William of Malmesbury, *Gesta Regum*, Rolls Ser., II. 314. The highest amercement known to Kentish law under Henry II was forty shillings (Pollock and Maitland, *Hist. Eng. Law*, I. 106).

than a century after the Norman Conquest,[92] and there are numerous evidences of these in the judicial records of the thirteenth century.[93] Some of them possibly represented methods by which powerful Norman sheriffs transacted business, but there were still marked differences recognized between the laws of Mercia, of Wessex, and of the Danelaw.[94] Though central control more and more made for uniformity, traces of the old usage of county courts long remained.

A striking feature of local government in the Norman period is seen in its police methods. Upon the men of the village and the hundred were enjoined drastic regulations for the apprehension of criminals. These imposed upon the mass of the English population a severe discipline in the matter of law enforcement to which probably no other European people has been subject. This result was effected through a responsibility of vills, but also through two other devices, the murderfine and frankpledge.

This responsibility of the vills assumed two forms. When a crime was committed, the men of the community were expected to raise the hue and cry and to pursue the offender.[95] When the public authorities wished to make inquiry to detect crime, they brought together for the purpose a few men of each of the four neighboring vills. This was an old English usage developed and improved by Norman officials.[96]

The murder-fine (*murdrum*) was devised to protect Normans[97] in England from assassination. Murder in this sense

[92] Glanville, XIV. 8.

[93] See the method of presenting Englishry (Gross, *Sel. Coroners' Rolls*, Selden Soc., p. xliii) ; also the privileges of the men of Kent (*Eyre of Kent*, Selden Soc., I. 52; Vinogradoff, *Eng. Soc. Eleventh Century*, 93).

[94] See *Leis Willelme*, 2, 21 : 2-4.

[95] *Leis Willelme*, 4.

[96] Gross, *Sel. Coroners' Rolls*, Selden Soc., p. xxxviii.

[97] Ten articles of William I, sect. 3; *Leis Willelme*, 22. The writer of the *Leges Edwardi Confessoris* (16, 16 : 1) represents this as a scheme originally instituted for the protection of Danes when Canute sent his army away. A passage in the coronation charter of Henry I (sect. 9) seems to assume that it was a part of the law of England before the Conquest. There is a very different version in *Dialogus de Scaccario*, Oxford ed., 99. The whole practice for centuries bears the stamp of a

was secret killing. The rule enforced was that, if the slayer in such a case were not given up in seven days, the heavy payment of forty-six marks was collected from the whole hundred [98] in which the crime occurred. The murder-fine was exacted only when the slain was French or Norman, not when he was an Englishman, but the law for this purpose reputed every man French [99] unless his English descent was proved. The process of submitting this proof, under the name of presentment of Englishry, was destined to remain a part of English law until 1340. It is certain that the murder-fine was being collected in the reign of William the Conqueror.[100] Upon Norman officials fell the duty of enforcing it, if necessary, by seizing property of men of a wide community.[101]

Frankpledge was an outgrowth of the *borh* system of the Anglo-Saxon kings, which afforded a pledge to lead the freeman of lower rank to justice in case he committed a crime. It is quite probable that before 1066 this was effected in more than one way by the lord or by neighbors.[102] It seems clear that William the Conqueror revived the law which required every man to be in *borh* and that he added some new

Norman origin. It was not introduced in the counties of the northern Danelaw (Morris, *Frankpledge System*, 51). Its absence from Shropshire, a palatinate until 1102, suggests that it arose only in the Norman period.

[98] In 1130 (*Pipe Roll, passim*) from 10 to 28. According to the *Leges Henrici* (91 : 2-2a) this may conceivably fall upon a manor, but upon the hundred if the manor is not sufficient. If the manor is on land which renders ferm to the king (91 : 3), he may have the fine levied upon the whole hundred; if the slain person is found in the open fields (91 : 4), this is the sole procedure. Cf. the so-called laws of William I, sec. 22. The *Leges Edwardi Confessoris* (15 : 2) are less explicit and seem to imply that this fine may be collected from any vill. The Ten Articles of William I (3 : 1-2) hold that the lord must make the arrest and that his property is liable if he does not; if his property fails, the hundred is to pay in common what remains. This is merely another expression of the responsibility of the vill or manor.

[99] *Leges Henrici*, 92 : 6; cf. *Dialogus de Scaccario*, Oxford ed., 99.

[100] Davis, *Regesta*, no. 202. It was specifically retained by Henry I and Stephen (Stubbs, *Sel. Charters*, 101, 121).

[101] *Leges Henrici*, 91 : 2, 91 : 2a; *Leg. Edw. Conf.*, 15 : 4.

[102] Cf. *Leis Willelme*, 3, where the pledge in Mercia is seen to be one person and not a group. The Anglo-Saxon police tithing was apparently only a West Saxon institution.

features.[103] In the time of Henry I it is described in a new fashion. One of the earliest Norman writers to mention the plan says that all villains are to be in frankpledge.[104] Others show that those who do not belong to the immediate household of some lord, who is thus responsible for them, are appointed to groups known as tithings, the members of which are mutual sureties for each other. If one of them commits an offense, it is the duty of the others to produce him.[105] The better known descriptions of the time represent the tithings as consisting of ten men,[106] but one of these tells that the number may be greater according to local custom.[107] In the light of the facts brought out by later records, it is apparent that the frankpledge tithings were constituted in two different ways according to locality. In the southern part of the former Danelaw as a rule they were groups of ten men, and in the shires of the old kingdom of Wessex they included, it seems regularly, all the men of a given village.[108] A head man, or as he was called, a capital pledge, supervised the police duties of the tithing.[109] If the men of the group failed to produce their guilty associate they were responsible, and a money payment was exacted from them.[110] The effect was to place collective responsibility upon the men of the village, just as the murder fine placed it upon the men of the hundred.

The revision of the tithing lists each year took place at a great session of the hundred,[111] probably held now by the

---

[103] Ten Articles of William I, 8, 8a. Group pledging is here assumed.

[104] *Leis Willelme*, 20 : 3a.

[105] *Consiliatio Cnuti*, II. 19, 2a. *Leges Edwardi Confessoris*, 20 : 1-1a.

[106] *Ibid.; Leges Henrici*, 8 : 1-1a.

[107] *Consiliatio Cnuti*, II. 19, 2a : ten, twenty, or thirty.

[108] Morris, *Frankpledge System*, 86-88. In the time of Henry I the tithing men and men of four tithings might take the same place as the reeves and men of four vills (*Leges Edwardi Confessoris*, 24 : 1-2, 38 : 2). Frankpledge was not introduced in the northern part of the Danelaw (Morris, *ibid.*, 45-53).

[109] *Leges Edwardi Confessoris*, 20 : 3; *Leges Henrici*, 8 : 1a (here called *aldremannus* or chief man).

[110] William of Malmesbury, *Gesta Regum*, Rolls. Ser., I. 130. The statement that Alfred instituted frankpledge tithings is of course an error.

[111] *Leges Henrici*, 8 : 1.

sheriff as at a later day, but in any event, like everything else in the hundred, under his general supervision. He or his agent called upon the men of the village to make payment for default of frankpledge obligation. The scheme was well planned to provide the peace suretyship for the peasants which no Norman lord would undertake to give, and to restrain the men of the community from violence and crime.

Frankpledge suretyship fits so well into the police scheme of the Norman rulers that at first sight it appears to have been originated by the Conqueror. Various authorities, however, notably Liebermann, hold that it grew up in the late Anglo-Saxon period. Liebermann shows reason for holding that the old English police tithing by Canute's time was also employed as a suretyship tithing. He also holds that the statements of chroniclers and law writers of the twelfth century prove the existence of the tradition that frankpledge is of pre-conquest origin.[112] The latter naturally assumed that it was identical with the *borh* system mentioned in the laws of Canute,[113] but this will hardly serve as an adequate explanation of its origin. Like the responsibility of the four vills, it must be regarded rather as an institution developed from old English beginnings by Norman authorities.[114] There is good reason to doubt whether *borh* before 1066 was the same as the frankpledge described by Norman writers.[115] The Conqueror is credited by a fairly reliable authority with the enactment of a new measure on the subject. Various details of the system as given by Norman writers are not known to be of English origin and some can hardly be so. The administration of the matter under Norman sheriffs obviously gave it a peculiar Norman tone. Its success depended upon a power-

[112] Liebermann, *Gesetze*, II. article "Zehnerschaft."
[113] II Canute, 20. See Morris, *Frankpledge System*, 15, 33-34.
[114] Gross, *Sel. Coroners' Rolls*, Selden Soc., p. xxxviii; Morris, *Frankpledge System*, 7-8, 25-27, 29-36.
[115] In one respect only may the identity be shown to be complete. The lord's pledging of the members of his household (Canute II. 31) was continued. This is sometimes loosely called frankpledge; more correctly it is mainpast.

ful sheriff of the Norman type. There were safeguards against collusion between the fugitive and his neighbors [116] which do not occur in the Anglo-Saxon codes. Like the murder-fine, the frankpledge system shows a suspicion of the lower classes of English which bears a Norman stamp. Moreover, *borh* seems never to have grown into frankpledge in the western counties,[117] which formed palatinates in the Conqueror's time and which were thus removed from his direct control. Whatever the origin of the system, its organization and operation by Norman officials were thoroughly characteristic of Norman rule in England.

AUTHORITIES

The source materials for the local government of the Norman period are, first, the legal works of the early twelfth century. These are quite unofficial in origin, but they attempt to state the existing English law. The chief of them are the *Leis Willelme,* the so-called ten articles of William I, the *Leges Henrici Primi* and the *Leges Edwardi Confessoris.* The last named is the least reliable, and occasionally contains statements which can be shown to be incorrect. The best edition of all these collections is that by Felix Liebermann in his *Gesetze der Angelsachsen* (vol. I. 1898). Those which bear the name of William I, though not the others, are included in Miss Agnes J. Robertson's *Laws of the Kings of England from Edmund to Henry I* (1925).

The writs and charters issued by the Norman kings also throw light on local government, giving the names of sheriffs, and also exemplifying their duties. This material is widely scattered. Some is published in Dugdale's *Monasticon,* some in the various chronicles of the period, some is preserved in the British Museum in its original form, and some appears in manuscript chartularies preserved originally by monastic houses. The best approach to it for the first two Norman reigns is through the calendared collection edited by H. W. C. Davis, the *Regesta Regum Anglo-Normannorum* (vol. I. 1913). A similar calendar, *An Outline Itinerary of the Reign of Henry I* (1921), was arranged by William Farrer. This appeared originally in the *English Historical Review,* vol. XXXIV. (1921), but was also issued separately.

Domesday Book throws some light on local government, as do occa-

[116] Ten Articles of William I, sec. 8a; *Consiliatio Cnuti,* II. 19, 2a; cf. *Leges Edwardi Confessoris,* 20 : 3.
[117] Morris, *Frankpledge System,* 51, 53-55.

sionally the monastic chronicles, particularly those of Abingdon and Ramsey.

Of the secondary writers, Stubbs deals with local government only incidentally. Haskins, *Norman Institutions* (1918), gives some new information. The various writings of J. H. Round, especially his *Feudal England,* and his *Geoffrey de Mandeville* treat many points of detail. George B. Adams occasionally touched upon questions of local government in his various works, especially in *The Origin of the English Constitution* (1912) and *Council and Courts in Anglo-Norman England* (1926). Other constitutional historians such as Gneist and Hatschek have dealt only cursorily with the subject. The most detailed treatment of the boroughs is Adolphus Ballard, *The Domesday Boroughs* (1904), which develops still further the general viewpoint presented by F. W. Maitland in his *Domesday Book and Beyond.* New material on municipal history with criticism of older views is presented by Carl Stephenson in the *American Historical Review,* XXXII. 10-21 (1926). James Tait in the *English Historical Review,* XLVI., gives a useful treatment of some matters of borough administration. W. A. Morris, *The Medieval English Sheriff* (1927), chaps. 3-4, contains a detailed account of this official in the Norman period. The same writer's *Frankpledge System* (1910) holds to the origin of this institution in Norman England. A few of the conclusions require modification in the light of Liebermann's treatment (art. "Zehnerschaft" in his *Gesetze,* vol. II.).

CHAPTER IX

THE NORMAN MONARCHY AND THE CURIA REGIS

The dominant feature of the constitution in Norman England was strong monarchy. The state became fully centered in the king. To quote Stubbs,[1] "It is from the person, the household, the court, and the council of the king that all constitutional power radiates." The establishment of this powerful monarchy is a cardinal fact in English constitutional history. It disciplined the conquered race in adversity and held a naturally turbulent baronage in order. Constitutional progress was possible only under a strong regime and an effective administration. The chief branches of later English government are in the main offshoots from the Norman king's domestic establishment. England under autocratic rule began within a century and a half to strive for popular liberties and checks upon absolutism. Lands wherein feudal disorder was perpetuated reached the age of strong monarchy and centralized routine at a much later time, hence their movement to assure popular rights and constitutional government is of comparatively recent date. The paradox of English constitutional history is that a powerful Norman kingship ultimately made possible limited monarchy.

No single interpretation can explain the system of government established by William the Conqueror, for he derived his power and the elements of his success from diverse sources. His election and coronation as king of England enabled him to claim the rights and prerogatives of Edward the Confessor. He attempted no overthrow of existing institutions of government, but rather utilized the advantages which they offered him. The existing body of English law was necessarily re-

[1] *Constnl. Hist.*, I. 336.

tained, and this came to be known as the law of King Edward.[2] Norman law was not yet reduced to writing in the
Conqueror's time,[3] and codes like those of Edgar and Canute
were useful. They were studied by Normans, who needed the
information they contained, as the legal works of the next
generation well show.

The law and usage of England were supplemented by those
of Normandy. With feudalism came the feudal law important
to the upper classes, introduced as a matter of fact by the
Norman nobility accustomed to act according to its principles.
These claimed for the king the aid and counsel of his barons,
and they recognized him as chief suzerain and supreme landlord. Beyond the rights of the English king, the Conqueror
was entitled to those involved in his feudal headship. Over
and above the allegiance of all free men he demanded the
fealty of feudal vassals; in addition to the old danegeld he
claimed the new feudal dues; retaining for emergencies the
English *fyrd,* he depended regularly upon the feudal array.
William, moreover, introduced in England some of the method
and spirit of the central routine of the Norman duchy. He
brought in the same control of local government which existed
in Normandy. In England the earl soon ceased nearly everywhere to be at the head of the shire, and the sheriff came,
like the Norman *vicomte,* under the king's sole direction.
Only a few regions, mainly on the borders, were governed by
Norman earls who controlled administration as did the feudal
ruler of the Norman county.

The founder of the new monarchy in England employed
absolutist usages which were neither English nor purely feudal.
The Norman dukes had borrowed from Carolingian monarchy
something of an attitude derived from Roman law. King
William made use in both countries of judicial commissions,[4]

[2] Ten Articles of William I (no. 7) ; Charter of Liberties of 1100,
sec. 13. Cf. Bigelow, *Placita Anglo-Normannica,* 38.

[3] Haskins, *Norman Institutions,* 4.

[4] Below, pp. 207-208; for Normandy, Round, *Calendar,* no. 712. For the
non-feudal side of justice, Maitland, *Constitutional History,* 162-164.

somewhat like those represented by the *missi dominici* under Frankish monarchy, and he employed the sworn inquest or primitive jury, the idea of which came down from Roman law.[5] In his disposition to assume initiative and power lay the spark of administrative progress.

The new regime owed much of its success to the conditions under which it was established and to the personal endowment and experience of the Conqueror. He was able to establish his followers as a feudal nobility in a conquered land and to place them in the strong position occupied by the Anglo-Saxon thegns. This reduced the English to abject submission and made them unable to resist change. William was noted for his strength of will and his sternness toward those who opposed him. From his youth he had experience with feudal rebellion and learned wisdom and caution in dealing with his barons. He had maintained a strong ducal power and a well ordered scheme of government, and was already a remarkably successful ruler when the conquest of England gave him an opportunity unsurpassed in the feudal age.

So far did William and his successors press their authority that not only their English subjects but also their Norman barons felt aggrieved. It has often been pointed out that English liberty would probably have perished but for the fact that the succession to the Conqueror's crown was disputed. Against the claims of their elder brother, Robert, both William II and Henry I had to contend. Stephen set aside the hereditary rights of his cousin Matilda, the daughter of Henry I. King William's two sons and his grandson found it advisable to offer concessions to gain popular support. Both Henry I and Stephen embodied these in written charters which succeeding generations might cite as precedents.

The immunities granted throw light on Norman rule. William Rufus, the most unjust of the Norman rulers, to gain the aid of the English during the feudal rebellion of 1088, en-

[5] Stubbs, *Select Charters*, 86; Adams and Stephens, *Sel. Documents*, 2-3. See Brunner, *Entstehung der Schwurgerichte*, 87-97.

gaged to allow them their own laws as best they had stood in
the past, to forbid unjust imposts and to grant them liberty
of the chase. These promises were not kept, but the king made
others during a serious illness in 1093. He ordered the dismissal of pleas which had been instituted by his agents and
the pardon of sums which he claimed through these and other
devices. He also promised good laws, the inviolable observance
of right, and the cessation of the practice of selling churches.[6]
These concessions were issued under the king's seal, but were
later abandoned. The charter of liberties issued by Henry I at
his coronation in August 1100, and apparently reissued the
following year,[7] offered various classes redress,[8] notably to
the church, a remission of the usage by which William Rufus
had sold or placed at farm vacant bishoprics and abbeys; to
the barons, alleviation of the exorbitant reliefs demanded by
Rufus, and of the abuses of the king's control over the marriage of heiresses and widows; to the knights who held their
land by military service, exemption of their demesne from
gelds and labor dues; to the English, the law of King Edward;
and to the realm in general, a firm peace, a sound coinage and
freedom from the pleas instituted and debts unjustly claimed
by the king's predecessor. It is easy to show that King
Henry failed in various particulars to keep these promises,[9]
but his charter was great in its own day and was destined to become the model of a greater charter over a century
later.

The concessions made by Stephen at his accession are of less
consequence, yet they show how important he regarded such
promises to gain adherents to his cause. At his coronation in
1135 he issued a confirmation of the liberties and good laws
granted by Henry I and the laws of King Edward.[10] The next

[6] Eadmer, *Hist. Nov.*, 31-32; *A.-S. Chron.*, 1088, 1093.

[7] Riess in *English Historical Review*, XLI. 321-331.

[8] Liebermann, *Gesetze*, I. 521-523; Stubbs, *Select Charters*, 100-102;
Adams and Stephens, *Select Documents*, no. 7.

[9] Round, *Feudal England*, 227, 310.

[10] Stubbs, *Select Charters*, 119. Henry of Huntingdon (Rolls Ser., 258)
represents Stephen as promising remission of danegeld to the church.

year the king issued a charter of liberties [11] designed primarily
to gain the support of the church. He undertook to respect
ecclesiastical rights and to assure canonical election of bishops
and abbots; at the same time he engaged to abolish new
forest claims made by Henry I, to forbid the injustice and
exaction of officials, and to observe good laws and ancient
customs in matters of justice. Norman rule at its best stood
for some excellent principles, but every Norman king was so
high-handed that he or his successor might hope to gain strong
support by undertaking to redress stored-up grievances,
whether popular, ecclesiastical or baronial.

Under this masterful regime the national assembly under-
went a fundamental change in its character and, at least for a
time, a marked diminution of its power. It continued to be
called the *witan* by English writers of the period, but this need
imply nothing beyond a continuance of its national character.
Latin chronicles refer to it as a council,[12] but they sometimes
borrow Norman terminology and refer to it as the king's *curia*
or *curia regis*. It now met in the French fashion [13] with greater
frequency, regularity and splendor than in the past. According to the Anglo-Saxon Chronicle King William was accustomed to wear his crown on the three great church festi-
vals of the year. Easter he observed at Winchester, Whitsuntide at Westminster, and Christmas at Gloucester. On these
occasions the chief men of the realm were gathered about him.
Mass was celebrated and the crown then placed upon the king's
head by a bishop or an archbishop.[14] Ceremony gave way to

[11] Stubbs, *Select Charters*, 120-121.

[12] As to identity of *curia* and *concilium*, Round, *Peerage, and Pedigree*,
I. 347-48. There appears no attempt to find names to distinguish between
a great and a small council before the reign of Henry I. The term
magnum concilium (Florence of Worcester, II. 43, 51) was at first used
only of ecclesiastical assemblages. The great council is referred to thus:
concilio totius regni (*Monasticon*, I. 242); *communi celebrato consilio*
(Farrer, *Itinerary of Henry I*, no. 660); *magnum placitum*, 1131
(Henry of Huntingdon). For other formulae of designation, below, n. 20,
and Farrer, *Itinerary of Henry I*, no. 92.

[13] Liebermann, *National Assembly*, 88; Luchaire, *Institutions Monarchiques*, I. 256-257.

[14] Cf. Farrer, *Itinerary of Henry I*, no. 245; Eadmer, *Hist. Nov.*, R.S.,
212; Florence of Worcester, II. 84.

festivity [15] and festivity to business. Henry I came to omit some of the three stated annual assemblies, but they were regarded as the rule until the reign of Stephen.[16] The king called sessions at other times when he so desired, and these might coincide with the gatherings of the baronage called out to render military service.[17]

The membership of these assemblies, as shown both by the statements of chroniclers and the names of those in attendance,[18] consisted virtually of the great men of the kingdom. It comprised, besides the king, and sometimes his wife and sons, the highest clergy, the lay magnates and a few others who were present because of their position in the king's household. The prelates who came included archbishops and bishops, often among these one or more occupants of Norman sees, together with some of the abbots. The lay lords were earls and other men of rank. The official group often represented the king's Norman as well as his English household establishment, and, so far as its members were not high clergy or important lay lords, they were usually churchmen of minor position. The impressiveness of these gatherings was enhanced by the appearance of some who were not members of the great council, notably knights and the vassals of members, who as lords had the right to call upon their men to attend and to advise them.[19]

A definition of the national assembly based upon contemporary descriptions would declare, almost in the words of a much later formula, that it was a body of archbishops, bishops,

[15] A state banquet was held until in the reign of Henry I (William of Malmesbury, *Gesta Regum*, II. 335; Milo Crispin, *Vita Lanfranci* in Migne, *Patrologia Latina*, vol. 150, p. 53; Eadmer, *Hist. Nov.*, 79; Liebermann, *National Assembly*, 82, n. 1).

[16] Liebermann, *ibid.*, 82.

[17] Davis, *Regesta*, no. 315, and Adams, *Council and Courts*, 12, 36, cite apparent instances.

[18] Davis, *Regesta*, nos. 22, 23, 26, 123, 125, 168, 170, 172, 315, 319; Farrer, *Itinerary of Henry I*, nos. 26, 512, 660; Round, *Feudal England*, 482-484; Stubbs, *Select Charters*, 121.

[19] Adams, *Council and Courts*, 6-7, 37-38, 61. It is probable that a quota of knights was exacted from tenants-in-chief to be present on these occasions (*Ramsey Chart*, I. 235).

abbots, earls and other lay magnates,[20] but it is possible to find other significant terms. The lay magnates were often denoted by colorless words which meant merely chief men,[21] but in more technical language they were called barons. Official statements of the Conqueror's day occasionally represent the national assembly as consisting of but two groups, the king's bishops and his barons.[22] The same usage occurs also under Henry I,[23] but by his reign the single word barons was used both in the king's documents [24] and in law works [25] to describe the entire membership.

The Norman king, then, regarded his great council as an assemblage of his barons. It was in one aspect the king's court for the trial of their causes by judgment of their fellow barons. The mere status of the king's vassal probably afforded the only qualification which would cover every case; [26] but the render of homage to the king in return for land held of him was a working test which would practically meet the situation.[27] In the Conqueror's time the word baron did not imply

---

[20] *A.-S. Chron.*, 1087: archbishops, bishops, abbots, earls, thegns, and knights; Florence of Worcester, II. 8: *coram rege, et Doruberniae archiepiscopo Landfranco et episcopis, abbatibus, comitibus et primatibus totius Angliae.* Eadmer (*Hist. Nov.* 53, 58) refers to the baronial element as *principes.* A legislative enactment of the Conqueror was decided upon (Liebermann, *Gesetze,* I. 485) *Communi concilio et consilio archiepiscoporum, et episcoporum et abbatum et omnium principum regni mei.*

[21] *Principes, primores, primates, optimates.*

[22] Davis, *Regesta,* no. 139; foundation charter of Battle Abbey (Migne, *Patrologia Latina,* vol. 149, p. 1289): *concilio etiam episcoporum ac baronum meorum.* Cf. Eadmer, *Hist. Nov.,* 58.

[23] As in *Chron. Monast. Abingdon,* II. 161.

[24] Charter of Liberties of Henry I, secs. 3, 10, 13; *Chron. Monast. Abingdon,* II. 113.

[25] In the Quadrapartitus (Liebermann, *Gesetze,* I. 533) Edward the Confessor agrees to Canute's laws *totius Angliae baronibus.* The *Leges Edwardi Confessoris* (prologue) claim authority of the *barones.* Cf. Florence of Worcester, II. 125. A late version of the *Leges Edwardi* (Liebermann, *Gesetze,* I. 635) says that the king ought to do justice *per consilium procerum regni sui.*

[26] Adams, *Council and Courts,* 8, 36. R. R. Reed (*Eng. Histor. Rev.* XXXV, 161) shows that there might be barons who were not tenants-in-chief.

[27] Round (*Peerage and Pedigree,* I. 337) holds that the status of tenant-in-chief constituted the actual qualification. Later feudal service

high rank and might be used to designate one of the king's men of no particular consequence.[28] Soon after the Conquest, however, the assembly inevitably became in effect a body of great tenants-in-chief. Although nearly all of these owed the king military service, most of them a heavy quota, this of itself was not essential to baronial status.

It has often been pointed out that some members of the great council were not barons, but these were certainly few. Papal legates and other distinguished visitors not in the king's fealty [29] were sometimes present, but need not be taken very seriously as members. The chancellor and the clerks of the king's chapel obviously attended because of administrative usefulness rather than baronial standing, although by the time of Henry I the chancellor was sometimes a fairly important tenant-in-chief. The attendance of the barons' men, the rear vassals, at the assembly on Salisbury plain, where they swore fealty to the king, has been taken to indicate that they were members of the great council, but the account in the Anglo-Saxon Chronicle shows that this was not the case.[30]

The status of bishops and abbots presents more difficulty. In the early years of the Conqueror they must have attended, according to custom, as *witan*.[31] William I, however, required that newly elected prelates take an oath of homage to him,[32] consequently as fast as English bishops and abbots were replaced by Normans the latter could be regarded as barons. The Conqueror's later documents sometimes class certain bishops and abbots as barons.[33] The king maintained that

was regarded as springing from homage for land: *quantum homo debet domino ex homagio tantum illi debet dominus ex dominio* (Glanvill, IX. 4; cf. IX. 1, 2).

[28] See Davis, *Regesta*, no. 67. In the king's writs to the county courts *barones* is merely a translation of thegns.

[29] Stubbs, *Constnl. Hist.*, I. 386.

[30] *A.-S. Chron.*, 1086. They are distinguished from the *witan*.

[31] Stubbs, *Constnl. Hist.*, I. 386; Liebermann, *Natnl. Assembly*, 79-80.

[32] Eadmer, *Historia Novorum*, Rolls. Ser., 2, 237. Cf. Liebermann, *Natnl. Assembly*, 79, n. 1.

[33] Adams, *Council and Courts*, 36-37; Davis, *Regesta*, nos. 129, 221. See *barones regis*, *Domesday Book*, IV. 497, and compare with *ibid.*, III. p. vii.

these held lands of him, for in Domesday Book all the bishops and some forty of the abbots appear among his great tenants.[34] According to the usage of the period the newly elected prelate received from the king the lands held by his predecessor.[35] Moreover, the bishops and some twenty-four of the abbots [36] from about 1070 seem always to have owed the king military service. William Rufus in 1095, after the death of the last English bishop applied feudal doctrine in dealing with the lands of his see during the vacancy, collecting a relief from his tenants,[37] as if an episcopal estate were an escheated fief. There were of course differences between a bishop as prelate and a bishop as baron, and bishops sometimes claimed that their status in the assembly was not baronial. Odo of Bayeux in 1082 and William of Durham in 1088 claimed the privileges of their order as a bar to trial before the king's barons, but both were overruled.[38] Whatever bishops and abbots might claim, they had come to be regarded from the royal and the feudal point of view as barons and as tenants-in-chief. When in 1164 it was represented as a rule of the reign of Henry I that prelates who held lands of the king were tenants by barony, owing the same services as other barons, the greatest English champion of ecclesiastical privilege did not seriously contest the claim.[39]

The counsel given in the national assembly must have been regarded as that of the whole body of barons,[40] but this was far from the fact. Later history shows that the lesser as well

[34] The famous requirement (*Domesday Book*, IV. 497-528) that an inquiry be made concerning lands when King William gave them is known through its application to the estates of the abbot of Ely.

[35] Necessarily from the time of Rufus (below, p. 253) ; probably from 1066 as a part of their investiture (p. 250).

[36] Above, p. 138.

[37] Round, *Feudal England*, 309; Adams and Stephens, *Select. Docs.*, no. 5.

[38] See Adams, *Council and Courts*, 32, ff., 46, ff.

[39] Constitutions of Clarendon, sec. 11; *Materials for Life of Becket*, Rolls Ser., II. 380; V. 73-79.

[40] Above, note 20. See Adams, *Origin of English Constn.*, 65 ; *Council and Courts*, 5. The vassal's obligation to a baronial lord of *observacio Consilii* (*Leges Henrici*, 55 : 3) may mean secrecy.

as the greater tenants-in-chief might come, and their right
to do so under Norman rule is not to be questioned, for every
vassal was entitled to justice in his lord's court. Their right to
appear as regular members at any time is not so clear. Moreover it is easy to show that attendance of the mass of barons
was out of the question. The king's tenants-in-chief, according
to Domesday Book, numbered above five hundred, and it has
been reckoned that there were about a hundred and seventy
barons of some consequence;[41] yet the maximum number of
persons who witness any known document at a great council
is seventy-five,[42] and the number often falls under fifty.[43]
These lists of witnesses substantiate the statements of writers
who represent the great council primarily as an assemblage of
magnates. Informed chroniclers sometimes say that all the
great men are accustomed to attend the three annual assemblies.[44] The statement may have been a concession to theory,
but more probably these writers took into account only a
limited circle of prelates and important lay barons who were
usually present.[45]

This may be illustrated by the cases of the abbots. Not all
abbots were, like the bishops, of the higher baronage. Not all
rendered military service to the king. Only a few are mentioned in attendance, although it is significant that some of
these are not on the list of those known to have owed knight
service.[46] Certainly not all could afford to attend, and William
the Conqueror is said to have conferred upon the abbot of
his newly founded monastery of Battle an allowance to support the latter when he came to court at Easter, Whitsuntide

[41] W. J. Corbett, *Cambridge Med. His.*, V. 511.
[42] In 1101 (Farrer, *Itinerary of Henry I*, no. 28). Under William II
there appear over 60 (Davis, *Regesta*, no. 315).
[43] *Ibid.*, nos. 22, 23; Round, *Geoffrey de Mandeville*, 262-263; Stubbs,
Sel. Charters, 121; Madox, *Exchequer*, I. 13.
[44] *A.-S. Chron.*, 1087; Eadmer, *Hist. Nov.*, Rolls Ser., 29; Malmesbury, *Gesta Regum*, II. 335; cf. II. 528.
[45] Not all these attend: Eadmer, *Hist. Nov.*, 53.
[46] The abbots of Battle and Gloucester in 1191 (Davis, *Regesta*, no.
315) and in addition the abbot of St. Mary's, York, in 1101 (Farrer,
Itinerary of Henry I, no. 26).

and Christmas.[47] Attendance must have been quite as burdensome for many of the lesser tenants-in-chief. The presence of these in any number may be assumed only on unusual occasions. The well-known meeting of 1116, in which Henry I required fealty to his son, was probably the only general assembly of tenants-in-chief for the whole period.[48]

Appearance at the king's assembly to give him counsel was a feudal obligation, apparently on the same footing as military service, which was rendered when the king demanded it through his summons. Attendance at the three regular sessions of the year is represented as customary, and nothing very specific is said as to summons but its employment can hardly be doubted.[49] When Robert Mowbray, fearing prosecution for rebellion, refused to attend the Easter court of 1095, William Rufus ordered him to come at Pentecost on pain of the king's ban.[50] Summons to assemblies held at unusual times and places was obviously a necessity. It is mentioned in the reign of Edward the Confessor and several times under William II and Henry I;[51] furthermore the Anglo-Saxon Chronicle in its account of the great council held in February, 1123, states that summons was by the king's writ. That some barons were summoned by name seems to be brought out in the story of Robert Mowbray's refusal to come. Moreover, a contemporary of Henry I, writing years after the death of that monarch, mentions a definite group of persons who in this reign had been called up by name.[52] This conforms with contemporary usage in France.[53] The king's summons explains why certain

[47] Davis, *Regesta*, no. 60. The authenticity of this document has, however, been questioned by Round.

[48] Round, *Peerage and Pedigree*, I. 334-336.

[49] William of Malmesbury (*Gesta Regum*, II. 335) says that the magnates came in the time of Rufus because of the king's *edictum*. Cf. Luchaire, *Institutions Monarchiques*, I. 253.

[50] *A.-S. Chron.*, 1095.

[51] Eadmer, *Hist. Novorum*, 53, 80, 231, 237 (Feb. 1095; Aug. 1097; Sept. 1115; Mar. 20, 1116) ; *A.-S. Chron.* (Feb. 1123).

[52] Stubbs, *Constnl. Hist.*, I. 608; cf. Pasquet, *Essay on Origins of House of Commons*, trans. Laffan, 2, n. 1.

[53] Luchaire, *Institutions Monarchiques*, I. 253-255.

magnates could be thought of as regularly present,[54] and why the number who came to the great council could be so small, for when taken with other facts, it implies that the lesser barons were not personally called to attend.

The national assembly in becoming a body of tenants-in-chief was radically altered both in personnel and in nature. Norman magnates replaced those of English birth. Nearly all the great landholders after 1067 and practically all the bishops after 1070 were Norman, and spoke a language which the English could not understand. Prelates and magnates in the newly conquered land were dependent upon the king as no *witan* ever was dependent upon an English king. They owed their lands and dignities to the crown. The lay members were crown vassals and the bishops and abbots in practically the same position. The *curia regis* might be regarded as the national assembly, but in a real sense it was the king's own assembly. It now corresponded to the feudal *curia ducis* of Normandy.

The functions of the great council were necessarily affected by the new conditions. As might be expected, its powers suffered a decline, although detailed accounts of various events in the reigns of the Conqueror's two sons show that they were real.

Feudalism involved the loss of some functions performed by the *witan*. The granting of lands now belonged to the king in his capacity of supreme suzerain. Concerning this there was no necessity of consulting the great council, although important grants of lands and privileges continue to be witnessed by its members, and are occasionally said to be made upon advice of the barons.[55] The creation of earls was now in the king's province without the participation of his council. Nomination of bishops and archbishops seems to have remained upon the old footing, often being made by the king,

[54] Above, p. 189; also note 45.
[55] Davis, *Regesta*, nos. 26, 163; *Chron. Monast. Abingdon*, II. 109; cf. *Monasticon*, V. 12; *Bigelow, Placita Anglo-Normannica*, 15; also above, note 22.

though on numerous occasions under the Conqueror's successors with the counsel of the baronage.[56]

The great council's control over direct taxation seems to have been slight. There is no mention of assent to the levies of danegeld, which were renewed. Florence of Worcester speaks as though the first Norman levy, in 1067, was purely the king's act, and the Anglo-Saxon Chronicle frequently speaks of gelds in the same way.[57] There are instances in which the great council authorized feudal impositions. In 1096 the barons gave to William II a grant to conquer Normandy which is by one writer designated as an aid.[58] To Henry I they also conceded an aid, presumably the strictly feudal one, which he took in 1110 for the marriage of his daughter to the Emperor.[59]

The legislative phase of activity seems to have continued without much change. Certain modifications of the Conqueror's time in the law of King Edward are retrospectively mentioned as made by the counsel of his barons,[60] and his legislation separating the jurisdiction of lay and ecclesiastical courts was also ordained by their counsel.[61] Two writers who produced law codes which they attributed to the Conqueror, felt it necessary to represent that these had the consent of the great council.[62] One important piece of the Conqueror's legislation, introducing trial by combat, is enacted without mention of baronial counsel, and the same may be said of the enactment of Henry I concerning the sessions of local courts and that concerning false coinage. But enactment of legislation by the king was the regular form, as it continued to be for ages, and this creates no presumption that the barons

[56] See Liebermann, *National Assembly*, 77.

[57] Below, pp. 216-218; Stubbs (*Constnl. Hist.*, I. 618) is doubtful as to whether assent was or was not given to the levy of such imposts.

[58] Below, p. 218.

[59] Stubbs, *Constnl. Hist.*, I. 400. Below, p. 218.

[60] Coronation Charter of Henry I. sect. 13.

[61] Liebermann, *Gesetze*, I. 485; Stubbs, *Select Charters*, 85; Robertson, *Laws of English Kings*, 234-35.

[62] Above, note 20.

were not consulted. The decree concerning the coinage was indeed issued at a time and place usual for the meeting of the great council.[63]

The assembly also assumed a national aspect when it approved the succession of a new king. A series of disputed successions to the throne made formal election important. Of the four Norman kings all except William II based some claims upon election, although this might be the merest formality. The Conqueror was chosen king in 1066 by the Anglo-Saxon *witan* after his victorious military progress compelled them to withdraw support from Edgar the aetheling, previously their choice. The designation of Henry I in August 1100 was obviously made by a small group of friendly ecclesiastics and barons who happened to be in attendance, or in the neighborhood of Winchester, when Rufus was killed. The assent of the barons to the king's coronation was apparently assumed,[64] though the next year he seems to have been crowned again by their counsel. The claim of election by clergy and people was ostentatiously employed to justify the seizure of the crown by Stephen in 1135, although there was no meeting of the council, and the church and the Londoners apparently assumed the initiative. The partisans of Matilda six years later also advanced the claim of election in her interest, but only an ecclesiastical assembly was held.[65] Henry I sought, like the earlier Capetians in France, to assure the succession of his heir through designation in his lifetime. In 1116 the barons of England did homage and took the oath of fealty to his son William, the higher clergy also doing fealty and

[63] Liebermann, *Gesetze*, I. 523; Robertson, *Laws of Kings of England*, I. 284-85.

[64] There was no opportunity to assemble a great council. The archbishop of York was unable to reach London in time for the coronation (*Historians of York*, Rolls Ser., II. 107), three days after the election. Cf. Farrer, *Outline Itinerary of Henry I*, first entry. In his coronation charter of 1100 Henry claims to have been crowned with the counsel and consent of the barons, but this has been held to be fiction (Riess, in *Eng. Histor. Rev.* XLI. 327, 329).

[65] Stubbs, *Select Charters*, 120; Stubbs, *Constnl. Hist.*, I. 356. See Adams, *Council and Courts*, 102-106.

promising homage when the king should die.[66] After the death
of the young prince the magnates of the realm, in January
1127, took the oath of allegiance to his sister, the former em-
press Matilda.[67] The great council was also consulted by
Henry I concerning the matter of the king's second marriage
in 1121,[68] though not concerning the second marriage of his
daughter a decade later.[69]

The assembly appears as guardian of national liberties and
of the public welfare. The idea that it chose the king tended
to associate the great council in the popular mind with the
charters of liberties which they usually issued to gain popular
support. Liebermann believed that the relation of the barons
to the retention of the laws of King Edward in the coronation charter of 1100 stood out clearly enough to make them
appear corporately as guardians of English liberty and as
successors to the *witan*.[70] In this charter Henry I undertook
to give heiresses in marriage together with their lands by the
counsel of the barons.[71] The great council maintained the
national interest in the matter of England's relations with
Rome, and approved the more important acts by which Henry
I strove to end his differences with the papacy.[72] The king
once wrote the pope that the barons even against his personal
will would not suffer detriment to the crown.[73] Further con-

[66] Florence of Worcester, II. 69; Orderic Vital. ed. le Prevost, IV.
416; Eadmer, *Hist. Nov.*, 237. The liege homage of all freemen whosesoever vassals they might be: Malmesbury, *Gesta Regum*, II. 495. According to Orderic Vital, II. 294, the Conqueror in 1078 exacted the homage
and fealty of the Norman barons to his son Robert.

[67] Florence of Worcester, II. 84-85; William of Malmesbury, *Hist.
Nov.*, 528-29. Round, *Geoffrey de Mandeville*, 31-32. The fealty to
Matilda was renewed at her marriage in 1131 (Malmesbury, *ibid.*,
II. 534).

[68] Florence of Worcester, *continuatio*, II. 75; Orderic Vital, IV. 422;
Eadmer, *Hist. Nov.*, 290.

[69] Malmesbury, *Hist. Novella*, II. 530. Henry of Huntingdon represents
the barons as consenting to the marriage when it actually occurred in
1131.

[70] Liebermann, *National Assembly*, 84. But King Henry professes to
hold the forests as they were under the Conqueror *communi consensu
baronum meorum* (Coronation charter, sec. 10).   [71] Sec. 3:1.

[72] Florence of Worcester, 1107; Eadmer, *Hist. Nov.*, 231-234.

[73] Liebermann, *Natnl. Assembly*, 76.

sultation which is mentioned had to do with the election of an archbishop of Canterbury and an abbot of Westminster,[74] and with administrative matters such as military affairs in Normandy[75] and the custody of Rochester castle.[76]

The judicial activity of the national assembly not only continued in some respects as before the Conquest, but was enlarged because of new conditions. Even in this aspect the body might be called a council.[77] In some civil cases Anglo-Saxon charters and the custom of the past, as set forth by the testimony of Englishmen, were adduced as evidence.[78] Disputes between prelates were laid before the great council, as for instance matters at issue between Canterbury and York[79] and a cause in 1131 between two Welsh bishops.[80] One of the earliest recorded causes tried before it after the Conquest was that in which the bishop of Worcester proved by ancient charters his right to certain lands claimed by the archbishop of York.[81]

The body often acted as a feudal court. In this capacity it replaced the *witan*, using Norman procedure and Norman law. Bishop Odo in the Conqueror's time and an archbishop and a bishop, in the reign of William Rufus, were tried as feudatories.[82] It is specifically stated that Roger, earl of Hereford, for his rebellion of 1075 was sentenced to perpetual imprisonment according to the laws of Normandy[83] and certain of his fellow rebels at the assembly of the next Christmas to blinding or banishment. For his part in the rebellion of 1095, William of Eu was accused before the great council by Geoffrey

[74] Davis, *Regesta*, no. 91.
[75] In 1123, Symeon of Durham, R.S., II. 267-268.
[76] Florence of Worcester, II. 85.
[77] *Ibid.*, II. 5-6, 8.
[78] Bigelow, *Placita Anglo-Normannica*, 7, 9, 136.
[79] Malmesbury, *Gesta Pontificum*, 41; Florence of Worcester, 1116.
[80] Henry of Huntingdon, 1132. So also Bigelow, *Placita*, 136.
[81] Florence of Worcester, II. 6-8; Bigelow, *Placita Anglo-Normannica*, 2-4.
[82] William of Durham (below, p. 250) and Anselm of Canterbury (below, pp. 253-254).
[83] Orderic Vital, ed. le Prevost, II, 264; cf. Florence of Worcester, *anno* 1074.

Bagnard. The issue between the two was decided by the Norman method of trial by combat [84] with the result that William was vanquished and punished by mutilation according to Norman usage, said to have been introduced by the Conqueror.[85] High treason was an offense triable before the great council throughout the period.[86] Accounts of the assembly sitting as a feudal court show that its procedure was informal [87] and that judgment was given by the assembled prelates and barons. In this relation appears the earliest evidence of successful constitutional opposition to a Norman king. William Rufus in 1095 had Anselm, archbishop of Canterbury, arraigned on a charge of disloyalty, and the king succeeded in browbeating the bishops in the *curia*, but the barons sturdily refused to condemn Anselm,[88] and the prosecution failed.

The national assembly thus appears as a council and as a court;[89] but its judicial functions were conciliar, and there was no basic distinction. The great *curia* is to be regarded, so Liebermann has shown,[90] as a continuation of the *witan* in spite of the fact that there was change in almost every feature. The Conqueror was elected king by the *witan*, and the older membership continued to sit until they were excluded by the appointment of Norman bishops and earls and the occupation of the lands by Norman barons. Moreover, the body retained the same functions whenever these were still useful, and in time came to preserve a national tradition. The great change was effected through the introduction of feudalism, which made the assembly a body of barons and gave it the duty of apply-

[84] *Anglo-Saxon Chron.*, 1096; Florence of Worcester, II. 39.

[85] Ten Articles of William I., sec. 10.

[86] An accusation of treason was made at the Easter *curia* of 1130 (Henry of Huntingdon, R. S., 252).

[87] Adams, *Council and Courts*, chap. 2. As to procedure cf. also Bigelow, *Placita*, 83.

[88] Eadmer, *Hist. Nov.*, R. S., 53-64; but cf. Valin, *Le Duc de Normandie*, 61-63; Orderic Vital, ed. le Prevost, IV. 459-461.

[89] For the word *curia* as a judicial court, see *Chron. Monast. Abingdon*, II. 116; for the baron's *curia* and summons thereto, *Leges Henrici*, 55.

[90] *National Assembly*, 75-82.

ing Norman law, of passing feudal judgments and of dealing with feudal aids and other feudal payments.

The initiative and influence of this body are difficult to determine. The duty of the assembled barons was that of giving counsel to the king, and this implies chiefly a consideration of what he laid before them. Barons brought up their law cases for determination and accused those guilty of disloyalty to the king.[91] It was for the monarch to say when he would proceed in such cases, but for the assembly to decide the issue. The formation of a baronial interest and class spirit in England along with the doubtful claims of William II and Henry I to the throne made it inadvisable for the king to flout the wishes of the higher nobility in other matters. It was not mandatory that he seek their advice, but the decision of difficult points of policy and the enactment of legislation by their counsel gave the monarch moral support. The levy of feudal and military aids by their consent was practically involved in the feudal order of things and might even be risky unless they were consulted. In some cases the king could not carry out what he had proposed without their consent. Their advice, when offered in a matter of real concern to them, was not to be ignored.[92] Under the strong-willed Conqueror real consultation occurred,[93] and under his sons there is evidence of plain speaking.[94] Some initiative seems apparent when, at Christmas 1092, the barons take counsel about the appointment of an archbishop of Canterbury, and William Rufus, though ill-disposed, consents to their desire for public prayers in the matter.[95] Ideas of prescriptive right appear. When Henry I in 1123 called upon the assembly to choose an archbishop of Canterbury and permitted the choice of the bishops to prevail against that of other classes,[96] there was

[91] Above, pp. 195-196.
[92] Adams, *Council and Courts*, 22. McIlwain, *High Court of Parliament*, 9-10.
[93] Adams, *Council and Courts*, 39-40.
[94] Especially in accounts of trials (Eadmer, *Hist. Nov.*, Rolls Ser., 63-64; Valin, *Le Duc de Normandie*, 62. [95] Eadmer, *ibid.*, 29.
[96] *A.-S. Chron.*, 1123; Symeon of Durham, Rolls Ser., II. 268.

complaint. Because the same king permitted his daughter to be married to the count of Anjou without baronial consultation, it was argued that this violated Henry's undertaking in the matter and nullified the oath of fealty [97] the barons had taken to the king's heiress. When to baronial interest was added the weight of popular approval upon deliberation concerning matters of public welfare, the position of the assembly was correspondingly strengthened.

The *curia regis* in the wider sense of the term included much more than the king's great assemblies. The word *curia* was used with the various meanings which have attached themselves to the English word court. It had originally meant a place,[98] then a body of persons associated with this place. In Norman England it might designate the king's hall or place of residence,[99] the persons included in the king's household,[100] and the assemblies held there whether for judicial or other purposes. As applied to administration it signified the persons about the king employed in the conduct of his business. In this sense there was necessarily a permanent and not merely a periodical *curia*.

The names of those in attendance upon William I or William II from time to time show a varied and changeable court personnel. The king's administrative writs were witnessed usually by one or two attendants, who were either household officials, magnates in the king's confidence, or administrators of no official status otherwise known. His formal grants were witnessed by a larger group, consisting usually of a few bishops and nobles of high rank along with one or more

[97] William of Malmesbury, *Historia Novella*, Rolls Ser., II. 530.

[98] A courtyard or enclosure: *Domesday Book*, I. 154 b. Cf. McIlwain, *High Court of Parliament*, 29-30 and 30, n. 2.

[99] *Leges Henrici*, 80: 7a. Cf. Latin version of II Canute, 59; also *Dialogus de Scaccario*, Oxford ed., 89.

[100] *Chron. Monast. Abingdon*, II. 80; *curialis juventus:* Eadmer, *Hist. Nov.*, 48; *curiales clerici:* Orderic Vital, IV. 11; *curialibus suis:* Malmesbury, *Gesta Regum*, II. 487. The *A.-S. Chron.*, 1103, calls the great council the king's *hired* or household. Cf. Liebermann, *Natnl. Assembly*, 75. n. 6.

household officials or lesser barons attached to the king's curial service. The king employed a small educated element which included an occasional English or Norman bishop in addition to the chancellor and other priests attached to the royal chapel. The chancery afforded a training-ground for the king's clerks, and the bishops active in administration were as a rule former royal chaplains.[101] The more important household officials and other curial agents were nearly all barons of secondary rank. They represented the class to which most of the sheriffs belonged, and some of the latter were employed at court.[102] Aside from the clerks trained in the king's chapel, these rough and ready men of all work, attached to the *curia* by special ties, provided the best talent available for the usual work of government.

The activities of the great number who were employed at court are obscured by the great poverty of official nomenclature. Only the occupants of the principal offices in the king's household or his clerks are mentioned by any official designation. Ranulf Flambard managed the most important business of William II as the holder of no known post except that of chaplain.[103] One baron who served over forty years as sheriff, who was sometimes employed as a royal justice [104] and who appeared repeatedly in the king's train, is never designated by any court title.[105] Even the Conqueror's commissioners who took the Domesday Inquest were mentioned only as barons. The title of justice or judge, sometimes given to persons who rendered temporary judicial service, was still one of vague import.[106]

The king as yet had only a loosely organized routine of

---

[101] Tout, *Chaps. in Administrative History*, 16; below, p. 225.

[102] Morris, *Med. English Sheriff*, 47.

[103] Below, note 134.

[104] This is Urse d'Abetot. See Morris, *Med. Eng. Sheriff*, 46, n. 47, 48, n. 49.

[105] Once designated as *minister* (Davis, *Regesta*, no. 10), apparently meaning *thegn* or merely *baron*. Compare the *palatini* at the French court (Luchaire, *Institutions Monarchiques*, I. 196-203).

[106] Below, pp. 207-209.

government, and he himself was the centre of administration. His writs and charters were issued wherever he happened to be, in England or in Normandy. When he was absent from England he left in charge of affairs his wife, a bishop, a baron, or even two or more persons in his confidence,[107] a temporary custodianship from which gradually evolved the office of justiciar. It is impossible to say whether the changing circle of earls, bishops, household officers, barons and chaplains about the king who witnessed his grants did so as a small assembly, for this was not certainly action upon which advice was essential.[108]

The king none the less did take counsel with such groups, especially in judicial matters. He heard causes as he travelled about, and judgment was found by his barons. An instance of this, wherein Duke William and his court gave judgment between two contending communities of monks, is recorded before the conquest of England.[109] In 1080 certain monks, learning that William was at Caen, came to lay their claims before him, and he ordered the bishops and abbots present to hear the case.[110] In 1085 a suit between a baron and an abbey was decided in the king's presence in Normandy, and those who decided the cause on his behalf were two abbots, a few barons and the royal butler.[111] Similar usage appears also in England. In 1086 King William devoted a whole day to the hearing of a civil plea at a manor of William of Eu in Wiltshire, those present numbering about thirty and including fifteen persons of the highest rank and two household officials.[112] Some years earlier the king commissioned Bishop Geoffrey of Coutances to preside in his place at a famous trial

[107] Stubbs, *Constitutional History*, I. 374-375; Davis, *Regesta*, xxviii. At William's death Lanfranc was *princeps et custos Angliae* (Milo Crispin, *Vita Lanfranci*, in Migne, *Patrologia Latina*, vol. 151, p. 55).

[108] Apparently the assumption of Corbett, *Cambridge Med. Hist.*, V. 515.

[109] Round, *Calendar of Documents*, no. 1172.

[110] *Ibid.*, no. 1114.

[111] *Ibid.*, no. 116. No. 165 is a similar case.

[112] Round, *Calendar*, no. 114; Davis, *Regesta*, no. 220; Adams, *Council and Courts*, 36-37.

between the Bishop of Worcester and the Abbot of Evesham.[118] It is more than once shown that judicial matters taken up on the king's travels were decided by counsel of his barons,[114] as was done in the great council. The disposition of causes by those in attendance upon the king thus reveals a small council in action.

There are some further traces of the conciliar activity of groups ordinarily about the king.[115] Reports that William Rufus took the counsel of imprudent youths or of clever but unscrupulous persons,[116] apparently record only rumor concerning the influence of the king's private companions and others who had access to him. In the summer of 1093, however, the king, then on a journey, took the counsel of those who attended him concerning his reply to Anselm's demand for a restoration of the lands of Canterbury.[117] An assembly in which Anselm some two months later did homage to the king and received investiture was apparently not a great council, and a charter issued by the king the next day in what seems to be a second session is witnessed by only eight bishops, barons and household officials.[118] There is in this a fair presumption that the king transacted various kinds of business with the aid of a small council of barons, and that he was following a Norman practice [119] introduced in England by the Conqueror.

In Normandy administration grew out of the duke's household, and the only permanent central offices at first distin-

[113] Bigelow, *Placita Anglo-Normannica*, 17-18; Adams, *Council and Courts*, 70-78. Davis, *Regesta*, no. 423, seems to represent parallel procedure.

[114] Round, *Calendar of Documents*, nos. 165, 1190; Bigelow, *Placita*, 123; cf. above, note 25.

[115] For a discussion of this see the writer's note in *American Histor. Rev.*, XXXIV. 772-778.

[116] Henry of Huntingdon, 1100. For the king's private associates, Eadmer, 48.

[117] Eadmer, *Hist. Novorum*, Rolls Ser., 40. This and the body mentioned in note 118 can hardly both be great councils.

[118] *Ibid.*, 41; Davis, *Regesta*, no. 337.

[119] Adams (*Council and Courts*, xix-xxi, 122-123) says originally Frankish and derived in Normandy through Capetian monarchy.

guishable were those pertaining to this organization. At the French court positions which were originally menial took on dignity, and their holders became officials of state. At the Norman court, which was much influenced by French usage, the principal offices were those of the seneschal, the chamberlain, the butler and the constable. The first two of these in particular appear as important administrative officers.[120] The household of the Norman king in England followed the French and Norman plan. Since the king had to direct much Norman government from England and *vice versa*, he was often attended on either side of the Channel by household officials from the other side. The best opinion holds that the same chancellor and chancery served the two countries in common.[121]

The greater household offices were held by barons, and tended to become hereditary. Even under the first two Norman kings some were passing from father to son.[122] Their holders waited upon the king and performed duties which preserved a suggestion of the origin of their offices, but these duties had apparently become nominal and ceremonial.[123] The various offices were represented by several officials bearing the same title, and for a long time there appears to have been no attempt to designate one of these as outranking the others.[124]

The official corresponding to the Norman seneschal in England held the less important post of *dapifer*, the best Eng-

---

[120] Haskins, *Norman Institutions*, 49-51.

[121] Tout, *Chaps. in Administrative History*, 135; Haskins, *Norman Instns.*, 54. This was true also of one of the chamberlains of Henry I and of Humphrey de Bohun, the dapifer (*ibid.*, 112).

[122] Davis, *Regesta*, xxvi. William fitz Osbern succeeded his father as seneschal of Normandy (Haskins, *Norman Instns.*, 51) William de Tancarville his father Ralph as chamberlain (*Notes and Queries*, Ser. 13, I. 246). As to some of the dapifers, Davis, *Regesta*, xxiii-xxiv.

[123] A familiar story of the dapifer who served the king's meals is overthrown by Round, in *Eng. Histor. Rev.*, XXXVII. 1-34.

[124] Round, *King's Serjeants*, 64. Robert Malet was not certainly grand chamberlain until the time of Henry I (Round, *Geoffrey de Mandeville*, 180; see *Notes and Queries*, Ser. 13, I. 245).

lish translation of which is the old title sewer. He was the steward, whose function was symbolized by the ceremonial duty of placing the dish on the king's table in the banquet hall.[125] The greater part of the dapifers of William I and William II were notable barons who occupied a prominent place in the king's administrative circle.

The chamberlain was a more important official. One or two of those mentioned in the first two Norman reigns were very prominent persons.[126] The chamberlain, as in the time of King Edward, was in charge of the king's household chamber or *camera* where of old his treasure was kept. There can be little doubt that he was also the official custodian of the treasury proper, the depositary of the king's funds now located at Winchester. The treasurer mentioned was as yet an obscure person, a subordinate, of the chamberlain. An officer of the time of William II and Henry was designated as chamberlain and treasurer.[127]

The butler of the Conqueror was a prominent person,[128] but his office of itself did not often bring him in contact with general administration. The constables were notable men who performed important military functions similar to those of the old English staller.[129] The constable appears as the king's principal military official, but also as a sort of quartermaster for a travelling court. In the time of Henry I there were apparently four of these officials, three with duties at the court. The title might be used also to designate the keeper of a local castle. All the lines of constables of the Norman period were keepers of royal castles, but these offices were different from those held at court.[130] After the time of Henry

[125] Round, *King's Serjeants*, 67, 69-73. [126] Davis, *ibid.*, xxiv-xxv.
[127] Tout, *Chapters in Administrative History*, 72-81.
[128] Davis, *Regesta*, introd., p. xxvii.
[129] Larson, *King's Household*, 149-150. The marshal was probably his actual successor (*ibid.*, 199) ; see also Round, *King's Serjeants*, 76-77 ; Davis, *ibid.*, xxvi. As to other duties in the twelfth century, see *Dialogus de Scaccario*, Oxford ed., 71-72.
[130] G. H. White, *Notes and Queries*, vol. 151, p. 383. See Davis, *Regesta*, introd., p. xxvi ; *Red Book of Exchequer*, Rolls Ser., III. 812 ; *Chron. Monast. Abingdon*, II. 80.

I there is distinguishable a high constable.[131] The marshals, both in Normandy and England were obscure persons, subordinates of the constable, but closely in contact with what went on. At court they preserved order in the king's hall and kept record by tally of expenditures of his officials. A chief marshal in whose department were four lesser marshals, may be traced from the reign of Henry I.[132]

The king's chapel after the Norman Conquest evidently became a larger establishment.[133] The importance of the service rendered by chaplains is shown by the fact that of nineteen bishops consecrated during the Conqueror's reign at least seven may be identified as priests formerly attached to the royal chapel. Maurice, bishop of London, a former chaplain and chancellor, remained prominent in administration. Under the Conqueror's sons two chaplains, Ranulf Flambard and Roger of Salisbury, became the king's principal ministers. From his earlier years Flambard was attached to the chapel, nor does it seem possible to show that he ever held an office in any other department at court.[134]

The chancery, also headed by the chancellor, was not originally one of the great offices. Herfast, an early chancellor of the Norman period, had been the Conqueror's chaplain before the Conquest;[135] but Regenbald, the chancellor of Edward the Confessor, remained for a time in William's service, so in chancery personnel there was some continuity. This is dis-

---

[131] Claims of rival houses to this dignity were not yet settled (Round, *King's Serjeants*, 79-81).

[132] *Red Book of Exchequer*, III. 812. Round, *King's Serjeants*, 63, 82-84. Cf. Luchaire, *Manuel*, 526-27 ; Larson, *The King's Household*, 150 ; Haskins, *Norman Instns.*, 51, 89 ; Davis, *Regesta*, p. xxvi-xxvii.

[133] Davis, *Regesta*, nos. 22, 315. In 1068 nine chaplains beside the chancellor witness a document, under Rufus appear eleven.

[134] See Stubbs, *Constnl. Hist.*, I. 324-327. That he was the king's treasurer (Davis, *Regesta*, 318) is very doubtful. There is nothing to show that he was chancellor (Davis, *Regesta*, p. xviii). He sometimes served as one of the king's justices (*Monasticon*, II. 497), but (despite *Chron. Monast. Abingdon*, II. 39) was hardly chief justiciar in the later sense. (See below, p. 207 and note 157 ; also p. 233, note 124).

[135] Haskins, *Norman Institutions*, 52-53 ; Davis, *Regesta*, introd., p. xvi.

tinctly true of the forms followed in drawing up the king's documents. It is apparent that the old chancery forms were followed almost exactly in the English writs, which continued to be issued for a time, and ʾ. ery closely followed in translation in the businesslike judicially-worded Latin writs of all the Norman kings.[136] The use of the king's seal to attest his documents is an English usage older than 1066, but one of which there are still earlier traces in Normandy.[137] The successors of Herfast[138] were better known men, whose services practically without exception gained bishoprics for them. The chancellor disposed of some ecclesiastical patronage.[139] In the time of Henry I he became one of three great officers of state. By this time he had a special deputy at the head of the writing office who was in charge of the great seal.[140] A writer of the time of Henry I, who was in a position to know the facts, says that Flambard was custodian of the seal[141] in the chancellorship of Maurice (1083-1085), his patron.

The treasury was in the castle of Winchester. In the Conqueror's day monies received in payment of danegeld were transported thither.[142] William Rufus upon his accession distributed treasure there in memory of his father, and Henry I at his brother's death appeared before the castle to claim its

[136] See Hall, *Eng. Official Histor. Documents*, 208-226 and app. IV.

[137] Haskins, *Norman Institutions*, 53; Tout, *Chaps. in Administrative History*, I. 126.

[138] Davis (*Regesta*, introd., p. xviii) shows that the Conqueror's chancellors were: Regenbald (1067), Herfast (1068-1070), Osmund (1072-78, perhaps both earlier and later), Maurice (1083-85 and earlier), and possibly Robert Bloet (1086-87). The first chancellor of William II was Robert Bloet (*Eng. Hist. Rev.*, xxvi, 84), who became bishop of Lincoln in Feb. 1094. His successor was Gerard (Raine, *Historians of York*, II. 109, 365; Davis, *Regesta*, no. 345; *Eng. Hist. Rev.*, xxxv. 387), nephew of Walkelin, bishop of Winchester (Orderic, ed. le Prevost, IV. 12), who in 1096 was made bishop of Hereford. The third chancellor of the reign, William Giffard, remained in office until after the accession of Henry I. when he was made bishop of Winchester.

[139] Round, *Calendar of Documents*, no. 4.

[140] Tout, *Chaps. in Administrative History*, 131-132.

[141] *Historians of York*, Rolls Ser., II. 102.

[142] . . . *qui debebant geldum portare ad thesaurum regis Wintonie* (*Domesday Book*, IV. 65).

contents. There also Domesday Book was deposited.[143] The
persons mentioned as treasurers in the first two Norman reigns
were laymen, attached to the chamberlainship, and not clerks
of the chancellor's clerical staff.[144] A century later it was still
a chamberlain who issued tallies by way of receipt for public
monies paid in.[145] It may be assumed that sheriffs, as at a
later day, delivered at the treasury sums due from their
ferm and from the king's judicial income not included therein.[146] They probably handled sums received from the smaller
reliefs, although barons dealt directly.[147] A special privilege
allowed the abbot of St. Albans to collect gelds in his franchise
and bear them to the treasury.[148] Towns are sometimes recorded as making their annual render of *ferm* to the sheriff
at Easter or Michaelmas,[149] and collectors are mentioned as
accounting to the treasury for the danegeld at Easter.[150] The
treasury force included some expert laymen, for from before
the Norman Conquest [151] it had been the custom to test the
quality of coins presented by a process of melting and refining
known as blanching. Doubtless the clerks necessary to keep
treasury records were under the direction of the chancellor,[152]
but there was probably little writing to be done. Receipts
and accounts were not far above the stage at which wooden
tallies sufficed. A high clerical element, influential in adminis-

[143] Florence of Worcester, 1087; Orderic Vital, IV. 87; Round, *Feudal
England*, 142-146.

[144] Tout, *Chaps. in Administrative History*, 74-76. For the older point
of view: Stubbs, *Constnl. Hist.*, I. 382; Larson, *King's Household*, 197-
198, 199-200.

[145] *Dialogus de Scaccario*, Oxford ed., 73. The chamberlains of the exchequer were now under the treasurer (*ibid.*, 72).

[146] Cf. *Leges Edwardi Confessoris*, 15 : 4 for a possible exception.

[147] The well-known references in *Domesday Book*, I. 280b, 298b, apply
to thegns. See, however, *Dialogus de Scaccario*, Oxford ed., 151-152.

[148] *Eng. Histor. Rev.*, XXIV. 427.

[149] *Domesday Book*, II. 107, 290.

[150] Round, *Domesday Studies*, ed. Dove, I. 89-91; Ballard, *Domesday
Inquest*, 249. In King Edward's time it was collected locally half at
Christmas, half at Pentecost (*Domesday Book*, I. 56).

[151] *Dialogus de Scaccario*, Oxford ed., introd., pp. 22-23, 28-31, 32-33;
Round, *Commune of London*, 65-66.

[152] Stubbs, *Constnl. Hist.*, I. 381.

tration, apparently worked for the improvement of treasury methods. Certain bishops of Lotharingian origin, more or less attached to the English *curia* after 1079, were expert accountants skilled in the use of the abacus.[153]

In the first two Norman reigns no permanent official stands at the head of the administration of justice. It is clear that the king might designate persons to preside at trials in his place and to pronounce judgment. Under William I and Henry I the queen sometimes presided in the king's absence [154] and authorized the writs necessary to enforce judgment. In the latter reign the king's son also appears in this capacity.[155] In the reigns of the Conqueror and Rufus various regents or lieutenants of the king are found in charge of government during his absence, as for instance Bishop Odo of Bayeux and William fitz Osbern in 1067 and, according to one account, William of Warenne and Richard de Bainfaite in 1075. Later writers sometimes refer to these dignitaries of the Conqueror's time as justiciars.[156] William Rufus once sent word in regard to a judicial matter to four persons, whom he addressed as justiciars of England and who were apparently in charge of affairs during his absence.[157]

It is often difficult to distinguish between these regents who carried on the government temporarily and the royal commissioners, later known as justices, sent out by the king to try special causes. The employment of the latter was clearly a Norman usage. There are about fifteen known instances in which justice was done locally under William I by such com-

[153] Haskins, *Eng. Histor. Rev.*, XXVII. 101-106.

[154] Davis, *Regesta*, no. 155; cf. no. 161; Round, *Feudal England*, 142-143; Bigelow, *Placita*, 33.

[155] Farrer, Itinerary of Henry I., nos. 584A, 586; Bigelow, *Placita*, 33.

[156] Odo is *justitiarius et princeps totius Angliae* (Henry of Huntingdon, 1087); William and Richard, *praecipuos Angliae justitiarios . . . in regni negotiis* (Orderic Vital, II. 262). The direction of affairs in 1075 seems to have been actually in the hands of Lanfranc (Davis, *Regesta*, nos. 78-81), but possibly he was only a medium of communication (Macdonald, *Lanfranc*, 208-210).

[157] Davis, *Regesta*, no. 424; cf. no. 423, Flambard and Bishop Walkelin are said to have been regents during the king's absence in 1096 (*Annales de Wintonia*, 1096).

missioned justices.[158] In some cases they sat in a county court, but in others they pronounced a decision by the judgment of special bodies of barons.[159] It is not clear that they might as yet find judgment solely upon their own authority.[160] The court thus held at the king's order was his court, and proceedings there were said to be *in curia regis*.[161] Certain persons were employed repeatedly for such service, Geoffrey, Bishop of Coutances, both in England and in Normandy. Ranulf Flambard is mentioned in this capacity in the time of Rufus.[162] The work of taking the famous Domesday inquest in 1086 was entrusted to commissioners of this kind, some of them lay barons, some ecclesiastics. For this purpose England was divided into districts or circuits, in one of which Bishop Geoffrey and Walkelin, bishop of Winchester, acted together.[163]

For the next forty years there is occasional mention of justices who try causes locally, but no further reference to their employment in systematic fashion. Moreover, in most instances they are mentioned as disposing of but one case. King William's Domesday commissioners were called barons at the time, but in his reign the title justiciary or justice was used, and in that of Henry I it frequently occurs.[164] The two words were employed interchangeably.[165] It is the fact that this type of official was known as a justiciary or justiciar which has made it difficult to distinguish him from the chief justiciar of the kingdom. A chronicler of the reign of Henry I even calls the Domesday commissioners justiciars.[166] In this

[158] Adams, *Council and Courts*, chap. 3.

[159] Davis, *Regesta*, no. 129. For judgment by county court, Bigelow, *Placita*, 7; Davis, *Regesta*, no. 221.

[160] Adams, *Council and Courts*, 94-97.

[161] Davis, Regesta, nos. 92, 132, 423.

[162] *Monasticon*, II. 497; Davis, *Normans and Angevins*, 523.

[163] *Domesday Book*, III. p. vii.

[164] *Justitia:* Bigelow, *Placita*, 130; Henry I, London Charter, sec. 1; Morris, *Med. English Sheriff*, 102, n. 240, 243. For the *justiciarii* of the Conqueror, *Foedera* (Record Com.), 1, 2.

[165] Ramsey, *Chart., Rolls* Ser., I. 149.

[166] *Justitiarii:* Henry of Huntingdon, 1085. For use of the same word merely in the sense of justice, Bigelow *Placita*, 63; *Chron. Monast. Abingdon*, Rolls Ser., II. 116, 119.

reign Roger of Salisbury became permanent chief justiciar, and the official title capital justiciar was used both in England and in Normandy.[167] Through lack of precise designation it is impossible to say whether Richard de Lucy, justiciar in Stephen's time,[168] was an official successor of Bishop Roger or the holder of a less exalted position. Numerous persons are called justiciars in King Henry's time, some of them even justiciars of all England,[169] who can be no more than justices likely to be sent by the king to any part of the realm. In the first two Norman reigns the justices were often experienced persons who possessed higher qualifications than ordinary administrative barons. They were not so technically trained as some of the staff of the chancery or the treasury, but they mark an important trend toward expert service within the king's undifferentiated curial establishment.

AUTHORITIES

The chief sources for the Norman monarchy and *curia regis* in England are the chronicles, the royal writs and charters, and the so-called *leges*, which are private compilations.

Of the chronicles the most useful are the *Anglo-Saxon Chronicle* which was continued down to 1154; the *Historia Novorum* (Rolls Series, ed. by M. Rule, 1884) written by Eadmer, a monk of Canterbury, who was concerned primarily with the relations between Anselm and the two sons of the Conqueror; the *Chronicon* of Florence of Worcester (English Historical Soc., ed. Thorpe, 1848) who died in 1118, but whose work was continued by other writers to 1154; and two works by William of Malmesbury, the *Gesta Regum* (Rolls Ser., ed. Stubbs, 1887-1889)

[167] Rymer, *Foedera*, I. 12. This may be *capitalis justicia*, rather than *justiciarius*, but Norman usage points to the reverse. The former expression was used as late as the time of Henry II to describe the chief justiciar (*Dialogus*, Oxford ed., 67). Stubbs (*Constnl. Hist.*, I. 420-421) shows that the adjective is applied to his subordinates, but this is unofficial usage. In Stephen's time Geoffrey de Mandeville was *capitalis justitia* of Essex (Round, *De Mandeville*, 105-106). For Normandy, Valin, *Le Duc de Normandie*, 109; Haskins, *Norman Instns.*, 87, 114.
[168] Madox, *Exchequer*, I. 33, n. (r); cf. Farrer, *Early Yorkshire Charters*, I. 96-97.
[169] Stubbs, *Constnl. Hist.*, I. 377; Henry of Huntingdon, Rolls Ser., 318; *Chron. Monast. Abingdon*, II. 170. So in Stephen's reign (Farrer, *Early Yorkshire Charters*, I. 96-97).

completed with additions about 1142, and the *Gesta Pontificum* (Rolls Ser., ed. Hamilton, 1870) completed about 1125. The *Historia Anglorum* of Henry the Archdeacon of Huntingdon (Rolls Ser., ed. T. Arnold, 1879) also gives contemporary information concerning the reign of Henry I, but is not so painstaking nor accurate. Orderic Vital, a monk of St. Michel in Normandy, but a native of England, wrote in the time of Henry I a much longer work, *The Historia Ecclesiastica* (Société de l'Histoire de France, ed. A. le Prevost, 1838-1855), dealing with Norman history and adding a considerable amount of detail bearing upon English affairs. A complete list of the chronicles of the period, including the lesser ones, may be found in Charles Gross, *Sources and Literature of English History* to about 1485 (1900; 2ᵈ ed. 1915).

The royal writs and charters of the Norman period are found in many places, but there are now useful guides (see above, end of chapter viii). The *Calendar of Documents Preserved in France 919-1206* (ed. J. H. Round Rolls Series, 1899) contains a useful collection for Normandy. The king's legislation was promulgated in writ form, and such writs may be consulted in Liebermann, *Gesetze der Angelsachsen*, vol. I (1898), or in Agnes G. Robertson, *Laws of the Kings of England from Edward to Henry I* (1925). Some were reprinted also in William Stubbs, *Select Charters of English Constitutional History*. Many of the king's documents are witnessed by numbers of his household or of his baronage and afford information concerning the constitution of his *curia*. M. M. Bigelow, *Placita Anglo-Normannica* (1879), is a useful collection of writs and excerpts from chronicles bearing on judicial matters.

The so-called *leges* are occasionally useful for this subject chiefly because of the theories which they set forth. Concerning them see note at end of chapter viii.

There are numerous secondary works, some of great importance. The general account of the central government of the Norman period in William Stubbs, *Constitutional History of England*, chap. 11, though now out of date in various ways, is still very useful. The best account of the great council is that in sections 63-70 of *The National Assembly in the Anglo-Saxon Period* (1913) by Felix Liebermann. T. F. Tout presents valuable material on the lesser *curia*, the chancery and the treasury in the earlier sections of his *Chapters in Medieval Administrative History* (vol. I. 1920). George B. Adams in his *Council and Courts in Anglo-Norman England* (1926) gives a scholarly feudal interpretation of the greater and the lesser *curia* and affords much information concerning the central judiciary. There are useful comments in the various works of J. H. Round, particularly on the feudal aspect of Anglo-Norman institutions. His genealogical researches have brought out information concerning various important families and official personages of the period. His *King's Serjeants and Officers of State* (1911) is a helpful contribution toward the history of the king's official household. Some phases of the personnel of this organization have been critically treated by Geoffrey H. White, in *Notes and Queries,* Ser. 13, I. 223, 245, 263 (1923), and vol. 151, p. 381 (1926). C. H. Haskins in his *Norman Institutions* deals with the ducal household in Normandy and H. W. C. Davis in the introduction to his *Regesta Regum Anglo-Normannorum,* vol. I., with that of the royal household in England. W. A. Morris in the *American Historical Review,* XXXIV. 772-778 (1929), deals with the problem of meetings of a small council under William I and William II. Achille Luchaire in the first volume of his *Histoire des Institutions Monarchiques sous les Premiers Capetiens* (2 vols. 1883, 2ᵈ ed., 1891) gives a highly useful account of the French national assembly and also of the king's special court.

CHAPTER X

THE NORMAN ADMINISTRATIVE SYSTEM
AND THE SPECIALIZATION OF THE LESSER CURIA

The loosely organized scheme of central administration
maintained by William the Conqueror had to do largely with
military affairs and finance. The preservation of the peace
was another matter of great importance, but this fell in the
main to sheriffs and other local authorities. Sheriffs, though
royal agents of only minor importance in military affairs,
were the king's chief dependence in much fiscal, judicial,
and police routine. On the other hand, the officials at court,
aside from their household duties, might be employed in military, judicial, and general administrative business.[1] Along with
others who ranked as barons, they constituted a council and
court which was potentially permanent. As yet the really expert element at court was confined narrowly to a limited force,
including a few prelates and some chaplains and clerks. The
ordinary business of central government was nearly all entrusted to a circle of barons of second rank, the same type of
men, and sometimes the same men, who held the office of
sheriff. By the time of William Rufus there occasionally appears a professional administrator, and by the later years of
Henry I a force of curial experts had been formed, through
whose activities the work of central government assumed new
effectiveness, that of the king's court was widely extended,
and the management of the revenues vastly improved. It is
now time to examine the principal activities and the temper
of the Norman king's administration and to trace these newer
curial developments.

[1] Adams, *Council and Courts*, 10.

Feudal military service was rendered at the king's summons. The constable of William II, operating with five hundred knights in Normandy, is called his *princeps militiae*, but there is no reason to believe that he was ex officio commander in chief.[2] According to Norman usage knights were marshalled by the unit known as the *constabularia*, which seems to have included ten warriors, although the actual unit may have been only five.[3] The period of service which the knight in England rendered at his own expense is not mentioned. It was probably forty days, but it could be, and often was, extended for a longer period with payment. This is one reason why expeditions of William II and Henry I to regain and to hold Normandy fell as a heavy burden upon the nation.[4] The Conqueror in 1067 is said to have given liberal wages to the knights who had accompanied him when he first crossed to England,[5] and Henry I at his death arranged for payment to the knights then in his employ.[6] For failure to render military service due there had been a fine,[7] and by 1100 there is mentioned on church lands a payment, known as scutage,[8] taken by the king when the due quota of knights was not provided. In the time of Henry I, it was already the custom when military service was not rendered to collect scutage.[9] In Stephen's reign this was a payment levied at either a mark or a pound on the knight's fee.[10]

The expense of military administration was increased by the fact that the Norman kings not only retained the customary

[2] Orderic Vital, *Hist. Eccles.*, IV. 60; G. H. White, *Notes and Queries*, vol. 151. p. 384.

[3] Round, *Feudal England*, 259; Haskins, *Norman Institutions*, 17-19.

[4] *A.-S. Chronicle*, 1090, 1100; Henry of Huntingdon, 1100; *Chronicon Beccense*, 1098, in Migne, *Patrologia Latina*, vol. 150, p. 650.

[5] Orderic Vital, II. 167.

[6] *Ibid.*, V. 50.

[7] Round, *Feudal England*, 270; *Domesday Book*, I. 172. Cf. *Instituta Cnuti*, III. 46: *forisfacti belli quod Angli vocant ferdwite in terra omnium suorum.*

[8] *English Historical Review*, XXXVI. 45-46.

[9] Round, *Feudal England*, 268-270.

[10] Round, *Studies on the Red Book of the Exchequer*, 1-16 (or *Ancestor*. VI. 176).

force of knights beyond their regular term of service, but also employed mercenary troops. Henry I had Bretons in his pay in 1123,[11] and Stephen brought across the Channel light-armed Flemings and Bretons and knights from various countries.[12] It is told in the Anglo-Saxon Chronicle that in 1085, when William the Conqueror expected attack from Denmark, he brought from Brittany and France the largest army of horse and foot that ever came to England and quartered them upon his vassals to be supported by each according to the amount of his lands. The archers, who from the battle of Hastings appear as part of the Norman fighting force,[13] presumably served also for hire.

The custody of the king's castles was a matter of the highest importance. Castles were often committed to sheriffs for keeping, just as in Normandy they were placed in charge of *vicomtes*. In the time of William I the chief castle of the county was often constructed by the sheriff.[14] In the beginning some of the strongest royal castles were placed in charge of special custodians who were chosen from among the most powerful and the most trusted of the Conqueror's followers.[15] Castle guard both for royal and for private castles was a special form of military service imposed upon knights of given baronies.[16]

The principles of the Anglo-Saxon military system were not entirely abandoned. The ship *fyrd* as well as the land *fyrd* was occasionally employed. William the Conqueror called out the old-time naval levy against the rebels at Ely in 1071, as did William II at the time of his Norman expedition in 1091.[17] The Norman duke had power to call out the *heerban* or

[11] Symeon of Durham, Rolls Ser., II. 274.
[12] William of Malmesbury, *Hist Novella*, 540, Sym. of Durham., II. 331.
[13] As in Orderic Vital., V. 45.
[14] Morris, *Medieval English Sheriff*, 59.
[15] Orderic Vital, II. 166, 184-186.
[16] *Victoria History*, Northampton, I. 295. Cf. Corbett, *Cambridge Med. Hist.*, V. 512-513; *Pipe Roll* of 1130, 44.
[17] *A.-S. Chronicle*, 1072, 1091.

general levy of the population, and naturally retained this feature of the old English *fyrd*. Such a local force appears under a sheriff during the rebellion of 1075.[18] The Anglo-Saxon Chronicle shows that during the revolt of 1088 William II was much strengthened by English troops of this kind. The effective service of the men of the northern counties against the Scottish king in 1138 is well known. English levies were still supported by their own communities as before the Norman Conquest. This is illustrated in a famous instance in 1194 when William Rufus ordered out twenty thousand Englishmen to aid him in Normandy. When they reached the sea they were dismissed but required by Ranulf Flambard at the king's order to turn over the ten shillings each which they had brought to meet their expenses.[19]

The arbitrary temper and methods of the Norman rulers are quite apparent in matters of finance. Here the Norman genius for exaction appears at its height. This was given wider rein by the revolts of the English in the earlier years of the Conqueror and no doubt by the fear of subsequent risings. In 1070 William I is said to have appropriated the treasure deposited in the monasteries by the more well-to-do English because of the king's severity.[20] The Norman scheme of government provided no safeguard for the protection of the lower classes, and the financial demands upon them arising from military and other exactions were heavy. The English writer of the Anglo-Saxon Chronicle declared that the Conqueror and his leading men were covetous of gold and silver and cared not how it was acquired. He asserts that the king let his own lands at rent to him who would offer most and reckoned not how sinfully the reeves collected from poor men, nor how many illegal deeds they did. He accuses them also of levying unjust tolls.[21] The dues collected upon the king's lands were systematically increased. The amount of

[18] Florence of Worcester, 1074.
[19] *A.-S. Chron.* and Florence of Worcester, 1094.
[20] *A.-S. Chron.* and Florence of Worcester, 1070.
[21] *A.-S. Chron.*, 1087.

the *feorm* which the English king had collected from groups of villages on his own land was increased nearly fifty per cent during the first two decades of Norman rule.[22] If the Norman barons exploited the peasants on their lands as severely, it is not difficult to understand the rapid decline of this class. Exactions of labor for castle building [23] and other forms of public service were also burdensome.

There was much complaint of the more formal exactions laid upon the land. The chroniclers constantly tell that the kings imposed these as if they did so of their own personal initiative. Some of them were regarded as illegal. Early in 1067 King William renewed the levy of danegeld, and the tax was repeated the next year.[24] It is tempting to see in the revival of this military imposition a direct relation to the generous payment made by the king to the Norman forces that had been serving him in England. The levy was apparently regarded as a breach of faith on the part of one who had undertaken to rule as an English king. Because of it William is said to have been cursed by Archbishop Aldred who had crowned him.[25] The danegeld of 1084 amounted to six shillings a hide, treble the amount traditionally said to have been levied before the Norman Conquest.[26]

Closely related to this tax was the Domesday Inquest which the king instituted, after consultation with the great council at Christmas, 1085. The king's commissioners, called barons at the time and justices by a chronicler writing twenty-five years later,[27] visited the various counties and called upon

---

[22] Morris, *Med. English Sheriff*, 68.

[23] *Ibid.*, 90, n. 139; cf. Davis, *Regesta*, no. 354; *Ramsey Chron.*, 202.

[24] *A.-S. Chron.*, 1066 (actually done in 1067), 1067 (actually 1068). The latter was the *vectigal importabile* (Florence, 1067) identified with the geld by *Chron. Monast. de Abingdon*, I. 450.

[25] William of Malmesbury, *Gesta Pontificum*, Rolls Ser., 252-253.

[26] *A.-S. Chron.*, 1083; Florence of Worcester, 1084; *Dialogus de Scaccario*, Oxford ed., 110. The levy in Berkshire was but seven pence a hide in King Edward's time (*Domesday Book* I. 56), in Dorset a shilling (*Ibid.*, 1. 75; Liebermann, *Gesetze*, II. 345, sec. 6c).

[27] Henry of Huntingdon, 1085: *justiciarios*. For those in Worcestershire, *Domesday*, III. p. vii.

juries composed of men of the shire, of each hundred, and of
the priest, the reeve and six villains from each vill, to give
testimony regarding the extent, the holders and the value of
all lands.[28] The returns were formulated for each county
under the names of the king and his tenants-in-chief, enumer-
ation being made by hundreds of the lands held by these and
the lands held of them by their tenants. This information was
assembled in 1086 to form the famous Domesday Book, the
greatest of all witnesses to the vigor of Norman administration. The aim in all probability was the reassessment of the
geld upon a uniform basis to replace the uneven and artificial
plan which had hitherto prevailed.[29] The record was deposited
in the treasury [30] and used for reference in deciding cases involving the king's revenue. Apparently no readjustment of the
levy was made, though the writer of the Anglo-Saxon Chronicle, who regarded the assembling of the data as a shameful
thing, obviously feared increased taxation.

There is reason to believe that from the time of Canute
until about 1050 the geld was taken somewhat regularly. By
the time of Henry I it was regarded as an annual levy.
Records show that the Conqueror just before 1086 [31] collected
it almost every year, and Henry I just before 1130 yearly.
Henry of Huntingdon speaks of gelds under William II as
continuous [32] and says that Henry I collected them very frequently in the period of his expedition to Normandy, beginning in 1117. A legal work of about 1115 states that the
danegeld was an annual tax.[33] It is said that Stephen at his
accession in 1135 promised to abolish the exaction, at that
time amounting to two shillings a year on the hide.[34]

[28] *Domesday Book*, III. pp. vii-viii; Stubbs, *Sel. Charters*, 86; Florence of Worcester, 1086.
[29] Round, *Domesday Studies*, (ed. Dove) I. 110; cf. *Feudal England*,
93-96; Maitland, *Domesday Book and Beyond*, 461-470.
[30] Henry of Huntingdon, 1085; *Chron. Monast. Abingdon*, II. 116.
[31] Round, *Domesday Studies*, ed. Dove, I. 87-88.
[32] *Anno*, 1100.
[33] *Leges Henrici*, 15. Cf. *Leges Edwardi Confessoris*, 11a.
[34] Henry of Huntingdon, 1135. So *Dialogus de Scaccario*, Oxford ed.,
110.

It seems necessary to conclude that danegeld was in the main arbitrary in nature as the chroniclers imply. Payment was made in two equal installments.[35] The incidence was such that the tax fell upon the demesne lands of the barons as well as upon those held by their peasant tenants, but it was easier for the former to gain special or temporary exemption.[36] To the geld of 1106, so it is told, burghers and villains contributed.[37] The traditional amount of the levy, two shillings on the hide, was possibly the usual rate. The heaviest danegeld recorded was that taken by the Conqueror in 1084. About the middle of the reign of Henry I a well informed law writer says that the geld is a levy of a shilling on the hide, but this writer probably has in mind the rate of the semi-annual payments.[38] The payment which William II by grant of his barons received in the year 1096 to aid in the acquisition of Normandy was made, so far as church demesne lands were concerned, at the high rate of four shillings on the hide. Some chroniclers regard this as an ordinary geld, but it was also called an aid.[39]

The earliest feudal aid mentioned, that taken in 1110 for the marriage of the king's daughter, was a land tax, but was levied at the rate of three shillings on the hide, and was formally granted by the king's barons.[40] Both William II and Henry I in the course of their Norman wars demanded payments similar to the later non-feudal aids, and it is possible that a military aid was already a recognized form of exaction.[41] There is no evidence that such a grant was formally

[35] Round, *Domesday Studies*, ed. Dove, I. 89.

[36] *Ibid.*, I. 94-116; Ballard, *Domesday Inquest*, chap. 14.

[37] *Chron. Monast. de Abingdon*, II. 70. Cf. 69.

[38] *Leges Henrici*, 15; cf. *Leges Edwardi Confessoris*, 11a; Round, *Domesday Studies* (ed. Dove), I. 92.

[39] William of Malmesbury, *Gesta Pontif*, 432; cf. his *Gesta Regum*, II. 371-372; *Chron. Monast. de Abingdon*, II. 38; *Leges Edwardi Confessoris*, 11 : 2. Cf. Adams, *Council and Courts*, 41.

[40] Henry of Huntingdon, *an.* 1110; *Chron. Monast. de Abingdon*, II. 113.

[41] Ramsey *Chart.*, I. 147. But *auxilium expeditionis* may refer only to military service or to scutage. It was clearly not a geld.

made by the great council, if exception is made of the instance
in 1096. This levy appears to be the source of the complaint
in the Anglo-Saxon Chronicle that the year 1098 was a sad
one because of manifold unjust imposts. For such emergencies
the king made special demands upon the clerical estate. William Rufus in 1093 refused an offer of five hundred pounds
from Anselm when those about the king advised that the
amount should be a thousand or even two thousand.[42] On this
occasion, according to Eadmer, the king was collecting a large
sum on all sides. Subsequently, when in 1096 he asked ten
thousand marks of the realm to gain possession of Normandy,
Anselm upon the advice of two bishops attached to the *curia*
contributed two hundred.[43] It is recorded that some of the
prelates found it necessary to despoil sacred objects to meet
the royal demands.[44] A few years earlier, during the vacancy
of the archbishopric following the death of Lanfranc, the
king is said to have made annual and even monthly exactions
upon the church of Canterbury.[45] These probably represent
an early form of the tallage paid to the king by churches,
which under the name of *donum* [46] appears in the Pipe Roll
of 1130. This document shows another form of contribution,
made by boroughs, apparently in lieu of the military service
and danegeld formerly rendered,[47] and called *auxilium* or
aid, though later it also was called tallage. A similar arbitrary
exaction assessed on the lands of the county according to their
hidage, as a corrective and supplement to the danegeld, dates
from the earlier years of Henry I.[48]

The king's ordinary income, as contrasted with his special
levies, was derived from the *ferm* of the shire and the borough,

---

[42] Eadmer, *Hist. Nov.*, 43.
[43] *Ibid.*, 74-75.
[44] William of Malmesbury, *Gesta Regum*, II. 371-372; possibly because
of the heavy geld (*importabile pensionis*, *Gesta Pontif.*, 432) of this
year.
[45] William of Malmesbury, *Gesta Pontificum*, 77.
[46] Cf. Round, *Feudal England*, 275-277.
[47] Stephenson, *Eng. Histor. Rev.*, XXXIV. 457-475.
[48] Haskins, *ibid.*, XXVII. 104. This was the *communis assisa*.

the income from pleas which belonged particularly to him, tolls, profits of the coinage and feudal dues, and also from a few minor fiscal claims of Norman origin which included the rents of forests, treasure trove, and certain varieties of great fish when they were caught.[49] Wreckage of the sea, moreover, was a perquisite of both the English king and the Norman duke.[50]

The power of the monarch to do justice both as king and as feudal suzerain was turned strongly to his advantage. For disloyalty or other breach of feudal obligation the vassal might be condemned to forfeiture of his lands. These as well as other offenses might be compounded by payments. The Conqueror permitted some of the English to redeem their lands. The abbot of Peterborough, who had recognized the claims of Edgar Aetheling, gave the king forty marks for reconciliation, and William laid a heavy fine on the monks of Ely for their participation in Hereward's rebellion.[51] The Anglo-Saxon Chronicle says that the Conqueror obtained great treasure from his subjects when he could make any accusation either with justice or otherwise.[52] Under William II the king's justice was notoriously perverted to financial ends,[53] and the impleading of his subjects became a favorite device to establish fiscal claims. The very day when Anselm was installed as archbishop Ranulf Flambard, the well known agent of the royal will, instituted a plea against him.[54] Flambard is described as the procurator and the impleader of all England, who drove and supervised *gemots* throughout the realm.[55] Eadmer says that, when the death of William II was expected in 1093, the king pardoned debtors the moneys he had claimed, but upon his recovery pleas and offenses resumed their former

[49] Below, p. 233, note 130; *Dialogus de Scaccario*, Oxford ed., 129.
[50] Above, p. 132; Haskins, *Norman Institutions*, 39.
[51] *A.-S. Chron.*, 1066; *Liber Eliensis*, 246.
[52] *A.-S. Chron.* 1086.
[53] Florence of Worcester, II. 46.
[54] Eadmer, *Hist. Nov.*, R. S., 39, 41.
[55] See *A.-S. Chronicle*, 1099; Florence of Worcester, 1099. Henry of Huntingdon, 1099, adds *exactor et exustor*.

status.[56] Robert Bloet, the bishop of Lincoln, gave the king three thousand pounds for a concord in one matter.[57] Another abuse of the time is shown in the coronation charter of Henry I, which declared that, except in cases of treason or felony, a vassal of the king should no longer incur the forfeiture of all his property, but that he should henceforth pay an amercement, fixed according to the gravity of the offense. A scale of penalties, resembling that of the Anglo-Saxon period, was thus to be re-established.[58] King Henry's charter in renouncing various abuses of his brother's reign included also the pleas and debts which he had claimed. But even under the rule of Henry, called the Lion of Justice, the exactions of the courts were so general that the "very name of plea" has been declared to have become a "terror to all men." [59] Before the great days of the itinerant justices legal technicality already had its extortionate side.

The Norman kings with the exception of Stephen were famous for the firm peace which they maintained. Even the complaining English chronicler commends them for this. William the Conqueror inflicted savage punishments to enforce his forest law, and this was one of the grievances of the period.[60] Henry I meted out heavy punishment to thieves, counterfeiters and merchants who used false measures.[61] After the accession of Stephen both native knights, who hated King Henry's peace, and rapacious mercenaries [62] asserted themselves.

The great importance of the king's peace already comes into the foreground. It expired with the king's death, so Henry I could justify his hasty coronation on the ground that this

---

[56] Eadmer, *Hist. Nov.*, 31, 38.

[57] *Historians of York*, Rolls Ser., II. 106.

[58] Charter of Liberties, sec. 8. Cf. McKechnie, *Magna Carta* (1914), 285-286.

[59] Round, *Geoffrey de Mandeville*, 105. A grant of the king (British Museum, Faustina A iii, fol. 75d) exempts certain church lands from pleas and lawsuits.

[60] Henry of Huntingdon, *anno* 1087; cf. Davis, *Regesta*, no. 347.

[61] William of Malmesbury, *Gesta Regum*, II. 487.

[62] William of Malmesbury, *Hist. Novella*, 540.

was necessary to prevent disorder. At his death again there was much robbery.[63] In his coronation charter he proclaimed the establishment of a firm peace and the pardon of those who had taken property since the late king's death on condition that immediate reparation be made. A law writer of the reign shows that the king's peace assumed many forms. It ran everywhere for eight days after the king's coronation and for the same period at Christmas, Easter, and Pentecost. It prevailed always upon the four great highways of the land and on navigable waters leading to cities and boroughs. Moreover, the king might promulgate it by his hand and seal, as King Henry did in his coronation charter. He might give his peace by his writ,[64] a process which allowed its extension to protect certain places, like fairs or markets, or communities of persons or even to punish certain classes of offenses. In the enlargement of its scope the monarch found an easy means of extending the authority of the central courts to ordinary cases. The king's peace had not yet become identical with the peace of the land, but it was already the strongest influence which made for law and order.

Norman administration was moulded by its rough feudal setting. Its tone was rude and its method often harsh and violent; it was characterized by strength rather than equity and dominated by the spirit of absolutism. The king's financial necessities bore heavily upon traditional English rights, yet new exactions upon the church, the boroughs and the realm in general, became fixed features of the king's fiscal system. Justice too often presented the aspect of barter to regain favor. The new forest system and the savage forest laws were real grievances. The English peasants were oppressed by Norman lords and officials, upon whom there was no effective check. The English church in Norman hands, as will appear later, had much cause for complaint. Even the king's dealings

[63] *Historians of York*, Rolls Ser., II. 107; *A.-S. Chron.*, 1135.

[64] *Leges Edwardi Confessoris*, 12. For example, Davis, *Regesta*, no. 377; *Hist. Monast. S. Augustine Canterbury*, Rolls Ser., 358, 366; *Monasticon*, II. 501.

with his Norman tenants-in-chief, had an arbitrary side which did not disappear with King Henry's vague promise that reliefs should be just and his undertaking that his brother's abuse of the feudal incidents should not continue. As was shown above, grievances were always so heavy that a king might gain popularity and support by pledging himself to some remission.

Norman kingship, on the other hand, has to its credit, except in Stephen's time, the suppression of feudal disorder, the maintenance of a firm peace and all the other advantages of a strong central government. The Norman kings were powerful enough and able enough to found an efficient state and to devise new and direct methods of attaining administrative aims. Moreover, Henry I effected a reorganization of the institutions of central government which is of basic and lasting importance in the history of the English constitution.

The every-day work of government in the hands of the Conqueror's circle of trusty barons naturally followed more or less the primitive methods known to the feudal baronage of the continent. The small clerical element with technical training and experience was confined largely to the chancery, although an occasional bishop was active in the king's service. By the end of the reign it is clear that a few barons and bishops, attached to the *curia*, were gaining unusual skill. The formation of a curial circle, of experts, including ecclesiastics and other new men who had risen rapidly to prominence, was advanced by the Conqueror's two sons, although both continued to make use of loyal barons of the older group. Under William Rufus the employment of an occasional layman or clerk of obscure origin becomes significant.[65] Orderic Vital, who dwells upon King Henry's subjugation of rebellious members of the older nobility, says of those who took their places in the government that they were men of lowly birth raised from the dust who possessed lands and riches far be-

---

[65] Hugh of Buckland is one of the earliest laymen. See Morris, *Med. Eng. Sheriff*, 48, n. 49, 52, 56. Flambard is a notable clerk of this class.

yond those enjoyed by their fathers.[66] By 1130 the routine of government had largely passed into the hands of this new court nobility, official in nature. A *curia* largely consisting of a group of experts whose sole business was administration, acquired continuity of personnel, and was thus enabled to make rapid progress along judicial and administrative lines.

By the later years of Henry I the hereditary household offices held by the baronage had lost much of their relative importance in the work of government. With the work of the butler the student of constitutional history is hardly concerned. The marshal[67] and the constables[68] were of greater importance, but were not officials of the highest rank. The *dapifer*[69] was one of the highest dignitaries at court, but he failed to attain the importance of his earlier counterpart, the seneschal in Normandy.[70] The baronial official who in the last years of Henry I occupied the place of greatest administrative import was the chamberlain.[71] Of equal dignity with the *dapifer* and the chamberlain by 1130 were the chancellor and a new official of state, who had recently appeared, the treasurer.[72] Above these in power and influence, though not a household official, was the justiciar, now the king's chief minister of state.

The reigns of William II and his brother mark an increase in the importance of the chancery. The three chancellors of

[66] Orderic Vital, ed. le Prevost, IV. 164.

[67] John, who was chief marshal in 1130 (*Red Book of Exchequer*, III. 812), purchased from the king the office which his father had held (*Pipe Roll of 1130*, p. 18).

[68] Round, *King's Serjeants*, 79; *Notes and Queries*, vol. 151, pp. 381-384; for the constables at court, *Red Book of Exchequer*, III. 812; *Chron. Monast. Abingdon*, II. 80.

[69] In 1091 are named five (Davis, *Regesta*, no. 315), probably one of these for Normandy.

[70] In the time of Henry I Humphrey de Bohun held the office for both countries (Haskins, *Norman Institutions*, 113).

[71] Robert Malet may possibly have been great chamberlain in the reign of William Rufus (Round, *Geoffrey de Mandeville*, 180; but cf. Tout, *Chaps. in Administrative History*, I. 91; also *Red Book of Exchequer*, III. 811).

[72] *Red Book, ibid.*

Rufus [73] were all notable clerks [74] who became bishops, one ultimately an archbishop. The chancellors of Henry I were chaplains of more obscure origin, but apparently very active in general administration. Circumstances illustrate the importance of these persons, whose office by 1130 stood in the front rank at court. William Giffard was in 1101 made bishop of Winchester. Roger, his successor, in 1103 was given the see of Salisbury and subsequently the office of chief justiciar of England. Waldric, the next chancellor, took Duke Robert of Normandy prisoner at Tinchebrai,[75] and later became bishop of Laon. The next chancellor, Ralph, in the office from 1107 to 1122, was a great personage, who formed court connections and was closely enough associated with the administration of justice to be denounced as an oppressor.[76] His successor, Geoffrey Rufus, paid a large sum for the custody of the seal,[77] and, unlike the Norman chancellors who preceded him, seems to have retained that office after becoming a bishop.[78]

Some of the chancellor's subordinates of the time of Henry I were also persons of consequence in administration. Two chaplains, first Richard and then Robert, were in turn keepers of the king's seal [79] and masters of his *scriptorium* or writing office.[80] The former was promoted to a bishopric. Certain of the other chaplains stood high in favor during the reigns of the Conqueror's two sons. Ranulf Flambard [81] and Roger of Salisbury are the two best known examples, but Thurstin,

[73] Above, p. 235, note 138.
[74] Gerard was a nephew of bishop Walkelin (above, *ibid.*), William Giffard of Eudo the *dapifer*.
[75] Round, *Feudal England*, 480-481.
[76] Florence of Worcester, II. 77; Henry of Huntingdon, 1123. See Round, *Feudal England*, 485; Orderic Vital, II. 436.
[77] *Pipe Roll of 1130*, p. 140. Cf. *Annals of Margan*, R. S., p. 11.
[78] G. H. White, *Notes and Queries*, vol. 151; p. 382. Farrer, *Itinerary*, no. 698, shows him as bishop-elect and chancellor. Cf. Sym. of Durham, II. 285; Henry of Huntingdon, 253.
[79] Eadmer, *Hist. Nov.*, 290; Malmesbury, *Gesta Pontificum*, R. S., 304; Florence of Worcester, 1121.
[80] *Constitutio Domus Regis, Red Book of Exchequer*, III. 807.
[81] For his early life, Orderic Vital, III. 310-311.

created archbishop of York in 1114, is another.[82] Orderic Vital [83] in a well known passage complains that Rufus conferred ecclesiastical honor upon curial clerks like pay upon mercenaries.

To the chamberlain's office, at least until the later years of Henry I, pertained not only the control of the king's *camera*, as in the past, but also the direction of the royal treasury which was located at Winchester. There was a master chamberlain early in the reign, but the office seems to have been in abeyance prior to 1133 when it was conferred upon Aubrey de Vere.[84] The administration of the treasury was in the hands of sub-chamberlains.[85] At some time not long before 1130 the office of treasurer was separated from that of chamberlain, and the former was placed over the treasury.[86] The first known treasurer of England, William of Pont de l'Arche,[87] was one of the newer men and had been employed by Henry I for many years both in a curial capacity and in that of sheriff. The office of *camera curiae*, a special treasury of the household which also received and disbursed funds, continued to be headed by a chamberlain.[88]

More important still in the history of administrative development is the appearance of the office of capital justiciar. Bishop Roger of Salisbury, who held this position, not only stood next to the king, administering England in his absence,[89] like the temporary justiciars of an earlier period, but he was in charge of justice whether the king was in England or in Normandy.[90] He was distinguished from other justiciars by the

[82] Raine, *Historians of York*, II. 129.   [83] Orderic Vital, IV. 11.
[84] Farrer, *Itinerary of Henry I*, no. 698. Above, note 71.
[85] Cf. Malmesbury, *Gesta Regum*, II. 488; below, p. 239.
[86] G. H. White, *Trans. Royal Histor. Soc.*, 4th Ser., VIII. 56-59; but cf. Tout, *Chapters in Administrative Hist.*, I. 85-87.
[87] G. H. White, *Trans. Royal Histor. Soc.*, 4th Ser., VIII. 67-72.
[88] *Red Book of Exchequer*, III. 811. The marshal was employed there regularly, the treasurer occasionally (*ibid.*, 812).
[89] Malmesbury, *Gesta Regum*, II. 483. Henry of Huntingdon, 1123: justiciar of all England and *secundus a rege*.
[90] . . . *agebat causas, ipse moderabitur expensas, ipse servabat gazas; hoc quando rex erat in Anglia, hoc sine socio et teste quando . . . morabatur Normanniae* (Malmesbury, *Hist. Novella*, Rolls Ser., 558).

fact that he was above all judges. He was also occupied with financial administration. According to one writer,[91] the whole business of the realm in the days of King Henry was subject to his decision. The Anglo-Saxon Chronicle, after showing that in 1123 he controlled the election of an archbishop of Canterbury, adds that he was strong and ruled all England. As a former chaplain and chancellor he was thoroughly trained in the business of the *curia*, and he gathered about him a family group which long perpetuated its tradition. For one nephew, Alexander by name, he procured the see of Lincoln. Another, Nigel or Neel, who in 1133 became bishop of Ely, appears in 1130 as one of the officials in charge of the treasury of Normandy, and from the beginning of Stephen's reign as treasurer in England.[92] Roger's son, Roger the Poor, was chancellor in the earlier years of Stephen's reign.[93] The Bishop of Salisbury was the great figure in the administrative reorganization under Henry I. His family continued this control into the next reign, and in some respects much later.

In addition to these able men King Henry employed at court other active administrators, some of whom are especially well known on account of their judicial work. Geoffrey de Clinton, apparently a chamberlain, was one of the prominent royal justices. Ralph Basset and his son Richard are even better known in this capacity. Aubrey de Vere, unlike the others a descendant of a Domesday baron, was at the same time an administrator, a sheriff, and a man of consequence in judicial affairs.[94] Here as elsewhere the main responsibility for business had fallen chiefly to the new men who owed everything to the king's favor and their own exertions.

[91] Symeon of Durham, R. S., II. 302. As to his activity, especially at the exchequer, *Dialogus de Scaccario*, 90-91.

[92] Malmesbury, *Hist. Novella*, 558; G. H. White, *Trans. Royal Histor. Soc.*, 4th ser., VIII. 68-70.

[93] Henry of Huntingdon, 1130; Florence of Worcester, II. 108; another chancellor, Philip, was in 1140 made bishop of Salisbury (*Ann. Mon.*, II. 228), when he was succeeded by Robert of Ghent (*Historians of York*, Rolls Ser., II, 225).

[94] For some of these persons, Morris, *Medieval English Sheriff*, 84-87.

King Henry's was a government both of skilled officials and of dignified counsels.[95] Counsellors are mentioned, but these may have been consulted privately, and the title cannot as yet be shown to have official significance.[96] Orderic Vital contrasts King Henry with his predecessor by declaring that he sagaciously embraced the advice of *witan* like Robert count of Meulan, Hugh earl of Chester, Richard de Redvers, Roger Bigot and other strong men.[97] Florence of Worcester names seven counsellors of the king who died in 1107, several of whom appear as members of the permanent administrative circle.[98] The most influential of the king's counsellors until 1118 was Robert Count of Meulan.[99] So powerful was the opposition of Robert and his associates to the papal claims in regard to investiture, that the pope in 1105 threatened special action against them.[100] It seems fairly clear that some, if not all, of the so-called counsellors were actually included in the king's small council.

That King Henry was in the habit of taking the counsel of the persons in attendance upon him there is abundant evidence. Some household officials and other administrators of the *curia* accompanied him on his travels, and the names of the older nobility, who also witness his documents,[101] show that stronger baronial sanction was often at hand. It is not safe to assume that every charter or notification thus attested represents collective advice,[102] but it is clear that some were authorized in council.[103] The changeable groups about the king

[95] See Liebermann, *National Assembly*, 78, n. 14.
[96] Baldwin, *The King's Council*, 11: *consiliarii or consiliatores*.
[97] Orderic Vital, IV. 95.
[98] Bishop Maurice was former chancellor and Roger Bigod *dapifer*. Robert fitz Haimo and Richard de Redvers often appear at court, and Milo Crispin was a prominent baron.
[99] Orderic Vital, IV. 168.
[100] Eadmer, *Historia Novorum*, 163; Migne, *Patrologia Latina*, vol. 163. p. 156.   [101] As in Farrer, *Outline Itinerary*, no. 635.
[102] About a dozen persons witness a document issued in the king's park at Woodstock (*Chron. Monast. Abingdon*, II. 65).
[103] *Monasticon*, V. 12; Farrer, nos. 51, 53. No. 660 is in a great council. One grant (*Monasticon*, I. 242) of King Henry was in the council of the whole realm.

cannot be regarded as having continuous organization, yet in effect they constituted a permanent body which might be consulted at pleasure. Either the household or the purely baronial element might predominate, but usually it seems to have been the former.[104] A charter conferred by the king quite late in his reign and said to have been read before his barons, bears the names merely of fourteen of the king's administrators. Fifteen of these some two decades earlier found a judgment in the king's *curia* at Winchester.[105] That this, like the great council, was considered a baronial assembly appears not only in the fact that those present were called barons,[106] but also in the fact that judicial work begun in the larger body might be completed in the smaller.[107] Moreover, the members of the exchequer, a specialized form of the small council which met periodically to supervise collection of the king's revenues, were also known as barons.

The small council not only found judgment, supervised the king's revenues, and concurred in the issue of some of the king's grants, but it also gave advice concerning policy and executive action. King Henry was advised early in his reign to imprison Flambard [108] and to seek an interview with Anselm regarding the investiture issue.[109] Now, as well as later, the king might lay before the small council the same kind of business that came before the larger. It is probable that Henry I made various administrative and legal regulations in this way, though his right thus to enact permanent legislation seems not to have been admitted,[110] nor does that to levy new taxes in such fashion seem to have been assumed. The king

---

[104] As in *Chron. Monast. Abingdon*, II. 164-165. Cf. *Eng. Histor. Rev.*, XXXI. 487. Yet a ratification issued to Hyde Abbey (British Museum, Domitian A xiv. fol. 22) was witnessed by two archbishops, six bishops, and two earls.

[105] *Chron. Monast. Abingdon*, II. 116, 164-165.

[106] *Coram baronibus meis ad scaccarium* British Museum, Faustina A 111, fol. 74d; *Chron. Monast. Abingdon*, II. 134.

[107] Adams, *Council and Courts*, 123-124.

[108] *A.-S. Chron.*, anno 1100.

[109] Eadmer, *Hist. Nov.*, Rolls Ser., 165: *inito igitur cum suis consilio.*

[110] Adams, *Council and Courts*, 118-120.

recognized no theoretical distinction between the assembly of great magnates, called together three or more times a year to afford him counsel, and the smaller group of officials, ecclesiastics and other barons who chanced to be with him from time to time. For all but exceptionally important business he might employ the latter in place of the former body. The eleven bishops, earls, barons, and household officials, whose names appear as witnesses to the king's coronation charter,[111] to all intents and purposes stand in place of a great council. The group which chose Henry king at Winchester, when Rufus was killed three days earlier, must have been even smaller. Actually there was somewhat of a fiction in the assumption that the small council afforded the same baronial counsel as the national assembly, for the former was usually dominated by the men attached to the king's service who represented his administrative interest.[112]

The lesser council has been regarded as a permanent governing board. There is much to support this viewpoint, but its function was deliberative and not executive.[113] Liebermann holds that a sort of administrative revolution [114] was introduced by its taking over business from the great council. This parallels a contemporary development at the French court. A careful scholar has been able to find listed for the reign of Henry I an average of less than one session a year, which was certainly that of the national assembly.[115] A body meeting even much oftener could hardly attend to all matters which required counsel or judgment, and many of these naturally fell to the lesser council. Although this body, was not new, yet an appreciable part of its business was, for much of its work as an exchequer and as a law court represents a real growth of administration. Out of this undifferenti-

[111] See Robertson, *Laws of Kings of England*, 282 and notes.
[112] See Tout, *Chaps. in Administrative History*, I. 10-11. It is probable that the deliberation of the smaller body was more secret than that of the larger. See Malmesbury, *Gesta Regum*, II. 360, 483.
[113] Tout, *ibid.*, I. 11.
[114] Liebermann, *National Assembly*, 78.
[115] Adams, *Council and Courts*, 121-122.

ated type of *curia* in course of time the king's council, his courts and his exchequer took permanent form.

This institutional differentiation appears in the reign of Henry I in two directions, namely in the work of the itinerant justices and in that of the exchequer. With the Norman period in England the king assumes a direct responsibility for the rendition of justice. The king's duty to do justice to his vassal by the judgment of his peers was acquitted in the greater or the lesser *curia*, and in either case, whatever the minor exceptions, the court consisted officially of the king's barons. But the conception of the king as fountain of justice came to rest on a still broader basis. The old English king, like the Norman duke, bore a special responsibility with respect to his justice where it concerned the maintenance of his peace and the punishment of crime. The Conqueror asserted his authority in such matters through an enactment which prescribed that the Frenchman should have the right to be tried by duel. Henry I in his earlier years enacted some new penalties for offenses,[116] but as late as the middle of the reign pleas of the crown were handled so largely by the county courts as to gain for these the name of the king's county courts. From this time on, however, King Henry is found asserting for his own *curia* direct jurisdiction over breaches of his peace, offenses which directly involved the king's orders, and matters affecting his fiscal interest.[117] The existence of a body of pleas of the crown, the income from which accrued to the king over and above that farmed by the sheriff,[118] naturally called for unusual care with respect to their trial and the accounting for the sums which it produced. When the king's court came to dispose of these pleas of the crown, either in a central *curia* or in a local session, held by the king's justices, the monarch became in effect a fountain of justice for the whole realm. This was an important step in

[116] Cf. Liebermann, *Gesetze*, I. 483-485, 523, 524 (3 : 2-3).

[117] Theft by 1124 (*A.-S. Chron.*), offenses of moneyers, 1125 (below, p. 232), other offenses and interests of the king still earlier (below, p. 234).

[118] See *Leges Henrici*, 10 : 1-4; also *Domesday Book*, I. 172.

a process which ultimately caused all justice to be regarded as the king's and as done in his name.

In all probability the king's officials were beginning in the reign of William Rufus to deal directly with pleas of the crown, heretofore disposed of by the officials of the shire and the hundred. The activities of Flambard the impleader, the complaint that offenders bought off the king,[119] and the fact that considerable sums of money were due the king because of pleas and offenses, all indicate that Rufus, like his successor, may have found it advantageous to have matters which concerned him tried before his own justices.[120] The Anglo-Saxon Chronicle first brings the trend to light, however, only as late as 1124 when Ralph Basset, a prominent justice of the king, was sent to Leicestershire to hold an assize, the result of which was the execution of forty-four thieves in one day. The next year the chief justiciar brought to Winchester the false coiners of the realm to receive for their offense the grave punishment which the royal enactment had already provided.[121] Before 1130, as the Pipe Roll of that year shows, itinerant justices were extending widely throughout the realm the judicial activities of the king's *curia*.

This development, so far as the extremely scanty evidence permits one to trace it, belongs primarily to the reign of Henry I. William the Conqueror frequently sent one or more of his justices to try a cause in a court held locally, but existing reports deal only with civil cases and fail to show that these agents regularly disposed of more than one matter under each commission.[122] The Domesday commissioners received many inquests; royal commissioners are mentioned once as trying pleas in East Anglia at some time between 1076 and

[119] Florence of Worcester, II. 46; William of Malmesbury, *Gesta Regum*, II. 369.

[120] Below, pp. 234-235. The existence of the local justice (notes 125, 127) shows this trend.

[121] Liebermann, *Gesetze*, I. 523. As to the case cf. *Ann. de Winton*, Rolls Ser., 47; William of Jumièges, bk. VIII. chap. 23.

[122] Adams, *Council and Courts*, chap. 3. So apparently in the early years of Henry I: *Ramsey Chart.*, II. 59.

1079 and again under Rufus in 1095;[123] but these seem to
be exceptions. In the reign of Rufus, despite the well known
activity of Flambard in judicial matters, there has been dis-
closed only a second occasion, in 1096, when itinerant justices
are said to try the king's pleas.[124] There is nothing here to
indicate that such justices were trying many pleas locally
or that the royal courts had to do directly with the enforcement of the peace.

A significant factor in the situation, first traceable in the
reign of Rufus, was the presence of a royal justice resident
within the shire.[125] Reference to so peculiar an official has led
to the suggestion that he was the sheriff,[126] but the existence
of a resident justice, other than the sheriff is well established
for the time of Henry I, both in England [127] and in Normandy.[128] At some time before 1102 the justice in Norfolk
and Suffolk is known to have sat with the sheriff to try a
royal plea.[129] According to the so-called Leges Henrici either
the sheriff or the justice had jurisdiction over theft, robbery,
arson and other crimes.[130] In his charter to London, Henry
I conferred upon its citizens the right to elect their own
justice, who to the exclusion of all other persons, even sheriffs,
was to hold the pleas of the crown.[131] A charter of Matilda
in 1141 made Geoffrey de Mandeville justice of the pleas and

[123] Miracula S. Edmundi, ed. Liebermann, secs. 42, 62; Round, Feudal
England, 329; Davis, England under Normans and Angevins, app. II.

[124] Monasticon, II. 497; Bigelow, Placita, 69. Flambard was present
when a local plea was held (Chron. Monast. de Abingdon, II. 39) and
was once among the four justiciars who acted in the king's absence
(Davis, Regesta, no. 424).

[125] Page, London, 203; Davis, England under Normans and Angevins,
app. ii; Morris, Med. Eng. Sheriff, 103; below, n. 129.

[126] Stubbs, Constnl. Hist., I. 420, note 1; Liebermann, Leges Edwardi
Confessoris, 73.

[127] Monasticon, II. 501; cf. Round, Geoffrey de Mandeville, 110, 373;
Morris, Med. Eng. Sheriff, 102-103.

[128] Haskins, Norman Instns., 100.

[129] To decide the king's right to a certain great fish (Ramsey Chron.,
267; Ramsey Chartulary, I. 149). Ralph Passelewe was justice here as
early as the time of William II (Ramsey Chron., 211, no. 188).

[130] Leges Henrici, 66. 9. Cf. 52. 1; Ramsey Cart., I. 241.

[131] Liebermann, Gesetze, I. 524-525; Stubbs, Select Charters, 108.

forfeitures in Essex pertaining to the crown. Stephen a few months later conferred upon him the same office in two other counties.[132] This type of local justice appears still later even in the reign of Henry II.[133] His known functions correspond to those of the later coroner.[134] His action, more than that of an occasional visiting justice who tried pleas, seems to have constituted the actual groundwork for the judicial circuits of 1130. It is altogether probable that his office arose through the efforts of Rufus and Flambard to enforce the king's fiscal claims and to augment his judicial income.

The development of judicial circuits under Henry I seems to have been the work of Roger of Salisbury. In 1116 one of the king's justices held pleas at Huntingdon, among them one touching an offense against the crown.[135] The fact that a *curia regis* lawyer, author of the *Leges Henrici*, in or a little before 1118, made a list of the pleas of the crown [136] and the rights which accrued to the king therefrom, is significant in this respect. Round has found itinerant justices holding pleas in Devonshire and Cornwall well before 1130.[137] The Pipe Roll of 1130 shows that in this year and the years immediately preceding justices had held pleas in nearly every English county, and their names show that they were experienced members of the king's *curia*. Although practically nothing is said concerning the kinds of cases tried, there is evidence that they dealt with treasure trove, breach of the peace, falsification of the coinage and forest offenses.[138] Ralph Basset's as-

---

[132] Round, *Geoffrey de Mandeville*, 92, 109-110, 141-142, 166.

[133] D. M. Stenton, *Cambridge Med. Hist.*, V. 584.

[134] He seems to have inquired into crime (Morris, *Med. English Sheriff*, 102) ; he kept the pleas of the crown in London according to the charter of Henry I (sec. 1) ; and he held these pleas, as the coroner might do until 1215.

[135] The concealment of treasure trove. See Farrer, *Outline Itinerary*, no. 370; Orderic Vital, *Hist. Eccles.*, ed. le Prevost, III, 126.

[136] *Leges Henrici*, 10 : 1-4.

[137] *Eng. Histor. Rev.*, xiv. 420-421.

[138] *Pipe Roll of 1130*, pp. 13, 18, 32, 47, 57, 91, 97, 112 113. For a list of forest pleas see *Leges Henrici* 17 : 2; for the pleas of the crown, *ibid.*, 10 : 1-4.

size of 1124 in Leicestershire so startled the writer of the
Anglo-Saxon Chronicle that it may be regarded as one of the
first for the punishment of crime upon a large scale. These
justices apparently called the reeve and four men of each
vill to assist them. At any rate a writ of Henry I alludes to a
current usage by which four men from each wapentake were
being summoned to the king's pleas and to his [139] sessions
of the county court.

That the itinerant justices of the latter half of the twelfth
century were fiscal as well as judicial officials has long been
established. There is nothing to show that under Norman
kings they assessed tallages [140] as they did in the time of
Henry II,[141] yet the information which they possessed concerning sums imposed before them, and sums promised the
king [142] for one reason or another, was clearly of great assistance to the exchequer authorities when the sheriffs were
summoned to give an accounting concerning these matters. The
itinerant justices might be regarded thus as agents of the exchequer. Their visits to the shire reduced both the judicial
and the fiscal independence of the sheriff and furthered the
process, apparently begun by the resident justice, of placing
him under control.

The exchequer was a second permanent branch of the
lesser *curia* which appeared in the reign of Henry I. It combined two functions which originally may have been distinct.
It was a board of accountancy and at the same time a royal
court for the king's revenue cases. In the former of these capacities it represented an outgrowth of the work of a receipt
department in which the chamberlain's officials issued notched

[139] *Monasticon*, VI. part 3, 1272, no. 20. Here two men from a half
wapentake. The usage is older than 1123. For a similar use of men of the
vill, above, p. 170.

[140] Mentioned by that name under William Rufus (*Eng. Histor. Review*, XXXVI. 45-46).

[141] Stubbs, *Benedictus*, II, preface, lxx, shows that Henry II held some
eyres that were purely fiscal.

[142] *Conventiones*. For a list of instances, see Bigelow, *Placita Anglo-
Normannica*, 140-142.

wooden tallies as vouchers for amounts paid in.[143] At some time before 1110,[144] and probably after 1080,[145] an adapted form of the abacus came to be employed in the work of computation. This employed columns or spaces ruled off across a table to represent such units of value as pence, shillings, pounds, and twenty pounds.[146] When counters or pawns were arranged in the proper spaces on one side of the table to show the amount claimed by the king's officials and another set on the opposite side to represent the credits to be allowed, as indicated by the tallies produced, the general effect was that of a game between the king's officials and the king's debtor. The Latin name *scaccarium*, originally that of a chessboard,[147] was used to denote the exchequer board or table, and through the French form of this comes the word exchequer.

The work of accounting at first seems to have been in the hands of treasury officials who received monies and issued receipt tallies, but the receipt office of the treasury remained merely an office.[148] By or before 1110 there was superimposed upon it an accounting board, the members of which sat about the exchequer table, imparted to their findings concerning amounts paid or payable the effect of a judicial decision, and employed judicial procedure to enforce collection of debts due the king. The recording of exchequer accounts, as opposed to mere preservation of duplicate tallies or counterfoils, has been traced as early as about 1116.[149] Later

---

[143] *Taleas quoque de eadem recepta a camerariis factis (Dialogus de scaccario*, Oxford ed., 62). The place of meeting was said to be at the tallies (*ad taleas*) before it was named for the exchequer board (*ibid.*, 60). The use of the tally is mentioned in Normandy (Round, *Cal. of Docs.*, France, no. 426). For the making of tallies in the time of Henry II, see *Dialogus*, Oxford ed., 74-75.

[144] Below, p. 237.

[145] Haskins, *Eng. Histor. Review*, XXVII. 105-106. Cf. Poole, *Exchequer*, 42-57; Round, *Commune of London*, 63-64.

[146] *Dialogus de Scaccario*, Oxford ed., 38-42.

[147] *Nulla mihi verior ad presens occurrit quam quia scaccarii lusilis similem formam habet (ibid.*, p. 60).

[148] As in *ibid.*, pp. 61-62.

[149] Poole, *Exchequer in Twelfth Century*, 37-38.

there appears a great roll of the exchequer,[150] prepared annually to show the state of accounts as they stood when the fiscal year closed. This record, which came to be known as the Pipe Roll, throws welcome light upon the finances of the medieval English kings. But one of these rolls for the reign of Henry I has survived, the Pipe Roll of the year 1130. This document follows stereotyped terms and methods which had obviously been in vogue for some years.

The establishment of the judicial side of exchequer activity has been attributed, naturally enough, to Roger of Salisbury, but it probably came previous to his justiciarship.[151] To be sure, a deputation to some representative of the king of due authority, like that of the justiciar, was important to the holding of the king's judicial sessions at fixed intervals. Moreover, trials other than those of revenue cases, were also held before the barons of the exchequer,[152] who constituted one form of small *curia regis*. This organization, nevertheless, must have been effected earlier than has been supposed. There was a meeting at a place called the tallies, so it is related,[153] before the name exchequer was used, yet a writ of the year 1110 was addressed by the king to the barons of the exchequer, ordering them to exempt the lands of a church from contributing to a feudal aid.[154] The judicial powers of these barons were well known in the latter years of King Henry's reign. The Pipe Roll of 1130 shows the exchequer remitting a certain sum collected and also imposing a penalty upon the sheriff who carelessly attended to the king's fiscal affairs.[155] The latter circumstance affords explanation of the fact that sheriffs well before 1125 are repre-

---

[150] The *rotulus annalis* (*Dialogus de Scaccario*, Oxford ed., 104).

[151] Roger's grandnephew does not claim that he originated the body, but merely that he was assigned for duty there by the king (*Dialogus de Scaccario*, Oxford ed., 90).

[152] Bigelow, *Placita Anglo-Normannica*, 127; Poole, *Exchequer*, 39, n. 4.

[153] *Dialogus de Scaccario*, Oxford ed., 60.

[154] *Registrum Antiquissimum*, Lincoln Cathedral, f. 5, no. 32; Farrer, *Itinerary of Henry I*, no. 256a (*Eng. Histor. Rev.*, XXXIV, 578).

[155] *Pipe Roll*, 31, Henry I, pp. 2, 96; cf. *forisfactura scaccarii*, p. 91.

sented as coming up to the exchequer with trepidation.[156]
It was holding them for their collections, their accounts and
their administration of the royal estates. A royal charter in
1131 mentions the particular form of justice which this body
enforced in collecting the king's *ferm*.[157] The exchequer was
already known as a *curia regis* which followed peculiar
methods.

In the time of Henry I this body almost certainly assembled twice a year as it did later. One session is known
to have been held at Michaelmas,[158] which was the end of
the fiscal year. On this occasion the sheriffs and other officials
paid what was still due from their *ferms* for the year, and the
great roll which showed the state of the annual revenues
was made up.[159] Another, and less important session was apparently held at Easter, which in the time of the Conqueror
had been the date for the final accounting of collectors of
danegeld and for partial payment of the *ferms*.[160] Some of the
king's revenues were due at this time, but accounts were due
in full at Michaelmas. Since Easter was the date when the
king regularly assembled the great council each year at
Winchester, the seat of the treasury, this was a favorable
time to hold a special meeting for fiscal business after the
large assembly broke up.[161] It is striking that the most important session of the exchequer was not held at this season
but at Michaelmas, when the king was usually on his travels
with his court. If Bishop Roger can not be designated as

[156] Round, *Commune of London*, 123. A form of summons was already
used (*Dialogus de Scaccario*, Oxford ed., 114. Cf. p. 113).
[157] Round, *Calendar of Documents*, France, nos. 1387, 1389.
[158] Round, *Calendar of Documents*, no. 1387; cf. *Domesday Book*, II.
290b. Michaelmas is September 29.
[159] *Pipe Roll*, 31, Henry I, ed. Hunter, introd., pp. xv-xviii; cf. Round,
Calendar, no. 1052.
[160] Rymer, *Foedera*, I. 12; Round in *Domesday Studies*, ed. Dove, I.
91-92; *Domesday Book*, II. 107.
[161] The geld rolls of 1086 were probably compiled by just such a body
after Easter (Round, in *Domesday Studies*, I. 91). The exchequer, however, was not as yet stationary at Winchester (Tout, *Chaps. in Administrative Hist.*, I. 96, 97).

the founder of the exchequer, at any rate he directed its
activities [162] and must have had an important part in its
development.

Concerning the personnel of the exchequer in the time of
Henry I there is little definite information, but the justiciar
presided over its deliberations, and the chancellor was regularly a member.[163] The presence of the chamberlains of the
treasury and also of the treasurer, when this official appears in
the later years of Henry I,[164] was no doubt essential as at
a later day, since these were the custodians of the king's
treasure, who gave receipts for funds and had knowledge of
disbursements. Both the treasurer and the chamberlain attended the Norman exchequer of the time,[165] as did the constable and the marshal. The two last named officials performed important functions touching the expenditure of funds
in the king's household.[166] Thus all the household officials
who regularly sat as barons of the exchequer in the time
of Henry II [167] seem to have been essential in the reign of
Henry I. These officials were reinforced by other barons, as
was usual in the small council.[168] The exchequer, however,
differed from other forms of the lesser *curia* because the
predominance of the official element was essential, and also
because the sessions were at regular intervals and the nature
of the main business was fixed.

[162] He is said to have sat each year at the exchequer which flourished
sub eo. With the king's consent he changed one of the methods employed
(*Dialogus de Scaccario*, Oxford ed., 90-91).

[163] *Pipe Roll*, 31, Henry I, 140; cf. Farrer, *Itinerary of Henry I*,
no. 681.

[164] William of Pont de l'Arche in 1130 held both the office of treasurer
and one of the chamberlainships of the treasury besides (G. H. White,
in *Trans. Royal Histor. Soc.*, 4th ser., VIII. 67-71).

[165] Round, *Eng. Histor. Rev.*, XIV. 426; Haskins, *Norman Instns.*,
88-90.

[166] The marshal kept tallies to show household disbursements both from
the treasury and the *camera*. (*Red Book of Exchequer*, III. 812). The
constable had to do with military expenditures (below, p. 329).

[167] See below, pp. 323-24. W. J. Corbett assumes (*Cambridge Med.
Hist.*, V. 523-524) the same attendance under Henry I.

[168] In 1128 the Earl of Gloucester and Brian fitz Count heard the treasury account at Winchester (Pipe Roll, 31 Henry I. 130, 131).

The exchequer was important because of its effective procedure in collecting moneys due the king. It was strong enough to make sheriffs afraid of its power and to reduce them to a strict accountability. Barons were subject to its authority. Its judicial power was constantly asserted and felt in all counties except the palatinates, at a time when this was but occasional so far as the *curia regis* in general was concerned. It was the earliest branch of the *curia* to accumulate a recorded body of precedent. Although it enforced hard bargains struck by the king, exactions made by his justices, and arbitrary impositions levied by him, it gave to his financial exaction a semblance of regularity and law which was lacking in the days of the Conqueror and of William Rufus.

Here as in other phases of his *curia* the king was establishing his own jurisdiction above that of the ancient folk-motes. His rights of justice were in part regarded as feudal, but they were by no means limited to the lands of his demesne nor the causes of his tenants-in-chief. They might be exercised over individuals in common.[169] Above local usages and customs stood the pleas of the king's court, the usages and customs of which were held everywhere to preserve immobility.[170] The doctrine was asserted that no man might question its record.[171] Some misdeeds, not breaches of feudal law, were offenses against the king, which placed a man at his mercy.[172] There was a long list of offenses, pleas of the crown,[173] the amercements from which directly increased the royal income whether they were tried before the king's justices, the sheriff or the hundred reeve.

The king in some measure was also extending his direct authority to the old local courts. Some county courts were held for the purposes of his business, and some pleas tried

---

[169] *Leges Henrici* 19, 2-3
[170] *Ibid.*, 9 : 10a.   [171] *Ibid.*, 49 :4.
[172] The list of these includes breach of the peace given by his hand, contempt of his writs, injury to his person, the killing of a member of his household, disloyalty and treason, erecting a castle without license, outlawry and theft punishable by death (*ibid.*, 13).
[173] *Ibid.*, 10 : 1-4.

there were his pleas. Introduction of his methods in the *gemots* which enforced the old English folkright may be traced. Occasionally a justice is recorded as trying a cause in the county court by the feudal judgment of barons. William the Conqueror authorized the introduction of trial by battle in England so his French followers might have their customary mode of trial.[174] This was employed in the *curia regis*, and King Henry directed it to be used in certain land cases in the county court between vassals of different lords.[175] Again, the inquest jury which is so familiar because of its employment in the Domesday inquest, was a royal institution, the use of which was enjoined upon sheriffs or justices by the king's writ.[176] It would be easy to overestimate the judicial activity of the king's court. Its business was no doubt small in volume, and until well in the reign of Henry I quite small. The county and hundred courts disposed of far more cases, but they transacted some of their business in the new way the king had prescribed. This combination of Norman methods with English as well as feudal law was to become the key to the legal development of the future.[177]

AUTHORITIES

The source material for most of the topics covered in this chapter is provided by the chronicles, the more important of which are described in the note at the conclusion of chapter ix. The royal writs are more authentic and often of value. *The Chronicle of the Monastery of Abingdon* (Rolls Series, 1858) and the *Chronicle of Ramsey Abbey* (Rolls Series, 1886) are especially useful because they incorporate writs of the Norman kings which illustrate administration. The same is true of the *Ramsey Chartulary* (Rolls Series, 1884-1893). The *leges* (see above, p. 178) throw some light on judicial history and afford bits of information.

Two special documents are of first-rate importance to the study of specific topics. The *Constitutio Domus Regis,* written after the death of Henry I, is a brief statement of the wages and allowances of the members of the king's household organization, especially as it stood in

---

[174] Liebermann, *Gesetze*, I. 483-484.
[175] *Ibid.*, I. 524, sec. 3. [176] Morris, *Med. Eng. Sheriff*, 58.
[177] Cf. G. B. Adams, *Yale Law Journal*, XXXIX. 115-128.

King Henry's later years. This gives useful information concerning the principal household officials, their duties and their relative rank. Two versions exist and there are slight textual differences. One appears in the *Liber Niger Scaccarii*, edited by Thomas Hearne (1728), pp. 351-359, the other in *The Red Book of the Exchequer*, Rolls Series, edited by Hubert Hall (1896), III. pp. 807-813. The *Magnum Rotulum Scaccarii*, or great roll of the exchequer, for the thirty-first year of Henry I, edited by Joseph Hunter (1833), was made up after Michaelmas, 1130. It is the only survivor of a series of such annual rolls, and gives detailed information concerning the king's revenues for the fiscal year, 1129-1130.

Of secondary accounts, that in Stubbs, *Constitutional History*, vol. I. chap. 11, is still useful, though it requires to be supplemented by more specialized works of recent date. J. H. Round, *The King's Serjeants and Officers of State* (1911) throws light on the royal household, and Round's essay on the "Introduction of Knight Service" (see above, p. 154) provides valuable material concerning military administration. T. F. Tout, *Chapters in Administrative History*, vol. I (1920), presents a useful treatment of the king's permanent *curia*, especially the chancery and the exchequer. J. H. Round in his paper on "Danegeld and the Finance of Domesday" in *Domesday Studies*, ed. P. Edward Dove, vol. I (1888), shows the financial basis of the exchequer system, and Round's chapter on "The Origin of the Exchequer" in his *Commune of London* (1899) marks the beginning of recent reconstruction of the history of this institution. G. H. White in *Notes and Queries*, vol. 151, pp. 381-384 (1926), presents a careful study of the "Officers of First Rank under Henry I." R. L. Poole, *The Exchequer in the Twelfth Century* (1912), deals with the Norman period in chaps. 2-4 and added materially to existing knowledge of the subject. C. H. Haskins in an article in the *English Historical Review*, XXVII, "The Abacus and the King's Curia" (1912), shows the probability that the exchequer is older than has been supposed. G. H. White's paper on "Financial Administration under Henry I" in *Transactions of The Royal Historical Society*, 4th ser., VIII. 56-78 (1925) is a highly important contribution which deals with the offices and officials involved, and establishes their personnel for the period about 1130. G. B. Adams, *The Council and the Courts in Anglo-Norman England* (1926) affords the most comprehensive examination of the lesser council under Henry I, particularly in its judicial aspect. H. W. C. Davis, *England under the Normans and Angevins* (1905) contains (appendix ii) a useful account of the king's local justice. W. A. Morris, *The Medieval English Sheriff* (1927), in chapter 4 presents an account of the local work of the king's justices and also deals with the local administrative bearing of the reforms of Henry I.

CHAPTER XI

CHURCH AND STATE IN NORMAN ENGLAND

Norman rule brought to the English church new life and vigor, which appear in many phases of its activity. This was due in the main to active and able bishops and abbots from Normandy, who soon displaced those of English race. It was in part the result of some lessening of secular control and a restoration of papal and ecclesiastical rule which made the church less national in character, more like that throughout the rest of western Christendom. The Norman period of English history was in the beginning one of ecclesiastical reform, supported by the king. The power of regulation passed from the *witan* to ecclesiastical officials and councils. England was placed in accord with the canon law and the reforming influences of the day. The king, however, by no means conceded all papal claims nor agreed with all the aims of the reforming party; and he retained much control over the personnel of the higher clergy and over their acts, individual and collective, which touched the interests of the state. In the maintenance of such a policy lies a striking exemplification of the vigor and the resolute strength of the Norman monarchy.

To a reform of the sluggish and backward church in England the Conqueror was committed not only by his own inclination and by current usage in Normandy, directed by strong ecclesiastical leaders, but also by the prompting and support of the Holy See. The papacy from the middle of the eleventh century was intent upon shaking off the control of secular princes, and expected thus to increase the spirituality and effectiveness of the church. In the days of Edward

the Confessor there was much in English religious life and in
the relations between church and state to cause grave concern. The continental reformers might well regard the church
in England as the most unsatisfactory of any in Western
Europe so far as its leadership, discipline, and polity were concerned. The control of the pope over the English church was
weak. Peter's pence was no longer paid at the papal court.
Ecclesiastical legislation and judiciary and the appointment
of prelates were largely under secular control. Edward the
Confessor had appointed a few foreign bishops of ability, but
prelates sometimes obtained their charges through simony
and held them in plurality. Illiterate English bishops were
mentioned, and one who attended a council on the continent
was almost deposed because he did not know the ritual of his
office.[1] Powerful magnates were able to appropriate church
property. The rule of clerical celibacy was ignored, and
churchmen might perform military service in person.
Complaint had been registered through papal letters against
the maintenance of the seats of dioceses in villages rather
than in cities, as was required by canon law.[2] No reform was
to be expected from the *witan* whose members both lay and
ecclesiastical profited from this laxity. The archbishop of
York was in 1061 called by papal action to answer for ir-
regularities.[3] Moreover, Stigand, the primate of the English
church, through his influence with the house of Godwin held
his office uncanonically in succession to the Norman Robert,
banished as a result of the overthrow in 1052 of the ruling
Norman party. In consequence Stigand had been placed under
the ban by five popes,[4] and the bond between the papacy
and the archbishopric of Canterbury was broken. Under the
circumstances it was easy for Duke William to gain for his
invasion of England the sanction and support of pope Alexander II. The Roman *curia* regarded the enterprise as a

[1] Henry of Huntingdon, 1050; Malmesbury, *Gesta Pontificum*, 36.
[2] Böhmer, *Kirche und Staat in England und in der Normandie*, 82.
[3] *Ibid.*, 82.
[4] *Ibid.*, 67.

holy war,[5] and looked to William to set the church in order in his newly acquired realm.

The Conqueror did much to fulfill these expectations. By the time England had been fully subdued the work of reform was undertaken. At Easter and Whitsuntide 1070 were held church councils, the former called by the king at Winchester, the latter at Windsor. In the presence of papal legates Stigand was formally deprived of his office along with one of the bishops he had consecrated.[6] Three English bishops [7] and several abbots were deposed on other grounds. The dependents of Godwin and Harold were disposed of, and the way was open to reorganization. The process was furthered by the death in 1070 of Aldred, the archbishop of York. To the two archbishoprics and to five bishoprics were now chosen Norman ecclesiastics, four of them members of the king's chapel.[8] The Italian Lanfranc, abbot of Caen, William's great counsellor in ecclesiastical matters, an especially notable father of the Western Church of that day, was in 1070 designated archbishop of Canterbury. The archbishop of York was in 1072 directed to make a profession of obedience to him [9] and to attend councils called by him within the see of Canterbury. Lanfranc worked in close accord with the king. The influence of the former directed the work of reform along lines acceptable to the monarch. Since some foreigners had been made bishops in King Edward's time, there remained but three of English birth. Two of these soon passed away, and only one English bishop, the venerated Wulfstan of Worcester, long survived the new organization. Henceforth the bishops as well as the abbots appointed were Normans or Lotharingians.[10] The English clergy were excluded from the highest ecclesiastical position.

[5] Orderic Vital (II. 122-123) says the pope sent William the banner of St. Peter by the merits of which he should be defended from all peril.

[6] Ethelric of Selsey (*A.-S. Chron.*, 1069).

[7] Leofwine of Lichfield, Ethelmar of Elmham, Ethelwine of Durham.

[8] Böhmer, *Kirche und Staat*, 87.

[9] William of Malmesbury, *Gesta Regnum*, II. 349-352; *Gesta Pontificum*, 39-45. [10] Böhmer, *Kirche und Staat*, 89.

The best usage of the Norman church now gained expression. One of the great changes made by Lanfranc was the restoration of church councils to their earlier position. Their canons again legislated for the church.[11] Discipline, culture, church buildings, all profited vastly. The councils of bishops and abbots,[12] called by the archbishop of Canterbury, became the chief instrument of the reform movement. The holding of diocesan councils each year to restore discipline and remedy abuses was also ordered. No longer did the secular power depose bishops and abbots nor regulate the life of the church. The papal headship became a matter of reality. Spiritual matters were fully restored to ecclesiastical authority. The canon law system of the Roman church was made to apply in England, and the evils of simony were denounced by the church, and this with that of plurality almost uprooted.[13] Peter's pence was again paid.[14] A church council at London in 1075 decreed that in accord with the decisions of ancient councils episcopal seats in England should be in cities rather than villages and that three should accordingly be transferred.[15] The removal of others followed within a few years. The treatment of clerical celibacy was more in line with the moderation of Lanfranc than the rigor of Hildebrand, but the marriage of the parochial clergy was partially restrained.[16] Later church councils in the time of Henry I enacted a number of canons which virtually completed this reform.

[11] Macdonald, *Lanfranc*, chap. 7.

[12] After 1075 no one except a bishop or abbot might speak in a church council without the license of his archbishop (William of Malmesbury, *Gesta Pontif.*, 68).

[13] Malmesbury, *Gesta Pontif.*, 68. Both evils occur under Henry I (Symeon of Durham, R. S., II. 283; *Gesta Stephani*, R. S., III. 17).

[14] Rev. O. Jensen in *Trans. Royal Histor. Soc.*, new ser., XIV. 187; XIX. 209-215.

[15] Malmesbury, *Gesta Pontificum*, 67-68. Two others had already been transferred, one to Exeter in 1050, the other to Lincoln in 1072-1073. Cf. Macdonald, *Lanfranc*, 101.

[16] In 1076 marriage of the clergy was forbidden for the future, but existing marriages were recognized. Cf. Macdonald, *Lanfranc*, 103-107. The canons passed under Hildebrand's personal direction in 1078 were much more severe (Z. N. Brooke, *Cambridge Medieval History*, V. 73).

Just as King William restored to church councils and church officials their appropriate place in spiritual concerns, he also followed the requirements of the canon law in establishing ecclesiastical courts. This was done with the consent of the great council by a famous enactment issued at some time between 1070 and 1076,[17] which separated ecclesiastical from secular jurisdiction. It directed that no bishop or archdeacon was henceforth to hold pleas affecting the episcopal jurisdiction in the ordinary local courts, and that no case which pertained to the realm of souls should be brought to secular judgment. Those summoned concerning any matter pertaining to the ecclesiastical jurisdiction were to appear only at the place designated by the bishop and were to answer not according to the usages of the hundred court but according to canon and episcopal law. The refractory person who refused to appear in the bishop's court in response to the third summons was to be excommunicated and the authority of the king or the sheriff was to be employed by way of constraining him to obedience.

Although the king respected the conviction of the times as to what was justly due the church, yet he refused to yield claims which trenched upon his sovereignty. With the more advanced principles of the Hildebrandine reform he had no sympathy. He was not in the least disposed to yield to the doctrines of the great monk which held that the pope was above all princes. Hildebrand, who became pope Gregory VII in 1073, had no doubt hoped from before the Conquest that William could be induced to hold England as a papal fief and in this way advance the temporal power of the papacy. Papal claims of suzerainty over Hungary, Spain and Corsica were made by the pope, and the Norman ruler of Apulia accepted such an arrangement. Gregory VII in 1080 made the demand of the Conqueror, who subsequently rejected it, hold-

<hr/>

[17] Liebermann, *Gesetze*, I. 485; Robertson, *Laws*, 234-236. A bishop was forbidden by a church council of 1126 to judge the parishioner of another bishop (Symeon of Durham, R. S., II. 280).

ing that fealty to the pope had not been promised by himself nor rendered by his predecessors.[18]

William had restrained the power of the Norman church in matters touching his political interest. According to Eadmer [19] he followed in certain respects the same principles on both sides of the Channel. He would permit the recognition of a new pope or the settlement of ecclesiastical matters with him only by his own consent. He would agree that the canons enacted by the archbishop of Canterbury in a general council of the bishops should be valid only when they had his approval and were ordained by himself. He would not be embarrassed by the impleading or excommunication at a bishop's hands of one of his servants or his tenants-in-chief, even for the commission of grave offenses against morality. Eadmer declared that all affairs both ecclesiastical and secular awaited the king's pleasure, but Eadmer of course had in mind matters of state policy and not ordinary ministrations and discipline of the church. Where the interests of the king and the nation were concerned William claimed supremacy, and his sons abated nothing of the claim. He once ordered the bishop of Chichester to induct the abbot of Battle Abbey which he had founded.[20] Pope Gregory decided that a dispute concerning the obedience of the archbishop of York to the archbishop of Canterbury should be settled in England by judgment of the bishops and abbots of realm, but the king's *curia* ultimately passed upon the matter.[21] On the whole, however, the king's policy was just and moderate, and it was furthered by the co-operation of Lanfranc.

With respect to the election and investiture of prelates the Conqueror's usage was directly in conflict with one of the foremost tenets of Hildebrand. It is of interest that in this the

[18] Macdonald, *Lanfranc*, 222-226; Makower, *Constnl. Hist. of Church of England*, 14, and note 5; Rev. O. Jensen in *Trans. Royal Histor. Soc.*, new ser., XIX. 213, 215-217; *Eng. Histor. Rev.*, XXVI. 223-238.
[19] Eadmer, *Hist. Novorum*, Rolls Ser., 10.
[20] Bigelow, *Placita Anglo-Normannica*, 14.
[21] Malmesbury, *Gesta Pontificum*, 41.

great pope did not make the demand for compliance with the new programme, a demand which a generation later caused a conflict. King William and his sons named bishops and abbots as freely as King Edward had done. There is some reason to believe that down to the time of Stephen the royal abbeys were virtually regarded as part of the king's hereditary domain.[22] In such cases free election of abbots was out of the question. Chancellors and other members of the king's chapel filled a good proportion of the vacancies in bishoprics. Many a case recorded in the chronicles testifies that, whatever reformers might hold in regard to the rights of cathedral and monastic chapters to elect, the king decided the appointment when he so desired.

The higher clergy, moreover, were gradually drawn into feudal relations with the king. Domesday lists bishops and abbots along with the other great landholders of the realm. Upon the bishops and some of the abbots the Conqueror imposed military service,[23] and these must have been regarded as holding feudal fiefs. When the bishop of Durham in 1088 adhered to the party of the rebellious barons, the king seized his lands as a forfeited fief, although the bishop claimed them as part of his bishopric. The great council by its judgment sustained the act.[24] Since about forty bishops and abbots owed feudal service to the king, it was natural that he should insist that the prelates who occupied so important a position in his scheme of government should be satisfactory persons. In Normandy it was customary for the lord to invest the abbot with his temporal possessions.[25] Frequently, if not regularly, the Norman king issued a writ which granted an English diocese or an abbey and its lands to the newly elected prelate.[26]

[22] Böhmer, *Kirche und Staat*, 391. Cf. Davis, *Regesta*, no. 329.

[23] Above, p. 137.

[24] Symeon of Durham, *Rolls Ser.*, I. 171-172, 180-184; Adams, *Council and Courts*, 46, 53-64.

[25] Böhmer, *Kirche und Staat*, 272.

[26] *Historians of York*, ed. Raine, Rolls Ser., III. 32; Davis, *Regesta*, nos. 104, 106.

Just as a king thus conferred lands, so for forty years he insisted upon investing the newly elected bishop or abbot with the ring and the staff, the symbols of spiritual office. This of course Gregory VII and his successors opposed because it gave the temporal power a function which belonged to the spiritual. It made the prelate the man of the temporal ruler and not of the pope. A papal decree against lay investiture was passed in 1075, but enforced by no rigorous action for several decades. So far as both bishops and abbots are concerned, the usage in England is clearly stated by an historian who was in a position to know it well.[27] From the coming of Duke William, with but two exceptions, bishops of Rochester who looked to the archbishop of Canterbury as their lord, the new prelate did homage to the king and received from him the pastoral staff. As to this no question seems to have been raised until the year 1093. It is clear that for his own purposes the king had ground to treat the bishop as a baron if he chose to do so. It has been shown earlier that bishops and abbots are sometimes classed as barons in documents of the Norman kings.[28]

The ecclesiastical theory of the case was often different. The bishop was primarily an ecclesiastical person, and might claim the privileges of his order. When Bishop Odo of Bayeux was seized for a rebellious act, Lanfranc justified the measure by declaring that he was imprisoned not as bishop but as earl of Kent.[29] In the reign of William Rufus, William bishop of Durham denied, though unsuccessfully, that he might legally be tried before the king's *curia* and judged as a baron by the king's barons. It is interesting to note that in this case also Lanfranc accepted the secular viewpoint and opposed a reference of the matter merely to the bishops.[30] The question how far the bishop or abbot might be treated as a baron was of fundamental importance under the Conqueror's sons.

[27] Eadmer, *Hist. Novorum*, Rolls Ser., 2.

[28] Above, p. 187.

[29] William of Malmesbury, *Gesta Regum*, II. 361. See Symeon of Durham, I. 184.

[30] Symeon of Durham, R. S., I. 171-172, 180-181, 184.

The reign of William Rufus marks the strongest claim to ecclesiastical supremacy made by any king before Henry VIII. The struggle between Gregory VII and the emperor Henry IV brought the occupation of Rome by the latter in 1084, and Pope Gregory died in exile the following year. After the Conqueror's death relations between England and Rome were broken, and until 1095 no successor to the papal throne was recognized by an English king.[31] Since, according to the royal contention, no business might be transacted with a pope until he was so recognized, and since after the death of Lanfranc in 1089 there was no archbishop of Canterbury, the king remained for a time the ultimate arbiter of ecclesiastical matters. Rufus strove to retain this position. He even declared in 1093 when he was asked to designate an archbishop of Canterbury that for the present there should be no archbishop except himself.[32] His action, like his theory, was often drastic. He temporarily took the episcopal staff from the bishop of Thetford to whom he had previously sold it.[33] Moreover, two bishops of Lincoln gave the king money to assure a favorable decision when the archbishop of York claimed their diocese as subject to himself.[34]

William II strained his rights and advanced new claims, the most famous of which were of a fiscal nature. He took over the lands of a bishopric or abbey with their income during a vacancy, except the portion which provided the food and clothing of the monks. Despite a formal renunciation of this right by Henry I in his coronation charter, it nevertheless remained a permanent prerogative of the English king. It was appropriated also by the king of France,[35] where it came to be known as the right of *regale*. The widespread indignation

[31] Böhmer, *Kirche und Staat*, 150.

[32] Eadmer, *Hist. Nov.* 30.

[33] William of Malmesbury, *Gesta Pontif.*, 151; *A.-S. Chron.* 1094. According to *Monasticon*, II. 429, this bishop purchased Hyde Abbey for his father.

[34] Henry of Huntingdon, 1093; Florence of Worcester, 1092.

[35] Luchaire, *Manuel*, 49-50, 511. See Luchaire, *Louis VI*, p. clxi, for an instance in 1099.

occasioned by this claim of William Rufus was due in part
to its novelty,[36] but probably even more to its abuse. On the
advice of Flambard, as it was believed,[37] the king deliberately
kept bishoprics and abbeys vacant so he might profit by the
fact. The lands of these churches were let to farm, and the
business was administered by Flambard. A later chronicler
says that he paid three or four hundred marks for each of
these estates and that in 1098 he had thus in charge sixteen
churches without pastors.[38] Rufus on the day of his death held
in this wise the archbishopric of Canterbury, the bishoprics
of Winchester and Salisbury and eleven abbeys.[39] In 1095,
following the death of Wulfstan of Worcester, the king levied
a feudal relief [40] upon the tenants of the bishop, a right which
could belong only to their overlord. Ecclesiastical estates were
thus treated like baronial fiefs. When the king seized the
lands of the bishop of Durham he granted away some of
them [41] as if they had already been forfeited according to
feudal usage. The king showed an alarming disposition to
apply to the lands of bishops feudal principles supposed to
hold only for lay baronies.

The personal property of a deceased bishop, heretofore distributed by the archbishop for charitable or other pious objects, was also claimed by William Rufus. The former plan
for disposing of such property was abolished, it is said, also
at the instigation of Flambard.[42] The king's agents took over
the treasure and other possessions of the late bishop [43] as they
did the lands which had belonged to his church. This right,

[36] Previously the bishop was in control of a vacant abbey (Orderic
Vital, III. 313). According to Florence of Worcester (II. 46) the king's
usage was *contra jus ecclesiasticum*.

[37] Orderic Vital, III. 312.

[38] *Annales de Wintonia*, 1088, 1092, 1097; cf. Orderic Vital, IV. 9-10;
Eadmer, *Hist. Nov.*, 26; Florence of Worcester, 1100.

[39] *Anglo-Saxon Chronicle*, 1100.

[40] Round, *Feudal England*, 309; Adams and Stephens, *Sel. Documents*,
no. 5.

[41] Symeon of Durham, Rolls Ser., I. 171, 172.

[42] Orderic Vital, III. 313.

[43] *Ibid.*, III. 313; IV. 10, 54.

known as the *jus spolii* [44] was exercised also by Henry I but abandoned by Stephen.

The ecclesiastical policy of William II was also oppressive and tyrannical in other respects. This appears clearly in his relations with the archbishop of Canterbury. After a vacancy in the office for about four years, the king during a serious illness in the spring of 1093 was induced to designate to this position the noted Anselm, then abbot of the Norman monastery of Caen. According to custom he was invested by the king with the pastoral staff and the lands of his see.[45] The archbishop yielded to what was now the usage of the realm and did homage to the king before he was inducted into his office.[46] Anselm was committed to the papal plan of reform, his principles were fairly rigid and his tact none too great. Difficulties soon beset him on every hand. Rufus refused to return to him all the lands which Lanfranc had held; he incurred displeasure by failing to contribute liberally enough to the royal war chest; the king refused him permission to hold a general council to reform morals and manners; when he asked that vacant abbeys be filled the king declared that they were his and not the archbishop's.[47] In 1095 the archbishop sought permission to visit the pope to receive his *pallium*, and William asked, "Which pope?" The answer was, "Urban," and the king declared that he had not yet recognized him. He had favored another claimant to the papal throne.[48] Anselm persisted and was placed on trial before the great council on what was tantamount to a charge of disloyalty, although he maintained that the archbishop of Canterbury might be judged by no man but the pope. The king and his party contended that his ring and staff should be taken from him and he should be expelled from the realm. The barons, however,

[44] Böhmer, *Kirche und Staat*, 147. For the *jus spolii* in France, see Luchaire, *Manuel*, 49-50.

[45] Eadmer, *Hist. Novorum*, Rolls Ser., 32-37.

[46] *Ibid.*, 41.

[47] *Ibid.*, 43-50. Cf. Glanvill, VII. 1.

[48] William of Malmesbury, *Gesta Pontif.*, 85-86.

refused to find him guilty.[49] The king, apparently in the hope of gaining sanction for his own acts, recognized Urban II, and then asked a papal legate to depose Anselm. He also attempted in vain to induce the latter to accept from his hand the *pallium*,[50] the archbishop's insignia of office which had long been conferred by the pope. By again refusing Anselm permission to visit Rome in 1097 William II virtually forced him to leave England. The bishops were overawed and declined throughout the controversy to support the archbishop.[51] The king refused to reinstate him at the papal command, and, despite the threat of excommunication from the pope in 1098,[52] held firmly to his policy until his death. One mark of favor to the papacy appears in 1096, when, probably in an attempt to aid the royal cause against Anselm, Peter's penny was collected by the king's aid and was sent to Rome, for the first time in years.[53]

The accession of Henry I brought a new attitude on the part of the crown and some improvement of the situation, but was soon followed by a renewal of conflict. Henry promised at his accession not to sell churches nor place them at farm nor during a vacancy to impose exactions upon their men. The vacant bishoprics and abbeys were filled. Anselm was soon invited to England to take up his duties as archbishop, but the latter was now strongly committed to the Gregorian policy of opposition to lay investiture. In his exile he had attended in 1099 a council at St. Peter's Church, Rome,[54] held by Pope Urban II, which had issued decrees against prelates who received lay investiture of laymen and who rendered homage to them in order to receive ecclesiastical possessions. The issue

[49] Eadmer, *Hist. Novorum*, 52-64; Malmesbury, *Gesta Pontif.*, 87-88.
[50] *Ibid.*, 89-90; Malmesbury, *Gesta Pontif.*, 68-69, 71-72.
[51] William of Malmesbury, *Gesta Pontif.*, 87-94. The king in 1197 required Anselm to swear not to appeal his case to the pope, but he declined (Eadmer, 83).
[52] *Ibid.*, 97, 100.
[53] *A.-S. Chron.*, 1095.
[54] Eadmer, *Hist. Nov.*, Rolls Ser., 112-114; William of Malmesbury, *Gesta Pontif.*, 103; Florence of Worcester, II. 43.

came up quickly upon Anselm's return. The king was by no means disposed to yield, and in 1101 demanded that Anselm become his man and consecrate the bishops and abbots who had been designated or else leave the land.[55] The archbishop at Westminster in 1102 [56] presided over the bishops and abbots in a council at which he undertook some reform of the church, but in 1103 returned to the continent. The king undertook to procure through the archbishop of York the consecration of the bishops whom he had invested. One of these, William Giffard, the late chancellor, refused, was deprived of his position, and went into exile. The other bishops remained unconsecrated.[57]

The controversy over investiture was followed by a series of negotiations between the king and Anselm, in which the pope, Paschal II, participated. A temporary agreement was reached in 1105,[58] and the next year Anselm returned to England [59] at the king's request, on the eve of Henry's final struggle with his brother Robert. In August, 1107, a settlement embodied the provisions of the temporary compromise. Anselm formally gave his adherence at a great council of the realm held in London. King Henry agreed that for the future no bishop nor abbot in England should be invested with ring and staff by the king or any other layman. Anselm conceded that no one elected to a prelacy should be denied consecration because of the homage which he did the king.[60] The archbishop of York now took an oath by which he renewed his obedience to the see of Canterbury, and five bishops were immediately consecrated.[61]

The compromise of 1107, the forerunner of a still more

[55] Florence, 131.

[56] William of Malmesbury, *Gesta Pontif*, 118-121.

[57] Florence of Worcester, 1103. According to Malmesbury (*Gesta Pontif.*, 110), William was blessed and received his staff from Anselm.

[58] Böhmer, *Kirche und Staat*, 160.

[59] Florence of Worcester, II. 55.

[60] *Ibid.*, II. 56; Eadmer, *Hist. Nov.*, 186.

[61] *Ibid.*, 187. One of these, Rainold bishop of Hereford, had offended the king by returning to him the ring and staff which he had conferred (Malmesbury, *Gesta Pontif.*, 303).

famous one between emperor and pope in 1122, left to the temporal power most of the actual advantages of a victory. King Henry had simply applied in one more instance his favorite method of conciliation which gained him much and lost him little. He parted with a certain amount of prestige in abandoning the investiture of bishops and abbots with the symbols of ecclesiastical authority; but they were required to become his vassals before they were consecrated. Moreover his influence in determining their election remained as great as that of his predecessors;[62] and he retained the usage of conceding formally to the newly consecrated bishop or abbot the temporal possessions of his church.[63] The king had gained an admission of his right to regard the chief persons of the church of England as his barons, and inferentially to exact the royal rights which their homage implied. He was powerful enough to dictate in many instances as to who should fill the most important positions in the church. In case his wishes were opposed, he was in a position practically to annul the election made, for his good will was necessary to gain for the person chosen the lands in the hand of the king since the death of the last occupant of the position.

Henry I was in general tenacious of ecclesiastical prerogatives claimed by his predecessors. That he curtailed the authority of the pope in England is shown by a letter of Paschal II, written in 1115 to the king and the English bishops. This holds that papal rights are being contravened and proposes as a remedy that church councils be held only with the pope's knowledge; that papal confirmation be given when bishops are elected or translated to other dioceses; that final decision be reserved to the pope in all judicial proceedings against bishops; and that freedom of appeal to the pope be allowed.[64]

[62] In 1123 the pope objected to the election of an archbishop of Canterbury in a great council and in opposition to the wishes of the monks of the cathedral church (Symeon of Durham, II. 272).

[63] Böhmer, *Kirche und Staat*, 161-162. In 1126 abbots and priors were forbidden to receive any ecclesiastical benefice from the hand of a layman without consent of the bishop (Symeon of Durham, R. S., II. 279).

[64] Eadmer, *Hist. Nov.*, 232; Jaffé, *Regesta*, I. no. 6453; cf. 6450.

None of these concessions seems to have been made. Appeals to the papacy were frequent only in the next realm. King Henry, like his two predecessors, enforced the rule that no one should receive papal letters except by his consent.[65] Moreover, there are cases mentioned in which the decrees of church councils are drawn up with the consent of the king and his secular barons.[66] The king in 1129 thwarted the decrees of a council relative to clerical celibacy, not by refusing his assent, but by accepting payment in accord with earlier Norman usage to let clerks keep their wives.[67] Various church councils of the reign, however, dealt with the danger that church property, following feudal custom, might pass to the sons of clergymen.[68] In 1107 the pope authorized Anselm to recede from a canon forbidding the ordination of the sons of priests, on the ground that almost the better and greater part of the clergy of England might be judged to be married men.[69] The council of this year forbade priests to marry or keep wives, although the regulation was evaded. Very much more effective were the canons enacted during the reign which made it impossible for the clergy to contract lawful marriage, and denied to those who retained wives or concubines ecclesiastical honor and rank.[70]

With the papacy the English church was of course in direct relations in the reign of Henry I as it had not been in the time of Rufus. Bishops and archbishops seem freely to have proceeded to Rome on business. After 1119 they took part in councils held by the pope, as they could not have done under the Conqueror and Rufus.[71] King Henry recognized papal

---

[65] Makower, *ibid.*, 236, n. 4. Cf. *Materials for Hist. of Becket*, Rolls Ser., VI. 79. Henry I in 1125 forbade an archbishop to enter a plea at Rome (*Historians of York*, ed. Raine, II. 212).

[66] Makower, *ibid.*, 20, 359, notes 25, 26.

[67] Henry of Huntingdon, 251; Böhmer, *Kirche und Staat*, 286.

[68] Jaffé, *Regesta*, I. no. 6152; Migne, *Patrologia Latina*, vol. 163, p. 219.

[69] Symeon of Durham, II. 255-256, 279.

[70] Malmesbury, *Gesta Pontif.*, 119; Böhmer, *Kirche und Staat*, 283-286; Florence of Worcester, II. 83, 87.

[71] Böhmer, *Kirche und Staat*, 299.

authority in most ecclesiastical matters.[72] He refused, however, to recognize the powers of visiting papal legates in England except under restrictions and claimed that this was a rule of his father's time. When in 1116 the pope sent a legate to reside in England and thus to thwart its archbishops, the king forbade him to enter the country. In 1119 the pope agreed that no one should perform the office of legate in England except at the king's request. In 1126 another legate was permitted to enter the kingdom only after being detained some time in Normandy.[73]

The question of the precedence of the see of Canterbury over that of York also brought conflict between king and pope. Thurstin, the archbishop of York, in 1114 refused obedience to Ralph of Canterbury, and at the instance of the king was forced to resign his see. The pope protested and five years later consecrated Thurstin as archbishop. The latter upon his return to England was banished by King Henry, who was induced to reinstate him only after the pope threatened to excommunicate the king and to suspend the archbishop of Canterbury.[74] As a result of the old disputes concerning the precedence of Canterbury its archbishop, in 1126, attained appointment as papal legate.[75] Since he now clearly outranked his rival, his claim to the formal profession of the obedience of the archbishop of York fell into abeyance. The presence of a resident legate facilitated closer relations with the papacy and an increase in papal authority in England. As late as 1131, however, Pope Innocent II wrote sharply in regard to the misuse of the right of *regale* and the *jus spolii* in England and threatened with excommunication English and Norman prelates who concurred in these abuses.[76]

[72] Thus in 1130 the pope authorized the archbishop of York to unite or divide sees (*Historians of York*, ed. Raine, Rolls Ser., III. 57).

[73] Makower, *Constitutional Hist.*, 26; Symeon of Durham, Rolls Ser., II. 276; Jaffe, *Regesta*, I. no. 6788; Eadmer, 258.

[74] William of Malmesbury, *Gesta Pontif.*, 262-266.

[75] Makower, *Constitutional Hist.*, 20, 285; Symeon of Durham, R. S., II. 281.

[76] Makower, *ibid.*, 301.

The support of the church was one of the chief influences through which Stephen gained his hold upon the throne. His reign brought a rapid decline in the ecclesiastical prerogatives of the English monarch. Formal recognition of the new ruler was soon accorded in papal letters, although Innocent II demanded that Robert, earl of Gloucester, remain true to the oath of allegiance which he had taken to his half-sister, Matilda, the daughter and heiress of Henry I.[77] Stephen's brother, Henry, bishop of Winchester, and other prelates arranged for his coronation. The king in his charter of 1136 sought to bolster up his position by mentioning the papal confirmation of his election to the throne. An increase in the freedom of the church was in accord with the spirit and trend of the times; but it was due in the first instance to formal concessions made by the usurping monarch. At his coronation, so it is said, he made certain promises which he renewed a little later at Oxford. When bishops died he would not retain their churches in his own hand. Canonical election should immediately be held, and the king would invest the new prelate with his church. Moreover, he would no longer hold the forests either of clergy or laity, as was done by King Henry, who impleaded them if they took venison from their own forests.[78] Provisions to this effect do not occur in the second charter of liberties which Stephen issued at Oxford in 1136, but the statements bearing upon the *regale* and upon freedom of election seem to be an interpretation or paraphrase of promises which do appear in this document. In it the king declares [79] that when churches are vacant he will commit them and all their possessions to the custody of clerks or worthy men of these churches until the pastor is canonically replaced. Arrangements made by bishops and abbots for the disposition of their personal property are to be accepted, and

---

[77] Böhmer, *Kirche und Staat*, 333-335; Malmesbury, *Historia Novella*, 545; Richard of Hexham, Rolls Series, 147.

[78] Henry of Huntingdon, 258; cf. William of Malmesbury, *Hist. Nov.*, R. S., II. 542.

[79] Stubbs, *Select Charters*, 120-121.

if any die intestate the distribution of his goods is to be made by his church. Thus the *jus spolii* is renounced.

In this charter were also made other promises of importance to the church. The king was not to commit nor permit simony in ecclesiastical affairs. Jurisdiction over the clergy and their property was to rest with the bishop, and the authority of the ecclesiastical courts was thus potentially widened. Stephen was in no position to uphold the rigid control maintained by his predecessors, and the church was in a position to gain a degree of autonomy heretofore denied. Subsequent history shows that it profited by the situation. It is interesting to observe that, although the king in the first year of his reign gave direction concering the work of a church council, this followed the tenor of papal instructions.[80]

Stephen, like Henry I, did not live up to the letter of his promises made to the church. Civil war soon broke out, and he found himself in a weak, sometimes in a desperate, position. He countenanced simony, and he did not check the seizure of church property by warring barons.[81] Churchmen later regarded him as a tyrant.[82] Suspecting the loyalty of the late justiciar, Roger, bishop of Salisbury, the king in 1139 seized and for a time imprisoned him, as also his nephew, the bishop of Lincoln, taking over their castles. In this he directly violated the promise that ecclesiastical courts should have jurisdiction over ecclesiastical persons. These acts did much to alienate the church and to weaken the king's position. At a council held the same year by Henry, bishop of Winchester, the king's brother who was now papal legate, the reinvestiture of the bishops was demanded [83] until their rights were settled, but the king prevented them from appealing to Rome.[84] In the course of the civil war of the reign, the clergy

[80] Symeon of Durham, II. 288.
[81] William of Malmesbury, *Hist. Nov.*, R. S., II. 543.
[82] Böhmer, *Kirche und Staat*, 328; John of Salisbury, *Polycraticus*, VI : 18.
[83] William of Malmesbury, *Hist. Nov.*, R. S., II. 553-554.
[84] Böhmer, *Kirche und Staat*, 341-342.

were sometimes divided because of rivalry between Bishop
Henry, the legate, and Theobald, archbishop of Canterbury.
Bishop Henry held a council at Winchester after his brother,
the king, had been taken prisoner, and sought the papal interdict against the followers of Matilda,[85] but in time he lost his
influence at Rome, and in 1143 ceased to be legate. Theobald,
his rival, espoused the cause of Matilda and her son, Henry of
Anjou, and in the end was influential in effecting the succession of the latter to the English throne.[86] To insure the succession of his son Eustace, the king in 1151 convoked an assembly of bishops and peers at London and proposed that the
prince be crowned. Since the pope had forbidden the archbishop to crown the usurper's son, the bishops refused, and it
was in vain that the king and his heir attempted to intimidate
them.[87]

The long warfare between the partisans of Stephen and
those of Matilda together with the weakness of the king
ultimately made for the freedom of the church. Just as the
baronage strove to shake off the control of the monarchy, so
did the prelates. Left largely to shift for itself, the church of
England was drawn closer to the papacy. Its legal system, released from secular control under Norman rule, looked thither
for headship. Before the end of the reign the English clergy
came to regard the pope as the supreme lawgiver and judge.
The doctrine of the supremacy of the pope over all temporal
powers was furthered by his leadership in the crusades and
gained acceptance. Interference of the latter in affairs of the
church was regarded as improper and even sacrilegious. The
English church became a realm within the realm. It gained
under the papal headship a solidarity which it had not known
before, and it was in a position to oppose future intrusions
into its affairs. Subsequent struggles of the state with the ecclesiastical order were to assume a much more serious aspect.

[85] Böhmer, *Kirche und Staat*, 345.
[86] *Ibid.*, 348-364. Bishop Henry was friendly to Henry of Anjou after
1153 (Symeon of Durham, R. S., II. 331).
[87] Gervase of Canterbury, Rolls Ser., I. 150-151.

In certain specific directions the increasing freedom of the church may be traced in Stephen's reign. The king's brother, the bishop of Winchester, who was papal legate from 1139 to 1143, increased the pope's power in England. The appeals to the papacy in ecclesiastical matters mentioned in the earlier Norman reigns, had not been permitted.[88] According to Henry of Huntingdon, Bishop Henry introduced the practice of carrying appeals to Rome. This chronicler relates that a church council held at London in 1151 was thrown into a turmoil by fresh appeals, three being made to the pope on this occasion.[89] Furthermore, the disorder of the times required that the church find a means of protecting the clergy and their property. The immediate effect was that excommunication was more widely used, nor was the king able to restrain the action of the church in this particular as his predecessors had done. A church council held at Winchester in 1139 passed decrees to protect the clergy, and authorized action against those who laid a hand on them or their property.[90] Another council, at London in 1143, in passing a canon to restrain assaults on the clergy, declared that those guilty of this offense might be absolved only by the pope.[91] When the king's mercenaries robbed churches,[92] or when great nobles seized an abbey, or made a castle of it,[93] and the king was unwilling or powerless to act, excommunication was the only recourse. It was also used by a papal legate against a bishop who wrongfully occupied a see.[94]

When King Stephen died in 1154 the position of the papacy was well established in western Christendom. Canon law was formulated and bound the different branches of the church together. In England the free election of bishops by cathedral

[88] As in the case of William bishop of Durham (Symeon of Durham, I. 184).
[89] Henry of Huntingdon, 282.
[90] Symeon of Durham, II. 301.
[91] Henry of Huntingdon, 276.
[92] William of Malmesbury, *Hist. Nov.*, II. 540, 561.
[93] Cf. Symeon of Durham, II. 314; Henry of Huntingdon, 277.
[94] Symeon of Durham, R. S., I. 146.

chapters, despite partisan issues, had made some headway. The pope had begun to confirm episcopal elections. The election of abbots were gaining more freedom, though still strongly under royal influence.[95] This influence was offset in some measure by the entrance into England of the orders such as the Cluniacs and Cistercians which constituted congregations with only one abbot at the head, the dependent houses being ruled by priors. Moreover, some monasteries and churches were obtaining bulls which placed them directly under papal protection, and these occasionally specified that elections of abbots were to be free.[96] Church councils and ecclesiastical courts functioned without restraint from the secular power. Ecclesiastical justice and jurisprudence were better organized and established than those of the king, and appeals to the papal *curia* freely took place. Papal letters came in without hindrance,[97] and prelates were not forbidden to go abroad. The clergy used spiritual weapons to protect themselves and their property. The control which the Norman kings had exercised in ecclesiastical affairs had broken down. The days when Rufus and Henry I dictated to Anselm were gone. The liberty of the church had become a rallying cry. When Henry of Anjou attempted to restore something of the control which had been lost to the crown in the period of the anarchy he faced a very difficult problem.

AUTHORITIES

The sources from which the relations of church and state are chiefly to be traced in the Norman period are the chronicles. To the monks who wrote these the church was naturally of pre-eminent importance. All of them include material of value to the ecclesiastical historian. A few stand out. Eadmer, a monk of Canterbury and friend of Anselm, in his *Historia Novorum* (Rolls Ser., ed. M. Rule, 1884) written about 1120, made it his object to record especially the relations between

[95] Böhmer, *Kirche und Staat*, 386-394.
[96] Z. N. Brooke, *Cambridge Historical Journal*, II. no. 3, 214-215; A. H. Sweet, *Catholic Historical Review*, new ser., IV. 400.
[97] Over a hundred letters and bulls were received during the reign (Böhmer, *ibid.*, 404, note 2).

Anselm and the two kings with whom the latter had to do. William of Malmesbury in his *Gesta Pontificum* (Rolls Ser., ed. N. E. S. A. Hamilton, 1870), written in the time of Henry I, gives an unusual amount of information concerning the personality and deeds of the Norman bishops. In his *Gesta Regum* and his *Historia Novella* (Rolls Ser., ed. W. Stubbs, 1887-89) he also includes important data. Especially useful also are the *Chronicon* of Florence of Worcester (2 vols. Eng. Histor. Soc., ed. B. Thorpe, 1848-1849), the *Historia Anglorum* of Henry, archdeacon of Huntingdon (Rolls Ser., ed. T. Arnold, 1879) and the *Historia Regum* of Symeon of Durham (2 vols., Rolls Ser., ed. T. Arnold, 1882-1885). The *Regesta Pontificum Romanorum*, edited by Philipp Jaffé (2d edition, 2 vols., 1885-1888, revised by S. Loewenfeld and others) includes a record of papal letters and acts touching English affairs, but practically all the material is collected from the chronicles. The letters of Lanfranc appear in Migne, *Patrologia Latina*. The writings of ecclesiastics of the period sometimes give their ideas of relations between church and state. Prominent among these is an anonymous York manuscript dating from the early years of Henry I, and published in Böhmer, *Kirche und Staat,* pp. 436-497.

One secondary work is outstanding because it deals purely with the theme of this chapter. Heinrich Böhmer, in his *Kirche und Staat in England und in der Normandie* (1899) gives an excellent and scholarly treatment of the whole subject. Felix Makower, *Constitutional History and Constitution of the English Church* (translation, 1895) presents useful material, but quite limited in amount. W. R. W. Stephens, *English Church from the Norman Conquest to the Accession of Edward I* (1901) affords a narrative, though it is not very strong on the institutional side. A. J. Macdonald, *Lanfranc* (1926) is a scholarly work of considerable value for the earlier topics treated in this chapter. Z. N. Brooke, "Pope Gregory VII's Demand for Fealty from William the Conqueror," *English Historical Review,* XXVI. 223-238, is an important study.

PART IV

ADMINISTRATIVE AND CONSTITUTIONAL DEVELOPMENT UNDER THE ANGEVIN KINGS, 1154–1216

CHAPTER XII

THE RISE OF THE JUDICIAL SYSTEM

Henry II (1154-1189), the son of Matilda and Geoffrey of Anjou, succeeded to a kingdom in a state of disorder. Though but twenty-one years of age, he was a strong man, able to restore peace and order. In a short time the marks of the anarchy of Stephen's time disappeared. The mercenaries were disbanded, the unlicensed castles destroyed, the refractory barons reduced to order and the orderly course of administration restored. From 1156 Henry, like his grandfather, was able to entrust administration to his justiciar and to spend much time on the continent.

The king's continental possessions, indeed, gave rise to his most difficult problem. Though wide in extent, they were without common tradition or homogeneity, and they so menaced the king of France that he took advantage of every opportunity which promised to break up this empire and to add part or all of it to his own domain. It included Normandy, which Henry had governed in person since 1150, Anjou of which he became count at his father's death in 1154, and the various parts of the great dukedom of Acquitaine, extending from the Loire to the Pyrenees, which had come to Henry in 1152 through his marriage to the duchess Eleanor. Subsequently, through the marriage of his son Geoffrey with the heiress of the duchy of Brittany, he came also to exercise lordship there. The various component parts of this great domain were feudal states, each with its own institutions. Their political unification and the establishment of strong government over them ultimately proved to be tasks too great for Henry and his two successors.

In England Henry was in 1163 drawn into a struggle over the rights of the church with Thomas Becket, the archbishop of Canterbury, and in 1164 caused to be drawn up the so-called Constitutions of Clarendon which set forth his claims in the matter. In this year the struggle became bitter and Becket fled to the continent. His return in 1170 was followed shortly by his murder, as a result of which the king had to renounce the main contentions of the Constitutions. In 1166 the king issued the Assize of Clarendon by which the administration of criminal law was reformed, and ten years later the Assize of Northampton which was a revision of that of Clarendon.

Henry's rule in England was marked especially by his judicial reforms which constituted his greatest work. Building on the foundations laid by Henry I, he advanced the organization to the king's courts. To him England owes the main features of her judiciary and the beginnings of the common law system. In 1181 he issued the Assize of Arms which provided a new basis of obligation for service in the *fyrd* and in 1184 the Assize of Woodstock, which reorganized the forest law. He also improved the central administration and further organized the royal finances. After the recapture of Jerusalem by the Turks in 1187 he agreed with the French king to go on a crusade and in 1188 levied the famous Saladin tithe, the first general tax on personal property in England.

A revolt of the feudal nobility both in England and the continental possessions of the Angevin house occurred in 1173 and 1174. This was suppressed by the energy of the king and in England mainly by the justiciar, Richard de Lucy. Subsequent risings on the continent, from 1182 to 1184, like this one, grew out of the discontent of Henry's sons, who were craftily encouraged in rebellion by the French king, Philip Augustus. In 1187 Richard, the elder of the king's surviving sons, was again in revolt, and in 1189 he formed an alliance with Philip Augustus by which Henry was forced in his last days to cede Auvergne and submit to other demands.

Richard I (1189-1199) was an absentee king with the spirit of a knight errant. But seven months of his reign were spent in England, which was of importance to him chiefly as a source of revenue. This he employed to enable him to take a leading part in the third crusade, from 1190 to 1192. He was taken prisoner when returning from Palestine by way of Austria, and unprecedented exactions were necessary to ransom him from the Emperor before he could be released in 1194. His energies during the remaining years of his life were largely absorbed by a struggle with the French king. Philip had plotted during Richard's absence with John, the brother of the latter, who had surrendered to him territories in

Normandy and Touraine. The war against Philip Augustus also demanded special financial levies in England.

Aside from its importance in the history of taxation, the reign of Richard is notable in England for the rule of the king's justiciars. The greatest of these was Hubert Walter, the archbishop of Canterbury, who carried on the government from 1193 to 1198. Upon him fell a large part of the responsibility for the taxation of the reign. He made some improvement in the judicial system and in 1195 assigned knights to aid in the preservation of the peace.

John (1190-1216), the brother of Richard, was accepted as king to the exclusion of the claims of Arthur the son of Geoffrey, John's elder brother. John was vicious, irreligious, treacherous and impulsive to the point of rashness. Philip Augustus, true to his policy of weakening the Angevin power, supported the claims of Arthur. A personal wrong done by John to the heir of the count of La Manche in 1201 brought a rebellion of the nobles of Poitou. Their grievances were carried to the French king, who as John's overlord summoned him in 1202 to answer and then asserted his rights by force of arms. The long struggle of the French king to break up the Angevin empire now met with success. The Norman barons turned against John. The disappearance in 1203 of Arthur, who had fallen into his uncle's hands, gave credence to the report that John had murdered him. The Bretons and Angevins joined Philip Augustus, who in 1204 conquered Normandy, Maine, Anjou, Touraine, and part of Poitou. Of the vast possessions which Henry II had held on the continent, little more than Gascony remained in the hands of the English king.

John was soon involved in a struggle with the church. A dispute over the election of an archbishop of Canterbury brought the king into conflict with pope Innocent III. In 1208 England was placed under a general interdict, and the next year John was excommunicated. He defied the pope, seized much church property and from 1209 to 1211 advanced his position in Wales and in Ireland. In 1212 the pope declared him deposed and supported Philip Augustus in a plan to conquer England. The following year John was glad to forestall the impending invasion by acceptance of the demands of Innocent III and by fealty to the papacy which made England its vassal state.

John now attempted to regain his continental possessions, and the English baronage found opportunity to demand redress of their grievances. Most of the barons refused to join an expedition to Poitou, and in 1214 the French badly defeated John's allies at Bouvines in Flanders. This worked to the advantage of the discontented barons in England, who in 1215 forced the king to concede their demands and to accept a great charter of liberties which they submitted. The armed struggle was renewed in a short time, and the barons attempted to depose John and place on the English throne Prince Louis, the son of Philip Augustus. John died in October, 1216, while the struggle was still in progress.

In the government of England, Henry of Anjou adopted the methods and the machinery which had been employed so successfully by Henry I. Administrative centralization advanced, and the royal judicial system was extended. Henry II, though a foreigner whose chief interests were continental, devoted much attention to purely English matters. He had abundant energy and a genius for organization. The judicial system which he established on firm and permanent foundations was destined to become a unique feature of English polity and an important buttress of English liberty. There is every reason to believe that Henry's judicial work was popular in his own day. He reaped his reward in the devotion of the English at the crisis of the reign, the feudal rebellion of 1173-74. England remained the strength of the Angevin kings amid the vicissitudes of their continental position. After 1174 their power in the British Isles was not again menaced until the baronage headed a movement with the approval of practically the whole realm to end the misgovernment of King John and set forth as a main objective the rule of law.

In the reign of Henry II the royal court gained an obvious ascendancy over the shire court as well as the seigniorial court. At the beginning of the reign the king's *curia* was a tribunal for great men and great causes; by the end of the reign it was a court of ordinary resort. Through this growth of jurisdiction, particularly through the regular mission of itinerant justices to the various shires, the usage of the central courts was extended outward until the custom of the county court ceased to be the main source of authority, and it was possible to speak of a common law of England. Had old local custom alone become the main basis of national law, England would have been in danger of running to a variety of sectional usages, such as still appear in the law works of the reign of Henry I, and the shiremote instead of the king's *curia* would have remained the centre of gravity in the judicial system. The primacy of the king's court was furthered by strengthening the *curia* which attended the king, by establishing a sedentary branch in addition to the exchequer, and by stressing the visits to the shires of the itinerant justices, who were given a part in the fulfillment of justice which in a number of important respects excluded sheriffs and other local officials. The competence of the king's court was widened through the requirement that some cases be tried nowhere else; it was still further extended by employment of new forms of procedure and improved methods of trial which attracted many causes.

The reign of Henry II from its earlier years brought new activity in the central courts. There is no reason to hold that the exchequer disintegrated in Stephen's time, as has sometimes been supposed, but certainly prior to 1154 it was not in a very flourishing condition.[1] It was immediately established upon a firm footing. The barons of the exchequer were still members of the court which the king held personally and were expected to aid him in his judicial work.[2] The activity of this latter court was clearly increased by the fact that Henry II himself not only took a lawyer's interest in judicial matters but liked to participate in the trial of causes. Maitland found that the justices were even inclined to encourage the settlement of cases in the king's own presence.[3]

[1] See Round, *Geoffrey de Mandeville*, 99-100, 154. In 1154 its buildings at Westminster were in disrepair (*Pipe Roll*, 2 Henry II, p. 4).
[2] Pollock and Maitland, *History of English Law*, I. 155. The king's justices at the exchequer sometimes dispose of ordinary judicial business (*Chron. Monast. Abingdon*, II. 297).
[3] Pollock and Maitland, *Hist. Eng. Law*, I. 159.

Concerning the dispatch of judicial business before Henry II interesting details are recorded for the early years of the reign. The year of his accession there was laid before the king and special members of his *curia*, a claim that the abbot of Abingdon had been deprived of certain lands.[4] Another case, in which the abbot of Battle was concerned, after waiting until the king's presence could be assured, was in 1157 argued before him and his justices.[5] In the course of the hearing the king showed a technical knowledge of charters and upheld the genuineness of the one which the abbot placed in evidence. In 1160 a dispute between two Norman churches was settled at Rouen before the king,[6] and those who aided him in this trial form very much the same kind of a group that appeared about Henry I on similar occasions. They were an archbishop, four bishops, the chancellor, the constable of Normandy and one other curial attendant who was a layman.[7] Five years later a *curia regis* at Westminster included a curial bishop, two archdeacons, a dean, and two justiciars, Robert, earl of Leicester and Richard de Lucy. Besides these six, who are all mentioned as justices, the treasurer, a chamberlain and three marshals were also present.[8] In the king's own court the clerical element was at times strong. The more powerful baronage was hardly represented.[9] The household element was the real nucleus of the court, and among its justices might be included the principal barons of the exchequer.[10] Toward the end of the reign even the justices of the king's court sitting at Westminster were called *familiares* or members of the royal household, but

[4] *Hist. Monast. Abingdon*, II. 184.

[5] Chron. *Monast de Bello*, 85-97; Palgrave, *English Commonwealth*, II. xliv-xlv. Bigelow, *Placita Anglo-Normannica*, 175.

[6] Eyton, *Itinerary of Henry II*, p. 50.

[7] An important case between the church of York and the church of Gloucester was in 1157 tried before the king and a fairly numerous body, consisting of two bishops, four abbots, nine lesser ecclesiastical officials, two earls, eleven others, designated as barons, a constable, and three dapifers (Bigelow, *Placita*, 190-191).

[8] Eyton, *Itinerary of Henry I*, 85. Since this was at Michaelmas, the body is probably a reinforced form of the exchequer.

[9] Pollock and Maitland, *Hist. Eng. Law*, I. 154.

[10] *Ibid.*, I. 155.

they were at the same time termed either liegemen (*fideles*) [11] or barons.

The contact of the king with his court led to striking progress, but it was too direct for ordinary administrative purposes. The difficulties in the way of a judicial hearing before a court which attended a king constantly on the move in England or on the continent are well illustrated by a famous case which involved the inheritance of one Richard de Anesty. Richard or his messenger sought the king across the sea at various times to obtain writs, and the matter followed the king's wanderings. In all it came to the attention of Henry II over twenty times, until after six years had passed, a vast amount of trouble taken by de Anesty, and a large sum expended in prosecuting the case, it was finally decided in favor of the claimant.[12] Apparently he had to seek the king abroad even for necessary writs, such as would supposedly be issued by his justiciar in his absence. One is impelled at once to agree with the conclusion of Maitland that for the first ten or twelve years of the reign "royal justice is very royal indeed." [13]

The difficulties of this situation were avoided after a time by the issue of certain writs which were obtained by litigants from the justiciar in the king's absence or by writs of course issued by the chancery with little formality or expense. The effectiveness of writ process nevertheless depended upon ready access to a royal court. This was afforded before many years in the sessions held by itinerant justices who at frequent intervals visited the various counties. The business which came before them was also said to be transacted *in curia regis*.[14]

---

[11] Glanvill, VIII : 3, mentions proceedings in 1177 in the king's court at Westminster before the bishop of Ely, the bishop of Norwich, Ranulf Glanvill *et aliis fidelibus et familiaribus domini regis*. Cf. *aliis baronibus domini regis* (Bigelow, *Placita*, 267).

[12] Palgrave, *English Commonwealth*, II. pp. v-xxvii; Hubert Hall, *Court Life*, chap. 7.

[13] Pollock and Maitland, *Hist. of English Law*, I. 159.

[14] Assize of Clarendon, sec. 6; G. B. Adams, *Origin of English Constitution*, 130-131, 130, note 20; below, note 15.

But a distinction was drawn between the king's capital court and that held before his itinerant justices.[15]

The incorporation of the itinerant justices as a permanent and essential part of the judicial system may be assigned to the year 1166. Henry II in his earlier years still had justices locally resident,[16] but he occasionally sent out his justices on circuit. An insult offered to one of them in 1163 by an ecclesiastic[17] made a profound impression at the time and seems to have had rather far-reaching effects. The local mission of the justices, it is well known, is mentioned also at other times in the earlier years of King Henry's reign. No more is known of their work, however, than of that of the itinerant justices of Henry I.

At Clarendon in 1166 Henry II issued a decree or assize which created a new situation. This clearly sprang from a desire to improve the observance of the criminal law. To aid in the process a form of jury was regularly to be used, to report upon oath who in the community was suspected of being guilty of certain crimes. Twelve men from each hundred and four from each vill were to be placed upon oath to tell whether in their community any were suspected of being thieves, robbers or murderers. The accusers from the vill seem to be derived from Norman usage.[18] Persons accused by jury were to be tried before the king's justices when they visited the shire. There was thus designated a group of criminal cases which might be disposed of neither before the sheriff, nor the bailiff of the hundred, nor that of the seigniorial court. Those accused by juries in their respective localities according to the provisions of the Assize of Clarendon were to come only before the king's justices, who were to send them to the ordeal

[15] Glanvill, IX : 11 : *in capitali curia vel coram justiciis regis ad tales inquisitiones faciendas in diversas regni partes. Curia Regis Rolls* (1922), I. 208 : *in curia domini regis coram justiciariis itinerantibus.*

[16] Doris M. Stenton, *Cambridge Med. History*, V. 584.

[17] Eyton, *Itinerary of Henry II*, 63 ; *Materials for Life of Becket*, III. 45.

[18] Above, chap. 11, p. 174. The sheriff apparently made use also of the heads of frankpledge tithings.

of cold water to decide their guilt or innocence.[19] The chattels of those convicted were to go to the king and all profits of this justice belonged solely to him.[20] The mission of the itinerant justices, or, as it is technically called, the eyre, was now a regular institution of the realm, an essential part of the judicial system.

Its work was easily enlarged by the simple process of adding items of business to the articles placed in the hands of the justices before they went out. This involved much less effort than the commissioning of special justices to deal with individual matters, although Henry II and his successors continued to follow the latter plan also in unusual cases. By the Assize of Northampton in 1176 the justices who visited the counties were ordered to include counterfeiting and arson in the list of crimes which they handled upon jury indictment;[21] they were also, when authorized by writ of the king or his representative, to determine all pleas and rights pertaining to the crown unless the matter was so great that it required the personal attention of the king;[22] moreover they were to inquire through juries concerning cases in which an individual had been dispossessed of property without judicial process. Within a decade after 1166 the eyre was being utilized to dispose of a considerable variety of matters, most of them pleas of the crown, but others affecting private property rights.[23] In 1194 it was employed to make inquest into the king's fiscal claims and interests in many forms, while at the same time it was required to deal with crime as usual and with jury cases involving title to land under the value of a hundred shillings.[24] By this time the form of the eyre was fairly well established.

[19] Assize of Clarendon, secs. 1, 2, 5, in Stubbs, *Select Charters*, 143; Adams and Stephens, *Select Documents*, no. 14.

[20] *Ibid.*, sec. 5.

[21] Assize of Northampton, sec. 1, in Stubbs, *Sel. Charters*, 150-51; Adams and Stephens, *Sel. Docs.*, 20-21.

[22] *Ibid.*, secs. 7, 9, 11, 13.

[23] *Ibid.*, sec. 5; cf. sec. 4.

[24] Stubbs, *Sel. Charters*, 259-263; Adams and Stephens, *Sel. Documents*, 29-33.

Henceforth there was merely a process of changing or adding articles or heads of pleas which the justices were instructed to take up.[25] The records of King John's reign show that, so far as criminal cases were concerned, it had practically reached its later form.

Much attention was given in the reign of Henry II to the detail of the eyre system. The various circuits were rearranged from time to time and the number of justices employed varied. In 1176 it was eighteen, in 1179, twenty-one.[26] A persistent effort was made for the improvement of the personnel and efficiency of this force.[27] Not only did their visits to the shire aid in establishing uniform legal usage and make the men of the shire familiar with the details of the king's business and the process by which it was transacted, but these circuits were of great administrative importance. The justices made inquest by jury to ascertain the king's fiscal rights, and they were ordered at times to undertake other duties which were purely administrative. The work of some eyres of the time of Henry II was purely fiscal.

The centralization of criminal justice in the hands of the itinerant justices enabled them to enforce some peculiar fiscal claims of the crown. The frankpledge obligation was enforced from 1166 through amercements laid by the justices upon the tithings which failed to produce an absconding member and upon communities which neglected to see that men were in tithing.[28] The Norman murder-fine was levied by these officials upon the hundred in which an unknown person was found dead. In the same way was enforced the responsibility of the vill to raise hue and cry when a crime was committed and that of vills and hundreds whose jurors failed to make due presentment of criminals. The amercement of a county court which gave false judgment was similarly carried into

[25] In 1176 the justices were sworn to observe the plan laid down (Benedict, I. 108). For the Articles of 1198, Hoveden, IV. 61-62.
[26] Benedict of Peterborough, I. 107, 238.
[27] Diceto, I. 434-435.
[28] Morris, *Frankpledge System*, 92.

effect.[29] Records of the criminal business of an eyre in the time of Richard or John,[30] are thus concerned with a considerable number of usages the maintenance of which brought an income to the king. All the necessary data were gathered for the justices by jury presentment, much of it before the sheriff in the county court and at his view of frankpledge in the hundreds. From the time of Richard I the record of these matters was preserved by coroners.[31] Under the Angevin administration of the pleas of the crown the justices enforced a series of legal and police regulations, some of them dating from the Norman period, through which almost any individual or community was liable to a pecuniary penalty imposed for a technical reason.

Because of the oppression of the justices, apparently through their wide power of levying amercements, there was set up the first central court of ordinary resort which did not follow the king. The exchequer tended to become sedentary at an earlier time, but it dealt primarily with fiscal cases. The king, after having in various ways districted the realm for purposes of the judicial circuit, in 1178 took the famous step of designating five justices, all members of his household, two clerks and three laymen, who were "not to depart from the *curia regis* and who were to hear the complaints of the realm and do justice." If any matter arose which they could not conclude they were to refer it to the king that it might be terminated before him.[32] There was thus established a sedentary court superior to that of the itinerant justices but inferior to the king's small council.[33] The justices on circuit did their work *in curia regis*,[34] the court at Westminster was referred to as a

[29] As in Pipe Rolls, 3-4 Richard I (Pipe Roll Soc., n. s. II), 39.

[30] See for example *Rolls of the King's Court*, no. 3 (Pipe Roll Soc., vol. 14, no. 3). *Select Pleas of the Crown*, Selden Soc., 23-36.

[31] Form of judicial visitation, 1194, sec. 20, Stubbs, *Select Charters*, 260; Adams and Stephens, *Select Docs.*, 30.

[32] Benedict of Peterborough, R. S., I. 207.

[33] See G. B. Adams, *Council and Courts*, chap. 8. Cf. Glanvill I : 13, *coram me vel justiciis meis apud Westmonasterium.*

[34] Above, p. 273.

capitalis curia regis, but above the latter was the court held *coram rege,*[35] that is to say, in the king's presence.

The justices of the new court are mentioned by Glanvill as remaining upon the bench at Westminster. It is probable that they were merged with the group attending the king personally when he was in residence. Certainly the line of cleavage between the jurisdiction of the two courts was not very distinct, and even in John's time cases might be transferred from either one to the other.[36] The rolls existing from 1194 onward show that there was a strong court meeting term after term at Westminster under the presidency of the justiciar and assigning matters to the itinerant justices. During the long periods of Richard's absence no court could actually be held *coram rege* in England,[37] and important cases had to be tried before the bench at Westminster. Probably for some such reason, in 1201 this court ruled that it might take up pleas specifically reserved for trial before the king or his chief justice.[38] On the other hand the king himself in this year held sessions of a court term after term which apparently disposed of the same kinds of business as the court at Westminster.[39] The later division between the work of the court of common bench and the court *coram rege* is not yet traceable. The court at Westminster can not well have been the later court of king's bench, as Stubbs holds, because it was neither a meeting of the council nor a court held in the king's presence. Moreover it can not have been identical with the later court of common pleas, because the work of the two courts was not well differentiated and the king might still hear common as well as crown pleas.[40] In 1215 this situation was cleared up somewhat

[35] Glanvill, VIII : 5.

[36] Adams, *Council and Courts,* 224-227.

[37] In 1199 some matters came up *coram domino rege ultra mare* (*Rot. Curiae Regis,* ed. 1922, I. 98, 256).

[38] *Ibid.,* I. 462.

[39] *Ibid.,* I. 254, ff., 374, ff., 413, ff. For the latest review of the situation, Adams, *Council and Courts,* 240-247; for the whole question concerning the court of 1178, *ibid.,* chap. 8.

[40] For the view of Stubbs, *Constitutional History,* I. 525, 645-646. For proof that this was not technically a council of magnates, Pike, *House*

when Magna Carta provided that common pleas should no longer follow the king but should be held in a fixed place.[41] Henceforth such pleas were confined to the sedentary court. Even later it might still be combined with the court *coram rege* either when the king was present or when he was a minor and held no travelling court.

The appearance of a body of professional justices and also of a permanent tribunal of sworn justices,[42] as well as the regular mission of justices upon eyre, greatly facilitated the conduct of the business of the king's courts and the rise of a common law. Justice in the king's courts now followed less the feudal principle of judgment by peers and became more frankly royal in character.[43] It was gaining a national aspect which set it off from the principles embodied on the one hand in the Code of Justinian and on the other in the canon law newly formulated by Gratian. The working of justice in the king's courts after a time appears in official record. A series of *curia regis* rolls begins in 1194,[44] and by the later years of John's reign there is already a considerable body of record which shows that familiar thirteenth-century procedure is being followed. From this judges and law writers, when they feel the need, will henceforth be able to seek precedents for their guidance. Thus the old Germanic principle of a self-developing law will hold the field against the code law of Rome, and the common law of England will stand out in marked contrast to the civil law followed in most continental states.

The common law naturally took for granted much feudal law and very much more of the usage of the old public courts held locally. The visits of the justices and the supremacy of the

of Lords, 254-255; Harcourt, *His Grace the Steward*, chap. 9, and *English Histor. Rev.*, XXIII, 732-740; Adams, *Council and Courts*, 219-225, 247-250. For Maitland's view that this is the later court of common pleas, *Select Pleas of the Crown* (Selden Soc.) pp. xi-xix.

[41] *Magna Carta*, sec. 17.

[42] Pollock and Maitland, *Hist. Eng. Law*, I. 154, 169-170.

[43] G. B. Adams (*Origin of Eng. Constitution*, 131) holds, however, that the itinerant justices held assembly courts.

[44] It is clear that concords or feet of fines were being recorded as early as 1175 (Round, *Eng. Hist. Rev.*, XII. 293).

king's courts made for uniformity. In case these agencies saw fit to suppress local tendencies or to introduce new principles of general application, they easily succeeded. Even in the Norman period the principle of the immobility and the superiority of the usage of the king's courts was well known. But against the ecclesiastical and the seigniorial courts the new judicial system had a struggle. The canon law was indeed of limited application, but this was hardly true of feudal justice. Against the latter in causes between subject and subject the king's justice prevailed only as it was made more effective and more popular than that of the lords. This process was greatly aided by Henry II through the introduction of improved forms of procedure and methods of trial which attracted civil causes. The royal prerogative and the king's ordinance were employed in some instances to reserve jurisdiction to the king's courts, but such action alone could not have rendered the king's courts nor the common law supreme.

This process, however, was necessary when Henry undertook to reduce the jurisdiction of the ecclesiastical courts. The real conflict was brief, extending over the period from 1164 to 1172. In the Constitutions of Clarendon in 1164 the king sought to establish a measure of jurisdiction over criminous clerks and to check the course of appeals to Rome in ecclesiastical causes. In both these matters he failed, although later a papal legate agreed that the king's courts should have jurisdiction over the clergy in cases involving breach of forest laws.[45] One or two jurisdictional claims made in the Constitutions of Clarendon the king fully vindicated as against the church. He ordained that jurisdiction should rest with the king's courts in pleas of debt even when there was involved a question of the breach of a customary form of oath by which the debtor promised to repay.[46] Moreover he successfully claimed for his own court the right to decide whether

[45] Below, p. 357.
[46] Constitutions of Clarendon, sec. 15, in Stubbs, *Sel. Charters*, 140; Adams and Stephens, *Sel. Docs.*, 14. Cf. Pollock and Maitland, *Hist. of English Law* (1899), II. 197-200.

land in dispute was held by lay or ecclesiastical tenure [47] and thus to determine whether the main issue should be decided in the royal court or the court Christian.[48] These were not great gains, but they would no doubt have been greater had it not been for the murder of Henry's great opponent, Archbishop Becket. The struggle resulted in drawing the line between the two jurisdictions much as it remained throughout the middle ages.

Legislative decree or administrative mandate accomplished still more in extending the king's jurisdiction in matters which were exclusively of secular concern. Even the Norman kings had thus regulated matters of jurisdiction.[49] Stephen made a grant to an abbot in which it was directed that the latter should plead concering his property rights only before the king.[50] Henry II not only asserted for his justices the sole right to try criminals indicted by jury, but he also introduced in proprietary cases the regular use of the writ *praecipe quod reddat,* an alternative writ, which ordered a person either to surrender the property in question to the claimant or to present himself before the king's justices for a determination of the matter at issue.[51] Another writ employed, the writ of peace, was a prohibition which estopped proceedings in a local court with respect to a proprietary cause assigned to or brought before the justices.[52]

The total effect of these prerogative measures would have been very much less had they not been accompanied by new methods of disposing of cases touching the possession of or title to property. Here Henry II introduced jury procedure, which could be employed by no one but the king or someone to whom he gave the right to use it.[53] By his assize or edict

[47] *Ibid.,* sec. 9.
[48] Below, p. 354.
[49] Above, p. 241.
[50] *Chron. Monast. Abingdon,* II. 181.
[51] Cf. Glanvill, I. 6.
[52] Glanvill, II. 8, 9.
[53] Henry once conferred this right upon an abbot (Pollock and Maitland, *History of English Law,* I. 143).

he specified that certain questions should be settled only by the finding of a jury before his justices.

The first of these specified forms of procedure, known as the assize *utrum*, he introduced in 1164, when he directed that the question whether a given piece of land was held as lay fee or by ecclesiastical tenure was to be decided by a jury of twelve before the king's justices.[54] Two years later he enacted a new assize, that of *novel disseisin*, which incorporated a usage sometimes enforced under Stephen and in King Henry's earlier years.[55] The principle applied was that no man might lose seisin or possession of his freehold tenement except by legal judgment. If he was thus dispossessed, the question became one for inquiry in the king's courts, again by a jury of twelve. If it was found that he had been dispossessed without due process of law, the king's court restored his seisin.[56] About the same time assize procedure was applied to a somewhat similar situation. By the assize of *mort d'ancestor* the heir was assured of the same seisin that the father had on the day of his death, and the justices upon complaint were required to ascertain by jury recognition what the father held at the time, so the son or other heir might be placed in lawful possession.[57] A third possessory assize, established at some time during the reign and known as the assize of *darrien* presentment, guaranteed the right to present or nominate the incumbent of a church living to the person, or the heir of the person, who had done so when the last vacancy occurred. In this case also the question was to be settled in the king's court by jury recognition to determine who the patron was that exercised this right on the occasion of the preceding vacancy of the church in question.[58]

[54] Constitutions of Clarendon, sec. 9.
[55] *Hist. Monast. Abingdon*, II. 184, 222, 223; cf. *Chartulary St. Peter of Gloucester* (Rolls Ser.), I. 242, 264.
[56] Cf. Assize of Northampton, sec. 5; Glanvill, XIII. 32-39; Pollock and Maitland, *History of English Law*, I. 146.
[57] Assize of Northampton, sec. 4, in Stubbs, *Select Charters*, 151-52; Adams and Stephens, *Select Documents*, 21-22; *Glanvill*, XIII. 2-7.
[58] Glanvill, IV. 1; XIII. 18, 19.

Under the assize *utrum* and the three possessory assizes the
king's writ was necessary to institute proceedings, and the
original writ which was issued ordered the justices to summon
a jury of twelve to answer one specific question. The only issue involved in the latter three cases was merely the right
to possession. With the matter of ultimate right or title to
property these proceedings were not concerned.

Right or ownership in land, so it has been shown earlier,
was decided according to the law of Norman England in the
king's court, the court of another lord, or in some cases in the
county court. Trial was by duel, a risky affair in which one of
the combatants was sometimes killed.[59] Moreover the vanquished not only lost the property in question but in addition
forfeited the rather high[60] sum of sixty shillings. All of this
was perpetuated until a much later period, but under Henry
II the requirement was made that, when right either to land
held by freehold tenure or to free service was claimed, a court,
even that of the lord, might hear the cause only when the
claimant produced a writ of right from the king or his justices.[61] Fairly late in his reign Henry II introduced an alternative to trial by battle. By counsel of his barons he enacted
what was known as the grand assize. This permitted the pos-
sessor whose title was questioned to submit his case to the
decision of an assize jury of twelve knights whose duty it was
to answer the question which claimant had the better right.
When the verdict of the knights settled this, right to the land
was permanently decided just as in the case of trial by duel.
The new procedure was safer and more rational. Granvill described it as a boon conferred by the prince upon his people.
It was a popular means of drawing cases to the king's court,
for only there were causes decided by assize juries. When the
defendant once declared before the justices that he placed

[59] For a thirteenth century instance, see *Calendar of County Court
Rolls of Chester*, Chetham Soc., 23; cf. Glanvill, II. 7.
[60] Glanvill, II. 3; cf. Liebermann, *Gesetze*, I. 484; Robertson, *Laws of
Kings of England*, 233 (2:2).
[61] Glanvill, XII. 2, 25; see forms of the writ, *ibid.*, XII. 3-5.

himself upon the grand assize, he might not turn back and must abide by the finding of the twelve knights in the king's court.[62]

The system of assizes is of vast importance in the history of English law. It rests upon the principle that if a freeman is dispossessed without lawful judgment his seisin shall be restored by authority of the king's courts. It follows the doctrine that the question of title or right of a man in possession may not be tried by duel before the king's writ of right has been obtained, and it encourages the defendant to choose the jurisdiction of the king's court. The enactment of the grand assize has been regarded as the greatest event in the history of English law. At one stroke it guaranteed in causes of basic importance to property right both the supremacy of the royal courts and that of jury procedure. It led the way to trial by jury in other civil matters. Trial by assize had heretofore been prescribed by enactment. The original writ which opened proceedings under the possessory assizes directed the use of an assize jury. Here it was unavoidable. The grand assize left it open to the individual to choose for himself a desirable course which led to jury trial. While use of the assize was mandatory, that of the jury was optional. The voluntary employment of anything so advantageous as the grand assize facilitated the voluntary submission of questions to juries in all sorts of cases. "In course of time the jury which has its roots in the fertile ground of consent will grow at the expense of the assize which has sprung from the stony soil of ordinance." [63]

There is very general agreement that the jury as it took root in England was introduced from Normandy by William the Conqueror and that it was derived from Frankish usage. In the form in which it appears in Frankish lands it was an inquest by which the Carolingian kings obtained information

---

[62] Glanvill, II. 6, 7; Pollock and Maitland, *History of English Law*, I. 147; II. 621. As to the date when the grand assize was instituted, see J. H. Round in *Eng. Histor. Rev.*, XXXI. 268-69.

[63] Pollock and Maitland, *ibid.*, I. 149.

useful to the crown or to crown officials.[64] The essence of the early English jury is that it was a body of men of a certain community placed upon oath before a public official to give a true answer to some question.[65] Unlike our jurors, these were witnesses to facts; unlike the compurgators of earlier English law they swore to tell the truth, not to assent to a fixed formula; unlike the doomsmen who found judgment, they merely gave answer to a specific question. While under the Norman kings the jury might be employed to make recognition of usage or fact useful in determining judicial causes,[66] its basic character was still that of a royal inquest. Its most important use was that which the king made for his own purposes, as when William I collected the Domesday returns by means of a wholesale series of local inquests upon the oaths of men of the various shires, hundreds and vills, or when Henry I placed twenty-four burgesses of Winchester upon oath to determine what were the king's rights there.[67]

An institution much like the jury is found among early Scandinavian peoples,[68] and there is a possibility that their usage in England, if left to itself, might have produced some of the essential elements. Of such a trend before the arrival of the Normans there is but one hint and this of very uncertain import. A law of King Ethelred, clearly designed to have effect in the Danish region, declares that the reeve and the twelve senior thegns are to take an oath in the court of the wapentake that they will accuse no innocent man and shield no guilty one.[69] Some have supposed that the men thus sworn constitute an accusation jury, but this is not clear. Early Germanic and Scandinavian law sufficiently recognized the right of any freeman to make accusations.

[64] Brunner, *Entstehung der Schwurgerichte*, 87-97; Pollock and Maitland, History of English Law, I. 140-141.

[65] Pollock and Maitland, *History of English Law*, I. 138.

[66] *Hist. Monast. St. Augustini* (Rolls Ser.), 353-4, 356; Davis, *Regesta*, no. 448; *Chron. Abingdon*, II. 84-85; *Ramsey Chartulary*, I. 247.

[67] *Domesday Book*, IV. 531.

[68] Pollock and Maitland, I. 142-143.

[69] III Ethelred, 3:1.

Not this but rather the finding of judgment, so far as known, was the duty of the senior thegns. It seems probable that this passage alludes to the fact that they passed upon the previous reputation of an accused person who was on trial.[70] Certainly they formed a permanent body, not a temporary one, like the later jury. Moreover no known link connects them with the accusation jury of the Assize of Clarendon. It is much more likely that the latter was derived from a body which more than two centuries earlier on the continent made accusations in ecclesiastical courts.[71] Before the accusation jury was established by Henry II for his own courts it was required in some matters before the bishop's court, in Normandy after 1159 and in England after 1164.[72]

But, whatever the manner in which this particular form of the jury was transmitted, all forms in the reign of Henry II represent essentially the idea of the Frankish inquest. They are varieties of the inquest or recognition by which the Norman king had gained information bearing upon his financial rights or otherwise useful in administration. The accusation jury performs a definitely specialized function when it answers the question as to who in the community is accused of crime, but for a long time to come the same juries of the hundred and the vill which do this before the justices will also answer various questions of concern purely to the king's fiscal interests.[73] The assize jury, or assize as it is more commonly called, is still more highly specialized, for it gives answer to but one specific question of fact and this decides a civil issue. Except for the assize the jury might still be regarded as an engine of despotism. It first associated the jury

---

[70] Above, pp. 94, 114. These lawmen according to *Leges Edwardi Confessoris*, 38 : 2, were actually so employed.

[71] Pollock and Maitland, *History of English Law*, I. 142.

[72] Haskins, *Norman Institutions*, 219, 220 ; Constitutions of Clarendon, sec. 6.

[73] See Assize of Northampton, secs. 9, 11, and Form of Judicial Visitation of 1194, prelude and secs. 2-6, 10-15. One set of juries even in the time of Edward I made answer to all the articles of the pleas of the crown.

with the maintenance of landed rights and some protection
of the weak against the strong.[74]

Trial by jury in one important class of cases which concerned the subject was not regularly introduced in the Angevin
period. Criminal causes were still disposed of by compurgation
or ordeal. The person accused by jury was sent by the justices to the cold water ordeal. This was the method of trial
also upon private accusations of serious offenses.[75] Compurgation long remained in local courts, especially in civil matters, but from the Assize of Clarendon it tended to give way
to the ordeal whenever crime was tried in the king's courts.
By 1200 the calling of a special jury to decide whether an accused person was guilty, appears as a special privilege allowed
the accused person who purchased it, but this method of disposing of a case came as a regular course of procedure only
after the death of King John. The ordeal by fire and water
received its death blow in 1215 when the Lateran Council
forbade the clergy any longer to participate. This rule was
formally recognized in England in 1219, and the justices,
deprived of the ancient mode of trial, found it necessary to
submit the question of the guilt or innocence of a prisoner to
a jury.[76] It was still essential that the accused formally place
himself upon the verdict of the country, as it was called. For
centuries it was necessary to apply pressure to compel a
defendant to accept this mode of trial if he objected. In 1215
trial by jury in criminal cases was not yet an ordinary part
of the law of the land. Moreover, it was long possible for the
person who was accused by an individual to challenge him in
the Norman fashion and to submit the issue to judgment by
duel.[77]

In some instances, however, before 1215, when charges were
preferred by the old method of private accusation or appeal,

[74] Pollock and Maitland, *History of English Law*, II. 604, 632.
[75] Glanvill, XIV : 1-2.
[76] Pollock and Maitland, *Hist. English Law*, II. 618-619, 619, note 2,
650-652.
[77] *Ibid.*, II. 632-634.

as it was called, the accused might escape a duel with the accuser by a resort to jury procedure. This he obtained by avoiding the main question and raising a secondary issue termed an exception (*exceptio*). If, for instance, he alleged that he was accused out of hatred and malice (*de odio et atia*), he might apply for the summoning of a jury to declare whether or not this was true.[78] In case the jury decided in his favor, he might then be admitted to bail to await the action of the justices.[79] So important was this right regarded that the barons in 1215 caused to be included in Magna Carta [80] a provision requiring that the writ *de odio et atia* be issued freely and without charge.

The reforms of Henry II mark the real foundation of the English judicial system. By the end of the reign writers speak of a common law or a custom of England.[81] Through the procuring of a writ of course at the chancery an individual might freely bring important matters touching his property rights into the king's court. By placing himself upon the grand assize he might effect transfer of an issue concerning his ultimate right in land from a county or a seigniorial court and bring this also before the king's justices to be decided by jury and not by ordeal. In several important respects jury trial was associated with the maintenance of the rights of the subject. There was a vast improvement in the means of rendering justice. The struggle of the barons against King John clearly brings out the fact that some of the reforms of his father were regarded as basic to the liberties of the landholding baronage.[82] They were equally available to all who held land by any form of freehold tenure.

From the new judicial system the sovereign profited even

[78] The usage is mentioned in 1198 (*Curia Regis Rolls*, 1922, I. 39), and again in 1200 (*ibid.*, 256, 342).

[79] Pollock and Maitland, II. 587-589.

[80] Sec. 36. See McKechnie, *Magna Carta* (1914), 361-362.

[81] Glanvill, XIII. 25; *Dialogus de Scaccario*, Oxford ed., 105.

[82] Pollock and Maitland, I. 146: "The most famous words of Magna Carta will enshrine the formula of novel disseisin." Cf. *Magna Carta*, sec. 39.

more. The extension of the activity of the king's courts, particularly the eyre, brought a notable increase in the king's income and his direct authority. The itinerant justices imposed a material check upon the sheriff's independence, both fiscal and judicial. In 1194 he was forbidden to serve as justice in his own county, and in 1215 to hold any pleas of the crown.[83] Something was gained at the expense of the ecclesiastical courts but more at the expense of the feudal lords. The Assize of Clarendon asserted the principle that in pleas of the crown no feudal franchise was effective as against the authority of the itinerant justices. Feudal lords found it necessary not only to admit the sheriff to make arrests on their lands in important criminal cases, but to allow their men of even the most highly exempt manor or honor to appear before the justices to make jury presentment of criminals. All matters which were the subject of jury presentment were tried before the justices and the perquisites including the chattels of those convicted belonged to the king.[84] The grand assize offered a constant inducement to litigants to remove one highly important class of case from the court of the lord to that of the king. Moreover the writ *praecipe quod reddat* might be used to remove many property cases directly into the king's court. This struck at the feudal principle that the lord was to do justice to his man.[85] When the barons had their day against King John, this alone of the judicial innovations of Henry II was subjected to alteration.

The administrative effects of King Henry's judicial reforms were quite as far-reaching, for they materially increased the king's income and his direct authority. The itinerant justices not only served as a check upon the power of the sheriff, but they assumed some administrative functions. They were employed to tender the oath of fealty at disturbed seasons, to supervise the destruction of unlicensed castles,[86] to levy tall-

[83] Form of Judicial Visitation of 1194, sec. 21 ; Magna Carta, sec. 24.
[84] Assize of Clarendon, secs. 5, 8-11.
[85] See Adams, *Origin of English Constitution*, 96, ff.
[86] Assize of Northampton, secs. 6, 8.

ages, to stock the king's manors, to secure jury presentment regarding the king's fiscal rights in an almost infinite number of instances.[87] The opportunities of making inquests of the Norman type were multiplied, and were extended both to offenses against the king's peace and to royal financial interests. The presentments made before the justices by the men of the hundred and the vill represent an advance in criminal law, but, more important still, they embody a scheme of administrative centralization. Monarchy was now reinforced by a powerful and effective scheme of royal supervision, and Angevin, as contrasted with Norman, absolutism, had gained an effective institutional support.

Innovations of wide significance for future constitutional development came in through these new measures. The presentment of juries representing local communities before the itinerant justices in the county court acquainted men with the details of the king's business and his methods of transacting it. Local juries on a few occasions were called upon by Henry II and Richard I to assess property for public purposes including taxation.[88] This plan was employed in 1198 to levy a new tax of nation-wide application. The inquest jury became the tap-root of the later parliamentary system. Before John's day the local juries, consisting of men of the county, the hundred, the vill or the borough, had been employed on notable occasions to aid the king in his fiscal work. The representative principle was thus early associated with the levy of taxation.

The law and usage of the royal courts sprang in part from old custom, but in part from the crown and the *curia*. It was natural that its execution should be profoundly affected by royal influence. The king and his council had not ceased making pronouncements. The usage of the justices so far as it protected the rights and secured the income of the king has

---

[87] Assize of Northampton, sec. 7; Form of Judicial Visitation, 1194, secs. 3-6, 10, 13-17, 19, 22; Stubbs, *Constitutional History*, I. 626-627.

[88] Assize of Arms, sec. 9; Ordinance of Saladin Tithe, sec. 2; Stubbs, *Constitutional History*, I. 626-628.

been called crown law as opposed to national law. How far the latter existed in 1215 is a question upon which authorities are at hopeless variance. Whether the law of the assize procedure was as yet merely a set of regulations to protect feudal tenure, or whether it was a usage which enshrined rights felt to be national, may not be accurately determined. The king might think of law as a series of regulations which he set forth, yet the realm in general was bound to regard it chiefly as well recognized usage. It was in this latter sense that Magna Carta marked the first great attempt to insist that the king himself should observe the law.

AUTHORITIES

The *Tratactus de Legibus et Consultudinibus,* by Ranulf Glanvill sets forth the procedure of the king's courts as it stood in the time of Henry II. The author was the chief justiciar of the kingdom, and the work was completed in 1188 or 1189. It is the earliest scientific work of the middle ages on the laws of any European country. The author makes, however, no attempt to cover the whole law, and is concerned with the procedure of the king's courts and largely with the use of various forms of writs which are being introduced to carry out the assizes.

A brief record of certain proceedings in the royal courts is occasionally found from 1175, but from 1194 the records are continuous. Two volumes of the earliest of these, edited by Sir Francis Palgrave, were published under the title *Rotuli Curiæ Regis* (Record Commission, 1833). F. W. Maitland published others of the years 1194-1196 in his *Three Rolls of the King's Court* (Pipe Roll Society, vol. 14, 1891), and in his *Select Pleas of the Crown* (Selden Society, 1888) published several rolls of itinerant justices belonging to John's earlier years. The British government has recently undertaken the publication of the remaining rolls of the king's courts for the reigns of Richard and John, and four volumes of *Curia Regis Rolls* (Record Commission, ed. C. T. Flower, 1922-1929) have appeared in this new series.

Some of the chronicles are especially useful for the information they give concerning the judicial reforms of Henry II. The best of these is the work known under the name of Benedict of Peterborough, covering the period to 1192. It was edited in the Rolls Series by William Stubbs (2 vols., 1867). This chronicle is especially useful because its author was well informed as to what went on at court and included many documents. The *Chronicon* of Roger of Hoveden, which comes down to 1201 also includes documents. The more important ones have been collected by Stubbs in his *Select Charters*. A good number of these appear in English translation in G. B. Adams and H. Morse Stephens, *Select Documents of English Constitutional History* (1901). Some useful cases, collected from the sources appear in the second volume of the *English Commonwealth* by Sir Francis Palgrave (1832), others in *Placita Anglo-Normannica* by M. M. Bigelow (1879).

An account of the judicial changes under Henry II was presented by William Stubbs in his introduction to Benedict of Peterborough (II. pp. lx-lxxvi), and in chapters 12, 13 of his *Constitutional History*. From the legal point of view the best account is that in F. Pollock and F. W. Maitland, *History of English Law* (1895; 2d ed. 1899). Some useful supplementary material will be found in the introduction to *The Earliest Lincolnshire Assize Rolls*, 1202-1209 (Lincoln Record Society, vol. 22, 1926), edited by D. M. Stenton. The standard history of the origin and introduction of the jury into Frankish, Norman, and English usage is Heinrich Brunner, *Entstehung der Schwurgerichte* (1872). G. B. Adams in his *Council and Courts in Anglo-Norman England* (1926) presents some new conclusions concerning the organization and work of the central courts in the Angevin period. James B. Thayer, in chapter 2 of his *A Preliminary Treatise on Evidence at the Common Law* (1898) gives an account of the development of trial by jury. The strongest attempt to prove that the jury is of Germanic origin is that of Ernst Mayer in his *Geschworenen Gerichts und Inquisitions Process* (1916).

CHAPTER XIII

THE GREAT AND THE SMALL COUNCIL

When the Angevin king is found holding a council the record usually makes it clear whether this is the lesser *curia* or the great assembly. Sessions of the great council might of course be held whenever the king desired, but the ceremony of the solemn [1] Norman crown-wearing days still served to designate some of them. Under Henry II most of the stated meetings which are recorded were at Christmas or Easter, although such meetings at Whitsuntide are mentioned.[2] Some were observed with the old formality,[3] but these were not held regularly three times a year. The Angevin kings depended mainly upon sessions called at special times as occasion demanded. The ancient ceremonial meetings tended to fade into less significant observances,[4] to be revived only in special coronations, such as those of kings who had just succeeded to the throne, or that of King Richard in 1194 to symbolize his sovereignty after his return from captivity.[5]

The place of meeting varied to suit the king's convenience, and there was less fixity than in the Norman period. Two

[1] As late as Christmas 1180, *tenuit curiam suam sollemnem* (Benedict, I. 269). See below, notes 3, 4, 7.

[2] *Ibid.*, I. 240; Palgrave, *English Commonwealth*, II. p. xliv.

[3] . . . *diademata insignitus regali* (*ibid.*, II. p. xliv). Henry II observed Christmas at Bur in 1171 and *voluit ut magnifice festivitas celebraretur. Interfuerunt episcopi; abbates, comites barones et multa multis largitus est* (Robert de Torigni, Rolls Series, 253).

[4] Henry held *sollemne festum* on his last Christmas although some of the earls and barons had deserted him (Benedict II. 61). So Richard I at Bur, Christmas, 1190 (Benedict, II. 104). Cf. Stubbs, *Constnl. Hist.*, I. 603. As to ceremony, Benedict, II. 3; Hoveden, III. 240.

[5] For the coronation of 1170, Benedict, I. 5; Gervase of Canterbury, II. 219; for Richard's coronation in 1189, Benedict II. 79; for that in 1194, Gervase I. 524-525.

important sessions at Clarendon in the vicinity of a royal forest indicate that King Henry liked to find surcease from business in the pleasure of the chase. Meetings at Woodstock, at Pipewell and at Nottingham [6] offer the same suggestion. The royal residences of Windsor, Winchester and Westminster were frequently the meeting-places. Even the crown-wearing days were not celebrated in fixed places according to earlier custom. Henry II was entirely too active a king to observe such convention, and it broke down.[7]

The assembly was still called either *curia* or *concilium*, but the use of both words to designate also the lesser council was calling for more precise nomenclature. This was required, too, by the increasing employment of the word *curia* to indicate a court in the purely judicial sense, sometimes a court quite separate physically from either the national assembly or the king's more intimate council. The great assembly of the realm is called the great *curia* (*magna curia*) [8] but more frequently the great council (*magnum concilium*).[9] It is also mentioned under the name *colloquium*,[10] a fact of considerable interest because the idea of conversation or discussion, which was associated with the king's councils in the time of Henry II,[11] is the same as that expressed in the word parliament, a word already employed, especially by French writers,[12] to describe a conference or parley. The statement often made, that the great council was known as the common council of the realm, has been shown to be in error.[13] This arose from the fact that the decisions of the body were often

---

[6] Stubbs, *Constnl. Hist.*, I. 611.

[7] See Stubbs, *Outline Itinerary of Henry II*, Benedict II. preface, pp. cxxix-cxlviii.

[8] Robert de Torigni, I. 234.

[9] Benedict, 1, 4, 92, 132; *generale concilium* (*Chron. Monasterii de Bello*, 72; Benedict, II. 93); *conventus generalis* (Gervase, I. 162).

[10] H. G. Richardson, *Trans. Royal Histor.*, *Soc.*, 4th ser., 143, 146.

[11] Becket writes (Migne, *Patrologia Latina*, vol. 190, p. 851): *ob publica regni negotia . . . conversatio et procerum regni soleat frequentior esse conventus.*

[12] Richardson, *Trans. Royal Histor. Soc.*, 4th ser., 137-145.

[13] A. B. White, *Amer. Histor. Review*, XXV. 1-17.

said to be enacted by the common counsel (*commune consilium*) of those present.[14]

The great council of the Angevin period was regarded as an assembly of the king's tenants-in-chief. Even the king's household officials, with the possible exception of ecclesiastics might be so classified. The king's great barons in this period also took the counsel of their barons.[15] The bishops now admitted their baronial status, and at Northamption in 1164 one of them made a specific statement that in the great council they were barons and peers of the lay barons.[16] Potentially the national assembly was regarded as the whole body of the king's barons. To one assembly Henry II is said to have called all the tenants-in-chief.[17] Magna Carta at the end of the period required that for certain purposes all the tenants-in-chief be notified.[18] Only a fairly limited number of persons, however, seem actually to have been present, and these chiefly great magnates, as in the past. In 1164, although the list is not complete, some fifty bishops, earls and barons in attendance at Clarendon are named,[19] in 1177, thirty-one are said to have been present at an arbitration.[20] The magnates listed as present at the coronation of Richard I numbered just over sixty. These included archbishops and bishops, among them several foreign, Welsh or Irish prelates, and abbots as well as earls and barons.[21] The attendance corresponds in general to that mentioned in Magna Carta, which presupposes an assembly consisting especially of archbishops, bishops, abbots, earls [22] and greater barons.

[14] Either *concilium* or *consilium* might be used for council or counsel.
[15] *L'Histoire de Guillaume le Marechal*, Societé de l'Histoire de France, ed. P. Meyer, II. ll. 13376-13396.
[16] *Materials for Hist. of Becket*, III. 52.
. .[17] *Materials for Hist. of Becket*, Rolls Series II. 390.
[18] Sec. 14.
[19] Fourteen bishops, ten earls, twenty-eight barons (preamble to Constitutions of Clarendon).
[20] Benedict, I. 154: fifteen bishops, eight earls, eight barons.
[21] Benedict, II. 79-80. Cf. Stubbs, *Constnl. Hist.*, I. 610. For a great council in 1198, see Hoveden, IV. 63.
[22] David, brother of the king of Scotland was earl of Huntingdon, Richard, the king's son count of Poitou, and John, earl of Gloucester and Mortain in his brother's reign.

Not all these classes might be found on every occasion among the magnates who were present, and others might appear either as participants or spectators. Abbots are not very often mentioned in the time of Henry II and bishops were probably not essential. In John's time, from 1209 to 1213, there were only two bishops in England, and apparently one great council was held without a single bishop.[23] The assembly held by this king at Northampton in 1211 at the conclusion of a campaign in Wales could have included few, if any, English prelates. Such was probably the well known assembly held by Henry II in July, 1177, at Winchester. The tenants-in-chief who owed military service to the crown had been summoned to come with horses and arms prepared to accompany the king to Normandy. The chronicler states that when all were congregated the king decided to defer the expedition.[24] This was a strictly feudal assembly rather than a gathering of national representatives.[25] The tenant-in-chief was responsible for the service of all the knights of his barony although some of these held of rear vassals.[26] It was not unusual for these rear vassals to attend their lords at the king's court to give them advice.[27] The presence of the whole body of knights did not mean that all were entitled to take part in the proceedings. There is no good reason for assuming that any idea of general representation of the landed class was modifying ordinary usage.

The magnates who in large measure constituted the great council in this period might be described not merely as barons but also as tenants by barony. The more important tenant-in-chief held a fief known as a barony,[28] for which it was as-

[23] The bishop of Winchester was excluded (Gervase, Rolls Ser., II. p. cxi). See below, p. 367.

[24] Benedict, I. 177-178.

[25] As Stubbs (*Constnl. Hist.*, I. 605-607) seems to suggest.

[26] Below, p. 336; Mitchell, *Studies in Taxation*, 17-18, 27-28, 40-42.

[27] Above, p. 185. This was sometimes even their specific duty (Adams. *Council and Courts*, 37-38).

[28] Pollock and Maitland, *History of English Law*, I. 260, 279. Cf. *Dialogus de Scaccario*, Oxford ed., 155; for greater and lesser barons, *ibid.*, 135.

sumed that he rendered military service. In Magna Carta [29] not only are the estates of a baron who holds of the crown by military service termed a barony, but also those of an earl held in the same way. Moreover, according to a rule promulgated in 1164, archbishops, bishops and other ecclesiastics who hold lands directly of the king are reckoned as tenants by barony who owe the same kinds of service as other tenants of this class.[30]

Lesser barons may have been admitted to the assembly, but their number was so great [31] that only a small attendance might be expected. Henry II in 1157 is said to have convoked along with bishops and magnates some abbots and other persons of lesser order. When, in 1164, the king called barons of second rank to reinforce the great council for the trial of Becket, this was clearly regarded as unusual.[32] Under the plan prescribed by Magna Carta the lesser tenants-in-chief were to be summoned by a general notice but not by name, and consequently their attendance was left optional. This general summons was apparently new in 1215.[33] A chronicler once in a while implies that the barons generally were present, but this is not borne out by other evidence and sometimes is even contradicted.[34]

[29] Sec. 2.

[30] Yet they might not be required to take part in judgments involving loss of life or members (Constitutions of Clarendon, sec. 11). In 1166 the two archbishops, thirteen bishops and twenty-four abbots held of the king by military service (Round, *Feudal England*, 249, 251). In the middle of the next century the only bishops not tenants-in-chief by barony were those of Rochester and Carlisle (Thorpe, *Registrum Roffense*, 76-79). The former held of the archbishop of Canterbury. The diocese of Carlisle dated only from the time of William Rufus.

[31] Above, p. 189.

[32] Gervase, I. 167; *Materials for Life of Becket*, III. 67.

[33] G. B. Adams (*Origin of English Constn.*, 226, note 4) shows reason for rejecting supposed references to it of earlier date.

[34] The summons to all tenants-in-chief in 1164 (*Materials for History of Becket*, 390) elsewhere (*ibid.*, III. 67) means the addition of some barons of second rank. Even at the coronation of 1170 (Benedict, I. 6), *almost* all the earls, barons and more noble class. The presence of almost all the abbots, priors, earls and barons at the coronation of 1189 (Hoveden, III. 8) may be compared with a list of some sixty (see above), which, however, includes no priors.

The presence of knights graced coronations, crown-wearing occasions and other great assemblies.[35] They did not rank among the minor barons of the period,[36] but some were royal vassals who held lands directly of the king.[37] According to a good authority, knights in 1198 assented along with the prelates, earls and barons to a piece of legislation.[38] It is probable that many of those mentioned as present at the great council appeared merely in the trains of their lords and not as tenants-in-chief.

The attendance of abbots is not very often mentioned,[39] and to a great council held at the beginning of his reign Henry II summoned only part of them.[40] Well informed writers of this reign [41] sometimes speak only of bishops, earls, and barons on occasions when the heads of monastic houses were also present. The latter could hardly have been regarded as an important part of the assembly until about 1185 when plans for crusading taxes and other exactions required their attendance. At Richard's elaborate coronation in 1189 twelve abbots were in attendance,[42] about half as many as owed military service to the crown. At an assembly in 1197, wherein the justiciar took up ecclesiastical business, their group was represented,[43] and this was true also the next year.[44] At John's

[35] De Torigni, Rolls Ser., 216, 276; Benedict, I. 107; II. 79.

[36] See Round, *Magna Carta Commemoratn. Essays*, ed. Malden, 46-47; for the earlier view, McKechnie, *Magna Carta*, ed. 1914, p. 200.

[37] Diceto, I. 404: *coram episcopis, comitibus, baronibus, militibus et aliis hominibus suis.* Cf. Magna Carta, sect. 2.

[38] Hoveden, IV. 63.

[39] At Becket's trial (*Materials for Hist. of Becket*, IV. 41); at the coronations of 1170 (Gervase, I. 219) and 1172 (*Materials*, IV. 175); in 1177 (see below), 1185 (Benedict, I. 336), and 1189 (Gervase, I. 453).

[40] Gervase, I. 163; cf. Delisle, *Bibliothèque de l'Ecole de Chartes*, vol. 69, 547-48.

[41] Fitzstephen (*Materials*, III. 51-52) who was in Northampton for Becket's trial (cf. note 39). Benedict hardly ever mentions abbots in attendance.

[42] The abbots (Benedict II. 79) of Westminister, St. Albans, St. Augustine at Canterbury, St. Mary's at York, Hyde, Peterborough, St. Edmunds, Crowland, Battle, Rivaulx, Holme, and Holm Cultram. Of these St. Mary's, Crowland, Battle, and Holm Cultram owed no military service.

[43] Gervase, I. 549.   [44] Hoveden, IV. 63.

coronation in 1199 thirty-three were present.[45] In 1205, when
the form of the king's summons to the great council is first
known, that of abbots did not come directly from the crown
like the writ sent to other magnates, but from the bishops.[46]
At this time the great problem was military and financial, that
of national defense, and an expedition to regain the lost possessions in France.[47] In this year and again in 1207, when
John asked the clergy to agree to a novel levy on church property,[48] monastic priors, as well as abbots were summoned to
attend.

Archdeacons and deans as well as priors were present in
some cases before 1215, but it is doubtful whether they came
in any capacity except that of advisers and assistants to the
prelates. At the great council of 1177, held at London for the
purpose of an arbitration between the kings of Castile and
Navarre, there were present many abbots, deans, and archdeacons, but only those who were barons participated in
the actual judgment rendered. In 1213 priors and deans as
well as abbots attended the great council held at St. Paul's.[49]
In Magna Carta there is a definite requirement that abbots
be summoned directly by letters under the king's seal, but
this document makes no mention of the attendance of lesser
ranks of the clergy.

Henry II and John both went somewhat beyond precedent
in calling in to assist the great council clergy who were not
bound to come by feudal obligation; moreover John followed
the same plan with reference to laymen. The king's writ
was employed more than once to call up certain persons for
administrative purposes when there is no reason to believe
that the great council was in session. Certain clerks and monks
were ordered through the sheriffs to appear before the king
in 1212.[50] The next year those who owed money to the king's

---

[45] *Annals of Winchester*, Rolls Ser., 72.
[46] Stubbs, *Select Charters*, 282-283.
[47] See Ralph of Coggeshall, 153.
[48] *Annals of Waverley*, 258; Mitchell, *Studies in Taxation*, 86.
[49] Matthew Paris, II. 552.   [50] *Lit. Claus.*, I. 129-30.

Jewish debtors were by proclamation directed to come before
the king with all haste.[51] A well known writ of 1213 directed
the sheriffs to send the reeve and four men of each vill of
the royal demesne that they might certify to the losses incurred by bishops and abbots during the interdict.[52] In November of this year, however, the king combined this procedure
with summons to a great council. The sheriffs were directed
to send the barons to meet the king at Oxford and at the same
time four discreet knights from each county to discuss with
him the business of the realm.[53] Nothing is known of this assembly, but John's action was followed later in calling parliaments in the reign of his successor.

The king was said either to hold[54] or to celebrate[55] a great
council. The words were often interchangeable, but the latter
was used in speaking of coronations. The magnates, with the
exception at times of abbots, were called together by the
monarch's summons[56] in the form of an individual writ. The
chancellor claimed the right to attend without summons[57]
and the archbishop of Canterbury the right to the first summons. During Becket's quarrel with the king, in 1164, complaint was made that the archbishop did not receive the
solemn first citation to the council directed to him by letter
according to former custom.[58] To the council which Henry II

[51] *Ibid.*, I. 132.
[52] Wendover, II. 82; A. B. White, *Amer. Histor. Rev.*, XVII. 11-16.
[53] *Report on Dignity of a Peer*, app. 2, p. 2.
[54] Thus, *rex tenuit curiam suam in sollemnitate Paschale* (Benedict,
I. 4) ; *habito concilio de conquirendo regno Hiberniae* (De Torigny, 186).
[55] In January 1177, *magnum concilium celebravit cum episcopis et
comitibus et baronibus regni sui* (Benedict, I. 132-133) ; in 1164, *statuens
celebrare concilium* (*Materials for Hist. of Becket*, R. S., II. 390) ; so
John's two great councils of 1207 (Waverley Annals, 258) ; *magnum
celebravit concilium de coronatione Henrici fili* (Benedict, I. 4) ; *ad
coronationem suam celebrandam* (Gervase, I. 453). The archbishop is
said (Gervase, I. 147; Diceto, II. 169) to celebrate a church council.
[56] In Oct. 1164, *convenerunt illuc episcopi, comites, barones, totius regni
mandato regis urgente* (Diceto, I. 313) ; *jussit apud Clarendoniam pontificum et procerum cogi concilium* (Gervase, I. 176). In 1176, *ad summoni-
tionem regis* (Diceto, I. 407-408).
[57] *Materials for Life of Becket*, III. 18.
[58] *Ibid.*, III. 51.

held in June 1170 for the coronation of his eldest son it is especially mentioned that he caused to be summoned in addition to abbots, earls and barons the archbishop of York and other bishops to crown the young king.[59] In 1170, when the king was bent upon an investigation of administrative malfeasance, it is said that all who were summoned came in great fear.[60] The earliest extant writ of summons is that issued by John in 1205 to the bishop of Salisbury,[61] in which the latter is directed to attend at the specified time and place and also to have cited the abbots and monastic priors of his diocese. Probably the Magna Carta requirement that bishops, abbots, earls, and greater barons be summoned individually by letters under the king's seal was regarded as a security against the king's leaving the summons of abbots to the bishop or that of the greater lay magnates to the sheriff.

It seems apparent that at no time did the lesser members of the great council receive individual summons from the king; yet the minor tenant-in-chief had a right to attend for some purposes [62] and a presumptive right to know when the assembly was to convene. The situation is met in Magna Carta by the promise that the king will cause the whole body of tenants-in-chief to receive through the sheriffs and royal bailiffs a general summons,[63] such as would be proclaimed in the county court and probably also in the market places.[64] Whatever may have been the usage of Henry II, certainly under John a special procedure was needed to facilitate the attendance of the minor tenants-in-chief.

Under the Angevin kings the constitution and appearance of the great council clearly presented varied aspects from

[59] Benedict, I. 5-6; cf. Gervase of Canterbury, 219. In 1177 are recorded the excuses of the English and Welsh bishops summoned but not present (Benedict, I. 144-145).

[60] Gervase, I. 219.

[61] See Stubbs, *Sel. Charters*, 282-283.

[62] Above, pp. 188-189, In 1175 Henry forbade the late rebels (Benedict, I. 93) to come to court without summons, but this was not necessarily summons to the great council as Stubbs believed (*Constnl. Hist.*, I. 608).

[63] *Magna Carta*, sec. 14.

[64] Morris, *Med. Eng. Sheriff*, 153, 199, 217-18.

time to time. For ordinary consultation the bishops, earls and greater barons were called, apparently either with or without the abbots. Occasionally persons of lesser rank are mentioned. An assembly of those convened under arms for military service was likely to comprise few bishops or abbots, but included numerous lesser barons, and many knights and rear vassals were present as spectators. In 1207 the clergy was asked to make a grant in an assembly apart from the lay baronage, and during John's struggle with the pope they were almost ignored.[65] On the other hand, the clerical element was sometimes especially reinforced, as during the discussions of the Constitutions of Clarendon when all the bishops were expected to come,[66] and in 1177 not only these but the other clerics to secure an imposing attendance for the purpose of the Spanish award. A prior with his cathedral chapter might be summoned before the great council merely to declare their choice of a bishop or an archbishop,[67] but priors became regular attendants for other purposes in John's time.

Before the great council were summoned also accused persons or litigants who were non-members. Sheriffs and bailiffs accused of official misconduct thus appeared in 1170, together with their sureties.[68] On ceremonial occasions, like crown-wearing days or coronations, the magnates who came to honor the occasion were likely to be attended by knights, and at any meeting by their vassals. The most imposing assemblies of the period were undoubtedly those for coronations or for the taking of fealty to the king or his son. The coronation of the younger Henry in 1170 is said to have been attended by almost all the earls, barons, and more noble persons of the realm.[69] That of Richard I in 1189 stands out through a detailed list of notables of the realm who were present, and that of John was even more largely attended. On some

[65] See above, pp. 296, 299.
[66] *Materials for Hist. of Becket*, IV. 201, 206-207.
[67] Gervase, I. 169-170; Benedict, I. 352.
[68] Gervase, I. 219; Stubbs, introd. to Benedict, II. pp. lix, lxi.
[69] Benedict, I. 5-6.

occasions the populace are mentioned as spectators, especially in 1185, when they gathered to hear the crusading
appeal made to the great council by the archbishop of
Canterbury.[70]

The view once expressed by Henry II concerning the work
of councils, was that when anything arose which concerned
greater affairs counsel was taken, and the barons came together
to give support to his business.[71] The dominant idea of the
chroniclers was that the work of the *curia* was consultation for
the welfare of the realm. To treat concerning the condition or
the business of the realm is frequently stated as the purpose
of a given assembly. At the beginning of the period this included the establishment of peace, the demolition of castles [72]
and a renewal of laws and customs of former times.[73] But more
specific problems of administration are soon mentioned. In
1162 at a great council in Normandy the king complained
about the conduct of ecclesiastical and fiscal affairs.[74] After
the consideration of the status of the realm in 1170, the king
appointed barons to go on circuit to hold inquest concerning
the conduct of sheriffs.[75] In the great council held at Northampton in 1176 an assize or decree concerning judicial affairs was made, and a division of the realm into judicial circuits was set forth with the assent of the assembly.[76] At the
Easter assembly of 1179 another arrangement of judicial
circuits was determined by common consent.[77] Disagreements
between ecclesiastical officials [78] and questions concerning the
election of prelates [79] occupied some attention. The famous
statement of the rights of the church known as the Constitutions of Clarendon was presented before the great council and

[70] Wendover, I. 135.
    [71] Migne, *Patrologia Latina*, vol. 190, p. 852; *Materials for Hist. of
Becket*, V. 25; cf. *ibid.*, II 310: *convenientibus autem episcopis et pro-
ceribus regni ex mandato regis ad expediendas regni necessitates.*
    [72] Gervase, II. 160.
    [73] *Chron. Monasterii de Bello*, 72; Palgrave, *English Commonwealth*,
II. xxxi.
    [74] Robert de Torigni, 212.   [77] *Ibid.*, I. 238.
    [75] Benedict, I. 4; Gervase, I. 216.   [78] Gervase, I. 163, 410.
    [76] Benedict, I. 107.   [79] Benedict, I. 352.

there agreed to by the bishops.[80] In 1188 at a meeting of the same body regulations were set forth to regulate the conduct and other affairs of crusaders.[81]

Foreign affairs and military questions also came before the great council. Welsh [82] and Irish affairs were discussed. In 1154 the project of conquering Ireland for the king's brother was considered and rejected.[83] In 1171 Henry II took up with the barons the matter of his expedition to Ireland. At this time Strongbow agreed to hand over to the king Dublin and Waterford, and the king agreed to give him a high office in Ireland.[84] In a great council of 1175 Henry II made an agreement with the king of Connaught fixing his status as a vassal.[85] At an assembly in 1177 the king was advised to replace the custodians of his castles and, later in the year, to postpone an expedition to Normandy. On the latter occasion the king sent two ambassadors to France.[86] Papal relations were also laid before the assembly. In the midst of his conflict with Innocent III John convened and consulted the baronage regarding terms of peace with the pope, and they advised that he should make peace only on terms which saved the royal dignity.[87] It was by their counsel, according to the formal acts, that the king in 1213 made over to the pope England and Ireland to be held as a papal fief, and that in the next year he accorded to cathedral and monastic chapters freedom in electing prelates.[88]

The development of the judicial system under Henry I and Henry II apparently reduced the volume of business which came before the great council as a court of justice. When private causes could be tried in a court held by the king in

[80] Constitutions of Clarendon, introd.
[81] Gervase, I. 409-410.
[82] Eyton, *Itinerary of Henry II*, 74.
[83] Robert de Torigni, 186.
[84] *Ibid.*, 252.
[85] Benedict, I. 101-103.
[86] *Ibid.*, I. 160, 177-178.
[87] Pref. to Gervase, II. p. cxi.
[88] Stubbs, *Sel. Charters*, 285, 288; *Statutes of the Realm*, I. 5.

person on his journeys or by his justices in his absence, there was little need that the great assembly should give hearing to any but important state causes. Disputes between the bishops, however, still came before it.[89] In 1164 the constable, Henry of Essex, was accused here of treason. The charge was that in 1157 in the Welsh campaign he had dropped the royal standard, crying out that the king was dead. The accuser, Robert de Montfort, challenged him to combat and vanquished him, thus establishing his guilt.[90] In the same year, the archbishop of Canterbury, Thomas Becket, with whom the king was engaged in a great controversy, was confronted with various charges, and by judgment of the barons of the great *curia* formally declared to be at the king's mercy for all his chattels. [91] In 1194 a great council heard the charge of disloyalty made against John, the king's brother.[92] The noted Spanish award of 1177, which was a practical demonstration of the high reputation of King Henry's justice, was really an arbitration, but judgment was given in the accustomed form.[93] It is shown that in Becket's case judgment was feudal, for a bishop acknowledged that he and his brethren were present as barons.[94]

The rulers of the Angevin line apparently did not bring all legislative matters before the great council. Although it was recognized that measures enacted without the common consent of the barons could be valid only for the king's lifetime,[95] much could be effected merely by the king's executive order.[96] The formal enactments or assizes by which Henry II introduced his sweeping legal changes and the so-called constitutions of the period were in the form of administrative decrees rather than permanent amendments to existing law.[97] The

[89] Stubbs, *Constnl. Hist.*, I. 523.
[90] William of Newburgh, I. 108; Gervase, I. 165.
[91] Gervase, I. 183.
[92] Stubbs, *Constnl. Hist.*, I. 541.
[93] Benedict, I. 151.   [94] Above, p. 295.
[95] Adams, *Council and Courts*, 118.
[96] Pollock and Maitland, *Hist. English Law*, I. 136-137.
[97] Stubbs, *Constnl. Hist.*, I. 614-617.

greater ones were considered by the national assembly. In other cases action was probably taken upon the advice of the smaller council. The Assize of Clarendon is named for the meeting-place of the great assembly in which it was enacted.[98] This is true also of the Assize of Northampton, issued ten years later, which extended the provisions of the former assize, and which was regarded as a re-enactment of it.[99] King Henry's Assize of Arms, by which in 1184 means were employed to provide arms and armor to insure the effectiveness of the local *fyrd*, was also set forth after consultation with the great council.[100] Richard in 1197 issued an assize of weights and measures, so it is said, by petition and counsel of his bishops and all his barons, and John in 1205 issued an assize of money also by their assent.[101] Magna Carta itself shows that this was the most binding form of enactment, for the great charter of liberties is in form a document issued by the king with the counsel of the bishops and magnates.[102]

The imposition of financial burdens upon the realm from the Norman conquest had been so much a matter of prerogative power and administrative action that Henry II, in all probability, never regarded either his regular income or his war levies as matters which called for consultation with his greater *curia*. The demand for a feudal aid in the three customary cases was clearly the king's affair. The imposition of the first general scutage in 1159 seems to have been held purely a matter within the king's ordinary province. There is no indication that the danegeld, levied during the first eight years of the reign, was treated otherwise than as a customary tax which the king was entitled as a matter of right to take

[98] See Stubbs, *introd.* to Benedict of Peterborough, II. pp. lix-lxi; Stubbs, *Constnl. Hist.*, I. 521-22.

[99] Gervase, I. 257-258.

[100] Benedict, I. 269.

[101] Hoveden, IV. 33-34; *Rotuli Litt. Pat.*, I. 54. Cf. Norgate, *John Lackland*, 103. So also Richard's assize of the forest (Hoveden, IV. 63) and John's assize of 1205 (Gervase, II. 96-97) concerning national defence.

[102] The *Waverley Annals* (p. 282) speak of the assembly at Runnymede in the usual way as one of bishops, magnates, and barons.

year after year. It is only under circumstances involving new administrative problems that Angevin rulers are found making finance a matter of deliberation with the great council.

The crusades of the twelfth century first brought to the attention of the national assembly new methods of extraordinary levy of great significance for the future history of taxation in England. In 1166 King Henry by counsel of his bishops and barons in Normandy decreed along with Louis VII of France that to afford relief to Palestine there should be paid for each poundworth of chattels six pence, the persons liable to the charge to make oath concerning their property.[103] In 1185, when the king was urged by the patriarch of Jerusalem to go to the aid of the hard-pressed Latin king there, he declined to go. This decision was given in a great council held at London, but in order that the labor of the patriarch's great journey should not prove in vain, says the chronicler, the king promised him fifty thousand marks of silver for the defense of the Holy Land.[104] For this undertaking he seems thus to have had the assent of the magnates. In January, 1188, Henry II in the presence of the barons of Anjou, Maine, and Touraine enacted the well known ordinance of the Saladin tithe, providing for the collection by ecclesiastical authorities of a tenth of moveable goods as alms. A few weeks later he convoked the archbishop, the bishops, the earls, and the barons of England and took up the matter with them, causing to be read the same articles which had been enacted on the continent. Then, after archbishop Baldwin had preached the crusade and many had taken the cross, by counsel of his barons he chose collectors of the tenth and sent them through the various counties.[105] In this fashion was adopted the famous tax on personal property, the first systematic levy of its kind in England, destined long to influence national taxation.

The captivity of Richard I in 1193 and the necessity of providing a ransom entailed a heavy financial burden upon the kingdom, which could not be met by the ordinary feudal

[103] Gervase, I. 198.　　[104] Gervase, I. 325.　　[105] Benedict, II. 30-33.

aid for such a contingency. The magnates were summoned to meet at Oxford, but the necessary information was not yet at hand to enable them to provide for the required levy. A little later the queen mother and the justices ordered the collection of the money required, and the justiciars, to meet the end in view, set forth the details of the heaviest scheme of general taxation England had ever known.[106] Upon the king's return in 1194 he laid his demands for additional revenue before a council attended only by a few magnates.[107] In 1198 occurs the first recorded case of successful opposition to an English king's demands for money. Before a council of barons held at Oxford the justiciar, Archbishop Hubert, laid Richard's proposal that three hundred knights be provided for his war in Normandy to serve for a year, each to receive three shillings a day. The amount of the grant was unprecedented. Hugh the bishop of Lincoln refused assent on the ground that the lands of his church were bound to render military service only within England.[106] He was seconded by Herbert bishop of Salisbury, and the archbishop withdrew the proposal. The latter then proceeded, apparently without consulting the assembly, to levy upon the realm a revived form of danegeld, a carucage amounting to five shillings on each hundred acres of land.[109] For assent to taxation in novel ways John consulted the great council in 1204 to increase the amount of the scutage, in 1207 to make a levy of a thirteenth of the personal property of the realm,[110] and in 1205, apparently to obtain aid for an expedition to Poitou and Gascony.[111]

The great council under Henry II and his two sons can hardly be said to exercise a real elective function. Election

[106] Stubbs, *Constnl. Hist.*, I. 539-40. See below, p. 340. There is no evidence that the final action was endorsed by an assembly (Stubbs, *ibid.*, 540, note 1; cf. 619-20).

[107] Hoveden, III. 240-242.

[108] *Ibid.*, IV. 40. The obligations of ecclesiastics in such cases were not well defined at this time (Powicke, *Loss of Normandy*, 315-316).

[109] Stubbs, *Constnl. Hist.*, I. 547-49.

[110] Mitchell, *Studies in Taxation*, 63-64, 86.

[111] Stubbs, *Sel. Charters*, 281.

to the throne is said to have occurred at the accession of
Henry II, but [112] there was no defect in his hereditary title.
The barons had done fealty to him in his grandfather's lifetime,[113] and his succession was arranged through an agreement
made with his predecessor, who once more caused the barons
to swear fealty.[114] Moreover Henry followed this example and
that of his grandfather in arranging for recognition of his heir
in his lifetime by requiring that the barons do fealty to him [115]
and, in the case of his son Henry, by actual coronation. It
does not appear that Richard was recognized by any of these
formalities prior to his father's death. Probably his undutiful
and rebellious conduct was responsible. The barons took the
oath of fealty to John in 1191 and in 1192 recognizing him as
successor to the throne in Richard's absence and apparently
contrary to his intention.[116] Although John's claim could be
disputed by Arthur, the son of his elder brother Geoffrey, his
succession was assured through the efforts and promises of
three of the late king's ministers. The report that at his
coronation the archbishop advanced the elective principle
as a reason for his enthronement [117] is not mentioned by the
writers of the time. Had John owed his throne to election by
the barons, deposition to reverse that act would more readily
have been advocated at a later time. The elections of bishops
and archbishops before the great council are mentioned as a
rule only in exceptional cases.[118] Elections were ordered by
the king to be held elsewhere, and the royal chapel seems to
have been the usual place.[119] The investiture of bishops [120]
and earls before the great council was a formal act more
impressively performed here, but it indicates no elective power
in the hands of the assembly.

---

[112] Stubbs, *Constnl. Hist.*, I. 487. [114] Gervase, I. 157.
[113] *Ibid.*, I. 484. [115] De Torigny, 184, 216.
[116] Benedict, II. 214, 237; cf. Richard of Devizes, 415. Richard just
before his death caused those present to swear fealty to John (Hoveden,
IV. 83).
[117] Stubbs, *Constnl. Hist.*, I. 551-554; Norgate, *John Lackland*, 64-66.
[118] As the election of Becket in 1162 (Gervase I. 169-170).
[119] Below, p. 353. Cf. 361, 373. [120] Benedict, I. 352.

The most striking assumption of conciliar power appears in 1191. The bishops, earls and barons in King Richard's absence met, deposed William Longchamp, the justiciar, and placed Walter of Coutances in his stead. Moreover, the same assembly, which could not have been called legally,[121] made a grant of a new form of municipal organization to London and also swore fealty to the king and his brother John, thus recognizing the latter as heir to the throne.[122] The change effected in the executive was actually revolutionary, as Stubbs has declared,[123] but it provided the government of England for over two years. These incidents show that the magnates believed they were the proper authority to assume control in an emergency.

The great council of the Angevin kings assumed little authority in matters of state as against the king. The tenants-in-chief gave judgment in cases submitted to them, but, though often consulted, they hardly established the right to dispose of other matters. In the most important questions the king gained his own way. In the only great matter in dispute under Henry II, the issue between church and state, they decided for the king. Even the bishops were overborne by the wrathful monarch and were ready to join in the judgment against Becket. It has been supposed that at the beginning of the conflict, in 1163, Becket's opposition prevailed against the king when he wished to claim for his treasury what was known as sheriff's aid. This is not clear, and at any rate the king before long is found in possession of the source of income in question.[124] The two bishops could hardly have stood out against Richard on the matter of taxation in 1198 as they did against his justiciar. In this case the end was effected in another way by prerogative power, as was appar-

[121] Apparently by John (Benedict, I. 213; Stubbs, *Constnl. Hist.*, I. 538).

[122] Benedict, II. 214; as regent, according to Richard of Devizes, **Rolls Ser.**, 415.

[123] Stubbs, *Constnl. Hist.*, I. 539.

[124] Stubbs, *Constnl. Hist.*, I. 500; *Materials for Hist. of Becket*, IV. 23; cf. Morris, *Med. English Sheriff*, 114.

ently done in 1193. The opposition of the clergy to the heavy taxation of 1207 was largely averted and that of the barons soon overcome by John.[125] The barons before 1215 made attempts to place pressure on the latter king.[126] In 1205, at a time when the invasion of the realm was expected, the magnates, who had been convened at Oxford, successfully demanded that John promise to maintain the rights of England.[127]

The great council was a body of prime importance to Angevin monarchy. It provided deliberation upon new and difficult questions, such as the levies to aid the crusade, to provide funds for king Richard's ransom, or to meet the needs of king John. When strengthened by its assent, Henry II could proceed with confidence in his struggle against ecclesiastical privilege. It stood for the rights of the crown during John's controversy with Innocent III. To the king's important legislative decrees it gave an authority which nothing else could give. It afforded the widest sanction to be gained in the realm for the king's acts, and especially facilitated the collection of new and unusual impositions upon the realm. Consultation with it was a wise and politic act. The best results were gained under conditions which gave to the assembly a semblance of right. Henry II freely employed its counsel, and both Richard and John sought and obtained its assent to innovations in taxation and other important measures.

Usage touching the great council was still in the plastic stage. The barons in the time of Richard believed that they were the ultimate source of authority in an emergency; under John they came to assume that they were the guardians of national liberty, yet for most of the reign they were unable to establish such a position against the crown. It was not clear whether assent to measures in the great council was national or individual. The archbishop of York in 1207 refused the payment of a tax on his estates on the ground that he had

[125] Mitchell, *Studies in Taxation*, 86-87.
[126] Hoveden, IV. 161.   [127] Gervase, II. 97-98.

not promised it.[128] The barons found it advisable to specify in Magna Carta that the great council might proceed with matters of taxation even when all of those summoned were not present. Discussion was informal, and decisions were reached by rough and unconventional methods. Moreover, the composition of the body might vary considerably. The noted requirement of Magna Carta that the king summon by individual letters the archbishops, bishops, abbots, earls and greater barons, although it conforms to usage traceable earlier, applies in word at least only to the constitution of an assembly called for the purpose of levying scutages and aids. This provision does not specify whether the king is to summon all the abbots or only those who are tenants by barony; it says nothing as to whether the summons of bishops may include priors, deans and archdeacons; it leaves an option as to the number of lay barons that shall be summoned by name, but retains for any tenant-in-chief the privilege of attending. The calling of the assembly was too much a matter of the king's convenience to permit the laying down of rigid rules for generations to come. Furthermore, the functions and powers of the great council were as yet so incapable of exact definition that it was impossible to draw a line between the work of this body and that of the small council.

The lesser *curia* or council, highly essential to the king's ordinary work, may be traced under Angevin rulers and earlier in three phases, two of which appeared as it attended the king upon his progresses. It served as a council with which he might take advice upon business of state. It acted as a court *coram rege* which might hear or decide cases wherever he chanced to be and whenever he had time for such work. It operated under a definite organization, usually in the king's absence, as an exchequer, meeting twice a year, nearly always at Westminster.

[128] Stubbs, *Constnl. Hist.*, I. 619. For a bishop's successful opposition to a levy in 1221 on the ground that he had opposed it, McKechnie, *Magna Carta*, 255. Cf. Mitchell, *Studies in Taxation*, 130-133.

The more active members of the small council as a rule appear in two capacities, one purely official and one feudal. The lesser *curia* in practice seems usually to be a domestic body,[129] familiar with administrative detail, but in theory it had to be a feudal body, which could pass judgment upon the king's tenants-in-chief. The household group was often reinforced by bishops or other members of the baronage not holding household positions.[130] The chancellor had the right to attend all councils,[131] and the justiciar took still higher rank. Constables, chamberlains and chaplains are found along with the king's relatives, his other barons of high rank, and some of his bishops and abbots. The permanent council long preserved its feudal tradition by exercising the power to levy pecuniary penalties upon earls and barons who claimed immunity from amercement not imposed by their peers.[132]

The exchequer shared the characteristics of the small council. Long after this period its working membership might still be reinforced by other members of the king's council whenever this was found necessary.[133] At the exchequer the king might be present in person, and judicial business quite beyond that of fiscal routine [134] might be transacted. There was a chamber of secrets near at hand whither the members might retire to deal privately with doubtful questions.[135] The judges, called barons of the exchequer, were qualified to pass judgment upon the baronage who claimed the right to be judged by their peers; [136] but the important members sat *ex officiis* and were officials of the court and household. These were the

[129] The names of the witnesses to the charters of Henry II (*Bibliothèque de l'Ecole des Chartes*, vol. 69, pp. 547-572) show that those who regularly attend the king are nearly always officials and persons in his employ.

[130] See *ibid*. Also Tout, *Chaps. in Administrative Hist.*, 11.

[131] *Materials for Hist. of Becket*, III. 18.

[132] McKechnie, *Magna Carta* (1914), 295-297; G. B. Adams, *Council and Courts*, 223-224, 247-250.

[133] As in Morris, *Med. Sheriff*, 241, n. 2, 242.

[134] Baldwin, *King's Council*, 9; *Rolls of King's Court, Pipe Roll Soc.*, vol. 14, p. 96. Cf. D. M. Stenton in *Cambridge Medieval History*, V. 514.

[135] *Dialogus de Scaccario*, Oxford ed., 92.

[136] *Magna Carta*, sec. 21. Cf. references above, in note 132.

justiciar, who presided, the chancellor and the treasurer, the two chamberlains of the exchequer, and the constable and the marshal or their representatives. Other persons were designated by the king as members from time to time.[137]

The conciliar and judicial activities of the lesser council were undifferentiated. As a court it might advise the king and as a council decide judicial issues.[138] The line of its activity was determined by the royal initiative. There was no oath of office and no definite delimitation of membership. Even in John's time the groups of councillors were still shifting, and the body lacked permanence, stability and organization.

In the judicial work of his earlier years Henry II, as shown above, was attended by a small number of members of his household, few or none of whom were of the class of greater barons.[139] This seems to have been true as a rule not only in this king's later years, but also in the reign of John.[140] Although on some occasions the lesser *curia* became a numerous assemblage of bishops, earls, barons, and household officials,[141] yet as a rule it is distinguishable from the great council. To the latter the magnates were necessarily summoned some time in advance, and many bishops, earls and barons were likely to be present. The lesser council, on the other hand, usually consisted[142] of those who happened to be about the king, and a considerable number of the bishops and lay barons

[137] *Dialogus de Scaccario*, Oxford ed., 67, 69-72, 112. The marshal attended the king when he tried a cause in 1164 (*Materials for Hist. of Becket*, III. 51).

[138] Cf. *Select Civil Pleas* (Selden Soc.), no. 190; *Curia Regis Rolls*, III. 124; Adams, *Council and Courts*, 230, note 36.

[139] Above, p. 272. See Palgrave, *English Commonwealth*, II. pp. xliv-xlv.

[140] Below, p. 317. Cf. Pollock and Maitland, *Hist. of English Law*, I (1899), pp. 154, 170.

[141] Fourteen bishops, abbots, earls, and barons, who are named, assisted the king when he tried a cause in 1157, and others were present (Palgrave, *English Commonwealth*, II. xlvi-xlvii). Fifteen are named later when the case is settled (*ibid.*, lxiv), nearly all prelates and members of the household.

[142] *Dominus autem rex consuluit super hoc illos qui tunc cum illo erant* (*Curia Regis Rolls*, II. 124). The periodical meetings of the exchequer apparently permitted regular summons in advance, and other small assemblies might be arranged in advance (see Palgrave, *English Commonwealth*, II. p. lxxxii).

would be at hand only under unusual or accidental circumstances.

The identity of those who ordinarily advised the king is not so clear as that of the barons of the exchequer or the judicial force which accompanied him, though it is of course apparent that at any meeting the same men might both advise the king and decide his cases. In the time of Henry II the king's counsellors [143] are mentioned, but it is still impossible to determine whether or not these were merely persons who discussed matters with the king privately and in an entirely extra-legal capacity. A chronicler of John's time names over thirty evil and subservient counsellors who gave the king advice in the period of his stand against the church.[144] These persons may nearly all be identified as officials at court or others in the king's employment, some as sheriffs, and most of them from time to time witnesses of documents which he issued.[145] From about 1205 this circle seems less variable than in the past. In it were many foreigners and other new men of lesser rank who owed their rise to the king's favor.

In numerous instances the Angevin king sought the advice of the narrower council on general matters of policy. In 1164 the king conferred secretly with members of his household [146] when Becket was on trial, once retiring with them into a further chamber. In 1177 Henry by their counsel called out the feudal military array to accompany him to the continent for a year.[147] When in 1191 Walter of Coutances was made justiciar he promised to do nothing except by the consent of his associates and the counsel of the barons of the exchequer.[148] It has been shown that in John's reign orders are recorded as issued by advice of the council or by that of the justiciar

[143] Benedict, I. 178. Here probably the great council. Used of the chancellor in *Materials for Hist. of Becket*, II. 365.

[144] Roger of Wendover, II. 59-60.

[145] Morris, *Med. English Sheriff*, 164 and note 192. See *Rotuli Chartarum*, I. part 1, *passim*.

[146] *Familiares*: Baldwin, *King's Council*, 11.

[147] Benedict, I. 138.

[148] Baldwin, *King's Council*, 9.

and other liegemen, or by that of Archbishop Hubert and others. Moreover, John in his will designated thirteen executors without whose advice he says he would ordain nothing, even though in good health.[149] Foreign policy was sometimes included within the scope of conciliar deliberation, for in 1209 letters from the Welsh prince Llewellyn were read before two bishops, the chancellor, the justiciar and others.[150]

The narrow council also performed a certain legislative function. In the earlier years of Henry II the judges admitted a distinction between a measure enacted by the king, valid for his lifetime, and a legal enactment approved by the great council which was permanently binding.[151] The distinction is similar to the later one between an ordinance and a statute. Writers of the Angevin period were quite familiar with the idea of a decree (*edictum*) [152] issued by the king to prescribe administrative arrangements. The judicial reforms of Henry were often made by temporary ordinances or decrees, and although, as shown above, some of these had the approval of the great council, there was no legal reason why most of them could not be issued upon the advice of the small council. Instructions to the itinerant judges effected real changes in law, though only in a few cases is the great council said to be consulted. Certain of the assizes of Henry II in the same way appear to be issued upon the advice of the smaller group. The court which sat at Westminster was established in 1178 by the advice of counsellors.[153] John in 1204 made and published regulations concerning the coinage two months before his so-called assize of money was issued upon the advice of the great council. In 1201 certain exchequer regulations were adopted after being recited before a small group of mag-

---

[149] *Ibid.*, 14; Rymer, *Foedera* (Rec. Com.) I. 144.

[150] Baldwin, *King's Council*, 14.

[151] Palgrave, *English Commonwealth*, II. pp. lxv-lxvi. As to legislation by ordinance, G. B. Adams, *Origin of English Const.*, 194-202.

[152] For *edicta* in this sense, Benedict, I. 93; Coggeshall, 60; *Waverley Annals*, 250; Palgrave, *English Commonwealth*, II. p. lxv.

[153] Benedict, I. 207: *per consilium sapientium regni.* For *sapientes*, cf. *Curia Regis Rolls*, III. 124.

nates.[154] John's successors continued to issue enactments in the same way.[155]

The aspect of the permanent council as a court *coram rege* is much more familiar.[156] When Henry II established the sedentary court at Westminster in 1178 he specified that difficult matters were to be reserved to the king and his circle of advisers.[157] In 1204 a case before the justices sitting in John's presence was postponed until the archbishop of Canterbury and other great men could be in attendance.[158] During Richard's absence in Normandy, there could actually be no court *coram rege* in England. For some time after his death the doctrine prevailed that the justices at Westminster might take up the type of cause which had been reserved to the king or his justiciar.[159] This temporarily confused theories, but it is still stated that certain matters are to come before the tribunal which attends the king wherever he may be in England.[160] The idea of maintaining a substitute for the court *coram rege* before long seems to be abandoned. Moreover, John at times greatly expanded its jurisdiction, sometimes observing the regular court terms and disposing of a large volume of business.[161]

It has been held, especially for the Norman period, that there was but one *curia regis*, contracting and expanding, and that the lesser could do whatever the greater could do. To the law of the Angevin as well as the Norman period the sanction of the various types of both the lesser and the greater council

[154] *Rotuli. Litt. Pat.*, 47-48, 54; Hoveden, IV. 152. But the grand assize and the assize of novel disseisin, bestowed by the counsel of the magnates (Glanvill, II. 7; XIII. 32), apparently had the assent of the great council as Stubbs (*Constnl. Hist.*, I. 616) held.

[155] Adams, *Council and Courts*, 145, n. 33, 322-325.

[156] Above, p. 272. Once in 1155 it consisted of the king's brother, the chancellor, the two justiciars, a steward, a constable, the king's physician, and Ralph de Sigillo (Palgrave, *English Commonwealth*, II. p. xlv).

[157] *Sapientioribus:* Benedict, I. 208.

[158] *Curia Regis Roll* (1925) III, 124.

[159] *Curia Regis Roll* (1922), I. 462.

[160] *Ibid.*, I. 463-465; cf. 261.

[161] See *ibid.*, III. 85-166, 337-347.

was the same, derived from the principle of baronial counsel and assent. There was nevertheless a very practical distinction between the assent of household officials and royal followers and that of the great assembly of magnates. The curial circle which attended the king could be regarded as a representative council neither by the barons nor the clergy. The Magna Carta requirement that scutages and aids shall have the assent of the great council shows clearly enough that the importance of the distinction was recognized. Whether the smaller body might do whatever the greater might do was not purely a theoretical matter. That in general it might handle the same categories of business, administrative, conciliar, and judicial, is clear. Whether it took the same place in government is a very different question.

The king had to decide which form of council would best facilitate the completion of a given piece of business, and until Magna Carta there was probably no actual barrier to a preference for either body except in making permanent legislation. The line of demarcation between the functions of the two bodies was destined to remain undefined for centuries, but a broad distinction is none the less evident. It lies not so much in the type of business transacted as in the degree of its importance. The court *coram rege* disposed of much judicial business and the great council could handle but little, yet the great trials of Becket and Robert of Essex were before the latter. The small council might advise the king upon any matter, but important deliberations upon foreign or papal policy or national defense took place before the magnates as a whole. The three feudal aids, the tallages, and probably the danegeld as well, were financial matters in the king's hands to manage as he saw fit, yet when he wanted assent to a new kind of tax, or wished to change the form of an older one, he took up the matter with the great council. He made various ordinances with the advice of his permanent *curia*, but the Constitutions of Clarendon, the great judicial innovations of Henry II and the greater legislative measures, including

Magna Carta, at least in form, came before the national assembly in accord with traditional usage.

The Angevin ruler was so largely an absolute king that he might do much without consulting the great assembly of the barons of the realm. Marked innovations in taxation, in legislation, in general policy, none the less called for this. Henry II habitually consulted the great council on almost every possible subject.[162] Matters of especial difficulty, matters which involved a radical departure from existing usage, were almost of necessity settled by the great assembly, and no just ground for opposition existed after this was done. Within a very important field the king could not ignore the great council, nor was it safe to do so. It was more largely attended and far more influential than the king's permanent council, and it represented the strongest power with which the monarch had to reckon.

AUTHORITIES

The greatest body of detail for the subject matter of this chapter is gained from chronicles. The most valuable of these is the work ascribed to Benedict, abbot of Peterborough, which covers in detail the period from 1170 to 1192. The author was well informed and included many documents in his narrative. The more recent edition of the work is by William Stubbs (2 vols. Rolls Series, 1867). Very useful also is the chronicle of Ralph de Diceto, the dean of St. Paul's, London. This is an original account for the period 1172 to 1201, and from 1188 on is a valuable contemporary record which contains many letters and documents. It was edited by Stubbs (2 vols. Rolls Series, 1876). A third work of major importance is the *Chronica* of Roger of Hoveden. The author was in the service of Henry II as early as 1174. The portion of his work covering the period 1169-1192 is a new version of Benedict of Peterborough with the addition of some important documents; the portion devoted to the years 1192-1201 is an original contemporary history which embodies documents in abundance. These three chronicles of the reigns of Henry II and Richard are supplemented by the history of William of Newburgh, begun about 1196 (ed. Richard Howlett, 2 vols. Rolls Series, 1884-1885) and the Chronicle of Robert of Torigni (also known as Robert de Monte), abbot first of Bec and then of Mont-Saint-Michel, whose work comes down to 1186 (ed. Leopold Delisle,

[162] Stubbs, introd. to Benedict, II. pp. ccvi-ccviii.

Société de l'Histoire de Normandie, 2 vols. 1872-1873; also Richard
Howlett, Rolls Series, 2 vols. 1889). The *Materials for the History of
Thomas Becket* (ed. J. C. Robertson, Rolls Ser., 7 vols. 1875-1885) is
frequently useful, especially for the study of the great council.

Of the chronicles of John's reign the best is that of Roger of Wendover, which is a contemporary authority for the whole period from
1200 to 1235. The portion of the work covering the period from 1154
appears in the Rolls Series (ed. H. G. Hewlett, 3 vols., 1886-1889), but
in a better edition (ed. H. O. Coxe, 4 vols., 1841-1844) in the *English
Historical Society* series. The writer was historiographer of the abbey
of St. Albans. His successor in that position, Matthew Paris, made
much use of his work in writing his chronicle at a later time. The
Chronicon Anglicanum, written by Ralph, the abbot of Coggeshall, is
valuable especially for John's reign. The part of his work from 1187 to
1195 was used by Roger of Wendover. His chronicle was published in
the Rolls Series (ed. Joseph Stevenson, 1875). Gervase, a monk of
Canterbury, wrote a chronicle of some value for the reigns of Henry II
and Richard, but important for the reign of John (ed. William Stubbs,
Rolls Series, 2 vols. 1879-1880). He died in 1210, but a continuator
brought the account past 1216.

The chronicles are especially valuable for the study of the great
council. A very useful guide for this purpose is the "Outline Itinerary
of Henry II" by William Stubbs, in the preface to vol. II of his edition
of Benedict of Peterborough. The best secondary account of the
national assembly is that of Stubbs in chap. 13 of his *Constitutional
History of England*. This has been supplemented in some particulars
by H. G. Richardson in *Transactions of Royal Historical Society*, 4th
ser., XI (1928); by A. B. White, "Was there a Common Council before
Parliament?" *American Historical Review*, XXV. 1-17 (1919), and "The
First Concentration of Juries," *ibid.*, XVII. 12-16 (1911); by J. H.
Round, "Barons and Knights in the Great Charter," *Magna Carta
Commemoration Essays* (ed. H. E. Malden, 1917) 46-77; and by various
passages in G. B. Adams, *Council and Courts* (1926).

The principal materials for the study of the smaller council as a court
coram rege are the various *curia regis* rolls and the cases collected in
Palgrave's *English Commonwealth*, vol. II. For these see note at end
of chapter xii. On the exchequer as a council, the classic work to be
consulted is the *Dialogus de Scaccario*, written just prior to 1179 by
Richard Fitz-Neal, treasurer of England. The best edition is that by
A. Hughes, C. G. Crump and C. Johnson (1902. In footnotes referred
to as the Oxford edition). The names of witnesses to the charters of
Henry II, which show the group in attendance upon him, are found
in Leopold Delisle's contribution to the *Bibliothèque de l'Ecole des*

Chartes, vol. 69, pp. 547-72. A calendar of Richard's documents for the years 1189-1191, providing a key to similar data, is published in A. Cartellieri, *Philipp II August., König von Frankreich* (1906), II. 288-301. The names of the corresponding group for John's reign occur in the various documents enrolled in the Charter Rolls (*Rotuli Chartarum,* vol. I, part 1, ed. T. D. Hardy, Record Commission, 1837). The Patent Rolls (*Rotuli Litterarum Patentium,* vol. I, part 1, ed. T. D. Hardy, Record Commission, 1827) occasionally throw light on John's council. R. W. Eyton, *Court, Household, and Itinerary of Henry II* (1878), though very incomplete, is useful especially because it gives lists of witnesses to the king's acts. The standard secondary account is in chap. 1 of J. F. Baldwin, *The King's Council in England during the Middle Ages* (1913). Some points are discussed in Adams, *Council and Courts* and in T. F. Tout, *Chapters in Administrative History,* vol. I (1920). The last-named writer holds that the small council in practice was a household rather than a feudal body.

CHAPTER XIV

THE ADMINISTRATIVE SYSTEM, TAXATION, AND THE ARMY

The permanent *curia* consisted of those persons of official or baronial status who were in attendance upon the king.[1] Collectively regarded, it was changing and unorganized, as the account of the lesser council, in the previous chapter, well shows. The part taken by the small council in administration, moreover, was not that of an executive. By its advice the king might decide upon supervisory arrangements, but it was a council, not an office.[2] In some respects its older work had ceased to follow the king. As a rule the exchequer now met and supervised the collection of the king's revenues in his absence. The itinerant justices also sat at a distance from his court, and this was usually true of the bench at Westminster. So far as the everyday detail of government at court was concerned, this belonged to individual household officials.

Within the *curia*, however, there developed by John's time, at the latest, an administrative department which followed the king. This was the king's *camera* or chamber, of which at first his household treasury and later his wardrobe office formed the most important part. The king's chamber became well organized, its members being chamberlains and clerks. By John's time it handled its own secretarial business and made use of a separate seal to authenticate its documents. It was the training-ground of a good number of those who rose to high administrative posts under Richard and John.[3] In this

---

[1] Above, pp. 313-315.

[2] Tout, *Chapters in Administrative History*, I. 10, 11; cf. II. 146-148.

[3] *Ibid.*, 107-119, 158-169; H. Jenkinson, *Magna Carta Commemoration Essays* (ed. Malden), 295.

latter respect its utility was even greater than that of the chancery of the Norman period.

The exchequer, although it still preserved the distinctive characteristics of the lesser council, and although its official figures were largely the same,[4] had entered upon a process of differentiation as early as the time of Henry I. As already shown, it was in theory a small council; and it might become identical with the council which attended the king, for it was sometimes held in his presence. For most purposes, however, it had become a distinct department, indeed the earliest department of government in any strict sense of the term. Unlike the lesser *curia* it met as a rule in one place, usually at Westminster.[5] Its work had apparently not ceased in Stephen's time, but the houses of the exchequer at Westminster were in disrepair at the accession of Henry II.[6] Its system was re-established by Nigel, bishop of Ely, the nephew of Roger of Salisbury. Nigel's son, Richard Fitz-Neal, later bishop of London, became treasurer of England in 1158[7] and continued for many years the administrative tradition of his family.

The body which gathered about the exchequer table twice a year, under the presidency of the justiciar, is known as the upper exchequer or exchequer of accounts. This employed judicial process in the collection and audit of the king's revenues. Although the greater officials, such as the chancellor or the constable, might be absent much of the time, it was expected that they be consulted in important matters.[8] There was also a lower exchequer, or exchequer of receipt, headed by the treasurer and the two chamberlains of the exchequer, which received and receipted the funds paid in and by the

---

[4] Above, pp. 313-314. As to the Norman exchequer, Haskins, *Norman Institutions*, 179-180.

[5] *Dialogus de Scaccario*, Oxford ed., 43-44. Sessions were occasionally held elsewhere (*ibid.*, and Tout, I. 96 n. 4; Poole, *Exchequer*, 71, n. 1).

[6] Pipe Roll, 2 Henry II, p. 4.

[7] *Dialogus de Scaccario*, Oxford ed., 96-97; D. M. Stenton, *Cambridge Med. Hist.*, V. 573, n. 1.

[8] *Dialogus*, Oxford ed., 69, 70, 72. As to the judicial character of proceedings, also 68, 112.

time of Henry II had control of the principal treasury of the realm. The exchequer thus absorbed the treasury. Located originally at Winchester, the latter was transferred to London in the Angevin period [9] and in John's time often housed at the Temple. For ages the treasurer and the two chamberlains of the exchequer upon receipt of proper authority jointly disbursed [10] the funds in their custody. The exchequer of receipt was the office through which a great part of the king's revenue was collected and paid out, but sheriffs might be ordered by writ to make immediate payment locally for special purposes, and for this were allowed due credit upon their annual account when it was rendered at the exchequer.[11] Moreover, certain kinds of payments were made at the king's *camera* which served as a household treasury.[12]

The work of the justiciar, the king's chief lieutenant, was executive as well as judicial and so was confined to no particular place nor department. Much of it was necessarily carried on in the king's absence and was separate from the *curia* which attended him. Thus the justiciar represented the king at the exchequer, and was his only representative in many high administrative and judicial matters when he was absent from the realm.[13] In the earlier years of Henry II he aided in the disposition of causes heard in the king's presence.[14] Later he presided over the new court at Westminster [15] and sometimes served as an itinerant justice.[16] He, as well as the king, might authorize the transfer of matters to the king's court and might sanction the issue of judicial writs. More-

[9] Tout, *Chapters in Administrative History*, 93-99; *Dialogus*, Oxford ed., 45.

[10] *Ibid.*, 61-62, 82; cf. D. M. Stenton, *Cambridge Med. Hist.*, V. 557.

[11] For example, Poole, *Exchequer*, 160-163; Morris, *Medieval English Sheriff*, 125-126, 149.

[12] Tout, *Chapters in Administrative History*, 100-108.

[13] *Dialogus de Scaccario*, Oxford ed., 67. See Constitutions of Clarendon, secs. 7, 9; for the Norman seneschal, Haskins, *Norman Institutions*, 183-184.

[14] Above, p. 278 .

[15] Glanvill, VIII. 2, 3.

[16] D. M. Stenton, *Cambridge Med. Hist.*, V. 574-576.

over, after the first decade of Henry's reign justiciars authorized the expenditure of funds from the treasury.[17] It is clear
that the justiciars of the period were strong men who were
not likely to be mere followers of routine at the exchequer,
in the law courts, and at the *curia*. Henry II at first followed
Norman usage in employing two. One of these, Robert the
earl of Leicester, was a valued counsellor of the king,[18] and
an honorary steward. Until the death of Robert in 1168 the
king apparently planned to make the steward an hereditary
justiciar like the Norman seneschal.[19] The other justiciar,
Richard de Lucy, more noted for his judicial activity, suppressed the feudal rebellion of 1173 in England.[20] His successor, Ranulf Glanvill, in office from 1179 to the end of the
reign, is credited with the active furtherance of judicial reform, and it fell to him as to his predecessors to manage affairs during the king's frequent absences. During Richard's
absence two ecclesiastics in turn carried on the government.
These were the chancellor, William Longchamp (1189-1191),
bishop of Ely, and Walter of Coutances (1191-1193), archbishop of Rouen, and former chancery official. Upon the third
ecclesiastical justiciar of the reign, Hubert Walter (1194-
1198) the archbishop of Canterbury and nephew of Glanvill,
devolved much of the burden of raising the funds for the
king's ransom and his war with France. He improved the
enforcement of the peace by a decree of 1195 and extended the
effectiveness of the itinerant justices.[21] Geoffrey Fitz-Peter,
Richard's last justiciar, was a baron trained in the school of
Henry II, who remained in office until his death in 1213.
He was influential in securing the succession of John, who
created him an earl, but who came to regard his influence as
one of unwelcome restraint. He sympathized with the barons

---

[17] Glanvill, VI. 7; IX. 6, 8; XII, 9, 25; Stenton, *op. cit.*, V. 576.

[18] Vernon Harcourt, *His Grace the Steward*, 50-51; Stenton, *op. cit.*, 576-578.

[19] Vernon Harcourt, *His Grace the Steward*, 40, 43-51.

[20] Stubbs, *Constnl. Hist.*, I. 516-517.

[21] See Stubbs, *Select Charters*, 258-264.

in their stand against John in 1213, enunciating principles of justice quite contrary to the trend of the king's policy.[22] The weakest of the series, the last justiciar of the period, was Peter des Roches (1213-1216), the Poitevin bishop of Winchester, a subservient placeman, disliked as a foreigner by the barons [23] and of little aid to his master in the struggle against them.

The chancery was still actually a household office to be regarded as following the king. Its activities were supposedly unified under one head, but in practice there was some division. There was already in the time of Henry II a second seal deposited in the exchequer.[24] In the time of John a third, the king's privy seal, was kept in the royal household and used to attest documents.[25] The chancellor was in a general way responsible for the work done by all those who used the seals. The keeping of the exchequer records as well as the custody of the exchequer seal was entrusted to a clerk.[26] The development of the king's wardrobe by John's time produced a force of chamber clerks over whom the chancellor's actual control could not have been great.[27] Moreover, the duties of this official as custodian of the great seal were sometimes discharged by persons in subordinate position. From 1162 to 1173, no chancellor was appointed, and the remaining chancellors of Henry II were not strong men. For a good part of the reign, moreover, the actual chancellor did not perform his duties in person.[28] The title vice-chancellor occurs, and although it is probably unofficial, the name gives a correct idea of the office. After 1159 such an official was often the working head of the chancery. In John's time even patents

[22] Below, p. 348.
[23] Coggeshall, 168.
[24] *Dialogus de Scaccario*, Oxford ed., 70-71; Tout, *Chapters in Administrative History*, I. 142-149.
[25] *Ibid.*, 151-157.
[26] *Dialogus de Scaccario*, Oxford ed., 69, 70-71; see also Tout, *Chapters in Administrative History*, 146-148.
[27] *Ibid.*, 160-162.
[28] *Ibid.*, 133-134.

under the great seal were sometimes issued by the chancellor's subordinates.[29]

Some of the chancellors of the Angevin period none the less had a strong influence in government. The office was not always one of the greatest in the kingdom, but its revenues from the issue of writs were large. Some of the chancellors of these three reigns were only of the rank of archdeacon; but some were bishops, one an archbishop and one the king's son.[30] Under Richard and John they came to hold office for life. Becket as chancellor during the early years of Henry II was a very influential person, and extremely active in secular administration, though his dignity was hardly second to the king, as one of his biographers claims.[31] He attended the king's councils without being called. Not only was he in charge of the great seal, but the king's chapel was in his disposition and care. Moreover, he received and administered the churches in the hands of the king, including those which fell to the crown by reason of a vacancy, although the latter did not belong to his office.[32] This account gives a good idea of the chancellor's office, but it describes what is practically the height of its power. A noted writer of the time of Henry II declares that nothing great is done or ought to be done either at the exchequer or in the *curia* without the consent or counsel of the chancellor,[33] but the statement seems to be based on Becket's influence at an earlier date. The next strong chancellor was William Longchamp, the bishop of Ely, who held office in Richard's reign and was also justiciar from 1189 until he was

[29] This was when Walter de Gray was chancellor in the period 1211-1213 (*ibid.*, 162). Cf. Round, *Calendar*, pp. 36, 537.

[30] The chancellors of Henry II were Thomas Becket (1154-1162), Ralph of Warneville (1173-1182), and Geoffrey, the king's illegitimate son (1182-1189) ; of Richard, William Longchamp (1189-1197) ; of John, Hubert Walter (1199-1205), Walter de Gray (1205-1214), and Richard Marsh (from 1214).

[31] Fitz-Stephen, *Life of St. Thomas*, in *Materials for Hist. of Becket*, III. 18.

[32] *Ibid.*, III. 18-20; Stenton, *Cambridge Med. Hist.*, V. 557.

[33] *Dialogus de Scaccario*, Oxford ed., 70. The chancellor of the time was relatively unimportant.

deposed from the office by the barons in 1191. After that time his influence could not have been great. Archbishop Hubert Walter, Richard's justiciar, was chancellor for the first six years of John's reign and was a power in the government, but his successors to 1216 were less able and independent.

The standing of individual chancellors as persons of weight in the king's councils obviously had little bearing upon the quality of the work done by their subordinates. In the time of Henry II this had attained a high level both in England and in Normandy. The king's writs were businesslike, concise and well executed. The reign of John reveals new forms of documents issued by the clerks of the king's chamber. Moreover, there began, chiefly when Hubert Walter was chancellor, a systematic transcript of certain documents. Three series are especially noteworthy. The king's letters patent and close and also the royal charters were enrolled as they were issued, so the chancery might retain official copies.[34] In this way was initiated the long series of Patent, Close and Charter Rolls. The Patent Rolls enrolled the king's Letters Patent, so named because they were sealed and delivered open. They were as a rule addressed generally and were intended to be shown repeatedly. They record on the whole the king's weightier acts, including his proclamations, his more important orders or edicts and the commissions which he issued. The Letters Close, recorded on the Close Rolls, were delivered sealed up, hence their name. These were addressed to individuals, whether officials or others, and could be used but once. They conveyed a large part of the detailed official instructions issued by the king. The Charter Rolls record the charters or solemn grants by which the king conveyed to individuals, churches, and towns either lands or privileges.

The hereditary official element in the king's household still persisted, although its place in the newer administrative arrangements was but rarely one of first importance. Constables,

[34] Haskins, *Norman Institutions*, 191; cf. Tout, *Chapters in Administrative History*, 135-138, 152.

dapifers and chamberlains evidently attended the councils of Henry II, for they appear among the witnesses to his acts. Among these only the high constable was an important dignitary of state throughout the period, his office standing next in rank below the chancellor.[35] He was the highest military official, serving actively in the field, as is well shown by the story of Henry of Essex, who was convicted of treason for dropping the king's banner [36] in battle. It was his duty to keep informed concerning the terms served by the king's knights and serjeants, for at the exchequer his representative along with the marshal attended to the payment of wages due them. Moreover, the constable produced at the exchequer the writs which had authorized the issue of funds from the treasury, although this duty was regularly delegated to a knight.[37] At court he administered his office either in person or through his clerk, a functionary who also had a regular post at the exchequer board, and who was an important person at the *curia*.[38]

To the constable's department belonged the marshal, whose duties were also performed both in the field and at court. He with the constable and the clerk of the latter formed a kind of board in charge of the detail of household expenditures. He witnessed payments made by the king's household officials, including those in charge of the king's hawks and falcons. He oversaw the payment of household salaries and wages. Under his direction were computed the amounts due the king's troops. At the exchequer his office, regularly filled by a knight, was indispensable, being charged with the administration of the oaths required, the delivery of writs of summons to be served, and the custody of the exchequer prison.[39] The first great marshal was William, who succeeded John, his brother, in

[35] Vernon Harcourt, *His Grace the Steward*, 41-42.

[36] Above, p. 305. For the succession of constables, *Dialogus*, Oxford ed., 25-26.

[37] *Ibid.*, 69, 71-72.

[38] *Ibid.*, 69, 84.

[39] *Ibid.*, 24-25, 71-72. He also had charge of the vouchers produced at the exchequer by accountants.

the office in 1194. Profiting by family connection as well as
by ability and knightly character, he became a leading figure
at court and through his marriage earl of Pembroke. He was
one of the three powerful men who secured the throne to John,
and after the death of the latter guided the government of a
boy king through a great crisis.[40]

Two hereditary stewards are mentioned in the time of
Henry II, both earls with honorary ceremonial functions
on state occasions. One of these, the earl of Leicester, was
employed in a higher office. In the reign of Richard I his
descendant appears with the titular dignity of high steward,
then known as seneschal.[41] At least one of the active stewards
of subordinate rank was employed by Henry II on weighty
missions of state.[42] The rank of master chamberlain was apparently maintained, but the office was honorary and not
active as in the time of Henry I.[43] The holders of several of
the lesser, non-hereditary chamberlainships achieved distinction in the king's service. In John's time their close connection with the business of the *camera* offered opportunity to
rise to higher position, as in the case of Hubert de Burgh.[44]

The itinerant justices, as already shown, acted not merely
as judicial, but in various ways as fiscal and executive agents
of the crown. One of the great administrative effects of the
judicial reforms of Henry II was to provide increased facilities
for inquest into the king's rights through these visiting representatives of the central power, who also supervised special
tasks and held sheriffs in check.[45] The form of their commissions was sometimes a matter important enough to be considered by the great council. After the rebellion of 1173 the
itinerant justices were charged with the duty of destroying

[40] *Dictionary National Biography*, art. "Marshall, William."
[41] Vernon Harcourt, *His Grace the Steward*, 40-43, 72. The title high
steward was not yet used.
[42] William fitz Audelin, *Dict. Natnl. Biog.*, art. "Fitzaldhelm, William."
[43] Tout, *Chapters in Administrative History*, 89-91, 109; cf. Haskins,
Norman Institutions, 183.
[44] Tout, *Chapters*, I. 159.
[45] For these matters see above, chap. xii.

unlicensed castles. They saw that ships and timber were not
sold out of the realm.[46] They assessed tallages,[47] they sometimes supervised the fiscal concerns of the royal demesne lands,
and they enrolled promises made before them to pay the king
sums for special privileges (*fines* or *conventiones*). The
amercements which they imposed were often regarded as oppressive. Their records showed the sources from which judicial
income was to be collected, and the rolls which they kept were
preserved at the exchequer.[48] Under Henry II appear a separate corps of forest officials and eyres of the special justices [49]
to enforce the forest law. This monarch revised the forest law
in 1184 through the Assize of the Forest, also called the Assize
of Woodstock, but its existence and administration remained
weighty popular grievances. Richard in 1198 issued a still
more severe assize.[50]

No account of Angevin administration would be adequate
without some notice of the part played in it by the sheriffs.[51]
Henry II soon appointed a force of these officials who were
satisfactory agents in local government. They were usually
persons devoid of feudal pretension who owed their position
to their fidelity and ability. Only for a time during Richard's
absence were they a group strong enough to wield a real
political influence. Under John they were subservient officials
who fitted perfectly into the king's scheme of government.
Practically all of them were English. John's misrule was not
based upon a shrievalty manned by foreigners, as has sometimes been supposed. Sheriffs of foreign origin were extremely
rare in his time until the period of his war with the barons
after Magna Carta.

The independence of the sheriffs was partly reduced through
their subordination to the itinerant justices. It was their duty

[46] Assize of Arms, sec. 12.
[47] *Dialogus de Scaccario*, I. 95; Mitchell, *Studies in Taxation*, 68, 76.
[48] *Ibid.*, 119.
[49] See Petit-Dutaillis, *Studies Supplementary to Stubbs Constnl. Hist.*,
II. 149-165.
[50] See Stubbs, *Select Charters*, 156-159; Hoveden, IV. 63-66.
[51] See Morris, *Med. English Sheriff*, chaps. 5, 6.

to serve a vast number of judicial writs and to carry out the orders of the justices. Thus their office became the ministerial agency upon which the new judicial system chiefly depended. Sheriffs, moreover, could be called to account by the justices, and Henry II in 1170 ordered the noted Inquest of Sheriffs for the purpose of investigating their peculation and financial exactions.[52] The result of this was the removal from their positions of nearly all the sheriffs and the substitution in most cases of men already connected with the *curia*. Richard I in 1194 contemplated a similar inquiry into the financial work of both sheriffs and justices, but the plan was never carried out. Sheriffs were forbidden to act as justices in their own counties in 1194,[53] and by a provision of Magna Carta [54] were forbidden to hold pleas of the crown. Thus the sheriff's importance in judicial affairs was limited, and his power to hold trials was now confined to the ordinary work of the local courts in his county except in matters wherein he was especially authorized to proceed under the king's writ.

The sheriff's duties, however, remained numerous. His position as a peace officer stands out more clearly than in the past. He was the custodian of prisoners. Like the justices, he received indictments in the courts which he held. His functions as a military leader within his county were retained, and he was still in many cases keeper of the chief castle in the county. Moreover he was responsible for carrying out many orders of the crown, involving not only judicial and financial matters but other executive acts as well. He was regarded as the superior of the reeves and bailiffs set over hundreds or towns, and passed on to them for service writs which he received. His office was the main executive agency of the crown in carrying out locally the detail of ordinary routine administration.

This was particularly true in the realm of finance. The

[52] See Stubbs, *Select Charters*, 147-150; also Stubbs, preface to Benedict, II. lxvi-lxix.
[53] Stubbs, *Select Charters*, 260.
[54] Sec. 24.

sheriff was almost the only collector of the king's revenues. The fixed farm which he rendered annually for his shire, unless he was otherwise directed, was paid at the exchequer, half at the Easter session, the remainder at the Michaelmas session.[55] For other sources of income he made a proffer or partial payment at the time of the earlier session, closing the account so far as he could make collection just after Michaelmas. The barons made individual bargains with the king concerning their feudal reliefs,[56] and might pay their debts directly at the exchequer.[57] The farmers of some royal estates and the officials of privileged boroughs also accounted at the exchequer separately.[58] In the time of John there appears one person who farmed the profits of the coinage for the whole realm.[59] The carucage of 1195 was levied in part by special collectors in each hundred, but who turned the money over to the sheriff.[60] The great bulk of the revenues were regularly collected by the latter official or his subordinate, and he was firmly held at the exchequer to the responsibility by the requirement of a periodical accounting.

The ordinary revenue of the Angevin king was much the same as that of the Norman period. It was derived chiefly from the fixed farm which the sheriff paid annually for holding his shire, from amercements imposed by the king's justices, from the farm of boroughs, from the feudal incidents (reliefs, marriage fines, wardships and escheats), from the revenues of vacant bishoprics and abbeys, and sums (*fines*) offered to the king for certain privileges. To the king also belonged the profits derived from the confiscated chattels of felons, wreckage of the sea,[61] treasure trove, the profits of the coinage, dues

[55] Morris, *Med. English Sheriff*, 147, 249, n. 52.
[56] *Dialogus de Scaccario*, Oxford ed., 134-135, 155.
[57] Round, *Magna Carta Commemoration, Essays* (ed. Malden), 51-76; *Dialogus*, Oxford ed., 133, 135, 155. In John's time the exchequer might demand security (Hoveden, IV. 152) for payment of a baron's debt.
[58] Morris, *Medieval English Sheriff*, 124.
[59] *Ibid.*, 124, n. 119.
[60] Mitchell, *Studies in Taxation*, 7-8.
[61] Round, *Calendar of Documents*, no. 452.

upon shipping, and some lesser perquisites. Danegeld was probably regarded as a part of the ordinary income of the king until it ceased to be levied after 1162. From these revenues the king expected to meet the usual expenses of government. The sum total in the earlier years of John's reign has been reckoned as somewhat under forty thousand marks a year.[62]

The usual revenues were insufficient in emergencies. A steady rise in prices at the end of the century, along with the increased cost of government and frequent expeditions to the continent, made it necessary for the Angevin monarchs to seek funds from additional sources. The extraordinary revenues were supplied chiefly by the three feudal aids, the scutage from military tenants who did not provide service when called upon, the tallage an imposition arbitrarily levied by the king upon the royal demesne, and special contributions known as *dona* or *auxilia*, similarly, though more seldom, exacted from Jews, prelates, religious houses and some others.[63] The aids and scutages thus in theory fell upon tenants-in-chief, and in general were likely to be levied from time to time upon a more or less uniform plan. The *dona* were fixed at round sums. Tallages varied in amount and were usually assessed by the itinerant justices. The amount might be collected by the sheriff, but the towns in some cases paid it at the exchequer.[64]

The most notable of these extraordinary finanical devices under Henry II was the scutage. This increased in importance as a means of raising war revenue, and John for the years from 1201 to 1206 inclusive made it an annual imposition. Under Richard and John there appear two new levies of importance, the hidage or carucage, a land tax which is in effect, though not in form, a revival of the danegeld, and in addition a tax of a certain fraction of the value of move-

[62] Mitchell, *ibid.*, 16.
[63] In 1157 upon the counties (Baldwin, *Scutage and Knight Service*, 19, cf. also p. 21.). *Donum* might mean aid, scutage, or tallage (*ibid.*, 21).
[64] Mitchell, *Studies in Taxation under John and Henry III*, p. 2.

able property. Through the latter tax Angevin monarchy prepared the way for a scheme of direct taxation in England which was long continued.

The first scutage of Henry II, that of 1157, was laid upon ecclesiastical tenants only. The first general levy in commutation of knight service was taken in 1159 for the king's campaign in Toulouse.[65] The former was at the rate of twenty shillings per knight's fee, the latter at the rate of two marks. Such a levy in lieu of knight service was repeated by Henry II on five occasions.[66] The amount soon fell to one mark on the knight's fee [67] but later rose to twenty shillings.[68] The levy of scutage was usually accompanied by that of a *donum*. An aid collected in 1168 for the marriage of the king's daughter took the form of a levy of one mark upon each knight's fee held by tenants-in-chief, supplemented by a tallage of towns and vills and by special contributions from prelates and others. This seems to be the heaviest and most systematic levy made by Henry II,[69] and it afforded precedents for the future.

The Angevin rulers devised means of making the scutage more profitable. The traditional allotment of service by the Conqueror was somewhat haphazard and not in proportion to the strength of baronies. In 1166 the king called upon the barons to report the number of knights they had actually enfeoffed, and when this number exceeded the number they had heretofore provided he charged accordingly.[70] The levy of 1168 occasioned some protest and the increase of service was soon partially abandoned.[71] Under Richard I scutage was

---

[65] Baldwin, *Scutage and Knight Service*, 18-23.

[66] In 1161, 1162, 1165 (expedition to Wales), 1172 (to Ireland), 1187 (to Galway). See Baldwin, *Scutage*, 23, 25-31, 44-53.

[67] In 1162 and 1165.

[68] In 1172 and 1187.

[69] Baldwin, *ibid.*, 32-44. This *auxilium* on knights' fees was also called *scutagium*. In this case the *scutagium* totalled about 4,000 pounds, the tallage of towns over 4500 pounds.

[70] Round, *Feudal England*, 236-237. This form of levy seems to have been made only in 1168 and 1172 (Baldwin, *Scutage*, 52).

[71] *Ibid.*, 52.

exacted several times,[72] and a payment of twenty shillings on the knight's fee was included in the feudal aid for the king's ransom in 1194. By his time wages of a knight had increased, and the scutage with the exception of that collected in 1159 and 1161,[73] had not been sufficient to enable the king to hire a knight in place of the one who paid for remaining at home. Accordingly the king made the attempt to collect from his tenants who did not take part in a campaign a larger sum. In Richard's time and possibly earlier, were received fines from important tenants who did not go on an expedition.[74] These were taken in place of the scutage and were greater in amount but there was not a fixed rate per knight's fee. The essential consideration seems to have been that the baron who failed to perform his military obligation deprived the king not only of a certain number of knights but also of his own services as commander. After he had made his fine with the king the tenant was excused from service and allowed to collect scutage from his tenants by way of partial recompense.[75] In John's time also the tenant-in-chief was often granted a writ permitting him to collect scutage from his tenants.[76] In the first instance the tenant-in-chief was responsible for the whole service of his barony.

The period of John's earlier war with France, from 1199 to 1206 inclusive, witnessed the levy of seven scutages. The only one of these years in which none was taken was 1200. These were true scutages [77] and not taxes levied generally upon

[72] Baldwin (Scutage, 73) says three, besides the aid of 1194.

[73] In the time of Henry II a fully armed knight was paid 8 d. per day, hence his wages for forty days amounted to exactly two marks (Vinogradoff, Eng. Society in Eleventh Century, 15-16). In emergencies the rate of payment rose to a shilling a day (Round, Archaeol. Journal, LIX. 147-148). See page 308.

[74] Fines ne transfretent or pro passagio.

[75] Mitchell, Studies in Taxation, 5, 17-18; Pollock and Maitland, History of English Law, I. 266-277.

[76] Mitchell, ibid., 34-35. In John's reign two plans were followed (ibid., 27). The tenant-in-chief either made a fine for his service and the right to collect scutage from his tenants; or he fined for his personal service and the right to collect scutage on his demesne, paying scutage on the infeudated portion of his holding.   [77] Mitchell, ibid., 11, 17.

knight's fees, as has sometimes been stated. But John increased the rate of the composition in some cases to two or, in 1204, two and a half marks per fee; he also took fines as explained above; he levied the payment at the beginning rather than the close of campaigns; and on some occasions he did so, as in 1201, when there was no fighting, or again, as in 1204 and 1205, when the forces were summoned but most of them not actually sent overseas.[78] The tenant was sometimes permitted to lead to the host a reduced number of knights which was regarded as the entire service due. The actual amount of the scutage collected was not large, but the rate of commutation for knight service was arbitrarily increased, especially so when many fines were taken, as they were in this period. The barons, therefore, had reason to fear that in time the king would apply what was in effect a very high rate [79] to the full military quota which they might be called to provide.[80] Scutages were levied respectively in 1209 for the expedition to Scotland, in 1210 for that to Ireland, and in 1211 for that to Wales. That of 1210 was at the high rate of three marks on the fee. By the date of the last of these the barons seem to have been so much discontented that John feared them. When the king resumed the war to regain his continental possessions, and made his expedition to Poitou in 1214, less than half of the available knights of the kingdom responded. A scutage was assessed at the rate of three marks on the knight's fee, but there was great difficulty over this matter. One chronicler says that it could not be collected from prelates. The northern barons especially refused to pay, holding the levy illegal on the ground that they did not owe service abroad.[81] The effect of this was to place them at the king's mercy, for if a tenant-in-chief failed to heed his summons to the host and did not pay his scutage

[78] *Ibid.*, 11-12, 19-20, 64-70.
[79] See *ibid.*, 39.
[80] *Ibid.*, 11-13.
[81] Mitchell, *ibid.*, 94-105, 109-116. The bishops (*ibid.*, 189) seem to have denied the obligation to serve abroad in 1230.

and offer a fine, the king might take possession of his lands.[82] The real grievance was that in these matters the monarch's power was arbitrary. The quarrel over the scutage led to the famous struggle between John and the barons.

The tallage under the name of *auxilium* or *donum* was not solely employed to supplement the scutage, but it accompanied most scutages.[83] That levied by John in 1214 is one of the exceptions in that it had no relation to the scutage of the year, its purpose being to raise funds to indemnify the church for its losses during the period of the interdict.[84] The tallage was in theory levied upon the royal demesne. It fell in the main upon the towns and upon religious houses which did not owe military service. In 1159 it was also collected from clerical tenants regardless of the fact that they were liable also to the scutage.[85] It was sometimes collected upon lands temporarily in the king's custody.[86] *Dona* from the Jews and moneyers of the kingdom were also taken. In the case of the towns and the royal demesne assessment was usually made by the itinerant justices. Upon religious houses and persons who were liable arbitrary sums were imposed.

The hidage or carucage first appears in the reign of Richard I. It was a land tax which was in effect a revival of danegeld upon a new basis. Technically it was regarded as an aid. The first tax of the kind was laid in 1194 as part of the aid for the king's ransom. Hide and carucate were names used in different parts of England for the ploughland. The carucage of 1194 was levied on the basis of the Domesday assessment.

In 1198 the tax was repeated to supply funds for Richard's war with France, the taxable unit being the carucate of one

[82] Cf. *ibid.*, 62.
[83] In 1156, 1159, 1161, 1162, 1165, 1168 (Baldwin, *The Scutage*, 18-19, 21-22, 23-24, 25, 27, 32) ; also in 1194, 1198, 1199, 1203, 1204, 1205, 1206, and 1210 (Mitchell, *Studies in Taxation*, 31, 54, 68, 76, 82, 100).
[84] *Ibid.*, 94, 116-117.
[85] Baldwin, *The Scutage*, 21.
[86] Mitchell, *Studies in Taxation*, 31.

hundred acres. A new assessment was made in each county by two royal commissioners. Before these and two knights chosen for each hundred the reeve and four men of each vill along with the bailiffs of barons holding lands therein, swore to the number of carucates in the vill. The money was collected and turned over to the sheriff by two elected knights and the bailiff of each hundred. The religious houses opposed the tax and refused to pay it, but the king took from them the protection of the courts, and they were compelled to barter for this and thus to furnish the funds required.[87] The only other carucage of the period, a tax of three shillings on each ploughland under cultivation, was levied by John in 1200 as an aid to provide the feudal relief which he had promised to the French king for his lands in France. Again there was opposition from the clergy, but the king seized the lands of the archbishop of York for refusal to allow them to be assessed, and he coerced the Cistercian monks who claimed immunity from taxation and refused to pay a fine in place of carucage.[88]

The tax of a fraction of the value of moveable property originated in a levy for a religious purpose, the relief of the Holy Land. In 1166 a levy of six pence upon the pound of the value of personal property was authorized for this purpose, though probably it was not systematically carried out.[89] The famous Saladin tax of 1188 enlarged the assessment, and became the first important tax on personal property. Though levied by ecclesiastical assessors, it was a national tax, was authorized by the great council, and consisted of a tenth of the value of the revenues and personal property of all men except crusaders, who were exempt. In case a person was suspected of swearing to a fraudulent return, the value of the property in question could be fixed by a jury of four or six men of the parish.[90] In 1201 a fortieth of revenues for one year was levied for the Holy Land, but this levy was far less

[87] Mitchell, *ibid.*, 7-8.
[88] *Ibid.*, 32-34. Coggeshall, 101-110.
[89] Mitchell, *Studies*, 6, and note 16.
[90] Stubbs, *Select Charters*, 160.

thoroughgoing. Churchmen paid it to the bishop of the diocese by order of the pope. The king granted a fortieth of the revenues of his demesne and asked the earls, barons, knights, and freemen to contribute, but each man calculated the amount of his own contribution.[91]

It was under the form of a special aid to the king, like carucage, rather than that of an ecclesiastical payment that the fraction of moveables was destined to become an important factor in English taxation. It was thus employed for the first time in 1194 as one of the means of providing the ransom of King Richard. A fourth of the value of moveable property was taken on this occasion, and it was thus more important than either the scutage or the tallage laid for this purpose.[92] The Saladin tithe had commended this form of tax to the king's ministers. The same plan was followed by John in 1203 when he levied a seventh of personal property, apparently under the pretense that this was a fine imposed upon the barons for deserting his expedition to Normandy. This tax, nevertheless, seems to have been collected from all the tenants-in-chief and the clergy as well. It is worthy of notice that in the same year a fifth of revenues for one year was collected on lands in the Channel Islands to provide for their defense.[93]

Of far greater consequence was John's later tax on personal property, the thirteenth of 1207, which the king asked as an aid to carry on the war against France. This was authorized by the great council though not without opposition, for John had just made a truce with Philip II and was already well supplied with funds. The barons were unable to resist the king, and the archbishop of York, who strongly opposed the levy, was compelled to leave England. Although the assent of the bishops and abbots was not given to the taxation of the lower clergy and the imposition of such an aid

[91] Mitchell, *ibid.*, 45-46.
[92] Coggeshall (p. 60) designates those who were to pay as all bishops, clerks, earls, barons, and also the abbeys and priories.
[93] Mitchell, *Studies in Taxation*, 63.

upon them was without precedent,[94] it was none the less collected from clergy as well as laity, the Cistercian order, however, remaining exempt.[95] Assessment was made by special justices, before whom individuals or their bailiffs swore to the amount of their property.[96] Notwithstanding the arbitrary features of the levy, its success was such that under John's successors the fraction of personal property became the chief basis of national taxation.

The Angevin as well as the Norman kings constantly employed their prerogative powers to their financial advantage. In collecting their more regular taxes as well as their scutages, they often accepted fines instead of fixed levies. When once the king placed on record his claims to a tax or any other amount due and began its collection through legal machinery, nothing could be done to stop him except to buy him off. The sums taken as an aid or *donum* and the fines offered to turn away the royal wrath might have much in common. Henry II after the revolt of 1173-1174 gained great profit by bargaining with the defeated party to restore them to his favor.[97] His action, however, in these cases was the purest justice when compared with John's fiscal methods. The exaction of the seventh in 1203 on the ground that the barons had failed to render military service was too ingenious. His manipulation of the scutage was sometimes unjustifiable, and the exactions he made upon the Cistercians after 1210 were sheer acts of despotism. Moreover, his levy upon the clergy in 1207, though questionable, was carried out with great determination and by drastic means. John went much farther in the course of his struggle with the papacy when in 1208 he forced most of the bishops to flee from the realm and seized upon the property of the church right and left.[98] So prosperous were the royal finances

[94] Mitchell, *Studies in Taxation*, 85.
[95] *Waverley Annals*, 258; *Annals of Winchester*, 79.
[96] Mitchell, *Studies*, 86-91.
[97] This came in for several years. See *Pipe Roll*, 26 Henry II., introd., p. xxii.
[98] Stubbs, *Constitutional History*, I. 559; cf. *Book of Fees*, I. 17, 35, 53; Mitchell *Studies in Taxation*, 106-107.

in consequence that there was no taxation, except scutages for service in the British Isles, until after John made his peace with Innocent III and restored the church property in 1213. Then he laid a tallage to enable him to repay the actual damage done to church property. Angevin rule had developed the basis of a system of taxation which was long to remain, and which of itself might not have been much resented except for its innovations and occasionally its heavy burden. John, however, enforced his claims not only in an arbitrary manner, but in such a way as to destroy confidence in his integrity.

The king's regular military force consisted in the first instance of those who owed knight service forty days a year or were employed by the king to render it. In 1181 it was formally required that the holder of each knight's fee have a coat of mail, a helmet, a shield and a lance.[99] Foot-soldiers were utilized, and the infantry assumed some importance in all three reigns.[100] An army regularly consisted of knights and serjeants, and the latter might be utilized as cavalry [101] or as infantry. Crossbowmen were also employed. The principle of the *fyrd* or general levy was still maintained locally and applied in emergencies.

The army in England was still in the main a feudal levy. Formerly the view was accepted that the prevalence of scutage tended to destroy this quality, since it afforded the king means to hire troops in place of those provided by the tenants who owed knight service.[103] It can be shown, however, that, except in the earlier years of Henry II and possibly in the case of a few of John's later scutages, the amount paid in the case of the knights who did not take the field

[99] Assize of Arms, sec. 1.

[100] Baldwin, *Knight Service*, 64-65.

[101] See Powicke, *Loss of Normandy*, 312; Willard, *Eng. Histor. Rev.*, XLIII, 618. In 1212, the tenants by serjeanty were summoned to appear with horses and arms (*Lit. Claus.*, I. 131). The pay of the foot serjeant under Henry II was a penny a day, that of the horse serjeant two pence (Round, *Archaeological Journal*, LIX. 148).

[102] Powicke, *Loss of Normandy*, 332-336.

[103] Freeman, *Norman Conquest*, V. 674; Stubbs, *Constnl. Hist.*, 1. 632.

was not sufficient to pay the wages of substitutes.[104] Thus the chief military effect of scutage was not to destroy the feudal conception of the army, but to keep it alive. By John's time the actual payment for knights owed by tenants-in-chief was often based only upon a fraction of the fixed quota. Apparently the scutage in practice now lessened the burden upon the baron and was designed to make him more willing to accept the old-time principle of military service.[105]

The actual levy of the feudal army was effected by the king's summons. In John's time the royal writ ordered the sheriffs to summon the military tenants-in-chief of the respective shires to appear at a given time and place equipped for the king's service. It is fairly clear that this was the usage also under Henry II.[106] The sheriff was assumed to have a roll of those who owed service so he might certify as to who had or had not come.[107] It was the duty of the king's constable to keep account of the terms of service, especially of those who served at the king's wages, and the duty of the marshal to attend to details of payment.[108] Returns regarding military tenants in the various counties demanded revision from time to time. In 1166 Henry II required the sheriffs to obtain from the tenants-in-chief information concerning the number of knights of the time of Henry I and the number enfeoffed since this reign.[109] There were other inquests of the same character.[110] A very complete one was taken in 1212, when John ordered the sheriffs to make inquest concerning all knight's fees and all tenements owing knight service or serjeanty together with the amount of service due.[111] By the

[104] Above, and note 73; Baldwin, *The Scutage*, 81-83; see Vinogradoff, *English Society in Eleventh Century*, 15-16.
[105] Baldwin, *The Scutage*, 16-17; Mitchell, *Studies in Taxation*, 302-304.
[106] Morris, *Med. Eng. Sheriff*, 117, 151.
[107] *Ibid.*, 152.
[108] *Dialogus de Scaccario*, Oxford ed., 71; as to Normandy cf. Powicke, *Loss of Normandy*, 367-369.
[109] Round, *Feudal England*, 236-241.
[110] Benedict, I. 138; *Book of Fees*, I. 1-57.
[111] *Ibid.*, I. 52-65.

time of Henry II the number of knight's fees from which service might be claimed seems to have been above six thousand.[112] There were a good many fractional knights' fees, so in many cases the provision of military service or of the funds to support it must have been a matter of joint arrangement by several landholders. Henry II in 1157 and Richard in 1194 called out only a third of the knights owing service, apparently for the sake of a threefold term of service. In 1205 the great council agreed to a plan by which every nine knights were to find a tenth, equipped with horses and arms in the usual fashion, and were to provide his wages at the rate of two shillings a day.[113]

Many knights and serjeants were in the king's pay.[114] This was necessary because of the duration of campaigns for more than forty days, and also because of failure on the part of some to render the service they owed, as witnessed by their payment of scutage. Richard I in 1198 made the unprecedented demand that the nation make him a grant to maintain three hundred knights in Normandy for a year with wages at the rate of three shillings a day.[115] All three of the Angevin rulers employed purely mercenary forces, particularly in their continental wars, but John also in his struggle with the barons after the granting of Magna Carta.[116] Some of the adventurers employed as captains in the war of 1215 and 1216 were famous, and had a reputation for carrying on war in an inhuman fashion.[117] During this struggle John even employed some of these men as sheriffs.

The keeping and defense of the royal castles was another important factor in the military affairs of the period. By, and probably before, the reign of John it had become the rule to confer upon the sheriffs of certain counties the custody of

[112] Mitchell, *Studies in Taxation*, 4.

[113] *Stubbs, Constnl. Hist.*, I. 631 ; Stubbs, *Select Charters*, 281-282.

[114] Cf. Round, *Calendar of Documents*, no. 70.

[115] Above, p. 308.

[116] Stubbs, *Constnl. Hist.*, I. 630-631 ; Coggeshall, 176, cf. Powicke, *Loss of Normandy*, 337-343.

[117] See Morris, *Med. Eng. Sheriff*, 162-163.

the castle of the principal town.[118] During the revolt of 1173 some of the sheriffs were in charge of the defense of these castles, holding forces of knights and serjeants for the purpose. But royal castles other than those in part of the county towns were usually committed to special castellans or constables. Once, in 1176, the king, after consultation with the great council took over the custody of the castles of his earls and barons, in England and in Normandy, appointing his own custodians.[119] These constables enforced the special military service known as castle guard.[120] They apparently were accustomed to collect money for this when those who owed ward of castle were willing to render or provide it, for Magna Carta [121] forbade this practice. John's constables were men of unusual military ability but were unscrupulous foreign adventurers, guilty also of other exactions. In 1215 and 1216 they levied a military charge known as tenserie, apparently upon the estates of those who opposed the king.[122] The Great Charter forbade them to commandeer grain or other chattels without making immediate payment, and bound the king to appoint no one to the position except those who knew the law of the realm and meant to observe it.[123]

Sheriffs were an especially important adjunct to military administration. Indeed, the importance of the sheriff in military matters stood highest in this period. In addition to their functions as mustering officers and custodians of castles they performed others when so required by the king's writ. They often purchased or provided military supplies and equipment and ships for transporting troops by sea. In the time of Henry II they were sometimes charged with the payment of the wages of those who garrisoned the king's fortresses. In John's time they were also called upon to furnish auxiliaries, in-

[118] *Ibid.*, 151.
[119] Benedict, I. 124.
[120] *Ibid.*, 152; Pollock and Maitland, *Hist. of English Law*, I. 278.
[121] Sec. 29.
[122] Morris, *Med. Eng. Sheriff*, 152.
[123] Secs. 28, 45.

cluding men for the king's galley service or men to wield axes or shovels.[124]

They were, moreover, regularly in charge of the *fyrd* or general levy so long as it was within the county.[125] This force was placed upon a regular basis in 1181 by the Assize of Arms,[126] which provided that each freeman should maintain military equipment according to his means. An inquest was to be held by the justices to determine who had an income of fourteen marks a year and who had ten marks. Persons in the former class were required to keep the same arms and armor as a knight; those in the latter class a fixed, though a smaller, amount. The burghers, moreover, and the whole body of freemen were required in similar manner to maintain a certain amount of military equipment. All who failed were to be punished in person and not by loss of land or chattels, and all were required to swear service for the protection of the king or the defense of the realm. Arrangements to marshal such a force were made in 1205, and it was called out in the southern counties, in 1213, when John feared an invasion of England by the French.[127]

The monarchy of the Angevin, like that of the Norman, kings was an absolutist monarchy, but its general effectiveness was far greater because it was an institutionalized absolutism. Through the restless energy of Henry II and his sons as well as that of their able ministers, administrative machinery and methods were constantly made to contribute to a process of centralization. As against this but one notable counter-movement may be traced, the grant of greater privileges of self-government to towns, a trend which was especially rapid under Richard and John.[128] Angevin centralization in the main brought increased efficiency of government. In the

[124] Morris, *Medieval English Sheriff*, 117, 152-153.

[125] *Ibid.*, 226-227, 234-235.

[126] Stubbs, *Select Charters*, 153-156.

[127] Gervase, II. 96-97; Wendover, II. 66-67; William of Newburgh, II. 514.

[128] Stubbs, *Constnl. Hist.*, I. 667-668; Ballard, *Eng. Histor. Rev.*, XIV. 97, 102-103.

centralizing process a variety of institutions were involved, the greater and the lesser council, the household offices, the exchequer, the central and even the local courts, the circuits of the itinerant justices and the offices of sheriff and castellan. Most of the agencies of government became professionalized and better organized. The earliest and perhaps the most far-reaching change came through a systematic use of itinerant justices which gave them great possibilities in government. Improvement by no means ceased with the famous acts of Henry II, for successful absolutism required good administrative arrangements. In Richard's reign the work was carried forward by Hubert Walter and under John even more rapidly, for advance may be traced in the *camera*, at the exchequer,[129] in the chancery and in the regulation of the shrievalty. The vice of John's rule, indeed, did not lie in an ineffective system of government but in the abuse of an extremely effective one. The great work of the Angevin kings, especially Henry II, was to correlate and improve the administrative agencies which had existed under Henry I. This institutional basis of the central government proved an enduring foundation, and remained the permanent groundwork of the English constitution.

Much depended upon the manner in which the monarch wielded the powerful machinery which had been constructed to meet his growing needs. Henry II was on the whole a ruler who showed justice and moderation. Barons who cut timber in the royal forests and in other ways broke the forest law were in 1175 heavily amerced, although the king had authorized this during the late war and some of the greatest personages in the land were among the offenders.[130] His sheriffs and his justices were accused of making wrongful exactions, but most of the sheriffs were on one occasion dismissed from office because of their dishonesty and oppression. The burden of taxation under Henry II was light as contrasted with that under

[129] Mabel H. Mills, *Trans. Royal Histor. Soc.*, 4th ser., IX. 151-161.
[130] Benedict, I. 92, 94; cf. *Pipe Roll*, 23 Henry II, p. xxi.

his sons.[131] In their time taxation was relatively heavy and sometimes levied in a despotic spirit. John in 1210 plundered the Jews and a little later the Cistercians. He lived extravagantly and collected the thirteenth of moveables when there was no immediate need. The excesses of his officials met little restraint. He employed foreign mercenary leaders who cared nothing for law. Magna Carta gives eloquent testimony concerning the exactions of foresters, castellans and sheriffs. The sheriffs especially were left almost free to impose upon the people and thus to obtain reward for faithful service to the king. Some of John's earlier charters brazenly admit this oppression and show certain counties bargaining for relief.[132] In 1213, after the beginning of John's quarrel with the barons, the justiciar, the bishop of Winchester and the magnates commanded sheriffs, foresters, and other officers of the king to refrain from extortion and injury,[133] but the prohibition obviously had little effect. Far from stressing the justice of his administration, John was willing to make capital of its injustice. It is clear that the great powers of the monarchy were being abused, and that its spirit had grown arbitrary and oppressive.

AUTHORITIES

The source materials are largely those mentioned at the conclusion of the last chapter. The materials bearing on the *coram rege* are covered at the end of chapter xii. For a detailed study of finance the Pipe Rolls are indispensable. The extant series begins with the year 1155. The three Pipe Rolls for the years 1155-1157 were published by the Record Commission (*Great Rolls of the Pipe*, 2, 3, 4 Henry II, ed. Hunter, 1844), and also that for the year 1189 (*Great Rolls of the Pipe*, 1, Richard I, ed. Hunter, 1844), and the chancellor's duplicate of the roll for the year 1201 (*Rotulus Cancellarii vel Antigraphum*, 1833). The Pipe Roll Society has published the remaining rolls to and including that for the year 1194 (41 vols., 1884-1928). The *Receipt Roll of the Exchequer for Michaelmas Term 1185* (ed. Hubert Hall, 1899) is apparently one of a series of receipt rolls made up in the lower exchequer.

---

[131] Cf. William of Newburgh, I. 282-283.
[132] Morris, *Med. Eng. Sheriff*, 145, 146.
[133] Wendover, II. 82-83.

For John's reign there are fragmentary rolls which pertain to the work of the king's camera, the Praestita Rolls, recording payments out of the treasury by way of advance or accommodation and the Misæ Rolls, containing an account of the daily expenses of the king's court (see, Gross, *Sources and Literature of English History*, 1915 ed., pp. 423-424; for a complete account of the financial records of this reign, H. Jenkinson in *Magna Carta Commemoration Essays*, ed. H. E. Malden, 1917, pp. 244-300). The records concerning knight's fees from 1198, arranged in orderly sequence and carefully edited under the direction of the Deputy Keeper of the Public Records, appear in *The Book of Fees, commonly called Testa de Nevill* (part 1, 1920). In addition to the two types of chancery record, the Patent Rolls and the Charter Rolls (noticed at the end of chap. xiii) there is a third series beginning also in John's time, the Close Rolls (*Rotuli. Chartarum*, 1199-1216, ed. T. D. Hardy, *Record* Commission, 1837), which further illustrates both the work of this department and the operation of the central government. Sir H. C. Maxwell-Lyte, *The Great Seal of England* (1926), pp. 299-304, explains the process of attaching the seal. This is illustrated both for Letters Patent (frontispiece, nos. 1-4) and for Letters Close (no. 5).

The most important secondary work on the central government is T. F. Tout, *Chapters in Administrative History* (vol. I. 1920). This deals with the chancery and the camera, but also contains useful material on the exchequer and on the permanent curia in general. R. L. Poole, *The Exchequer in the Twelfth Century* and the introduction to the Oxford edition of the *Dialogus de Scaccario* (ed. A. Hughes, C. G. Crump and C. Johnson, 1912) are scholarly accounts of the exchequer. L. W. Vernon Harcourt, *His Grace the Steward and Trial by Peers* (1907), is also useful for this period. The field of the military system and finance is partly covered in J. H. Round's account of the introduction of knight service (see above, p. 154) and in J. F. Baldwin, *The Scutage and Knight Service in England* (1897). The whole field of taxation is covered by S. K. Mitchell, *Studies in Taxation under John and Henry III* (1914). The treatment of military service and scutage in vol. I. of Pollock and Maitland, *History of English Law* (1895; 2d ed., 1899), is still of distinct service. F. M. Powicke, *The Loss of Normandy* (1913), in chapter 8 presents a useful account of the military system on the continent under Richard and John, which has a bearing upon conditions in England. Haskins, *Norman Institutions*, chap. 5, deals with the government of Normandy under Henry II. Chapters 4 and 5 of Morris, *The Medieval English Sheriff*, are devoted to the Angevin period. D. M. Stenton (*Cambridge Medieval History*, V. 572-585) provides a scholarly and recent summary of the administrative system of Henry II.

CHAPTER XV

THE ANGEVIN MONARCHY AND THE CHURCH

The reigns of Henry II and his sons mark a period of much conflict between church and state out of which emerged the main basis of relations as they were to remain until the Reformation. This conflict illustrates remarkably well the temper and methods of the Angevin kings. Papal power and control over the Western church were rapidly increasing in this period. Alexander III (1159-1181) was resolute in presenting his claims, and Innocent III (1198-1216), whose reign coincided almost exactly with John's, was the strongest of medieval popes. It was an age when popes defined their position, placed it upon a basis of law and precedent, and made strong assumptions regarding their power over secular rulers and secular affairs. The Angevin kings, on the other hand, held to the Norman ideas of royal control where matters of state were concerned, and made new and arbitrary assertions of their rights touching ecclesiastical affairs. It was impossible in the face of strong opposition to maintain their entire position or to return to that held by the predecessors of Stephen. The policy of national as opposed to papal or ecclesiastical control presents three outstanding objectives which occasioned controversy, the reduction of ecclesiastical jurisdiction under Henry II, the levy of new taxes upon church property under Richard and John, and control of the election of the archbishop of Canterbury under John.

Henry II from the beginning of his reign could scarcely have looked with favor upon the freedom of the church so recently established under Stephen. The brief charter of liberties which he issued at his accession passed over entirely the concessions which Stephen had made, and granted to the church as to all men the liberties and customs which Henry I had confirmed by his charter. A return to the Norman policy is witnessed by the fact that the king soon accused a bishop of an infringement of royal authority because the latter procured from the pope a bull to settle his dispute with an abbot.[1] Appeals to the papacy were made frequently in Henry's earlier years under the king's license. Apparently with some specific case in mind, the pope wrote in 1156 to Theobald, the archbishop of Canterbury, complaining that appeals were smothered, and that no one in the presence either of king or archbishop dared appeal to the apostolic see.[2] Here is a forecast of Henry's interest in restricting the jurisdiction of church courts. Within a decade various incidents occurred which convinced the king that a more strict administration of justice over clergymen and further regulation of ecclesiastical courts were necessary.[3]

An intimation of the king's decision to assume an advanced position appears in the fact that after the death of Archbishop Theobald he procured in 1162 the election of his intimate and chancellor, Thomas Becket,[4] to fill this high office. In 1163, after a five years' absence from England, Henry submitted to a synod at Westminster proposals limiting the right of priests and lower clergy to trial before ecclesiastical tribunals when accused of certain grave crimes.[5] The king is said to have declared that since the beginning of the reign more than a hundred homicides had been committed in England by clerks.[6] To these the jurisdiction of the king's courts did not extend,

---

[1] Stubbs, *Select Charters*, 135; Makower, *Constnl. History Church of England*, 21. For the bishop's case, Palgrave, *English Commonwealth*, II. lx-lxi.

[2] *Hist. Monast. St. Augustine, Canterbury*, R. S., 411; Jaffé, *Regesta*, 2d ed., II., no. 10128. As to the circumstances, see Z. N. Brooke, *Cambridge Historical Journal*, II. no. 3, 216-217. For the procedure of appeal, Palgrave, *Eng. Commonwealth* II. p. lxxix.

[3] *Materials for Hist. of Becket*, I. 12-13; III. 43-45, 264-266; cf. Davis, *England under Normans and Angevins*, 209.

[4] Hoveden, I. 218-219; William of Newburgh, I. 139-40.

[5] *Ibid.*, I. 140; *Materials for Hist. of Becket*, III. 266-275; IV. 39. The offenses were theft, felony, murder, arson.

[6] William of Newburgh, I. 140.

and ecclesiastical courts had a reputation for laxity in dealing with clerical offenders.[7] The archbishop strongly opposed
the innovation, holding that ecclesiastical courts ought to
retain full jurisdiction, and that convicted clerks would be deprived of their orders and thus in case of a second offense
would automatically be judged as laymen. It is clear that
Henry II also desired, like the Norman kings, to hold in restraint the bishop's authority to excommunicate crown vassals and officials. Becket had recently offended Henry by
excommunicating a tenant-in-chief in a dispute without certi-
fying the matter to the king.[8]

The king next approached these matters by asking the
bishops whether they would observe the customs of Henry
I.[9] They refused, and he then had drawn up and presented
to the great council at Clarendon in January, 1164, a document which professed to set forth usages of the realm as they
existed in the time of his grandfather. The prelates regarded
much of this as a statement of new law.[10] It can hardly be
questioned that these constitutions, as they were called, made
claims not in force under the elder Henry,[11] and his usage had
been greatly modified to the advantage of the church in
Stephen's time.

The Constitutions of Clarendon specified that clerks accused of crime, after a preliminary appearance before the
king's justices, should be tried in the ecclesiastical court.
The king's justice was to follow the case there, and if the
accused was found to be guilty the church should protect
him no longer.[12] This would enable the king's courts to
prescribe punishment. They might impose a more severe
penalty than the court Christian, for ecclesiastics were for-

[7] Newburgh, I. 140-141; *Materials for Life of Becket*, IV. 201-202.
[8] Ralph de Diceto, I. 311-312.
[9] *Materials for Hist. of Becket*, I. 13; II. 376.
[10] *Ibid.*, II. 380; III. 280-284; V. 73-79; Newburgh, I. 141.
[11] Below, p. 357.
[12] Sec. 3, Stubbs, *Select Charters*, 138; William of Canterbury, *Materials for Hist. of Becket*, I. 25; cf. Maitland, *The Canon Law in the
Church of England*, chap. 4.

bidden by canon law to give judgment involving the shedding of blood.[13]

The Constitutions of Clarendon declared also, in general terms of the usage under Norman kings, that no tenant-in-chief of the king and none of his officials might be excommunicated nor their lands placed under interdict unless the king himself, or in his absence his justiciar, was consulted, so the proper phases of the matter might be referred to the royal or the ecclesiastical court.[14] Excommunicated persons were not to be required to give security for future conduct, but only to make answer in the bishop's court.[15] Relations with the papacy were also safeguarded. Archbishops, bishops and other clergy were not to leave the realm without the king's license, and in that case were to give security that they would seek no ill to the king or kingdom.[16] Moreover, appeals to the pope were to be held in check. Ecclesiastical controversies were to go no farther than the archbishop's court without the king's assent.[17] The king's right to the revenues of vacant archbishoprics, bishoprics, abbeys and priories of the king's demesne was specifically asserted, and his control over elections to fill such vacancies was to be assured by the requirement that electing bodies should assemble in the royal chapel and choose with the king's consent. The prelate elect, as in the past, was to do homage and fealty to the king as his liege lord before his consecration.[18]

Minor provisions dealt with some further matters of jurisdiction. The king's officials, as in the time of William the Conqueror, were to aid in compelling laymen who failed to heed the summons of the bishop or archdeacon to make due appearance to answer.[19] On the other hand, laymen were safeguarded against oppression in the ecclesiastical court by the

---

[13] Cf. Assize of Clarendon, sec. 11; Jaffé, *Regesta*, 2d ed., II. no. 13811.
[14] *Ibid.*, sec. 7.   [15] *Ibid.*, sec. 5.   [16] *Ibid.*, sec. 4.
[17] *Ibid.*, sec. 8. According to Fitz-Stephen (*Materials for Hist. of Becket*, III. 47) this meant that the matter should come before the king's court.
[18] *Ibid.*, sec. 12.   [19] Sec. 10.

requirement that they should be duly accused only in the bishop's presence, and, if no one would or dared accuse them, the sheriff might be required to provide an accusation jury of twelve.[20] The king's courts were to gain jurisdiction in all pleas of debt, whereas in the past those in which the debtor gave security upon oath had been claimed by the court Christian.[21] Moreover, power to determine whether a given piece of land in dispute belonged to one or the other jurisdiction was to rest with the king's court.[22]

The bishops who were present at the council of Clarendon, though dissatisfied with the king's claims, nevertheless, consented to the document.[23] Becket himself yielded, but subsequently sought absolution from the pope for so doing.[24] After making a vain attempt to leave England in secret, contrary to the requirement of the Constitutions, thereby further rousing the king's ire, he was called to answer before the great council at Northampton in October, 1164, on charges chiefly concerning certain revenues which he had administered as chancellor. Judgment was given by default to the effect that he should forfeit his moveable goods to the king. He appealed to the pope, and it was subsequently decided that he should be imprisoned as a disturber of the peace. He appeared carrying his cross and bade the bishops pronounce excommunication against anyone who laid hands upon him,[25] yet the king required bishops as well as barons to find judgment.[26] It was not formally pronounced, for Becket, hurriedly leaving the court, crossed the sea to Flanders.[27]. Soon afterward the king ordered the sheriffs to take over the lands and revenues of any clerk or layman who appealed to the Roman curia.[28]

[20] Sec. 6.
[21] Sec. 15; Pollock and Maitland, *Hist. of English Law*, I. 128-129.
[22] Sec. 9.
[23] William of Newburgh, I. 141.
[24] Ralph de Diceto, I. 312; but he did not seal the Constitutions. Hoveden, I. 222; *Materials for Hist. of Becket*, I. 23-24; II. 383.
[25] *Ibid.*, II. 394-398; III. 52; Jaffé, *Regesta*, II. no. 11208.
[26] *Materials for Hist. of Becket*, III. 65.
[27] *Ibid.*, I. 39, 42.
[28] *Materials for Hist. of Becket*, V. 152.

Pope Alexander III, at this time resident in France and struggling against the power of Frederick Barbarossa, was in a difficult position. He was at first disposed to act with caution to avoid turning the king of England into an enemy. At the request of the latter Alexander appointed as papal legate Roger the archbishop of York, a man long unfriendly to Becket,[29] but wrote to Becket that the necessary letters were to be issued to Roger only with the consent of the latter, and also that he should direct the bishops not to give heed to anything the king might require contrary to the liberty of the church.[30] In a confidential letter the pope even exempted the king, his courtiers and his clerks from the spiritual authority of the archbishop of Canterbury.[31] The English bishops sent by the king as his advocates in the matter of Becket's appeal to the pope, were none the less coldly received, and, when the archbishop submitted the Constitutions of Clarendon to Alexander, the latter condemned most of them.[32] In 1165 the pope wrote to Henry reprehending him for preventing clerical judgments and establishing new laws, which he called old, for the oppression of the churches.[33] He also instructed two of the bishops to admonish the king for his prohibition of the visits of the English clergy to the continent, and the prevention of appeals to the papacy, and to ask the recall of the archbishop of Canterbury. The papal policy for the time being toward the king was one of tactful treatment and reproof, toward his impetuous archbishop, one of limited and not very successful repression.[34]

[29] *Materials*, II. 362.

[30] Migne, *Patrologia*, vol. 200, pp. 285, 287; Jaffé, *Regesta*, II. nos. 11004, 11006. [31] Migne, *Patrologia Latina*, vol. 200, pp. 426-427.

[32] Hoveden, I. 231; *Materials for Hist. of Becket*, III. 49; V. 73-79.

[33] Migne, *Patrologia*, vol. 200, p. 375; Jaffé, *Regesta*, II. no. 11206.

[34] In 1166 Becket was designated papal legate for England except the archbishopric of York (*ibid.*, II. no. 11270). He was in 1168 forbidden to pronounce sentence of excommunication, suspension, or interdict (*Materials for Hist. of Becket*, IV. 114; VI. 421) without receiving a special faculty. The next year, when he excommunicated two English bishops and various clerks and barons of the king, the pope commanded that these persons be absolved (*ibid.*, III. 87-93; Migne, *Patrologia Latina*, vol. 200, pp. 590, 643).

The conflict entered upon its final stage when in 1170 Henry II determined to have his son Henry crowned as king. For the archbishop of York to officiate at a coronation in the province of Canterbury was in derogation of the rights of Becket, and the pope had forbidden this.[35] Moreover, he directed Becket not to crown the king's son nor to permit another to do so unless the young king absolved all from observing the customs recently exacted.[36] The king, however, arranged to have the ceremony performed before the prohibition was published. A month later he became reconciled with Becket and ordered a restitution of the property of the see of Canterbury;[37] but the stubborn prelate angered the king as he landed in England by delivering papal letters which suspended from office the archbishop of York and excommunicated other bishops and a number of their aids[38] for participating in the recent coronation.

When, a few weeks later, four of the king's followers murdered Becket, Henry II was placed upon the defensive, and his chances of carrying out the Constitutions of Clarendon greatly reduced. There was a danger that the pope would excommunicate him or lay his kingdom under an interdict. When in 1171, however, he conducted an expedition to Ireland the pope approved his successes there and his measures making for a stricter control over the Irish church.[39] A papal letter also confirmed Henry's dominion over Ireland, previously conceded by Adrian IV, and the king granted the pope's request that Peter's pence be collected[40] there, as in England.[41] In 1172 Henry II met the papal legates at Avranches in Normandy, and an agreement was reached concern-

[35] *Materials for the Hist. of Becket*, II. 406; Jaffé, *Regesta*, II. no. 11267.

[36] Jaffé, *Regesta*, II. no. 11733.

[37] *Materials for Hist. of Becket*, I. 82-85.

[38] *Ibid.*, I. 89-94; Migne, *Patrologia Latina*, vol. 200, pp. 699, 713; Gervase, I. 222.

[39] Jaffé, *Regesta*, II. nos. 12162, 12163.

[40] *Ibid.*, II. no. 12174.

[41] *Ibid.*, II. no. 11205.

ing the matters at issue. The king took an oath that he had not desired nor commanded the death of Becket, and swore to go on a crusade unless released by the pope, to support two hundred knights one year to defend Jerusalem and to restore the possessions of the church of Canterbury. Concerning the specific issues which had led to the whole struggle Henry made two engagements. He promised not to hinder appeals to Rome in ecclesiastical causes, and he undertook to abandon the customs introduced against the churches of the land in his time.[42]

As a result of this agreement the limits between the secular and the ecclesiastical jurisdiction were fixed neither as Becket nor as Henry had contended they should be. In the matter of appeals the pope gained an important victory. From this time they seem to have increased in number, and they had an important part, through the appointment of delegated judges, in making effective in England the general canon law rather than just those parts of it which were enacted by church councils with the king's approval. The admission of freedom to appeal to Rome involved abandonment of the refusal to permit the clergy to leave the realm. It meant that papal bulls required no license for admission into the realm. It meant also that bishops, notwithstanding their fealty to the king, constantly received and obeyed instructions from Rome.[43]

Very important also was the effect of Henry's agreement as it bore on the question of criminous clerks. Henceforth a clerk arraigned in the king's court claimed his clergy and was turned over to his ecclesiastical superior for trial.[44] Benefit of clergy was thus to remain until modern times. In 1175, however, the itinerant justices held clerks for breaches of the forest law, and the following year the papal legate agreed that for such offenses and for failure to render lay service due the king they might be haled before his courts. To avoid a

[42] Benedict, I. 31-33; Gervase, I. 238-239.
[43] Z. N. Brooke, *Cambridge Historical Journal*, II. no. 3, pp. 215-225.
[44] Maitland, *Select Pleas of the Crown* (Selden Soc.) nos. 117, 118, 123, 159. See D. M. Stenton, *Cambridge Med. Hist.*, V. 560.

358 CONSTITUTIONAL HISTORY OF ENGLAND

situation which had enabled the murderers of Becket to escape punishment, it was also agreed that confessed or convicted murderers of clerks should be tried in the secular court in the bishop's presence.[45] The church as before retained its jurisdiction over laymen in purely spiritual cases and also in matrimonial and probate matters.[46] Henceforth bishops sometimes excommunicated the king's servants,[47] but in doing so they had to reckon upon the possibilities of his displeasure.

Henry II did not undertake to give up everything he claimed in the Constitutions of Clarendon. Bishops before consecration continued to do homage,[48] and the king continued to control their election. He still enjoyed the revenues of vacant bishoprics and abbeys. His courts retained jurisdiction over advowson cases and cases arising over the debts of laymen.[49] The right of the king's court to decide whether land was held as lay or as alms fee was established,[50] and writs of prohibition were issued to prevent the court Christian from dealing with secular matters. The jurisdiction of the royal courts was advanced in several respects, although the monarch's most striking claims were abandoned.

From 1172 peaceful relations with the papacy were restored. Papal intervention which has a political bearing occurs in a few instances. In 1173 the pope directed that, if the custody of the daughters of the French king, affianced to Henry's sons, then plotting rebellion, were not turned over to the latter within forty days, the province in which they were detained should be placed under an interdict.[51] In 1177 a papal legate

[45] Benedict, I. 105; Diceto, I. 402, 410; cf. Assize of the Forest, sec. 9 (Stubbs, *Sel. Charters*, 158).

[46] Pollock and Maitland, *History of English Law*, I. 125-131; II. 367, 372-374; Glanvill, VII: 13.

[47] Stephens, *Hist. of English Church*, 194; Benedict, I. 315-316; Hoveden, IV. 139-140.

[48] Glanvill, IX. 1. Afterward they might swear fealty but not do homage even for their baronies.

[49] Glanville, X, 1; XIII. 18-22; but see D. M. Stenton, *Cambridge Medieval Hist.*, V. 561.

[50] Glanvill, XIII. 2, 23-24. Cf. Jaffé, *Regesta*, II. no. 13106. For writs of prohibition, see Glanvill, XII. 21, 22.

[51] *Ibid.*, II. no. 12248.

was sent to lay all of Henry's dominions under an interdict to enforce the marriage as arranged between his son Richard and the French princess Alais, but the matter was settled through an agreement with the French king.[52] In 1184 Lucius III in a much more conciliatory spirit asked Henry II that in the interest of peace with the French king he settle the matter of the dowry and other property rights of Margaret,[53] the widow of Henry's deceased son and sister of the French monarch. In the same year the pope exhorted the king to go on a crusade. Henry II had been released from his earlier promise, but in 1188, after the capture of Jerusalem, he took the crusader's vow which was ultimately fulfilled by his successor.[54]

The king in this period is found asserting some claims against the church. One of these bore on the visits of papal legates. During the Becket controversy, Henry was able to procure the appointment of the archbishop of York as papal legate in England, though Becket's own province was exempted from this legatine jurisdiction.[55] To the visits of foreign legates uninvited Henry II made the objection offered by his Norman predecessors. In 1176, the pope appointed Cardinal Vivian legate *a latere* to visit Ireland and Scotland. The king accounted both lands his possessions, for in 1174 the King of Scotland had done homage to him. The Scots, moreover, had applied for a legate to decide the question of their dependence upon the church of England. Two bishops, sent by the king to meet Vivian, demanded by what authority he dared to enter the kingdom without leave. He was permitted to proceed to Scotland only after he had taken oath that he would do nothing against the king or his realm.[56] With the movement to increase papal power by granting monasteries exemption from the control of bishops the king also showed displeasure.

[52] Benedict, I. 180-181, 190-191.
[53] Diceto, II. 30-31; Jaffé II. no. 15150.
[54] Benedict, I. 332, 338; II. 30.
[55] Above, p. 355.
[56] Benedict, I. 118.

The monks of St. Augustine's Canterbury in 1179 obtained a papal privilege permitting that their abbot henceforth be blessed at his installation by the archbishop without making the profession of obedience [57] which had been customary. The king accused the abbot of making his church tributary to Rome by rendering an annual payment,[58] but the pope declared that this was not the usage of the Roman see.

King Henry, contrary to the canons of the church, made good the claim to control the selection of prelates as he had asserted it in the Constitutions of Clarendon. Moreover, he deliberately kept sees vacant that he might employ their revenues. During the Becket controversey, in 1169, Alexander III complained about the numerous vacancies, and asked him to allow freedom of election by refraining from the nomination of persons of his choice to cathedral chapters.[59] In 1173 Henry agreed that he would retain vacant bishoprics and abbeys in hand no longer than a year except in case of emergency and also promised greater freedom of election.[60] The situation at the time is shown by the fact that six bishops and an archbishop were all chosen within a short time.[61] Throughout his reign Henry often controlled the selection made by the chapters of cathedrals and abbeys, or refused to accept the persons chosen by these bodies.[62] The king's approval was necessary. The younger Henry in 1173 even attempted to prevent papal confirmation of an archbishop of Canterbury, unpopular in France, by declaring that the election had been made without his assent.[63]

There are numerous examples of the king's manipulation of elections. His own illegitimate son, though only an unordained

[57] Gervase of Canterbury, I. 163, 275; Jaffé, *Regesta*, II. no. 13294. A similar case arose at Malmesbury (*ibid.*, II. 12401).

[58] Ten marks a year (*ibid.*, II. no. 13293).

[59] *Materials for Hist. of Becket*, VI. 503-505; cf. IV. 125; William of Newburgh, I. 280-281.

[60] *Materials*, VII. 553; Diceto, I. 410.

[61] Diceto, I. 366-368.

[62] Benedict, I. 93, 299; cf. *Magna Vita S. Hugonis*, 78.

[63] Gervase, I. 245; Benedict, I. 69.

youth, was chosen bishop of Lincoln, and later was made archbishop of York.[64] In 1186 Henry gained the former see for the famous Hugh of Avalon against the opposition of the canons, who attempted to win the king over by naming three clerks in his service. Henry declared that all three were rich enough, and the chapter gave in.[65] The royal control was furthered by the process of calling chapters to court to elect. Thus in 1184 the canons of York cathedral were assembled in the chapter house at Westminster to choose their archbishop.[66] A little earlier the king gave the abbey of Thorney to the prior of Ely and the monks, says the chronicler, came to make the election according to the king's desire.[67] The king's procedure is illustrated in 1175, when a royal clerk summoned the clergy of the vacant see of Norwich and those of twelve vacant abbeys to come to the king to make elections. Each chapter was directed to send the prior with five or six of the wiser and more discreet members of the house, who were to bring a letter advising what they were to do.[68]

Henry II intervened in 1184 to settle a quarrel over the election of an archbishop of Canterbury. The bishops of the province and part of the Canterbury chapter were convened in the king's presence, and both groups claimed the right to elect. After a later conference had failed, the bishops chose Baldwin, bishop of Worcester. The Canterbury monks declared that this election was void, but the king persuaded them to accept the choice made by their opponents, and subsequently brought the prior and the better part of the chapter to London where, after reasserting their claims, they formally chose Baldwin as archbishop.[69] Thus, Henry procured an elec-

[64] *Ibid.*, I. 93, 271; II. 77, 99.

[65] *Ibid.*, I. 345-346.

[66] *Ibid.*, I. 319.

[67] *Ibid.*, I. 173. The new abbot swore fealty to the king.

[68] *Ibid.*, I. 93. So in 1188 (Diceto, II. 62). This and other elections (*ibid.*, I. 342) were made abroad.

[69] Benedict, I. 319-320, 321; Diceto, II. 22-24; Gervase, I. 309-25. The election of Becket in 1162 was actually made by the monks (*Materials for Hist. of Becket*, I. 8; II. 366-67). For that of Richard of Dover in 1173, Diceto, I. 369.

tion without overriding either party and without yielding his
right of assent. The question raised was nevertheless to
create great difficulty in the future.

The fiscal demands upon the church present new features in
all three of the Angevin reigns. Henry II in 1159 arbitrarily
laid upon clerical tenants-in-chief a contribution (*donum*),
apparently like those which under his Norman predecessors
were much resented.[70] In this reign the novelty lay in plans
for papal and crusading taxes in England; under Richard and
John it is found in new forms of national taxation imposed
upon church property.

In the period of his controversy with Becket Henry II began
to yield somewhat to the desires of Alexander III in regard
to ecclesiastical levies in England. In 1165 Peter's pence was
collected as usual throughout England.[71] In 1166 it was agreed
that a tax of six pence for the relief of the Holy Land should
be taken upon the valuation of each pound of personal property.[72] This appears, however, to have been merely a voluntary
contribution.

A new series of papal appeals, two decades later were
more successful. In 1184 Pope Lucius III requested the king
and the clergy in England to provide him an aid for the
defense of the patrimony of St. Peter against the Romans.
The matter was referred to the bishops, who reported that it
would not be to the advantage of the realm if papal nuncios
came to collect such an imposition. They recommended instead
that the king should grant the aid to the pope, promising to
make compensation in return, and to this Henry agreed.[73]
In the next year the patriarch of Jerusalem came to England

[70] Baldwin, *The Scutage*, 21-22.

[71] Jaffé, *Regesta*, II. no. 11205. Annual collection of this seems to have
been the rule since about 1133 (Rev. O. Jensen in *Trans. Royal Historical Soc.*, new ser. XIV. 184-186; see also Jensen, *ibid.*, XIX. 221-
228).

[72] Two pence a pound the first year and a penny a pound for four
successive years, reckoned at six pence in all (Mitchell, *Studies in Taxation*, 6 and note 16).

[73] Benedict, I. 311.

to obtain assistance to defend the Holy Land against Saladin. The great council refused to authorize a tax for the purpose, but advised that fifty thousand pounds be given the patriarch to repay him for his trouble.[74] Henry and the French king declined to lead a crusade but made promises of men and money. Heretofore no purely papal tax and no national tax for crusading purposes had been imposed. In 1188, however, after the fall of Jerusalem, the great council, following the precedent set in the king's continental possessions, authorized the Saladin tithe, a tax of a tenth of the moveable property of Henry's English lands, to be levied by ecclesiastical authorities, who were given the privilege of resorting to jury assessment if they regarded it as necessary.[75]

Richard I as a crusading king well deserved the favor of the church, but he was high-handed and hot-tempered, and on the continent after his return committed arbitrary acts so adversely affecting ecclesiastics that he was nearly involved in a struggle with Innocent III.[76] In dealing with the English church at times he was also arbitrary. He ordered the canons of York to elect Geoffrey, his illegitimate brother, as archbishop, and the pope confirmed the choice. Later this archbishop became involved in difficulties, and in 1196, in spite of the fact that the pope was favorable to him, Richard forbade him to administer his diocese.[77] The king had no difficulty in gaining the assent of both bishops and barons when he nominated Hubert Walter archbishop of Canterbury, nor in procuring appointment as papal legate for the bishop of Ely, left as justiciar in his absence. After Archbishop Hubert was made justiciar, the king gained for him, in 1195, the same distinction.[78] The next year Hubert set fire to a church in London in which an agitator had sought refuge and dragged

---

[74] Gervase, I. 325; Benedict, I. 335, 336-338; Wendover, I. 134-135.

[75] Stubbs, *Select Charters*, 160; Mitchell, *Studies in Taxation*, 6.

[76] Luchaire, *Innocent III*, Les Royautés Vassales, 149-155. Normandy was placed under an interdict (Hoveden, IV. 18-20).

[77] Benedict, II. 77, 209; Hoveden, IV. 8.

[78] Jaffé, *Regesta*, II. nos. 16505, 17202. He was thus at the head both of the royal and the ecclesiastical courts.

him away to be hanged. The protest aroused by this violation of sanctuary on the part of the archbishop was so great that he offered to resign the justiciarship, but the king was loath to part with his able minister, and he remained in office until in 1198 Innocent III forced him to resign by threatening to place England under an interdict.[79]

The one notable struggle between Richard and English ecclesiastics came over a matter concerning taxation. Archbishop Hubert in 1197 presented to a great council at Oxford the king's request that provision be made for three hundred knights to serve abroad with him for a year each with wages at the rate of three shillings a day. The proposal was defeated by the opposition of two bishops. The famous Hugh of Lincoln, noted as a champion of the rights of his church, declared that it owed military service only in England and that he would not pay this levy. Herbert of Salisbury supported him. The justiciar dissolved the assembly and in his report to the king charged his failure to the opposition of the two prelates.[80] This is the first instance in English history of successful opposition to a royal demand for a new tax. The king ordered the seizure of the possessions of the two offenders, but a little later seems to have become reconciled to them.[81] Another instance of clerical opposition to taxation occurred when the carucage was levied in 1198 to supply the funds needed for the war in France. The religious houses refused to pay until the king took from them the protection of the courts. Compelled to buy it back, in so doing they provided the funds desired.[82]

The clergy of England were far less in sympathy with Richard's successor than with the famous crusader king. John was regarded as frivolous, sinful and irreligious,[83] but Archbishop Hubert entered his service, and the instances of his

---

[79] Hoveden, IV. 6, 12-13, 48; Potthast, *Regesta*, no. 552.
[80] *Magna Vita St. Hugonis*, R. S., 249-51; Hoveden, IV. 40.
[81] *Magna Vita St. Hugonis*, 251, ff.
[82] Mitchell, *Studies in Taxation*, 7; Hoveden, IV. 66.
[83] *Magna Vita St. Hugonis*, 291-294; Matthew Paris, II. 565.

conflict with the English church prior to 1207 have to do almost entirely with the matter of taxation. It is a notable fact that, although the barons were dissatisfied with John's rule, the actual opposition from 1206 to 1213 was nearly all clerical. In 1201, as in 1198, difficulty arose over a levy of carucage. The archbishop of York refused to allow his lands to be assessed, and the king seized them. The Cistercians, relying upon a general immunity from taxation, refused to pay a fine in lieu of the tax without the consent of their order, and the king for a time deprived them of the protection of the courts.[84] In 1207 John asked the bishops and abbots to make him a grant from the revenues of the beneficed clergy. They refused to do so, and the king gained from the great council consent to a levy of a thirteenth of personal property and revenues. This the clergy paid either directly or in the form of a fine. The archbishop of York, who again refused, was compelled to leave England, and the king took over the property of his see. Other prelates who met the demand with refusal were compelled to pay by seizure of their goods. It is noteworthy that the Cistercians were exempt.[85]

Until the death of Archbishop Hubert in 1205 John worked in harmony with the higher clergy. Hubert had an influential part in placing John upon the throne. He had pronounced sentence of excommunication against those who broke the peace pending the new king's arrival in England.[86] Under him as chancellor the archbishop again had an influential position in government. The question of the election of his successor, as is well known, involved the king in his famous struggle against Innocent III. The great pope had several years previously twice threatened the king with an interdict because of his dealings with an Irish archbishop and a Norman bishop.[87] The younger monks of Canterbury in 1205 attempted to make good their claims to elect the archbishop by secretly choosing

[84] Mitchell, *Studies in Taxation*, 34; Coggeshall, 101-110.
[85] *Ibid.*, 88.
[86] Coggeshall, 98.
[87] *Papal Letters*, I. 14, 18.

their own candidate. John attempted to place his own nominee in the place through the election of the bishops, but election by cathedral chapters was becoming the rule, and the pope had already ruled that the bishops had no share in the election of an archbishop of Canterbury.[88] Since the monks had appealed to Rome, the king procured the mission thither of a deputation from their house with a secret understanding that they should choose his candidate. Innocent III in 1206 gave a decision that the election by the monks and that by the bishops had both been irregular. He then prevailed upon the deputation of monks to elect a strong man, Stephen Langton, an Englishman by birth and one of the cardinals. This arrangement deprived the king of his power of assent and control. John furiously declared that he would have nothing to do with Langton, who had been a resident in the territory of his enemy, the king of France. The pope nevertheless consecrated him as archbishop in 1207,[89] and the issue was joined in the third great struggle between church and state since the Norman Conquest.

Not only did John refuse to receive Langton as archbishop, but he proceeded to expel the monks of Christ Church Canterbury, who adhered to the choice of their delegates, and also confiscated their property.[90] The revenues of the see itself he of course already held in his own hand. To check action against him by any representative whom the pope might appoint the king also forbade the holding of papal pleas in England. Innocent threatened an interdict unless the archbishop was admitted and the monks restored. Three English bishops, commissioned to act in the matter, in March, 1208, proclaimed all England and Wales under a general interdict. The doors of the churches were closed to public services, its ministrations were largely suspended, except in the baptism of infants and the confession of the dying, and the dead were

[88] Powicke, *Stephen Langton*, 80.
[89] This story is presented in Roger of Wendover, *Flores Historiarum*, R. S., II. 10 ff., 36-40; see also Stubbs, preface to *Walter of Coventry*, II. pp. xlix, ff.
[90] Ralph of Coggeshall, R. S., 163; *Annals of Waverley*, 259.

no longer buried in consecrated ground.[91] Divine offices in private [92] were subsequently permitted once a week in monastic houses.

The king at once ordered that the possessions of bishops, clerks, and monks and other ecclesiastical property be confiscated, and sent his agents throughout each province to take it over. Immediate custody of this property was committed to men of the vill in which it lay, who were to provide for the subsistence of the clergy.[93] The three bishops, after giving sentence of excommunication against all who had laid hands upon the property of the church, fled overseas, as did also two others.[94] The archbishop of York was already in exile. The see of Lincoln was declared vacant and its revenues confiscated in 1208 because its bishop was consecrated abroad by Langton.[95] John de Gray, the bishop of Norwich, and Peter des Roches, the bishop of Winchester, two creatures of the king, held the only sees not in his hand. Through the absence of Gray in Ireland after 1209, des Roches remained the only bishop in England.[96]

For more than five years John tyrannized over the English church as not even William Rufus had done. From the bishoprics in his hands as well as from numerous abbeys he is known to have derived a considerable income.[97] In 1210 the pope wrote to the archbishop of York to induce the king to restore to the churches and charitable houses of the province, the thirteenth which he had exacted.[98] In this year, apparently upon pretext of recovering Normandy, John made upon monastic houses new exactions which are said to have been enor-

[91] Roger of Wandover, II. 46; *Canterbury Chron.*, app. to preface of Gervase, II. xcii-xciii; *Chron. de Melsa*, I. 342-343.
[92] Potthast, *Regesta*, no. 3608; *Chron. de Melsa*, I. 343.
[93] Coggeshall, 163; *Annals of Waverley*, 260.
[94] *Ibid.*, 261.
[95] Potthast, *Regesta*, no. 3788; Wendover, II. 54.
[96] Coggeshall, R. S., 162; II. 512; Norgate, *John Lackland*, 130, 149; cf. Potthast, *Regesta*, no. 3605. The bishop of Durham adhered to the king (Wendover, II. 60) but died in April, 1208.
[97] Mitchell, *Studies in Taxation*, 106-108.
[98] Potthast, *Regesta*, *no.* 3992. *Papal Letters*, I. 35, here in error.

mous.[99] The Cistercians declined once more to contribute to
an aid contrary to the privilege of their order. The king
refused to allow their abbots to attend the annual chapter
of the order, forbade any Cistercian to cross the sea, and
exacted a large sum from their various houses.[100] The next
year he is said to have extorted letters from them resigning
their property.[101] Until 1212 it must have appeared that John
had gained a great advantage through his quarrel with Innocent III. He had, to be sure, not taken over all church
property in England, and he could still threaten to appropriate
more; but he had decidedly increased his income from the
revenues of vacant sees and abbeys and from those of ecclesiastics who adhered to the papacy. The pope threatened
to proclaim the king's excommunication, but John professed
to care nothing for such a penalty. It has been pointed out
that he never appeared to be stronger or more successful than
in the days when he defied the greatest of the medieval popes.

Some sort of compromise was to the interest not only of the
king and the pope but also of the dispossessed clergy. Archbishop Langton was a man of high statesmanship whose influence postponed the launching of the excommunication.
Negotiations for John's recognition of the archbishop continued after the interdict.[102] As early as 1208 the three bishops
who acted as papal representatives were induced to cross to
England, but they were unable to see the king. In 1209 John
was willing to negotiate, apparently to forestall excommunication. The three bishops came to Canterbury. John's agents
were willing to make restitution of the manors of the archbishop and four of the bishops and to pay Langton an indemnity. But the king's form of peace was rejected because it did
not provide for complete restitution of church property. It

[99] Mitchell, *Studies in Taxation,* 105; Roger of Wendover, II. 57.

[100] According to the continuator of William of Newburgh (II. 510)
John took away their privileges and the protection of the law. See also
Coggeshall, R. S., 163; *Annals of Waverley,* R. S., 264, 265; *Annals of
Margan,* R. S., 29; *Chron. de Melsa,* I. 328-329.

[101] *Annals of Waverley,* 268.

[102] *Papal Letters,* I. 31; Potthast, *Regesta,* nos. 3419-3422, 3494.

was in vain that Langton himself came over to Dover later
in the year under a safe conduct. Upon leaving England the
bishops who accompanied him threatened to proclaim a papal
sentence of excommunication in the land within fifty days,
unless the king gave satisfaction. In November this was published in France,[103] but English ecclesiastics were held back
from the step by fear.[104] The sentence was known in England,
but this did not deter the magnates from assembling with
the king at Windsor at Christmas.[105]

After John's excommunication he was in a less conciliatory
mood. The heavy taxation of the church and the oppression
of the Cistercians in 1210 may be interpreted as an answer
to the papal act. In this year John again sent for Langton,
but the latter, who found the proposed terms fatuous, was
led to suspect treachery and failed to appear.[106] In 1211 the
pope wrote to John that severer measures would be taken if
the king did not accept his offer of peace. Two papal legates,
Pandulf and Durand, came to England commissioned to ab-
solve John if he would make amends in the matters for which
he was under excommunication. They came before the king
at Northampton in August, after he returned from a campaign in Wales, but John refused to take a form of oath required, so no agreement could be reached on the matter of
reparation, and the legates returned.[107] The execution of the
implied papal threat to publish John's excommunication and
declare his subjects absolved from their allegiance remained
the next step.[108]

---

[102] Gervase, R. S., II. preface, xcviii-cvi, 103-105; *Annals of Waverley*,
261-264; *Annals of Winton*, 80-81, Potthast, *Regesta*, nos. 3600, 3622.
   [104] Roger of Wendover, II. 52.   [105] *Ibid.*, II. 54.
   [106] Gervase, II. preface, cvi-cvii, cx-cxi, 105-106.
   [107] *Chron. Rotomagense*, Bouquet, *Recueil*, XVIII, 360; Gervase, II.
pref., cxiii-cxv; Wendover, II. 58; *Annals of Winton*, 81. Norgate (*John
Lackland*, 161, note 1) shows that this could not have been in 1212 as
the *Waverley Annals* have it.
   [108] The story that the legates in 1211 took this step in John's presence
and in that of the great council (*Annals of Burton*, 209-214; *Annals of
Waverley*, 268) is suspicious both on its face (see Stubbs, introd.,
Walter of Coventry, II. p. lviii, note 4; Ramsay, *Angevin Empire*, 430
and note 5) and in the light of other facts. Below, p. 370 and note 114.

The year 1212 marks the turn of the tide. The Welsh, probably under French influence, broke the peace recently made. The dominions of the rebel princes together with their allies were relieved of the interdict, and the princes declared by the pope released from allegiance to John.[109] In the spring the king closed nearly all the ports and ordered the sheriffs to prohibit the reception in religious houses or episcopal seats of any papal mandate directed against himself.[110] Later in the season he gathered his host for another Welsh campaign, but at Nottingham was informed that his barons contemplated treachery. Fearing the effect of the declaration of the pope that they were released from their allegiance, a declaration of which John had apparently just learned,[111] he dismissed the army,[112] and, returning to London, exacted hostages of the suspected magnates and proceeded to the outlawry of two of the number, Eustace de Vescy and Robert Fitz-Walter, who had fled from England under accusation of treason and who were supposed to be ringleaders of a conspiracy.[113]

The pope, failing in the attempt to stir up rebellion in England, next promoted a plan for an attack upon John from without. Toward the end of the year Innocent declared the king deposed.[114] John spent Christmas, 1212, at Westmin-

---

[109] Walter of Coventry, 206-207; *Brut y Tywysogion*, 273. A more careful statement than that of *Annals of Waverley*, R. S., 268.

[110] *Ibid.*, 267, 268.

[111] Roger of Wendover, R. S., II. 61. Cf. *Annals of Winton*, R. S., 400. A papal letter threatening John with ruin unless reconciliation comes before June 1 (Migne, *Patrologia Latina*, vol. 216, p. 773) has been dated 1212 (Potthast, no. 4395), but belongs to the year 1213 (Walter of Coventry, II. 209).

[112] The story that he shut himself in Nottingham castle fifteen days is false (Norgate, *John Lackland*, 169, n. 8).

[113] William of Newburgh, I. 513-514; Coggeshall, 165; cf. *Annals Monastici*, III. 33; Norgate, *John Lackland*, 289-293.

[114] According to Wendover (II. 63-65) in a council at Rome, held prior to January 1213, and attended by the cardinals and by Langton and the bishops of London and Ely. Norgate (*John Lackland*, 174) shows that in November, 1212, John's envoys offered to accept the terms offered by the legates the preceding year. Langton and the English bishops according to Coggeshall (165) had proceeded to Rome *contra nuncios regis*. Ramsay (*Angevin Empire*, 435-436) doubts the papal sentence of deposition, but apparently on inadequate grounds.

ster with but a small following of knights,[115] and Langton came from Rome into France in January, accompanied by two English bishops, to promulgate the papal sentence there. They declared that John was deposed. Innocent had already written the French king that he was to execute the sentence by expelling John and seizing his kingdom. Philip made ready his forces to invade England, and John issued a general military summons, assembling his army at Dover.[116] Pandulf and Durand under a private understanding between Langton and the pope were now sent to John with full conditions upon which his submission would be received. These he accepted, apparently to the letter, at Dover on May 13.[117] He undertook to receive in peace the archbishop, the five exiled bishops and Robert Fitz-Walter and Eustace de Vescy and to revoke the outlawry declared against ecclesiastics. Specified amounts of indemnity were to be paid to Langton, the five bishops and the monks of Canterbury. The lands of the church were to be placed in the hands of the papal nuncios.

The king, moreover, went farther. Two days later he conceded to the pope the kingdoms of England and Ireland to be held henceforth by him as a vassal of the Roman church. In lieu of all service and of Peter's pence he agreed to pay annually to the see of St. Peter a thousand marks, seven hundred for England and three hundred for Ireland. Furthermore he took the oath of fealty to the pope as his overlord.[118] By yielding everything John ceased to be an enemy of the papacy and came under its protection. Pandulf returned to the continent and, to the anger of Philip Augustus, admonished him to give up the intended invasion of England.[119]

John now turned his attention to an expedition to France to regain his lost territories, but the barons objected to fol-

[115] Wendover, II. 64.

[116] Wendover, II. 65; William of Newburgh, II. 514.

[117] Compare the papal form of submission (Migne, *Patrologia*, vol. 216, 773, 774) with that accepted by John (Wendover, II. 70-72). But John's envoys had been consulted by the pope (*Papal Letters*, I. 37).

[118] Stubbs, *Select Charters*, 284-286; Wendover, II. 74-76.

[119] Roger of Wendover, II. 77-78; cf. Coggeshall, 166.

lowing an excommunicated king. When the latter sent security
for the return of the exiled prelates, his absolution was pronounced at Winchester by Langton on July 20. John swore to
defend the church against all adversaries, to restore the good
laws of his predecessors, especially those of Edward the Confessor, to judge all his men according to just judgment of his
court, to restore the rights of individuals and to make full
restitution before the next Easter in all things pertaining
to the matter of the interdict.[120] The barons now refused to
follow him to Poitou on the ground of their poverty and
returned home. A great council was assembled at St. Albans
by the justiciar and the bishop of Winchester, to whom the
king in his temporary absence had entrusted affairs with the
proviso that they should take counsel with Langton. The injustice of the king's officials was denounced, a demand made
for the abolition of evil laws and a reference made to the
liberties granted by Henry I. On his return John gathered an
army to move against the barons as rebels, but the archbishop
protested that this was a violation of his oath to proceed
only after judgment of his court. The king angrily declared
that Langton had nothing to do with lay affairs, but the latter followed him, declaring that unless he desisted he would
excommunicate all the king's followers who made war before
the interdict was removed.[121]

Subsequently, at an assembly held at St. Paul's, London, in
September, the archbishop produced and read a copy of the
the charter of Henry I, suggesting this as a measure of the
liberties which the king had promised at his absolution.[122]
John's struggle with the church had raised up in Langton a
champion of the liberties of the realm. The effect was lessened
by Innocent's inclination to discourage baronial resistance to
the king. Especially was this true after the beginning of
July, 1214, when John made the promised restitution to the

[120] Wendover, II. 80-81.
[121] Ibid., II. 82-83.
[122] Ibid., II. 83-87.

church and secured a relaxation of the interdict.[123] Toward the end of that year, as a struggle with the barons became imminent, John strove for the favor of Innocent III by abandoning one more claim which was opposed by the church, namely the control of ecclesiastical elections.

Control over, or at least assent to, episcopal elections was a fundamental part of the policy of the Angevin monarchs. Although he had promised to remedy abuses, Henry II surrendered nothing of this power. Richard filled various vacant bishoprics according to his own desire.[124] The pope in 1205 admonished John to allow the monks and archdeacons of Winchester freedom in electing their bishop,[125] but the outcome was the selection of the king's devoted servant, Peter des Roches. During the interdict, although various prelates had died,[126] Innocent III vainly ordered chapters to elect.[127] In the one case in which this was done, the king refused to accept the bishop chosen because he had been consecrated by Langton.[128] Innocent III in 1213 threatened John with the loss of the revenues of vacant sees [129] in case this situation was prolonged. A chronicler [130] quotes the king as declaring to the papal legates in 1211 that his predecessors from their chambers filled bishoprics. The words may not be genuine, but they express John's view of the case, and it was truer to the facts than that of the legates themselves.

After the reconciliation with the papacy and the return of the surviving bishops, the king issued summons, as his father had done, to the chapters of vacant cathedrals and monasteries to come for election.[131] He also made to several abbeys a

---

[123] *Papal Letters*, I. 40; Wendover, II. 100-102; *Annals of Waverley*, 281. For Innocents' attitude in 1215 toward the baronial movement, Norgate, *John Lackland*, 225-226.

[124] William of Newburgh, I. 300, 391.

[125] Potthast, *Regesta*, nos. 2439, 3607.

[126] For a list of vacancies, Walter of Coventry, II. 213.

[127] As in Potthast, nos. 3606, 3607.

[128] Roger of Wendover, II. 54.

[129] Migne, *Patrologia Latina*, vol. 216, p. 774.

[130] *Annals of Burton*, Rolls Ser., 211.

[131] *Rotuli Litterarum Clausarum*, I. 150.

grant of the right of free election,[132] thus assuming that it was his to confer or deny that right. The quarrel with the barons, however, showed the need of strong papal support, and toward the end of the year 1214 John issued a charter [133] to all cathedrals and religious houses granting freedom to elect their prelates. In this he promised not to impede free elections when churches wished to make them, and in so doing seems to have renounced the summoning of chapters to court to designate their choice.[134] The king's leave to elect was still required, but this was not to be denied nor deferred. None the less the custody of vacant churches was specifically retained, and the royal assent to elections, so vigorously asserted in Langton's case, was still necessary, though it was to be refused only for due cause to be supported by demonstrable facts. The charter did not end abuses, which were flagrant under John's successor. The principles which John had set forth were often evaded in practice but remained binding in law until the Reformation.

A review of the main points at issue between 1154 and 1216 shows that the most novel contention of the monarchy, that in regard to the taxation of the moveable property of the church, was the one most easily established. The principle of the Saladin tithe was turned against the church by Richard and John and was permanently incorporated into the national scheme of taxation. The innovations presented in the Constitutions of Clarendon were in the main ended by a compromise through which the church gained for its jurisdiction vital and permanent concessions, although the monarch made substantial gains in other respects. The fundamental point over which John waged his five-year conflict with Innocent III, curiously enough was gained. In agreeing to give up

---

[132] *Annales Monastici*, III. 42. Cf. Richard's grant to St. Mary's, York, in *Monasticon*, III. 552.

[133] Stubbs, *Select Charters*, 288-289; Makower, *Constnl. Hist.*, 471.

[134] Powicke, *Stephen Langton*, 81-82. Assent to an election was actually refused by John in the case of a bishop in 1216 (*Papal Letters*, I. 40-41).

the abuses of the scheme by which he and his predecessors had controlled the election of prelates, John retained the right of assent to such elections.

This was one of the powers which from the king's point of view were essential to repel ecclesiastical intrusion and to preserve national rights. Henry II and Richard on some occasions forbade the use of papal mandates in matters of dispute between the English clergy.[135] Despite the conviction that the church should be free in its own sphere, the twelfth century accepted some royal control as a matter of course. The acceptance of the primacy of the archbishop of Canterbury on the part of the Welsh bishops in 1184 was naturally assumed to be an important step in establishing the lordship of the English king in their land. Conversely, the pope welcomed the rule of Henry II in Ireland because it would bring the Irish church under his control. After Henry became overlord of Scotland, he strongly resented the attempt of the Scottish church to maintain its independence. Secular overlordship and some ecclesiastical control were believed to be inseparable. Clement III in 1190 made William Longchamp, the king's regent, papal legate not only for England but also for Wales and the parts of Ireland under the dominion of the king's brother.[136]

All three of the Angevin rulers strove in England to advance this royal supremacy in one form or another. All three were wrathful and arbitrary when opposed in an important assertion of it. All three attempted to carry the point by despotic methods. The measures they adopted are among the strongest manifestations of Angevin absolutism, least pronounced under Henry II, of greater intensity under Richard, and so unjust and irresponsible under John that they demanded a powerful check upon the overgrown power of an arbitrary monarch. The exile of Becket and his friends and the unprecedented taxation of church property in 1198 were but mild

---

[135] Gervase, I. 376-377, 551.
[136] Jaffé, *Regesta*, II. no. 16505.

376 CONSTITUTIONAL HISTORY OF ENGLAND

episodes when compared with John's outlawry of the bishops, his seizure of church property and his continued oppression of the Cistercians.

Had these monarchs reckoned merely with the English church, they would no doubt have reduced the prelates to compliance. It was the papacy back of Becket and of Langton which in the end made them formidable. The pope maintained the right to confirm elections of bishops and archbishops and to consecrate the person chosen.[137] The papal claim to depose temporal rulers was so skilfully advanced by Innocent III that John cringed. Nevertheless papal interests and those of the national church were far from identical, a fact which is well shown by the attitude of the bishops in 1184 toward the proposed papal tax. Innocent was concerned with the claims of the English bishops to restoration and reparation, but Langton, not the pope, was the champion of English liberty. It was he who saw the deeper principles at issue in John's barbarous conduct toward ecclesiastics. It was he who first asserted that just judgment of court must hold for baron as well as clerk. The papal fulminations had encouraged baronial resistance to John's misrule. Through the pope's insistence the two baronial leaders and reputed plotters of revolt were permitted to return to England.[138] John's conduct toward the church had helped to lay the train which led to Magna Carta.

AUTHORITIES

The chronicles of the period all contain material on ecclesiastical history. For these see note on authorities at end of chapter xiii above. For Becket and his controversy with Henry II there is a special collection of biography, history and letters published in the Rolls Series, entitled *Materials for the History of Thomas Becket,* ed. J. C. Robertson (1875-1885). Papal relations with England to 1198 may be traced in vol. II of the *Regesta Pontificum Romanorum,* edited by Phillip Jaffé (2d edition revised by S. Loewenfeld and others, 1888). The period from 1198 is covered by the *Regesta Pontificum,* ed. A. Potthast (2

[137] See Benedict, I. 69.
[138] *Rotuli Litterarum Palentium,* I. 99.

vols. 1874-1875). The *Calendar of Entries in Papal Registers relating to Great Britain and Ireland,* Rolls Series (ed. W. H. Bliss, 1893) begins with the year 1198. The matter of appeals in ecclesiastical cases for the earlier years of Henry II is well illustrated in the letters of John of Salisbury, ed. J. A. Giles (1848). There are occasional cases of this kind for the period 1187-1199 with other matter illustrating ecclesiastical usage in *Epistolæ Cantuariensis,* vol. II, Rolls Series, ed. William Stubbs (1865). The letters of Innocent III in Migne, *Patrologia Latina,* vol. 216, occasionally throw light on affairs in England. The Constitutions of Clarendon are most conveniently consulted in Stubbs, *Select Charters.*

Of the secondary works, Felix Makower, *Constitutional History of the Church of England* (translation, 1895), presents useful material on the topic of this chapter, though it is quite limited in amount. F. W. Maitland, *Roman Canon Law in the Church of England* (1898) contains a chapter on the "Criminous Clerks" which is the standard treatment of this topic. Z. N. Brooke in an article in the *Cambridge Historical Journal* (II. no. 3, 1928) entitled "The Effect of Becket's Murder on Papal Authority in England," brings out the great importance of the renunciation by Henry II of the attempt to prevent appeals to Rome. F. M. Powicke, *Stephen Langton* (1898), throws new light especially on the disputed Canterbury election of 1206. Achille Luchaire, *Innocent III,* in the volume entitled *Les Royantés Vassales du Saint Siege* (1908) contains a chapter on the relations of Richard I with the church and another chapter on John's relations with the papacy. The most detailed and scholarly study of the latter topic is to be found in chapters 4 and 5 of Miss Kate Norgate's *John Lackland* (1902). Sir James H. Ramsay *The Angevin Empire* (1903) clears up some points. H. W. C. Davis, *England under the Normans and Angevins* (1905, etc.) occasionally introduces some new and useful material on the relations between church and state, as does Doris M. Stenton in *Cambridge Medieval History,* vol. V (1926), chap. 17. The best general survey of the ecclesiastical history of the period is W. R. Stephens, *The English Church from the Norman Conquest to the Accession of Edward I* (1901).

CHAPTER XVI

THE ANGEVIN MONARCHY AND MAGNA CARTA

Angevin monarchy, despite the restrictions upon it springing from legal usage and baronial power, revived and perpetuated the absolutist state of the Norman period. Henry
II when contrasted with his successor appeared as a just and
moderate ruler; [1] but in his reign as well as in the reigns of
his sons the monarch save in a few emergencies thoroughly
dominated the government. After the feudal rebellion of 1173
Angevin power was not again endangered in England for half
a century. The system of government built up by Henry II
was effectively carried on by justiciars in the king's absence.
The long-continued absence of Richard I severely tested the
arrangement, but on the whole it proved equal to the strain.
Richard and John felt secure in their power, and their attitude became more and more imperious. John was the first
monarch who assumed the style king of England in place
of that of king of the English. The lack of concern on the
part of these kings is shown by the fact that, unlike their
Norman predecessors, they did not grant charters of liberty
to win the support of the realm. Henry II at his accession
issued a brief charter in which he confirmed to the church,
to his earls and barons and to all his men the liberties which
Henry I had conceded with the same remission of evil customs
which his grandfather had made.[2] This, however, was the
last grant of the kind for over seventy years. All that was
exacted from Richard and John when they ascended the throne
was a repetition of the old-time promises of the coronation

---

[1] William of Newburgh, I. 280, 282-283.
[2] *Statutes of the Realm*, I. 4; Stubbs, *Select Charters*, 135.

oath. Stephen Langton did not intend that John should forget these, for when he absolved him in 1213 he compelled him in effect to swear to them anew.[3] They were, however, vague in effect and difficult to enforce.

The increasing boldness and sense of security shown in the conduct of the kings of the period are largely to be explained by the fact that their organizing genius or that of their able ministers had greatly strengthened the authority of the monarch. The rise of the new judicial system, which brought a new sense of legality and justice and an increased security for the free land-holder, as shown in an earlier chapter, gave a vastly wider authority to the king's courts; it weakened feudal jurisdiction and increased the royal revenue; and, particularly through the itinerant justices, it brought increased facilities for the conduct of, and the control over, administration. Moreover, the employment of sheriffs of the newer class, who owed their advancement to the favor of the crown, also made for centralization. Improvement in various agencies at court also provided stronger means of central control. The king had come to wield a powerful administrative organization.

In supplying their fiscal needs the Angevins showed an increasingly arbitrary attitude. The methods of taxation followed by Henry II conformed in general to the customary usage of feudal monarchy in England, although he seems to have stretched his feudal claims. But after the Saladin tax had brought the moveable property of the kingdom under contribution for an ecclesiastical object, the ransom of King Richard not only required a repetition of this form of taxation but brought a renewal of the land tax and with it other fiscal exactions which bore with unprecedented severity upon the church. Both Richard and John made demands which prelates believed to be in violation of the existing immunities of the church. To meet only a remote need John exacted one tax

[3] McKechnie, *Magna Carta*, (1914), 104. For John's coronation oath, Hoveden, IV. 87-88.

upon moveable property against the opposition of the church and some of the nobility. Moreover his frequent scutages were so collected as to alarm the baronage. John had a vision of an absolutist state, untrammeled by the restraints of feudal usage. The defense or reconquest of the king's continental possessions or the prosecution of his claims in Wales or Scotland were objects for which support was demanded regardless of precedent or complaint.

Angevin monarchy was most of all arbitrary when it faced troublesome opposition. Henry II showed himself high-handed in the prosecution of his claims against the church. Richard acted summarily when the prelates opposed his plan of taxation. Angevin temper and despotism ran wild in John's practical outlawry of the bishops and his wholesale seizure of church property to enforce his claim to approve the election of an archbishop of Canterbury. Moreover John's fury caused the outlawry and the confiscation of the property of barons [4] who offended him or aroused his suspicion. Enemies who fell into his hands sometimes met cruel and terrible deaths. He showed himself mean and despotic in many ways.[5] Under a king of primitive passions, no scruple and but slight sense of justice, the dreadful possibilities of unrestrained power became all too obvious.

Between the attitude of such a ruler and that of the baronage there was necessarily a conflict. The views of kings as to their powers must usually be interpreted from their actions. The high claims of John toward the church and toward certain matters of justice and taxation, enforced with reckless determination, speak for themselves. The assumption of some absolute power of control, though exercised with more discretion, also characterizes the reign of John's father.[6] It is clear, on

[4] As to the property of Robert fitz Walter and Eustace de Vescy, *Rot. Lit. Pat.*, 101.

[5] See above, p. 269; also the account of John's starving the wife and son of William de Braiose (*Annales Monastici*, II. 265); also Norgate, *John Lackland*, 131, 137.

[6] The forest regulations were regarded as absolutist expressions of the king's will quite distinct from the common law (Petit-Dutaillis, *Studies Supplementary to Stubbs*, II. 149).

the other hand, that monarchy was expected to observe the usages of feudal law. John's departure from principles of feudal justice, feudal military exaction and feudal fiscal demands conflicted with the custom of the age and the baronial idea of right and law. By feudal law the king was obviously supposed to be bound no less than the feudal baron.

Some discussion of the abstract question whether the king was subject to the law was taking place in the time of Henry II. John of Salisbury, writing about 1160, to support the supremacy of the church over the temporal power, declares that the difference between the tyrant and the king is in their obedience to law.[7] The prince is the public authority, an image on earth of the divine majesty, and his authority is derived from God. The authority of the prince, however, depends upon the law, and it is a greater thing than empire to submit the princely authority to the laws. There are some who whisper or even publicly proclaim that the prince is not subject to the law and that whatsoever pleases him has the force of law, but when they thus withdraw the king from the bounds of law they make him an outlaw.[8] It is well known that Glanvill, the justiciar of Henry II, years later quotes the maxim that what pleases the prince has the force of law.[9] This is hardly the language of pure absolutism, for Glanvill in the same passage recognizes that the laws of England are in the main unwritten and here refers to a certain class of laws which are promulgated by the counsel of the nobles and the authority of the prince.[10] A clerical administrator of Henry II, however, finds a purely divine sanction for the king's acts. He says that all power is from God and that the deeds of kings are not to be discussed nor condemned by their inferiors. Their hearts are in the hands of God. The care of their subjects being entrusted by God himself, their cause stands or falls by divine and not by human judgment.[11] They set forth proper laws

[7] John of Salisbury, *Polycraticus*, IV. 1.
[8] *Ibid.*, IV. 7.
[9] Stubbs, *Constitutional History*, I. 593.
[10] Glanvill, prologue.　　[11] *Dialogus de Scaccario*, Oxford ed., 56, 105.

of their own volition which are beyond the common law of the realm. In the days of John's conflict with the church, ecclesiastics were far less likely to accept these doctrines than those of John of Salisbury. When it is reported that John was called a tyrant,[12] the chroniclers show that this means a ruler who overthrows or disregards the law.[13] What was to become the fundamental constitutional issue of John's reign had been raised in an academic form long before Archbishop Langton or the barons brought forward the specific issues involving it.

So strong was the power of the king by John's time that baronial discontent was loath to express itself in action. The woes of the church seem to have awakened no baronial protest, and even the pope's absolution of John's subjects from their allegiance stirred up no baronial movement until there was insistence upon a revival of military service in the king's continental possessions.

There are not lacking indications of baronial discontent with the policy of all the Angevin kings. It is probable that even Henry II interpreted his feudal claims in an oppressive manner. A chronicler of John's time declares that Henry corrupted the laws of King Edward, and another that both John's father and his brother raised up evil customs for the oppression of the church and the realm.[14] This seems partially a protest against the loss of baronial jurisdiction and revenue through the rise of the king's courts. There is, moreover, no reason to believe that the straining of the king's general feudal claims was confined to John's time, for in 1215 are mentioned those who had been disseised without judgment by his two predecessors.[15]

Some symptoms of discontent appeared early in John's reign. In 1199 the justiciar along with Archbishop Hubert

[12] Matthew Paris, II. 562.
[13] At any rate this is the later interpretation. See *Annals of Waverley*, 282; *et ita pro lege ei erat tyrannica voluntas.*
[14] *Annals of Waverley*, II, 282; Coggeshall, 170.
[15] Articles of the Barons, no. 25.

Walter and William Marshal induced the barons ill-disposed toward John to swear fealty to him by promising that he would do them justice.[16] In 1201 their demands were revived. The king called out the feudal array for service in Normandy and the English earls, assembling at Leicester, declared that they would not cross the sea unless the king rendered to them their rights. John's response was a demand for the surrender of their castles.[17] These incidents, however, imply no more than attempts of powerful individuals to gain redress of private rather than common grievances through an exceptionally favorable opportunity for bargaining.[18] In 1203 John claimed that the earls and barons deserted his service abroad.[19] When in 1205 the realm was arming for defense and an expedition to France was being planned, the magnates in a great council at Oxford exacted of the king an oath to preserve their rights and those of the realm of England.[20] So unpopular was the expedition that, at the instance of Archbishop Hubert and others, it was abandoned when ready to embark, and a select force of knights sent instead.[21]

Although some barons strongly objected to the taxation of 1207, and although the scutage of 1208 for a war to enforce Scottish fealty to John might be regarded as illegal,[22] there is no sign that the king regarded further trouble with the barons as imminent until about the time of his excommunication by Innocent III, when late in the summer of 1209 he required a general oath of fealty.[23] During the Welsh rebellion of 1212, when a papal absolution of Welsh princes from their allegiance had been pronounced, the barons succeeded after the dismissal

[16] Roger of Hoveden, IV. 88.
[17] *Ibid.*, IV. 161.
[18] Powicke, *Loss of Normandy*, 316.
[19] Roger of Wendover, I. 318; Matthew Paris, *Chronica Majora*, II. 483.
[20] Gervase, II. 97-98.
[21] *Ibid.*, II. 99; *Annals of Waverley*, 256; Coggeshall, 152.
[22] Mitchell, *Studies in Taxation*, 93.
[23] *Annals of Winton*, 80; *Annals of Waverley*, 262; Wendover, II. 48. Of all men, clerk, and lay, holding land by free tenure: *Annales S. Edmundi*, Liebermann, *Ungedrückte Geschichtsquellen*, 149.

of the army at Nottingham in clearing themselves generally
of the charges of conspiracy which the king brought against
them.[24]

Only after the deposition of John was proclaimed by the
pope, and the king demanded a renewal of military service
abroad in 1213, did a determined opposition arise. The barons
refused to cross the Channel prior to John's absolution, asserting that they would not follow an excommunicated king,
but a little later they alleged as an excuse their poverty.[25]
The northern barons went still farther and declared, in terms
of Bishop Hugh's objection of 1198, that their lands owed no
service abroad.[26] John went to Guernsey without them, but
returned, and in the autumn of 1213 with a mercenary force
proceeded against them as rebels. As shown above, Archbishop Langton then intervened, holding that while the realm
was under interdict the king was bound to observe the oath,
made at his absolution in the preceding July, by which he
promised to judge his men by just judgment of his court.[27]
The issue between the king and the barons had reached
a new stage. John had only deferred his vengeance. Judgment in regular form had been shown by bitter experience
to be of vital importance to ecclesiastics, and it was now
becoming necessary to preserve the offending barons from
destruction.

The summer of 1213 brought forward the demand for
securities. At a great council held in St. Albans while John
was absent from England, the injustice of his officials was denounced, the abolition of evil laws was demanded, and mention was made of the liberties granted by Henry I. A little
later the coronation charter of Henry I was produced by
Langton before an assembly in St. Paul's Church, and this
henceforth came to be regarded as a concrete expression of
the liberties to be exacted and of those promised by John at

---

[24] *Coggeshall*. 165. They gave hostages (Wendover, II. 62).
[25] Matthew Paris, *Chronica Majora*, II. 549, 550-551; Coggeshall, **167**.
[26] *Ibid.*, 167.
[27] Above, p. 372.

his absolution.[28] In the light of the demands made later, it is clear that the main objects of baronial reform were now defined. The party had not forgotten the enlarged jurisdiction of the king's courts, which reduced that of their own. There was great discontent with military service abroad and the king's plan of collecting scutage in place of it. The injustice of the king's administration and the oppressive methods of his agents had become matters of protest. The securities which had been granted by Henry I were regarded as essential for the protection of feudal rights. Above all else loomed the question whether the cause of the refractory baron was to be submitted to the just judgment of the king's court.

Actual conflict was precipitated by the stand of a part of the baronage in 1214. The king led an expedition to Poitou in February, and it is said that few of the earls and a very large number of knights followed him.[29] In May he issued writs for the collection of scutage from those tenants-in-chief who were not rendering their military service.[30] The northern barons, who had withheld the service, refused to pay on the ground that they were not under obligation on account of the lands they held in England either to follow the king outside the realm or to aid him by paying scutage when he went.[31] Some of the prelates held the same view both earlier and later. In July John failed in his own military enterprise abroad, and his allies were decisively defeated by Philip Augustus at Bouvines. The king returned in October to face an opposition encouraged by his defeat. When he pressed for payment of the scutage they still refused.[32]

Both sides now prepared for a struggle. It is recorded by Roger of Wendover that the baronial leaders secretly conferred at Bury St. Edmunds under pretense of a pilgrimage, and

[28] Roger of Wendover, II. 83-84; Walter of Coventry, II. 217-218; cf. *Brut y Tywysogion*, Rolls Ser., 281.

[29] Coggeshall, 168.

[30] McKechnie, *Magna Carta* (1914), 31.

[31] Walter of Coventry, II. 217.

[32] Norgate, *John Lackland*, 225-226; Mitchell, *Studies in Taxation*, 112-113.

that the charter of Henry I, which they had previously received at London from the archbishop, was brought forth. It is also asserted by Roger that they took a solemn oath to withdraw their fealty and to wage war on the king, unless he granted their liberties.[33] There are other indications that meetings were held and that collective baronial demands were formulated this year.[34] John gathered mercenaries and sought to win the support of the church by issuing the charter which guaranteed to cathedral and monastic chapters the right of electing prelates.[35] Soon after Christmas the barons came to the king at London in military array and, according to Roger of Wendover, demanded that he confirm to them and to the church and the realm of England certain liberties along with the laws of King Edward as contained in the charter of Henry I.[36] The king obtained a delay until after Easter, promising then to grant reasonable satisfaction.

John was soon in straits, for the pleas of the exchequer and the county courts ceased, and the king's authority broke down. On January 15, 1215, he reissued the charter to the church and ordered the sheriffs to administer the oath of fealty in a stringent form. A baronial spokesman unsuccessfully sought of the pope that, as overlord of England, he would compel John to restore the ancient liberties. The king, early in March, 1215, took the vow of a crusader, evidently to render those who attacked him guilty of sacrilege. In April the northern barons met in arms at Stamford and after Easter marched south to Brackley in Northamptonshire. There they were met by Langton and William Marshal, who on behalf of the monarch asked for their demands. In reply they received a schedule which they took back to their master. It was backed by the threat that, unless he sealed it, the

---

[33] Roger of Wendover, II. 111-112; cf. Ralph of Coggeshall, 170.

[34] See Walter of Coventry, II. 217-218. Roger of Wendover (II. 86-87) even reports a rumor of an oath on the part of the barons in 1213 to strive to the death for the liberties contained in the charter of Henry I.

[35] On November 21. Above, p. 374.

[36] Roger of Wendover, II. 113.

rebels would constrain him by seizing his lands, castles and goods. When John heard its contents, he asked why the barons with these unjust exactions did not demand his kingdom, and declared with an oath that he would never grant them liberties which would make him a slave.[37]

Early in May the barons observed the ceremony (*diffidatio*) of formally renouncing their allegiance according to feudal custom as a preliminary to war with their overlord. They then chose Robert Fitz-Walter as their leader. A few days later John attempted to win over the people of London by granting a charter which conferred long desired privileges, and then issued a writ in which he promised not to take nor disseise the barons who were against him, nor their men, nor to go against them by force of arms, except by the law of the land or the judgment of their peers in his court until the matter had been submitted to a committee of arbitration.[38] The offer evidently produced no effect, for two days later the king abandoned the principle of judgment by peers and ordered the sheriffs to seize the lands, goods and chattels of his enemies. The barons now moved upon London, which received them. Many other towns went over to them, as did additional magnates. John could no longer hope to hold out, and at the end of the first week in June agreed to receive the representatives of the rebels. On June 10 he sent William Marshal and others to London to announce to the barons that he would accede to the laws and liberties which they asked. On June 15 began a five days' conference at Runnymede, on the Thames between Windsor and Staines. Apparently on that day the king accepted and sealed the preliminary articles which were submitted to him. On June 19 Magna Carta was issued, and on this day peace was made between the two parties.[39]

The fact is well recognized that Magna Carta is to be in-

[37] Wendover, II. 115. Here may be found the names of the baronial leaders.

[38] *Rotuli. Litt. Pat.*, I. 141.

[39] This account follows the careful treatment in McKechnie, *Magna Carta* (1914), 34-42.

terpreted as a series of concessions won from the king by the barons in arms. It is an aristocratic, not a popular, document. It is not a compact between the nation and the king.[40] It naturally has to do first of all with the reform of baronial grievances, but this reform is a reasonable one. Although John, and apparently the pope,[41] regarded it as an inadmissible infringement of the prerogatives of the crown, this but reflects the king's arbitrary attitude. Magna Carta as a whole is so moderate in tone that one finds it difficult to see how such a document could have originated merely among the leaders of the baronial revolt. There are exceedingly few radical sections, but one or two that seem reactionary. The great number of provisions call merely for the reasonable interpretation of existing law, particularly feudal law, much of which may be traced in the work of Glanvill twenty-five years earlier. The claim of the northern barons, the originators of the movement, that they were exempt from military service is entirely ignored, although, at least so far as this concerned service in Poitou, it had been advanced at some early stage of the negotiations.[42]

The Great Charter, moreover, is not to be regarded as a baronial document in too exclusive a sense. Its main trend was obviously suggested as far back as 1213. The form of its principal feudal provisions and that of a few others was borrowed from the charter of Henry I. Its most important section, that concerning due process of law, embodies the principle set forth by Langton. He, though formally neutral, had sympathized with the baronial demands, and, directly or indirectly, he had suggested many of them. Furthermore, he along with some of the bishops seems to have been active in the negotiations at Runnymede just as he was in those of

[40] See Jenks, "The Myth of Magna Carta," *Independent Review*, IV. 261, 267; Petit-Dutaillis, *Studies Supplementary to Stubbs Constitutional History*, I. chap. xii.

[41] G. B. Adams, *Magna Carta Commemoration Essays* (ed. H. E. Malden), 36.

[42] McKechnie, *Magna Carta* (1914), 171-175, 486 (sec. 7).

an earlier time.[43] Moreover, the interests of the classes which aided the barons in gaining the Charter could not well be overlooked. The towns, the under-tenants, the knights and the church were all remembered. The Great Charter was not a hasty formulation of the demands of hotheads, as might be expected, but a fair, practical statement of approved usage which represented sober thought and no little statesmanship.[44]

The opening section, like that of the charter of Henry I, concerns the rights of the church. A promise is made in general terms that the church shall be free and its rights and liberties observed, although no one could have thought of the freedom promised as that which the church had asserted in the reign of Stephen. The king also undertook to observe the grant of freedom of elections which he had already made. A subsequent section, by which any law-abiding subject was permitted freely to leave and enter the realm, released a prohibition upon clerks imposed by the Constitutions of Clarendon.

Sections two to eight inclusive deal, like corresponding sections of the charter of Henry I, with the feudal aids and incidents. The reliefs of earls, barons and holders of single knights' fees were fixed in amount as they had not been fixed in the charter of Henry I or the preliminary articles of the barons.[45] The wardship of minor heirs was safeguarded. The custodian was to have only the customary payments and reasonable services from the land without destruction or waste. The heir when he came of age was to have his land without payment of relief. Heirs were to be married without disparity. Widows were to have their marriage portion, their inheritance and their dowry within forty days of the death of their husbands. They were not to be compelled to remarry so long as security was given that they would not remarry with-

[43] Roger of Wendover, II. 87, 115, 118. The pope in March 1215 reproved Langton and the bishops for not checking the quarrel (*Foedera*, I. 127).

[44] As to its actual authorship, Norgate, *John Lackland*, 234, and Powicke, *Magna Carta Commemoration Essays* (ed. H. E. Malden, 108-109) offer suggestions.

[45] Cf. Adams, *Origin of the English Constitution*, 213-216.

out the lord's consent. A subsequent section [46] provided that for land held of an escheated barony in the king's hands no more relief nor service was due than had been rendered the baron formerly in possession. Lands of a mesne tenant convicted of felony were to remain in the king's hands but a year and a day [47] and after that to revert to the lord. The three feudal aids were to be reasonable in amount.[48] These concessions thus afford a definite idea of baronial liberties which had been infringed by the crown.

The obligation of military service abroad was not defined. Precedent was too clearly against the contention that it was not due the king. No one was to be compelled to perform greater service from a knight's fee or any other free tenement than was due from it.[49] Knights were not to be compelled to give money in place of castle ward if they wished to provide that service, and allowance for exemption was to be made while they served in the king's host.[50] In the main these were safeguards provided for the knight rather than the baron.[51]

The sharp practice and arbitrary claims by which John had abused his claims against property were assailed in a number of sections. The king and his bailiffs were to seize no land nor rent for debt so long as the chattels of the debtor sufficed.[52] No man and no vill, except those rightfully bound to do so, was to be compelled to make bridges over streams, as the king had compelled them to do to further his sport in hawking.[53] The chattels of the deceased person were protected by a provision that, if he died intestate, they might be distributed by his near relatives and friends under the oversight of the church, saving the debts which he owed.[54]

[46] Sec. 43. [47] Sec. 32. [48] Sec. 12.
[49] Sec. 16. [50] Sec. 29.
[51] Even the knight who held directly of the king was not classed as a lesser baron (above, p. 298, note 36).
[52] Sec. 9.
[53] Sec. 23. McKechnie, *Magna Carta*, 300-302; Morris, *Med. English Sheriff*, 219.
[54] Sec. 27.

Sheriffs and bailiffs in collecting crown debts were to levy on the chattels of deceased tenants-in-chief holding lay fiefs only to the value of the debt, leaving the remainder to fulfill the will of the deceased.[55] The king by virtue of his claims upon the wardship of an heir to a tenement held of the crown by leasehold or socage or burgage was not to claim guardianship also with respect to lands which were held of another by military service; nor was he to have the custody at all unless the land held of him owed military service.[56] All barons who had founded abbeys were to have their custody during vacancies.[57]

Economic and commercial interests of wide scope also received protection. The city of London and all other cities, boroughs, villages and ports were to have their liberties and free customs.[58] Fish-weirs, obstructions to the navigation of streams, were to be removed.[59] The uniformity of weights and measures for which King Richard had vainly striven,[60] was to be established.[61] Foreign merchants were to be safe and secure in England to enjoy the ancient customs free from evil tolls, and their freedom to come and go was to be curtailed only in time of war.[62] The lands which had been taken into royal forests in John's time were to be disafforested, and the river banks that he had fenced in for the sake of his falconry [63] were to be released.

The willful exactions of John's officials were attacked in various sections of the Great Charter. These had formed another blot on his reign. They had been denounced in the great council in 1213, and the justiciar had issued an order against them.[64] An attempt was made to prevent exactions of sheriffs and bailiffs by requiring that counties, hundreds, wapentakes and ridings be let at the ancient *ferm*, thus removing the temptation of these officials to recoup themselves

[55] Sec. 26.
[56] Sec. 37.
[57] Sec. 46.
[58] Sec. 13.
[59] Sec. 33.

[60] Cf. McKechnie, *Magna Carta*, 356-358.
[61] Sec. 35.
[62] Sec. 41.
[63] Sec. 47. Cf. references in note 53.
[64] Roger of Wendover, II. 82-83.

against an increase by imposing upon the community.[65] A limitation was also placed upon the exercise of the king's rights of purveyance. No constable or bailiff was to take grain or chattels without at once making money payment unless he could obtain postponement at the good will of the seller. No sheriff or bailiff was to requisition the horses or carts of any free man for official transport service except by permission of the owner. The king and his bailiffs were not to take wood for use in castles or for any other purpose except by permission of the owner.[66] The bad customs of foresters and warreners, of sheriffs and their bailiffs and of river banks and their custodians, were to be subjected to inquiry in each county by twelve knights chosen in the county court and were to be declared and destroyed.[67] Moreover, seven odious natives of Touraine, who seem to have been military adventurers,[68] were to be removed from their offices with their relatives.

The provisions of Magna Carta respecting the courts and the rendition of justice were nearly all of importance to the realm in general. Common pleas were no longer to follow the king's court about, but were to be held in a fixed place,[69] a provision which drew a new line between the work of the court *coram rege* and the bench at Westminster and marked the latter as a court of common pleas. No sheriff, constable, coroner, or other royal bailiff was henceforth to hold pleas of the crown,[70] which were thus reserved to the justices. The employment of John's subservient and ill-famed foreign favorites was struck a blow by the promise that the king would employ as justices, constables, sheriffs and bailiffs men who knew the law and were inclined to observe it.[71] Men who dwelt outside the royal forests were no longer to be compelled to attend the forest courts unless in response to a plea.[72]

[65] Sec. 25. Cf. McKechnie, *Magna Carta*, 317-319; Morris, *Med. English Sheriff*, 147, 155.
[66] Secs. 28, 30, 31.
[67] Sec. 48.
[68] Sec. 50. See McKechnie, *ibid.*, 444, 447.
[69] Sec. 17.   [71] Sec. 45.
[70] Sec. 24.   [72] Sec. 44.

Arbitrary and unreasonable exactions in the king's courts were to be checked by the requirement that amercements imposed were to be in proportion to the offense, and amounts were to be assessed not at the will of the justices but upon the oaths of men of the neighborhood. The amercement, moreover, was to save to a man his means of livelihood, to the merchant his merchandise and even to the villain his implements and outfit necessary for tillage.[73] A clergyman was to be amerced only according to his lay holdings and not according to the extent of his ecclesiastical benefice.[74] The rights of persons charged with crime were protected in several ways. The writ *de odio et atia* was to be issued without charge, to enable one accused through sheer malice to avoid the risk of duel with the accuser.[75] No one was to be imprisoned on the appeal of a woman except for the death of her husband.[76] No bailiff was for the future to send anyone to the ordeal[77] on his own affirmation unsupported by credible witnesses, who were apparently to certify to court proceedings in the case.

A few of the concessions bearing on judicial matters were designed primarily to protect interests which were either feudal or baronial. Earls and barons were to be amerced only by their peers, and in proportion to the offense,[78] a provision which removed from the courts of shire and hundred and those of itinerant justices the appointment of boards to levy monetary penalties upon barons declared at mercy, and confined this function to the court *coram rege* or that of the exchequer, whose members ranked as the peers of the greatest feudal tenants.[79] The holding of the possessory assizes was required four times a year by two justices sent to the county along with four knights elected in the county court. If these assizes could

---

[73] Sec. 20. [74] Sec. 22.
[75] Sec. 36. See McKechnie, *Magna Carta*, 359-364.
[76] Sec. 54.
[77] Sec. 38. See as to *ponat ad legem*, Morris, *Early English County Court*, 111. McKechnie, *Magna Carta* (1914), 370-375, seems too indefinite.
[78] Sec. 21.
[79] McKechnie, *Magna Carta*, 295-298; above, p. 313.

not be taken on the day of the county court, enough knights and freeholders were to remain to attend to this business.[80] Here is a striking proof of the popularity with the barons of the guarantees of seisin established by Henry II and of the importance attached to the assizes in securing the rights of property holders. But one provision sought to check the operation of the new system of royal courts, and this is the only part of the Great Charter which is unmistakably reactionary. The writ *praecipe* might no longer be issued concerning a free tenement to call cases into the king's court in such a way that the feudal lord lost his jurisdiction.[81]

The greatest of all the safeguards sought, described by Langton as just judgment of court, was set forth in words very closely resembling those used about a month earlier in John's writ, which aimed to give assurance to the barons. This guarantee constitutes the famous section thirty-nine. In the more acceptable translation it reads: "No freeman shall be taken and imprisoned or disseised or exiled or in any way destroyed, nor will we go upon him nor send upon him except by the lawful judgment of his peers and the law of the land." [82] This security had been demanded by the barons in the preliminary articles in a form which seemed to contemplate merely that they were to be judged by their peers in the king's court.[83] As finally stated, the concession might be interpreted as applying to the freemen of the realm, and was equivalent to a guarantee of due process of law.[84] Seventeenth-century lawyers, unfamiliar with the medieval meaning of judgment by peers, supposed this to be a guarantee of jury

[80] Secs, 18, 19.

[81] Sec. 34. See McKechnie, 346-355.

[82] Following the conclusions of McKechnie, *Magna Carta*, 381-382, *vel* is translated "and" after "taken" (*capiatur*) and also after "judgment of his peers" (*judicium parium suorum*). It is fairly clear that judgment of peers and the law of the land are not exclusive terms. See Adams, *Origin of English Constitution*, 262-274; and Vinogradoff in *Magna Carta Commemoration Essays* (ed. H. E. Malden), 80. But see Powicke, *ibid.*, 99-121.

[83] Articles of the Barons, no. 25.

[84] Adams, *Origin of Engl. Constn.*, 242-243; Vinogradoff, *op. cit.*, 83-86.

trial, which in 1215 was only one method of trial in civil cases and not usually a part of the law of the land where criminal matters were concerned. The judicial guarantee of this section was completed by that of the next in which the king promised not to sell, deny, or delay right or justice.[85]

Beside these great concessions stand in importance two others which deal with scutages and other extraordinary financial payments. Scutage was peculiarly likely to claim the attention of the barons, in view of the fact that no other general check upon the crown was prescribed in the Great Charter with reference to military service. Scutage was the crux of the problem, for it was the usual penalty the baron faced in case he refused to comply with an unreasonable demand. The new Angevin taxes were classed under the head of aid. Glanvill had questioned the lord's right to take such non-feudal aids even to carry on his wars.[86] Neither scutage nor aid, except in the three customary feudal cases, was henceforth to be levied except by the common counsel of the realm.[87] To make it certain that this consent was to be taken fairly, there was added as an afterthought the famous provision [88] for calling to the great council all the tenants-in-chief, by general summons through the sheriffs and bailiffs, but the archbishops, bishops, abbots, earls, and greater barons by individual letters under the king's seal. Summons was to be issued for a specified place at least forty days in advance, and was to state the reason of the summons.

Since the primary interest represented in Magna Carta was baronial, the great part of its provisions are feudal in bearing, as G. B. Adams has shown.[89] Baronial self-interest was the impelling force, but this worked for the repression of the grievances of the one class by relieving also other classes. The bishop and the abbot also were barons. The king's lay baron often, probably as a rule, held some land as an under-tenant.[90]

[85] Sec. 40.   [86] Glanvill, IX. 8.   [87] Sec. 12.
[88] Sec. 14. Not in the Articles of the Barons. See McKechnie, *Magna Carta* (1914), 248; Adams, *Origin of English Constitution*, 227-228.
[89] *Ibid.*, 208-210.   [90] *Ibid.*, 230.

The Great Charter conferred the principal privileges claimed by the barons upon the under-tenants as well, and required that all barons, lay and ecclesiastical, observe these toward their men.[91] The feudal reforms applied also to knights, and some special sections were inserted in their interests. The towns were especially remembered for their adherence to the baronial revolt, and all free men also profited by the judicial concessions and the checks upon John's sheriffs and other officials. The church was in the future repeatedly to appeal to Magna Carta against the exactions of the king. Baronial self-interest demanded some consideration of others, especially the allies of the barons. In estimating the importance of Magna Carta, moreover, it is necessary to go beyond baronial intent, for the effect was more important than the baronial party could have foreseen. The feudal nobility naturally gained most, but all classes profited, for even the villain was remembered in one section. The Great Charter in some real measure assured liberties to all men of the realm.

It has been asserted that in advancing feudal claims Magna Carta was reactionary and a clog upon government. Since the Angevin kings in judiciary and finance were advancing beyond the feudal stage, this was necessarily true. John's misgovernment, however, is not to be confused with constitutional or administrative progress. The real progress of the period was not impaired. It has been observed that there is little in the Great Charter that does not represent a statement or a reasonable interpretation of law which existed both before and after 1215.[92] This was true of nearly all the judicial guarantees and of the principle that aids other than the three customary ones required the assent of the lord's vassals.[93] It was true generally of the regulations concerning the feudal aids, incidents, and service. The fixing of these aids in amount was an innovation, though one which followed existing custom. The

[91] Sec. 60.
[92] Adams, *Origin of the English Constitution*, 249-250.
[93] Glanvill, IX : 8.

requirement of the consent of the great council to a scutage trenched upon the normal power of the crown, as did the requirement that existing privileges of towns be retained. The insistence upon the discontinuance of the writ *praecipe*, whenever it took from a lord's court judgment concerning a freehold tenement, was an extreme assertion of the feudal viewpoint against the king. But these instances of newly-made restrictions were few. Magna Carta really contained little that was novel in principle because it was in the main a statement of existing feudal law.

The English state of 1215 had not yet reached the point of transition from the feudal to the modern stage. The chief institutions, methods and theories of government were mainly feudal.[94] This holds true of the national council, of military service, of judgment by peers, of scutage and of everything involved in the feudal aids and incidents. With none of these features could the monarchy dispense. The departure from feudal methods prior to Richard's time had been in spirit rather than in form. The king's everyday administration and judiciary were largely centered in the household element of the small council, which remained nominally baronial. The king's growing financial needs were met in part by scutage and by some manipulation of the aids and incidents. Even the unusual taxes for crusading purposes were collected with the assent of the great council, which might authorize aids other than the feudal three.

With Richard absolutist methods sometimes superseded feudal sanction in matters of finance. Under John this was true also, though there was still some consultation with the great council; but in his arbitrary procedure without legal process, in his feudal exactions, in some of his scutages, and apparently in the levy of the seventh of 1203, John was openly flouting feudal rights. The same may be said of some of the judgments given against those who opposed him and of his proposed proceedings against refractory barons, both in 1213

[94] See Adams, *Origin of the English Constitution*, 144-148.

and in 1214. The tension to which feudal principles had been subjected under Henry II was followed by a series of shocks under his two sons.

The statement in Magna Carta was necessarily feudal. Feudalism was being defied, and no tangible nor just scheme had appeared to take its place. The balance of political power rested with the barons. They were the only class powerful enough to champion the rights, either baronial or national, which were being overridden. Their attitude was that their lord, the king, must obey the law and that if he failed to do this he might be constrained to do so. Feudal usage gave them the right to do this. In exercising that right they contended for the fundamental principle of Magna Carta, the supremacy of the law over the king.

Some defects are obvious in the Great Charter. It frequently lays down broad principles [95] which cannot well be applied in practice. It fails to define exactly even summons to the great council. It shows little grasp of constitutional principles. Above all else, it provides no adequate means of enforcement. Twenty-five barons were to be appointed to see to this.[96] Four of these were to be appointed to report infringements. If the king refused redress, the twenty-four were to levy war upon him. Compulsion was to enforce the liberties to which the king had been forced to assent. Warfare was a very unsatisfactory and uncertain method of upholding constitutional guarantees, but the only one that might be made operative against John. Moreover, the twenty-five barons were chosen from among the king's enemies, and the renewal of the conflict with a king who had yielded unwillingly became inevitable. Within a short time king and barons were once more at war, and the latter, despite excommunication at the hands of the pope, had fallen back upon the plan of deposing John with the aid of a foreign prince. Fortunately the death of John, in October, 1216, saved the barons from themselves and

[95] McKechnie, *Magna Carta* (1914), 129-131.
[96] Sec. 61.

made it possible for William Marshal, the regent chosen by the royalist party, to reissue the Great Charter in the name of a boy king.

This and subsequent reissues of Magna Carta differed somewhat from the document of 1215, but the fact detracts little from its value. The levy of scutage and non-feudal aids by consent of the great council was omitted, but the latter remained the rule and the former in part.[97] The levy of taxation by consent of the baronage was indeed good feudal law whether specified in a charter or not. This was true also of the safeguards concerning the feudal aids and incidents. The provisions for the reform of administration, and those relating to justice and the courts were retained. Even the provision concerning the writ *praecipe* was enforced and passed into the law of the thirteenth century.[98] To specific provisions of Magna Carta appeal was often made and its principles upheld by the courts of the next century;[99] furthermore they were subjected to new interpretation to meet the needs of successive centuries.

Later interpretation has often obscured the actual meaning of the Great Charter in its own day. It did not assure trial by jury nor taxation by parliament. A regular scheme of taxation to meet ordinary expenses of government was as yet unknown. As for the representative idea of parliament, even had the king been willing, the barons would almost certainly have opposed it.[100] The Charter, none the less, did provide for protection to property, for due process of law, for reform of misgovernment, for the observance of other rights dear to all free men. In almost every section it upheld the principle that the king must observe the law. It even marked in crude form the earliest assertion in England of the idea of limited monarchy, although the device of placing a new check upon mon-

[97] Mitchell, *Studies in Taxation*, 366-367.

[98] McKechnie, *Magna Carta*, 351-355.

[99] Faith Thompson, *First Century of Magna Carta*, 40-54.

[100] McKechnie, *Magna Carta*, 239-240; Adams, *Origin of English Constitution*, 217-223.

archy through baronial control, ultimately proved a failure. Limited monarchy in England was destined to come by another route, yet the practical value of Magna Carta is well enough demonstrated by constant discussion, reassertion and application of its principles [101] under John's immediate successors. In the history of English liberty it set a notable landmark.

AUTHORITIES

The more important accounts of the events leading to Magna Carta are in the chronicles of Roger of Wendover, Walter of Coventry and Ralph of Coggeshall. The text of the Magna Carta of 1215 may be conveniently consulted in Stubbs, *Select Charters*. English translations are easily accessible in G. B. Adams and H. M. Stephens, *Select Documents of English Constitutional History* (1908), or in D. J. Medley, *Original Illustrations of English Constitutional History* (1910). W. S. McKechnie, *Magna Carta* (1905, revised ed., 1914) gives both Latin text and English translation.

A detailed commentary on the document section by section is provided also in McKechnie's *Magna Carta,* which is the most complete book of the kind. The introduction to the work contains an excellent historical account of the baronial revolt leading to Magna Carta. This supplements the account in Stubbs, *Constitutional History* (I. chap. 12) and the scholarly account in Miss Kate Norgate, *John Lackland* (chap. 6).

Certain passages of Magna Carta are carefully elucidated in *Magna Carta Commemoration Essays* (ed. H. E. Malden, 1917). The chapters by Sir Paul Vinogradoff (on "Clause 39"), J. H. Round ("Knights and Barons") and F. M. Powicke ("Per Iudicium Parium vel Legem Terræ") are especially important and useful contributions. George B. Adams. *The Origin of the English Constitution* (1912), in chaps. 5 and 6, presents much material which is valuable to the student of Magna Carta, although his central thesis, that the Great Charter grew out of an attempt to enforce the feudal contract between the king and his barons, has not met with general acceptance. The same point of view was reiterated in Professor Adams' article "Trial by Peers Again," in *Yale Law Review,* XXVIII. 450-462 (1919).

The pioneer critic of the view of Magna Carta held by Stubbs was Edward Jenks, whose article, "The Myth of Magna Carta," appeared in the *Independent Review,* vol. IV. Charles Petit-Dutaillis in his

[101] Faith Thompson, *First Century of Magna Carta,* 54-67 and chap. 5.

Studies Supplementary to Stubbs' Constitutional History (vol. I. Trans. W. C. Rhodes, 1908; 2d ed., 1911) presents original interpretations, as does Charles Bemont, *Chartes des Libertés Anglaises* (1892). Faith Thompson, *The First Century of Magna Carta: Why it persisted as a Document* (1925), presents material of great value in estimating the importance of the document.

INDEX

INDEX

Abacus, 207, 236

Abbeys, vacant, control by Angevin kings, 333, 353, 360, 367, 368; by barons, 391; by Henry I, 254; by Rufus, 183, 251-252, 253

Abbot, 37, 58, 61, 62, 137, 138, 140, 340, 351, 365, 368; as baron, 187-188, 189, 191, 250, 295; deposition of, 245, 246; designation of, 101 and notes 10, 11, 102, 108, 129, 185, 186, 191-192, 248-249, 256, 263; election of, 195, 361, 373-374; exemption of, 360; in great council, 294, 295, 297, 298-299, 302; military service of, 188, 189 and note 46, 249, 297 note 30, 298, note 42; Norman in England, 196, 245; summons to, 299, 301, 312, 395

Abingdon Abbey, Abbot of, 272; knights of, 137

Absolutism,
  of Norman kings, 180-184; ecclesiastical prerogative, 248-249; in finance, 215-221; in general, 222-223; in justice, 280-281
  of Angevin kings, in feudal relations, 396-398; in finance, 338; forest regulations, 380, note 6; gains through judicial reforms, 288-290; the king and law, 381-382; tone of, 346-348, 378-381

Adams, George B., 123, 155, 179, 201, note 119, 210, 242, 292, 320, 400

Adams, Henry, 123

Adrian IV, 356

Advowson, right of, 282

Aethelings, 26, 27, 36, 40

Aid,
  Feudal, 397
    Great council and, 197; kings' initiative in, 306, 395; a land levy, 218, 338; in Magna Carta, 389-390; for marriage, 192, 335; in Normandy, 133-134; under Norman kings, 143; political effect of, 149-150; for ransom, 307-308; as extraordinary revenue, 334
  Non-feudal
    Cistercians and, 368; forms of, 218-219, 340, 395; great council and, 197, 312, 318, 399; to conquer Normandy, 192
  Papal, 362

Aldred, archbishop, 100, 245

Alexander II, pope, 244

Alexander III, 350, 355, 360, 362

Alexander, bishop of Lincoln, 227, 260

Alfred, king, appointment of bishops, 101; and judicial matters, 43, 55; laws of, 43, 44, 52, 60, 104, 107, 110; life of, 96; military changes of, 89; political situation at accession of, 25; region acquired by, 49, 79; reign and achievement of, 49; treaty with Guthrum, 61; and the *witan*, 60, 62, 68

Alms, free, land in, 148, 350; the king's, 167

Alms-penny, 116

Amercement, 173 and note 91, 331, 333, 393; of clergy, 393; of earls and barons, 393

Anesty, Richard de, 273

Angles, 21

dinates of sheriff, 332; summons to great council through, 301, 395

Bainfaite, Richard de, 207

Baldwin, bishop and archbishop, 361

Baldwin, J. F., 321, 349

Ballard, A., 97, 155, 179

Bamborough, high reeve of, 50

Barons, Preliminary Articles of the, 386-387, 389

Baronage, 185, 197, 269, 288

Barons, as administrators, 199, 202-204, 216, 222-224; aids of, 143; allies of, 389, 396; amercement of, 313, 347; assent of 318, 396, 399; authority of exchequer over, 240; bishops and abbots as 187-188, 256; counsel of, 201, 218, 230, 295; curial, 199, 200, 216, 228-229; of exchequer, 229, 237, 238, 271, 313, 315; in great council, 186-187, 188-189, 191, 253-254, 295, 296, 312; greater, 312, 395; judgment of, 240; judicial powers of, 160; as justices, 273; lesser, 188-189, 190-192, 228-229, 297 and note 34, 313; military obligation of, 134, 137-139, 343; of Normandy, 121, 131, 134, 135; the northern, 385, 386, 388; objects of baronial reform, 385; opposition to King John, 311, 337-338, 370, 371-373, 380, 382-387, 397-398; reliefs of, 142, 333, 389; as sheriffs, 164; in small council, 314; taxation of, 340; as tenants-in-chief, 140, 186, note 26; the twenty-five, 398; as under-tenants, 395-396; vassals of, 144; *see also Curia regis* and Military service

Barony, 138, 139, 145, 148, 159, 214, 296-297 and note 30, 312; escheated, 390; tenure by, *see* Tenure

Basset, Ralph, 227, 232, 234-235

Basset, Richard, 165, 227

Battle, Abbot of, 189-190, 248, 272

Battle, trial by, *see* Ordeal

Beauchamp, Walter de, 164

Beck, F. G. M., 17, 47

Becket, Thomas, chancellor, archbishop, 267, 297, 298, notes 39, 40, 300, 315, 319, 327 and note 30, 351, 352, 354-357, 361, note 69, 375, 376; judgment upon, 305, 306, 354; trial of, 318

Bede, 21, 22, 26, 46, 123

Bemont, C., 401

Bench, The, at Westminster, 278-279; the common, 278

Benefice, lay, 133, 393

Benefit of clergy, 351-352, 357-358

Bernicia, 22, 25, 50, 51

Bigelow, M. M., 210

Bigot, Roger, 228

Birch, W. de Gray, 46, 122

Bishop, arrest of, 250; as baron, 186-187, 191, 250, 295, 305, 395; and coronation of Stephen's heir, 261; at county court, 86, 87, 103, 106, 168; and customs of Henry I, 352; court of, 247, 286, 351, 353, 354; deposition of, 102, 245, 246, 251; designation of, 101, 108, 129, 184, 248-249, 255, 259, 262-263, 373; election of 61, 184, 358, 366, 373-374; ex-communication by, 248, 352, 358; as household official, 199, 200, 207, 219, 223; illiterate, 244; infringement of royal authority, 351; investiture of, 102, 309; in great council, 36-37, 58-59, 185-186, 187-188, 295, 302, 304, 306-308, 310, 312, 395; King John and, 341, 367-369, 370-371, 373, 388; judicial issues between bishops, 195; jurisdiction of, 105-106, 260; and legate, 359; military service of, 137, 138, 140, 188, 249; Norman in England, 196, 245; of Normandy, 134, 135, 185; offenses

418 INDEX

284; constitutional importance of, 290; of Domesday, 140, 216-217, 241; jury trial in civil actions, 281-284; in criminal cases, 286-288, 399; in Magna Carta, 288, 395; question of Scandinavian origin of, 285-286; sheriff and, 172; *see also* Inquest

Jus Spolii, 252-253, 258, 259-260

Justice, of duke of Normandy, 132; feudal, 144, 149, 150-151, 157, 158-159, 289, 382, 393, 394; feudal justice in great council, 195-197, 305; franchisal, 157, 158, 171; growth of royal, 231-234, 279, 379; king as fountain of, 55, 231-232; perversion of, 220; seigniorial, 150-151, 157-158, 173; as source of income, 151, 220, 222; not to be sold nor delayed, 395

Justice or justiciar,
of Angevin period, 272, 282-284, 290, 313, 332, 333, 341, 352, 357, 392, 393
of the bench, 278
of the forest, 331
itinerant, 168, 216-217, 231-232, 271; administrative work of, 289-290, 330-331, 334, 379; circuits of, 234-235, 270, 274-276, 277; chief justiciar as, 324; instructions to, 316; and sheriffs, 331
of Norman period, 156, 157, 170, 199, 204, note 134, 207-209, 208, note 166, 231-234, 240
resident local, 161, note 35, 233-234, 276
sheriff as, 172-173

Justiciar, chief, beginnings of the office, 200, 204, note 124, 207 and notes 156, 157, 209 and note 167, 233, note 124; of Henry II, 218, 325; of John, 325-326, 382-383; and narrow council, 315-316; president of the bench,

278, 348; of the exchequer, 239, 313-314, 323; of great council, 298, 308, 310, 372, 391; as papal legate, 363-364; of Richard I, 269, 325; the two justiciars, 272, 317, note 156, 325

Jutes, 21

Kemble, J. M., views of, 29-30, 46, 59, 62, 96; works, 46, 73, 96, 122

Kent,
kingdom of, 21, 22, 24-26, 41, 82; its institutions, 26, 28, 31, 36-38, 42; its laws, 26, 38, 31, 44, 45, 104
hereditary sheriffs of, 164

King,
early Germanic, 15
Anglo-Saxon, 21, 33-37, 52-57; election of, 52, 59-60; his house, 36, 54; household, 69-72; as lord, 52, 68-69, 109; his peace, 35-36, 37; his powers, 33-34, 45, 53-56, 69, 72, 74, 108, 120-121, 158; his resources, 35, 37-38, 63-65; succession, 52, 59-60, 182, 193-194; as the state, 57; his *wergeld,* 35
Frankish, 35
Norman king, and feudalism, 144-147; as liege lord, 145; resources of, 149
at exchequer, 313; *see also* Monarchy

Kingdoms, Anglo-Saxons, 21-25

Knight service, *see* Service, military

Knighting lord's eldest son, 134, 143, 150

Knights, arms of, 342, 346; assigned, 296; contribution of to fortieth of, 201, 340; the *constabularia* of, 213; elected, 339, 393; exemption of demesne of, 183; fees of, *see* Fees, knights'; forces of, 214, 345, 383; at great

428 INDEX

Villa, Roman, 32

Village, cathedral in, 244, 246; the dependent, 31, 32, 74; the free, 31, 111, 112, 120; the Germanic, 13-14; *see also* Village community

Village community, Anglo-Saxon, the dependent village, 31, 74, 111-112 (jurisdiction over, 74-75, 119; *see also* Vassalage); the free village, 31, 112; the hide, 30; lords of, 113; mark theory, 29-30; various names of, 30; relation to borough, 88; to the family group, 30; to the parish, 103; Seebohin's theory of, 32-33; works on, 46-47; *see also* Vill

Villain, 151, 153-154, 218; at county court, 169-170; in frankpledge, 176

Villainage, 149, 152-153

Villanus, 112, 116, 152

Vinogradoff, Sir Paul, views, 17, 46, 75; works, 46, 97, 123, 155, 400

Viscounty, the Norman, 132

Vivian, Cardinal, 359

Von Maurer, G. L., 16

Wages, of garrisons, 345; of king's household, 241-242, 329; of knights, 213, 336 and note 79, 344; of serjeants, 342 and note 101

Waitz, Georg, 16

Walcher, bishop, 147

Waldric, chancellor and bishop, 225

Wales, 24, 269, 380; allegiance of to John, 370, 383; the interdict in, 366, 370; marches of, 147; North Wales, 128; primacy over Welsh church, 375; South Wales, 24, 128

Walkelin, bishop, 205, note 138, 207, note 157, 208

Wall work, 38, 65, 89, 90, 115

Wallingford, treaty of, 130

Walter, Hubert, archbishop, 269, 316, 325, 327 and note 30, 328, 347, 363-365, 382

Waltheof, earl, 163

Wapentake, 80, 104, 170; reeve of, 81, 235, 285

War, private, 134

Wardrobe, the king's, 70, 322

Wards, of northern counties, 80

Wardship, of minors, 142, 144, 150, 333, 389, 391

Warneville, Ralph of, chancellor, 327, note 30

Warreners, 392

Waters, navigable, and king's peace, 222

Wealh, 29

Weights and measures, 103, 391

Welsh, as landholders, 31-32; as slaves, 29

Wendover, Roger of, 320, 385, 386, 400

Wergeld, 12, 13, 15, 44, 45, 92, 115

Anglo-Saxon, 27, 28, 30, 32, 35, 38, 44-45, 92, 106

Germanic, 12

Wessex, earls of, 51; kingdom of, 21, 22, 24-26, 49, 50; its institutions, 26-28, 31-32, 35, 36, 38-41, 43-44, 66

Westminster, 370; *curia regis* at, 184, 294; exchequer at, 323

Westmorland, 128

Whitby, council of, 23

White, A. B., 320

White, G. H., 211, 242

Whitsuntide, 184, 189, 293

Wick, 30, 89

Widows, dowry of, 389; under king's peace, 54; marriage of, 143, 144, 183, 389-390

Wight, Isle of, 21, 23

Wilfrid, bishop, 37

William, bishop of Durham, 188, 250, 252

William, count of Mortain, 147